The Parl
Battle over Brexit

Meg Russell and Lisa James

OXFORD
UNIVERSITY PRESS

OXFORD
UNIVERSITY PRESS

Great Clarendon Street, Oxford, OX2 6DP,
United Kingdom

Oxford University Press is a department of the University of Oxford.
It furthers the University's objective of excellence in research, scholarship,
and education by publishing worldwide. Oxford is a registered trade mark of
Oxford University Press in the UK and in certain other countries

First Edition published in 2023

Impression: 1

Published in the United States of America by Oxford University Press
198 Madison Avenue, New York, NY 10016, United States of America

British Library Cataloguing in Publication Data
Data available

Library of Congress Control Number: 2022946817

ISBN 978-0-19-284971-7

DOI: 10.1093/oso/9780192849717.001.0001

Printed and bound in the UK by
Clays Ltd, Elcograf S.p.A.

Acknowledgements

This book was made possible by the help and support of many people.

From 2019 to 2022, Meg Russell held a UK in a Changing Europe (UKICE) Senior Fellowship, funded by the Economic and Social Research Council (grant ES/T000929/1), which also allowed the Constitution Unit at University College London (UCL) to employ Lisa James. Without this there would have been no book at all. Membership of the UKICE network was also important to the research, including through our involvement in many public events, private discussions and other writing projects coordinated by Anand Menon and his top-class team at King's College London. Key insights have come from other Fellows in the network, including Catherine Barnard, John Curtice, Katy Hayward, Nicola McEwen, and Jill Rutter. The UKICE Brexit Witness Archive was also an invaluable resource.

Though we have made extensive use of the public record in conducting the research for the book, a thorough understanding of politics always depends on appreciation of the dynamics, relationships, and negotiations which exist behind the scenes. We are hence indebted to the many busy people who gave up their time to be interviewed as part of our research. They included John Baron, Kevin Barron, Gavin Barwell, Hilary Benn, John Bercow, Paul Blomfield, Ben Bradshaw, Graham Brady, Tom Brake, Chris Bryant, Yvette Cooper, Stephen Doughty, Oussama El Fatihi, Helen Goodman, Dominic Grieve, Philip Hammond, Dianne Hayter, George Hollingbery, Bernard Jenkin, David Jones, Stephen Kinnock, Colin Lee, Oliver Letwin, David Lidington, Robert Lisvane, Alison McGovern, Gina Miller, Ed de Minckwitz, Lisa Nandy, Dick Newby, Matthew Pennycook, Jacob Rees-Mogg, Raoul Ruparel, Philip Rycroft, Angela Smith, Julian Smith, Caroline Spelman, Rory Stewart, Gisela Stuart, Emily Thornberry, and Sarah Wollaston, plus others who preferred not to be named. Their insight and openness was essential to our analysis, and we are grateful for their willingness to revisit memories of a difficult period in recent history.

Several interviewees were generous enough to also read and comment on draft chapters, or to assist us with queries on points of fact or interpretation. Others who kindly did this included Tim Bale, Nick Barber, David Beamish, Graeme Cowie, Phil Cowley, David Gauke, Tom Hickman, Alexander Horne, Conor Kelly, Arabella Lang, Lee Marsons, David Natzler, Alan Renwick,

James Rhys, Robert Saunders, Simon Usherwood, Alan Wager, and Hannah White. Our colleague Tom Fleming deserves particular thanks for reading through the whole draft of the book, as do the two anonymous reviewers for Oxford University Press. This all resulted in numerous thoughtful and constructive suggestions which greatly strengthened the accuracy and acuity of the analysis.

We have enjoyed substantial background research support from within the Constitution Unit at UCL. First and foremost, great thanks are due to Sam Anderson, who made a major contribution to the initial information gathering for the book. We are also grateful for research contributions large and small from various others, including Emilia Cieslak, Flora Curtis, Will Knatchbull, Tom Leeman, Oli Maddison, Ben Matthes, Donya Mojtahed-Zadeh, Gil Richards, Matt Richardson, Eric Robinson, Joe Ryder, and Philip Wilson. More broadly, we have greatly benefited from the intellectually rich and supportive environment created by our colleagues at the Constitution Unit, and the wider UCL Department of Political Science.

Dominic Byatt and Jade Dixon at Oxford University Press were enormously helpful and encouraging throughout. We also thank Nivedha Vinayagamurthy at Straive and the rest of the production team. Those people who so kindly provided supportive comments for use on the cover and in publicity for the book have left us feeling both very grateful and flattered by their endorsement.

Finally, we thank our friends and family for their patience and support. Meg thanks above all Philip Carter for his tolerance while yet another book project encroached on both her time and good temper. Lisa in particular thanks her parents Dawn and Paul James, and Bella Gage.

Contents

List of Tables

1

Introduction

The UK's exit from membership of the European Union—the process that came to be known as Brexit—stirred up controversy of a kind that the country's politics had rarely seen. This extended far beyond the campaign surrounding the June 2016 referendum, and into the succeeding years. After the public's narrow vote to leave the bloc, by 51.9 per cent to 48.1 per cent, increasingly bitter arguments took place over how the result should be put into effect. Many of these were played out in parliament.

The Brexit process, and particularly parliament's role in it, led to very visible questioning of some of the fundamentals of UK politics. Parliament is the nation's central democratic institution, and traditionally sits at the heart of the constitution. But at times during the Brexit debates, media headlines referred to its members as 'saboteurs', 'wreckers', 'mutineers', and 'traitors' (Daily Mail 2017, Stevens 2018a, 2018b, Swinford 2017). When the courts stepped in to defend parliament's role, judges were branded 'enemies of the people' (Slack 2016). Three years on from the referendum, Conservative Prime Minister Boris Johnson sought to prorogue—or shut down—parliament for five weeks. This caused some MPs even within his own party to accuse him of mounting a 'coup' (Sky News Politics 2019). In turn, when the Supreme Court ruled the attempted prorogation unlawful, one senior minister reportedly described this as a 'constitutional coup' by the judges (Demianyk 2019), while another told returning MPs that they had 'no moral right to sit'.[1] In December 2019, Johnson's party manifesto alleged that the UK had been 'paralysed by a broken Parliament that simply refuses to deliver Brexit', and that 'MPs ha[d] devoted themselves to thwarting the democratic decision of the British people' (Conservative Party 2019a: 2, 47–8).

These were extraordinary events, and extraordinary allegations, in a country normally renowned for its long-standing, stable democracy. Despite some criticism, the Westminster parliament had long been an emblem of such democracy, not just in the UK but throughout the world. However, during 2016–19, events in parliament took a highly unusual turn. Theresa May's government suffered the biggest parliamentary defeat on record over her Brexit deal, which went on to be defeated twice more. Newspaper front pages accused MPs of 'seizing control' of the House of Commons agenda from the government, and the Commons Speaker was subject to intense criticism—particularly by Brexit supporters. Boris Johnson had been a leading light of the Vote Leave campaign, during which he celebrated parliamentary democracy as 'the most valuable British export'.[2] But having contributed to May's downfall, he assumed the premiership and attempted to prorogue parliament, subsequently suggesting that he might even refuse to comply with a law that it had passed.

So what went wrong? How did Brexit end up igniting such fierce arguments about the role of the UK's political institutions? Did it demonstrate fundamental flaws in the UK constitution, or were there ways in which things might realistically have been handled better? And to what extent have these tensions caused lasting political damage? Those are the central questions addressed in this book.

This first chapter summarizes the book's purpose, the questions that it will ask, and the kinds of research on which it is based, before briefly summarizing how it is structured and the events and topics that it covers. But first, given the book's central focus on parliament as a site of the arguments over Brexit, the chapter starts by setting out some context in terms of the institution's traditional place at the heart of UK politics.

Brexit, Parliament and the Constitution

The UK constitution can be described as uniquely parliamentary. Legislatures are central to all democracies as the institutions which represent voters, linking them to national political decision-making. The UK is classified by political scientists as a 'parliamentary democracy', meaning that it goes beyond this, to make the government's survival dependent on retaining the confidence of parliament. The same model applies to many countries across Europe and the Commonwealth, such as Germany, Italy, Canada, and Australia, distinguishing them from 'presidential democracies' in countries like the US (Lijphart 1992). But the UK constitution goes further still. Not only is the government dependent on the confidence of the House of Commons; parliament is also considered the ultimate authority in the constitution. This tradition of 'parliamentary sovereignty' is connected to the well-known fact that UK lacks the kind of identifiable written constitution that exists in most other states. Typically, such documents enjoy the status of 'higher law'—being difficult to amend, and hence constraining parliamentary decision-making. By contrast, in the UK, parliament traditionally has the final say. This results in a more flexible constitution, and a reduced role for the courts, when compared to many other democracies.

The Westminster parliament—and its two chambers, the House of Commons and House of Lords—has various functions, fairly typical of those ascribed to legislatures throughout the world (Kreppel 2014, Loewenberg and Patterson 1979, Norton 2013). One of them, already alluded to, is *representation*. Citizens vote for their members of parliament, who make decisions on their behalf. In the UK House of Commons, this representation is organized on the basis of 650 single-member constituencies. Legislatures are also sites of *deliberation*, as debating chambers for the nation. Crucially, much of this debate is conducted on the public record, providing transparency for voters. Connected to this is the function of *oversight* of the government and its policy plans, conducted for example through parliamentary questions and committees. Finally, parliaments have a *policymaking* function, which is most obviously demonstrated by the requirement for their assent in passing laws.

The Westminster parliament performs all of these functions, though the representation function applies less directly to the House of Lords. But while members of the Lords lack constituencies, most sit for political parties, which are crucial to the workings of both chambers. Indeed, the parties' central role contributes to a paradox concerning the UK parliament—that, notwithstanding its formal centrality, it is frequently seen as weak (Flinders and Kelso 2011, Kreppel 2014). Over the past hundred years the UK has usually had single-party majority governments, which tend to result in limited public conflict between ministers and MPs and can create an impression of parliamentary acquiescence. But significant influence may go on behind the scenes in parliament (Russell and Cowley 2016, Russell and Gover 2017). In particular, the practice of single-party majority government means that interactions within the governing party are crucial to the smooth running of the institution. As Anthony King (1976) pointed out decades ago, it is often misleading to talk in general about 'executive-legislative relations', because the relationships that matter to the government maintaining its majority are normally those between ministers and their own backbenchers. While much has changed since he was writing, that basic truth remains fundamental (Russell and Cowley 2018).

When it comes to policy, the government has substantial resources at its disposal, most notably through the civil service, which means that in important ways this is 'made' by ministers (Norton 2013). Hence Westminster is typically seen as a 'reactive' legislature, which scrutinizes, amends, and approves the policy proposals put in front of it by government (Mezey 1979). But other reasons to doubt the Westminster parliament's power and influence have also been much discussed (Flinders and Kelso 2011). In particular, it is often noted that parliament's 'sovereignty' has been challenged by various constitutional developments, which have seen policymaking power drain away from Westminster. These include the establishment of devolved legislatures in Scotland, Wales, and Northern Ireland post 1997, and an increasing role for the judiciary resulting from the Human Rights Act 1998 (Barber 2021, Bogdanor 2009, Elliott, M. 2019c). But one of the biggest contributors to concerns about sovereignty was the UK's membership of the EU (and its predecessor institutions) post 1973. This required compliance with European law, adjudicated by the European Court of Justice (ECJ), which placed a constraint on parliament's policymaking power, feeding claims that the principle of UK parliamentary sovereignty no longer applied (Barber 2011).

Concerns of this kind were a key driver of UK Euroscepticism, which demanded a return to greater sovereignty for the Westminster parliament—as characterized by the 2016 Vote Leave slogan 'Take Back Control'. The next chapter discusses how Eurosceptic tendencies long existed in UK politics but gained particular prominence from the early 1990s onwards. Proponents argued for a return of power to parliament, often doing so by demanding referendums—which led to the first nationwide referendum in the UK in 1975. But referendums introduced an unfamiliar logic to UK politics—of 'direct democracy', exercised by the people, rather than the more traditional 'representative democracy', exercised by those whom they elect to parliament. This created a risk of new tensions developing over parliament's role, placing its decision-making functions in potential conflict with the 'will of the people' (Weale 2018). Arguments around these questions became commonplace after the referendum of 2016.

Between the 1975 and 2016 referendums, parliament itself changed in various important ways. Frequently cited examples include the growing prominence of specialist 'select committees' in the House of Commons after 1979, and the removal of most hereditary peers from the House of Lords 20 years later. Meanwhile, more seats were won by MPs beyond the main two political parties, and party cohesiveness gradually declined—as witnessed by increasing 'rebellious' votes cast against the party line (Russell and Cowley 2016). All of these changes encouraged greater cross-party working by parliamentarians, and greater confidence to challenge the government, adding to a sense that the institution was getting stronger (Norton 2015).

Hence in some ways parliament was seen as diminished during this period, partly thanks to the UK's EU membership. On the other hand, its capacity for independence and scrutiny of government was growing. This helps to explain a notable irony of the Brexit years—that Eurosceptic pressures to return power to parliament ended with angry arguments about the need to contain parliamentary intervention after the referendum.

Purpose of the Book

The arguments over Brexit reached high media prominence—dominating the headlines for months on end. They have already been subject to analysis in various other books (e.g. Barwell 2021, Ford and Sobolewska 2020, Grey 2021, Seldon and Newell 2019, Shipman 2017a, 2017b). But these have tended to focus on relationships inside government, on the EU negotiations, on the role of public opinion, or on some combination of the three. Meanwhile, no book-length study has considered the particular impact of Brexit on parliament, and the role that parliament played in these developments.[3] Yet parliament was highly visible in the Brexit process, and its interventions significantly (and often controversially) affected what took place. This makes a proper appreciation of the institution's internal dynamics essential to understanding the politics of Brexit. In addition, given how these disputed events drew parliament's own role into question, Brexit raised doubts about some of the most central relationships in the UK constitution. Notably, the Conservative Party manifesto of 2019 (whose allegations about parliament were cited above) argued for a formal rebalancing between government, parliament, and courts (Conservative Party 2019a).[4] But evaluating such claims requires a proper understanding of what happened during the Brexit years.

Parliament's debates over Brexit took place, at varying levels of intensity, from the June 2016 referendum to the UK's formal departure from the bloc in January 2020. Throughout much of this period formal negotiations were going on between the government and the EU. Meanwhile, opinion polls showed that voters consistently considered Brexit the single most important issue facing the country (YouGov 2022b). Through its representation, deliberation, and oversight functions, parliament sought to explore the possible Brexit options, and to hold the government to account. Particularly at the later stages, it also took key policy decisions, which frequently reached the news. But the topics under consideration were often very complex, as was the nature of parliament's own procedures. In a highly polarized political environment, full of claims and counterclaims, this made it hard for external observers to judge reliably what was going on. Even those closely involved sometimes struggled to follow the intense and fast-moving developments. Opportunities for misunderstandings, generated either deliberately or inadvertently, were rife. The print media, with its eye-catching headlines, was itself extremely polarized over Brexit. Blame games were widespread, while the detail of developments was sometimes reported inaccurately, and often not at all.

This book hence seeks to provide a fuller and more even-handed account of the contested parliamentary developments over Brexit. This was a crucial period in UK political and parliamentary history, and the book endeavours to provide an accurate document of record. In doing so, it explodes some of the myths that became established in media accounts. In particular, it challenges the widespread impression that a 'Remainer' parliament stood in the way of the government delivering Brexit, which subsequently justified Boris Johnson in taking radical action to 'get Brexit done'. While many parliamentarians were undoubtedly unhappy about Brexit, some of whom might have been delighted to see the decision reversed, the most important arguments that stymied the process were between Prime Minister Theresa May and her own Eurosceptic backbenchers. Johnson and others who went on to serve in his Cabinet were among those who stood in her way. There are many fascinating twists and turns in the story described in the book, but this central aspect deserves more widespread attention—particularly given his perceived legacy of having been the man who broke the impasse to deliver Brexit, and the instability that his Brexit deal created with respect to Northern Ireland.

These were, as already emphasized, highly polarized debates. As far as possible, the book is built on objective evidence, as further described below. Its purpose is neither to defend nor to question the UK's decision to leave the EU. Nor does it set out to defend or attack the actions of any particular group. But it does take a position that respects parliament as the central democratic institution, upon whose authority the government's legitimacy is based, and upon which UK democracy depends. No democracy in the world exists without a parliament.

Methods and Sources

Parliament is, as already mentioned, by its nature an open institution. Unlike many other political bodies, its proceedings take place on the public record, and are transcribed and televised. This creates an invaluable resource for researchers. A first source of information in the book was therefore the Hansard record of proceedings in both chambers, alongside other parliamentary documents such as amendment papers and committee reports, and occasional government documents. These are all referred to in a way that will enable readers to trace the originals and, should they wish, to explore them for themselves.

In addition, the book uses numerous secondary sources, which appeared both contemporaneously with the events described—primarily through the popular media—and subsequently through reporting by other scholars and commentators. Again, full citation is provided for these sources.

A third and crucial source for the book is detailed interviews with many of the key protagonists. The authors conducted around 50 such interviews with parliamentarians, including ministers and shadow ministers, plus government and parliamentary officials. Interviews were conducted on a confidential basis, in order to encourage maximum frankness from interviewees; comments from them are reported anonymously throughout the book. Many of those interviewed are listed in the Acknowledgements section, though some preferred to keep their involvement completely off the record. In addition, the authors made significant use of the 'Brexit witness archive' gathered by the UK in a Changing Europe initiative at King's College London. This is an invaluable resource, comprising detailed on-the-record interviews with further protagonists, which readers themselves can explore. As these latter interviews are public, citations are provided.

These materials have been used to draw together as complete and accurate as possible an account of the parliamentary story of Brexit. However, various caveats should be noted. First, while the public record indicates reliably who said what and when, there is no guarantee of why they said it. Not all public statements can necessarily be taken completely at face value; parliamentarians may sometimes misunderstand points or speak from incomplete information; they may occasionally hide their true motivations—for example, omitting to mention whether they are taking a position due to pressure from party whips. At times they may even deliberately seek to mislead. Interviews, meanwhile, can be very useful for gleaning information that protagonists might be reluctant to provide publicly, or that they were not able to state at the time. However, memories can be unreliable, and interviewees may—consciously or unconsciously—present partial or biased accounts (Berry 2003, Richards 1996).

Authors must therefore exercise a degree of judgement and interpretation in presenting information from all these kinds of sources. Where possible, sources have been checked against each other—for example, statements in interviews being compared to the public record, or claims from other interviewees. Any plainly self-serving or factually incorrect statements are either presented as such or have been omitted altogether. But, as all good researchers know, this is not a perfect process. A further degree of interpretation will inevitably be placed on materials by the authors themselves, who may bring their own biases, and ultimately by the reader. But, within this world of necessarily imperfect information, the authors have striven to be fair.

A Word on Language

The term 'parliament' is used throughout the book to mean the House of Commons and House of Lords collectively. The book's focus is more often on the Commons than the Lords, but where only one chamber is referred to this is done explicitly by name. Various other technical parliamentary terms, particularly relating to procedure, also regularly appear. Brief explanations of their meanings are given in the separate Glossary.

The term 'Brexit', meaning British exit from the EU, was only popularized around the time of the 2016 referendum. In Chapter 2, which describes the period prior to the referendum, the term 'Eurosceptic' is used to describe those who wanted to loosen UK ties to the EU and its predecessor institutions. Many Eurosceptics did not at that time seek to break with the EU altogether. At the time of the referendum, the words 'Leaver' and 'Remainer' were coined to describe supporters of the two alternatives on offer. 'Remainer' continued to be used afterwards, for those who hoped to reverse the result, but 'Leavers' more often came to be known as 'Brexiteers'. The terms used in different chapters reflect these linguistic developments.

As outlined in Chapter 4, the terms 'hard' and 'soft' Brexit emerged only after the referendum, to describe options for the UK's possible future relationship with the EU. Different groupings in parliament, particularly within the Conservative Party, coalesced around different options (for more detail see Chapter 6). Within the book, the term 'hardliner' is often used to describe those who were determined that there should be a hard Brexit, while Conservative 'moderates' took a different view, and were mostly content to support a soft Brexit. But no such labelling is perfect, because political life tends to be more messy than this, and language itself can be disputed.[5] All such language should be read as the authors' best possible approximation.

Questions Asked by the Book

There are numerous questions that can be asked about the Brexit process. Many are beyond the scope of this book, and have received attention elsewhere. The central questions for this study relate to the relationship between Brexit and the functioning of parliament, and parliament's place within the constitution. As a principal venue within which many difficult arguments took place, examining proceedings in parliament can reveal a lot about the politics of Brexit, as well as about parliament itself. Generally the book seeks particularly to explore the following high-level questions.

1. *What actually happened?*
   As already indicated, the Brexit process was lengthy. Formally, the UK's negotiations with the EU took place within the framework provided by Article 50 of the Treaty on European Union, which specifies a two-year period for such talks. However, Article 50 was not triggered until nine months after the referendum, and by mutual agreement a further 10 months were added to the negotiating period. Hence parliament discussed the options on Brexit for more than three and a half years post referendum, in debates that became increasingly heated and divisive. Prior to the referendum, the UK's relationship with the European Union had been under discussion in parliament for years (while the consequences of Brexit are liable to be debated for many years to come). One primary purpose of the book is to document carefully what actually happened in parliament over those years, and where and how parliamentarians influenced the process. Since parliament by its nature includes a diversity of members, the book explores the role that was played by different groups—for example, government backbenchers, the opposition, the Commons, and the Lords.

2. *What went wrong, and what might realistically have happened differently?*
   The vocal attacks that were made on parliament over Brexit, as illustrated at the opening of this chapter, show how the process generated doubts about the core institutions of UK democracy. Throughout the process, blame was often assigned to different individuals and groups, depending on the critic's own perspective on Brexit. The book therefore also explores the extent to which parliament itself was a problem. Did MPs really seek to 'thwart the democratic decision of the British people', and if so, which MPs and why? How might such destabilizing

arguments have been avoided? Connected to this, the Brexit process included numerous knife-edge moments, beginning with the referendum itself. The narrow 52:48 result helped generate uncertainty about what should happen next, leaving government and parliament to navigate the alternatives. Many preferred a much 'softer' Brexit than ultimately occurred; others favoured a second referendum. Narrow parliamentary votes might on occasion have suggested that alternative ways forward could have been pursued. But was this really the case? Did key figures such as Prime Minister Theresa May, House of Commons Speaker John Bercow, or opposition leader Jeremy Corbyn clearly mishandle the situation? Were there errors on the part of political parties or other groups? Questions of this kind recur throughout the book.

3. *What does the Brexit process demonstrate about parliament's constitutional role?*

Brexit highlights important questions about parliament as an institution. As already indicated, the process began partly due to a desire to return power to the UK parliament; yet it ended with some of those who had most forcefully espoused such views condemning parliament's interference. How can these seeming contradictions be explained? During the process, tensions repeatedly arose over how parliament should conduct its role, and about its own internal rules. Often these related to the central balance of power between government and parliament; for example, the extent to which parliament should be able to set government policy, and the extent to which government should be able to determine what parliament discusses and when. Did government, parliament, or some other actor behave in ways that were constitutionally improper during the Brexit process? Or did Brexit just put strain on these institutional structures that was difficult to bear?

4. *What changes are needed in our institutions?*

This set of questions leads to others, about the strengths and weaknesses of the UK's constitution, and its broader politics. During the period when Brexit was being hotly debated, and afterwards, various participants and commentators—from a range of perspectives—have suggested that the process demonstrated flaws in UK constitutional arrangements. The extent of these discussions have been wide-ranging, but many have the role of parliament at their heart. There are important questions in particular about how the institution interacts with the roles of referendums, political parties, and the government. But concerns go wider, including for example relationships between the centre and the devolved institutions, and adherence to constitutional norms. Are there strains caused by Brexit that might need to be resolved?

5. *What have the battles over Brexit done to the culture of UK politics?*
    Finally, some suggest that Brexit forms part of a bigger cultural change, of reduced tolerance towards both political 'elites' and constitutional constraints. Other frequently cited examples of such trends include the election of President Donald Trump in the US, and attacks on democratic checks and balances in countries such as Poland and Hungary—described as having fallen prey to 'populism' and 'democratic backsliding'. In addition to, or instead of, seeking institutional fixes, does the UK now need to be concerned about its own political culture, and if so, what solutions can be found?

Each of these questions is addressed at various points throughout the book, and each is returned to in the concluding chapter.

The Structure of the Book

The rest of the book comprises 10 chapters. Nine are organized broadly chronologically, while the final one offers general conclusions. Each chronological chapter, after a short introduction, is framed by a theme. These themes, collectively, help to shed light on the developments in the book, in particular by drawing from previous academic analyses. But the thematic sections are short, and like all of the material in the book are intentionally written in an accessible way. Each chapter ends with its own conclusion, which reviews the material that has been covered and how this relates to some of the bigger questions identified by the book.

The next chapter, Chapter 2, summarizes parliamentary developments prior to the Brexit referendum. It takes a far longer view than other chapters, beginning with the UK's entry into the then European Economic Community (EEC) in 1973. It goes on briefly to cover debates under the Conservative governments of Margaret Thatcher and John Major, and the Labour governments of Tony Blair and Gordon Brown, before exploring at greater length the tensions under Conservative Prime Minister David Cameron post 2010. This ends with the 2015 bill that facilitated the referendum. The chapter's theme, which is central to the book, is parliamentary party cohesion. Both parties were divided on European matters, but this particularly applied to the Conservatives. In calling the referendum, Cameron was significantly influenced by parliamentary backbench pressure from Conservative Eurosceptics.

Chapter 3 deals with the referendum itself, including the campaign, the result, and the immediate political aftermath. Cameron had hoped that a promised renegotiation with the EU would result in a Remain vote, and campaigned for this. However, when—contrary to most opinion polls—Leave won the referendum, he departed the scene and was replaced by Theresa May. The thematic section in this chapter deals with referendums in UK politics, and points out that these are in various ways unusual in international terms. Most notably, the referendum was a one-stage process, with parliament itself not having voted in favour of Brexit, and it was held on a question of principle rather than a detailed prospectus for change. The referendum formally had no legal force, but was widely considered politically binding.

Chapter 4 considers the early months of Theresa May's premiership, and the early responses of parliament to the referendum result. Questions emerged quickly regarding whether parliamentary approval would be needed for the triggering of Article 50, for the UK's objectives in the negotiations, and for the final Brexit deal. The government was reluctant to concede these points. One consequence was the first Supreme Court case, taken by Gina Miller, which forced the government into presenting parliament with a bill to approve triggering the Article 50 process. The bill faced little parliamentary resistance, though around 50 MPs from Remain-voting constituencies opposed it. The thematic section of this chapter, accordingly, deals with constituency influence in parliament.

Chapter 5 covers the snap general election of June 2017. Having previously promised not to hold an early election, Theresa May justified her U-turn by arguing that parliament was attempting to block Brexit, which was ill-justified by the facts. Having hoped for an increased majority, May instead ended up heading a minority government with the support of the Northern Ireland Democratic Unionist Party (DUP). While some urged her to change course at this point, and pursue a wider cross-party approach to Brexit, she did not do so—and indeed, this would have been difficult. The theme for the chapter is the dynamics of minority government.

Chapter 6 begins to explore more fully the options for Brexit, and parliamentarians' attempts to influence the detailed Brexit outcome. Its theme, accordingly, is parliament's role in foreign affairs. When negotiations began with the EU, it became increasingly clear that there were tensions between the 'red lines' that Theresa May had set out shortly after becoming Prime Minister, and retaining Northern Ireland's stability, because the Belfast/Good

Friday Agreement relied on an open border with the Republic of Ireland. Through various mechanisms, parliamentarians sought to influence the negotiations, potentially to edge the Prime Minister towards a 'softer' Brexit. Groupings formed, often on a cross-party basis, to press for different outcomes, but no clear majority emerged.

Chapter 7 covers the agreement of Theresa May's Brexit deal with the EU, and pressures from parliament for a say on the final outcome of Brexit. This was achieved through inserting the requirement for a so-called 'meaningful vote' in the government's EU (Withdrawal) Bill. At this stage, moderate Conservatives feared that their hardline colleagues might force the Prime Minister into a 'no-deal' Brexit—which would trigger deleterious economic effects and the need for a hard Irish border—by refusing to approve her Withdrawal Agreement. Once the Brexit deal was reached, the House of Commons did indeed initially reject it by a huge margin, in January 2019, with a large number of Conservative rebels joining the opposition in voting against it. The great majority of these rebels were Brexiteers. The thematic section in this chapter discusses the traditional role of the opposition, which can rarely be expected to help the government out of a difficult situation.

Chapter 8 has as its theme the government's default control of the House of Commons agenda, which came under increasing pressure after the deal had been defeated, when other MPs sought to build alternative majorities. It includes discussion of the subsequent defeats of May's deal, where DUP and hardline Eurosceptic votes made a crucial difference. With a no-deal exit on 29 March 2019 remaining the legal default, MPs held multiple votes, expressing strong resistance to this outcome and sending May back to the negotiating table. Through voting on several occasions to take control of the Commons agenda, they facilitated 'indicative votes' on different Brexit options, but none found a majority. They also required the Prime Minister to seek extensions to the Article 50 period. But with no majority for any final resolution to the Brexit process, Theresa May ultimately resigned.

Chapter 9 begins with the Conservative leadership contest which resulted in the rise to the premiership of Boris Johnson. Throughout that contest, there was controversy about the idea of a lengthy parliamentary prorogation, possibly to force through a no-deal Brexit. Parliamentarians, including some of May's ministers, took action to try and prevent this. There were also suggestions that Johnson could be deposed and replaced by a cross-party government. However, these attempts had limited success, and a prorogation was sought, only subsequently to be overturned by the Supreme Court. MPs voted for a further Article 50 extension against Johnson's wishes, and he responded by threatening not to comply. The theme for this chapter is populism and democratic backsliding.

Chapter 10 deals with the final stages up to the UK's formal departure from the EU. First Johnson, under pressure, negotiated an alternative deal which included significant regulatory differences between Great Britain and Northern Ireland. This reneged on promises previously made to the DUP that there would be no potentially destabilizing 'border down the Irish Sea'. Having recanted and sought an Article 50 extension, Johnson then persuaded parliament to grant him an early general election, which he won with an 80-seat Commons majority. This allowed him to attain swift parliamentary approval for his deal. The theme for the chapter is the Fixed-term Parliaments Act, which had to be overridden to facilitate this election and has since been repealed.

Chapter 11 wraps up the arguments in the book, returning to the key questions listed above. It summarizes developments, concluding that what was often presented as an institutional argument between parliament and government was in fact, first and foremost, an internal one inside the Conservative Party.[6] The difficulties after the referendum led directly from its lack of clarity about what Brexit should mean. Theresa May negotiated a deal that many of her own Brexiteers refused to accept, but Conservatives on both sides of the argument preferred to paint the problem as one created by a generalized 'parliament'. May's successor Boris Johnson—despite having himself opposed her deal—stepped up this anti-parliamentary rhetoric.

The bitter arguments over Brexit hence resulted in significant reputational damage to parliament, which, despite its status as the UK's central democratic institution, has been increasingly sidelined since the referendum. The notion of 'parliamentary sovereignty' has become particularly contested and confused. Constitutionally, it is crucial that the UK both learns how to do referendums better and rebuilds its culture of government accountability to parliament. Brexit has also significantly exacerbated territorial tensions, particularly relating to Scotland and Northern Ireland. Perhaps most worryingly, it left a political culture of populism, built on the polarization created by the referendum, which has encouraged attacks on essential constitutional checks and balances. This fallout now needs urgent attention.

Notes

1. House of Commons Hansard, 25 September 2019, column 660.
2. These words, which were reproduced in Vote Leave leaflets, appeared in the famous article written by Johnson (2016) in the *Daily Telegraph* announcing his referendum position.
3. Barwell (2021) does give more space to this than others, though parliament is not the main focus of his book. The self-published book by Francois (2021) on the 'battle for Brexit'

provides a useful insider perspective from one set of protagonists, but unfortunately contains some grave factual errors (e.g. reporting that key motions were approved by parliament, when they were in fact defeated). Various academic authors have produced shorter pieces on different aspects of parliament's role in Brexit, many of which are quoted later in the book (e.g. Bale, Cygan, and Russell 2020, Fleming 2021, Fleming and James 2022, Lynch and Whitaker 2019, Quinn, Allen, and Bartle 2022, Russell 2021a, Thompson 2020, Thompson and Yong 2019).

4. This review never took place, partly due to the intervening Covid-19 crisis. But controversies about the role of parliament (and indeed the courts) remained high-profile under the government of Boris Johnson, as further discussed in Chapter 11.

5. For example, some supporters of a hard Brexit considered that this was the only form of real Brexit, and described all of those who opposed it as 'Remainers' (e.g. Francois 2021).

6. These internal party divisions were long-standing (as explored in Chapter 2) and remain very visible even now that the UK has left the EU (as touched upon in Chapter 11).

2

The Parliamentary Path
to the Brexit Referendum

This book's primary focus is the impact that the 2016 referendum had on parliament and on debates about parliament's role in the political system. After the referendum, some of the most bitter battles over how to proceed were played out in parliament. But parliament also had a very significant role in bringing about the referendum in the first place, particularly through the efforts of Conservative backbench MPs (and a few others) to pressurize their party leaders. These members used a wide variety of mechanisms to bring the issue of a referendum onto the parliamentary agenda, mirroring—as subsequent chapters will show—some of the tactics used later by parliamentary rebels when responding to the referendum result. Decisions made by the House of Commons Speaker, John Bercow, became controversial at those later stages—but he also played a crucial role before the referendum, in facilitating the voice of Eurosceptic MPs.

A key theme throughout this whole book is therefore how parliament operates when Britain's generally cohesive political parties are deeply divided. Both of Westminster's two main parties were split over how to respond to the referendum result. But significant splits in the parties on European matters dated back decades, as summarized in this chapter. The chapter therefore begins with a thematic discussion of divided political parties, and the extent to which rebel backbenchers can use parliament to exert their power, before moving to a chronological account of the European issue as fought out in parliament prior to the 2016 referendum.

This chronology starts with a brief account of parliament's role in the UK's original decision to join the European Economic Community (or 'Common Market') in 1973. Next it reviews developments under the Conservative governments of 1979–97, the Labour governments of 1997–2010, and the 2010–15 coalition government. It ends by describing parliament's approval of the legislation to facilitate the Brexit referendum, under the Conservative government of 2015. A consistent feature of this period was the steadily growing parliamentary pressure for referendums to be held on European matters. This began in the 1970s, and ended with David Cameron's commitment to facilitate the vote that took place in 2016. Both the UK's relationship to European institutions and the use of referendums in deciding these matters raised questions about the sovereignty of parliament.

Divided Parties and Parliamentary Backbench Power

Cohesion is the default setting for political parties in modern parliaments (Bowler, Farrell, and Katz 1999, Willumsen 2017). Members commonly join parties because of shared policy goals or common ideology, are socialized into them, and stand for election on a published policy platform. Adherence to this platform can then be important in providing accountability to voters—ensuring that they will get what they voted for (Carey 2007). In many countries party leaders have substantial means of imposing discipline on their MPs: rewarding loyal behaviour through appointment to ministerial office or prized committee roles, while denying rebels funding or speaking rights, or blocking them from running for future election. Such disciplinary mechanisms encourage parliamentary voting behaviour that is often highly predictable, with parties acting as stable blocs. This allows reliable governing majorities to form, by combining forces between such blocs.

Particular aspects of the UK parliamentary system are worth noting in this context. First, unlike in most other countries in Europe, the electoral system for the House of Commons is based on a logic of local representation rather than party proportionality. Under this 'first past the post' system, one MP is elected for each of 650 local constituencies, with the candidate who gains the greatest number of local votes winning the seat.[1] It is the aggregate of these local decisions that determines the make-up of the House of Commons, rather than any calculation of national vote share. Small parties with dispersed support (such as the Greens) consequently struggle to win seats, while large, well-established parties (such as Labour and the Conservatives), and those with more geographically concentrated support (such as the Scottish National Party) do much better. Since 1945, more often than not either the Conservatives or Labour have won a Commons majority and been able to govern alone—though this has been less the case in recent years.[2]

The Westminster electoral system creates an incentive for large parties to hold together, contributing to them being 'broad churches' containing a diversity of opinion. While party cohesion may be the norm, this can make it hard to maintain. In addition, the very decentralized system of selecting parliamentary candidates gives party leaders less scope than in many other systems to ensure that those elected will toe the party line. Policy differences within parliamentary parties will normally be resolved in private, but sometimes can spill out into the open in the media or on the floor of parliament. Scholars have noted a gradual decline in voting cohesion since the 1950s, and particularly since the 1970s (Russell and Cowley 2016). Under Tony Blair there were some significant backbench rebellions, peaking when 139 Labour MPs voted against the Iraq War in 2003. Subsequently, the unusual formation of a coalition government between the Conservatives and Liberal Democrats in 2010 triggered unprecedentedly high levels of rebellion in both of the governing parties (Cowley and Stuart 2012b). As touched on in the previous chapter, these intra-party relationships are absolutely central to the functioning of the House of Commons. Governments depend primarily on support from their own MPs to maintain their majority: if enough of their backbenchers vote with the opposition, ministers face defeat. Consequently, the core determinant of 'executive–legislative relations' in the UK is the subtle relationship between the government and its own backbenchers rather than the more visible one with the opposition (King 1976, Russell and Cowley 2018).

The recent growth in observable party dissent at Westminster can be linked to various factors. These include procedural changes in parliament (such as the development of the House of Commons select committees from the late 1970s, which encouraged greater evidence-based, cross-party working), the demographics of MPs (such as higher levels of education), and the wider environment (including changed public expectations, and the growth of social media). Meanwhile, whips and party leaders have limited and declining disciplinary tools at their disposal to manage dissent, when contrasted with many overseas parliaments. Parliamentary leaders do not control MPs' financial allowances, and the House of Commons Speaker is a politically neutral figure, leaving party whips largely powerless regarding which members are called in debates. Particularly following reforms in 2010, which introduced elections for the chairs and members of select committees, the whips' control over committee positions is also more limited than in many other legislatures. In theory, party leaders' ultimate sanction is to 'withdraw the whip' from recalcitrant members, effectively removing them from the parliamentary party. But while this can disadvantage such members, by barring them from standing as party candidates in future elections, in the short term it is self-defeating for leaders, and so in practice is rarely used. On some divisive issues, particularly those of 'conscience', such as abortion, internal division is instead managed by allowing MPs free (i.e. unwhipped) votes (Cowley 1998). Notably, even in these cases the level of party cohesion is generally fairly high, in part simply because party members tend to agree with each other. But crucially, because policy matters before parliament are often complex, it is organizationally efficient for members to take their cue from figures that they trust, which in normal circumstances includes party frontbenchers and whips (Cowley 2005, Willumsen 2017).

The policy in question is clearly an important factor in whether parties can hold together, and there has been no single issue more divisive at Westminster than the UK's place in Europe. In both main parties, these splits have caused significant backbench dissent against the party leaderships (Smith 2012). Such divisions reflect, to an extent, the UK's historically ambivalent attitudes towards membership of the EU and its predecessor institutions, when compared to other member states. Influential commentators have referred to the UK as the 'awkward partner', a 'stranger in Europe' or 'the Eurosceptic state' (George 1998, 2007, Wall 2008). Pre 2016, public opinion surveys consistently showed UK support for membership of the EU (and predecessor institutions) to be well below the European average (Goodwin and Milazzo 2015), which both reflected and helped to induce the Eurosceptic attitudes of political elites (Evans and Butt 2007). Suggested roots of these attitudes (e.g. George 2007, Spiering 2004) included the UK's history as an 'island nation'; its success in the Second World War; its uniquely Eurosceptic media; and its electoral system—which makes EU-style bargaining and compromise somewhat alien to its political culture. Whatever the causes, as this chapter charts, such ambivalence was reflected by frequent splits inside both of the main parties over Europe right from the very outset. Following the UK's entry into the bloc, divisions on the Labour side were initially very serious, but gradually declined (Smith 2012). Meanwhile, the European issue became increasingly divisive within the Conservative Party (Bale 2006, 2016, Heppell 2014), with the parliamentary party becoming progressively more Eurosceptic over time (Cowley and Stuart 2010, Heppell 2020). UK Euroscepticism in general also gradually became more extreme, with resistance to further integration increasingly giving way to calls for the UK to withdraw from the EU entirely (Usherwood 2018).

Although the timetable of the House of Commons is quite heavily controlled by the government (as further discussed particularly in Chapter 8), Westminster provides various mechanisms that backbenchers can use to get issues onto the parliamentary agenda. MPs can propose amendments to bills, and table motions for debate and parliamentary questions, all with relatively little sanction from the whips. As described later in the chapter, these opportunities increased post 2010. Not much can be achieved by a single individual, or small handful of rebels, but if rebels begin to organize themselves and act as a cohesive group, they can put significant pressure on party frontbenchers, and potentially influence the whole direction of party policy. Just how much could be achieved through such organization was demonstrated by Conservative Eurosceptic backbenchers in the run-up to the Brexit referendum.

Parliament and the EU to 2010

British Entry into the EEC

The UK was not among the six founding members of the European Economic Community (EEC) created under the 1957 Treaty of Rome.[3] However, it very soon sought entry to the bloc (Geddes 2013, George 1998, Young 1999). Two unsuccessful applications were made in the 1960s, by Conservative Prime Minister Harold Macmillan and Labour Prime Minister Harold Wilson respectively. Admission finally occurred in 1973, under the Conservative government of Edward Heath.

Parliament had a central role in these decisions, which were initially taken without the use of a referendum. Informing MPs of the government's desire to join the bloc in 1961, Macmillan promised that '[n]o agreement will be entered into until it has been approved by the House'.[4] In 1967, under Labour, the Commons in principle strongly supported entry. Ultimately, when Heath successfully negotiated entry, MPs were consulted again.

But there were visible internal divisions within both main parliamentary parties (Norton 2011, Saunders 2018). Heath managed this situation by allowing his Conservative MPs a free vote.[5] The Labour leadership claimed to support the principle of EEC entry, but some on the party's left saw the Common Market as a 'capitalist club' which might constrain the actions of a socialist government (Daniels 1998). Faced with its own internal divisions, the opposition found reasons to whip against Heath's proposal. However, 69 pro-European Labour MPs broke ranks to vote with the government on the principle of membership, while 20 abstained. To bring this decision into domestic law, the government next needed to pass the so-called implementing legislation, in the form of the European Communities Bill. On the Conservative side, Heath was forced to declare the initial Commons vote—at the bill's second reading—a matter of confidence, meaning that defeat would cause the government to fall. Even in these circumstances, 15 Conservative MPs voted against the whip, and the bill squeaked through only narrowly with the help of a few Labour abstentions. Its remaining Commons stages took five months and resulted in numerous Conservative rebellions (Norton 2011).

One notable amendment, proposed by a Conservative backbencher, sought to make entry into the European bloc conditional on prior approval in a referendum—a mechanism never before used at national level in the UK. The Labour Shadow Cabinet was split on whether to support this. Left-wingers, led by Tony Benn, won the argument, and the decision was taken to back the referendum amendment. But this caused several other Labour frontbenchers, including the party's deputy leader Roy Jenkins, to resign. He was among 63 Labour MPs who then chose to abstain on the Conservative rebel amendment, which caused it to fail. The UK consequently went on to join the EEC with parliamentary approval, but without a referendum.

However, the depth of Labour's splits meant that, when the party re-entered government in 1974, this was on a promise to renegotiate the membership terms and put these directly to the people. Party leader Harold Wilson had previously declared himself strongly opposed to referendums, as had various other key figures including soon-to-be Conservative leader Margaret Thatcher (Saunders 2018). Nonetheless, an in/out referendum was a key demand of the Labour left. Wilson conducted a brief renegotiation with the UK's European partners, and the referendum took place in 1975. Cabinet members were permitted to campaign on either side, with Benn and other left-wingers arguing for Britain to leave the EEC, while most, including Jenkins and Shirley Williams, argued for it to stay. The Conservative leadership, and great majority of the party's MPs, also supported continued membership, as did most of the media. The result was strong public endorsement of this position, by 67.2 per cent to 32.8 per cent.

The Thatcher and Major Years

In the years that immediately followed, Labour's travails over Europe remained significant, playing a major role in the breakaway by Jenkins, Williams, and others to form the Social Democratic Party (SDP) in 1981 (Crewe and King 1995). But they subsequently waned. Meanwhile, unease on the Conservative side grew, particularly in response to developments at the European level. Europe was changing, and further treaties often provided flashpoints, triggering divisions inside parliament and parallel political pressures outside.

The first major change was the Single European Act of 1986. This caused limited Conservative concern, being seen as consistent with the kind of market liberalization that the UK government espoused. But subsequently, attention increasingly shifted to greater regulation to promote a level playing field.

This began to change attitudes in both parties—being attractive to Labour, but less welcome on the Conservative side. In 1988, European Commission President Jacques Delors addressed the UK's Trades Union Congress (TUC), highlighting the EEC's potential to enhance social protection. The immediate riposte was Margaret Thatcher's widely cited Bruges speech, rejecting moves towards a federal political union (Young 1999). Thatcher had been a firm proponent of EEC membership in 1975, but now increasingly came to be seen as a Eurosceptic.

The peak of tensions came over the Maastricht Treaty, agreed in 1991. Its timing closely coincided with other key developments. First, Thatcher had been ousted as Conservative leader the preceding year and replaced by John Major, who was more relaxed about European integration. Second, in the midst of parliament's debates on the treaty, the UK was forced out of the European Exchange Rate Mechanism (ERM)—an arrangement designed to align countries in preparation for potential monetary union, about which Thatcher herself had been unenthusiastic. The UK's exit from the ERM followed major instability on the currency markets in the wake of a referendum in Denmark which rejected the terms of the Maastricht Treaty, and fears that the same would occur in France. In the UK these events were both politically and economically destabilizing.

A third contextual factor was not directly connected, but was also crucial to the changing mood. In the courts, the *Factortame* cases established definitively that UK law could not conflict with European Community law, and if found to do so must be set aside (Drewry 2016). The first ruling occurred in the European Court of Justice in 1990, and the second in the UK's highest court in 1991.[6] The cases underlined what now seems an obvious point— that while UK representatives could participate in and influence the European decision-making process, parliament had de facto ceded some of its traditional sovereignty to the European institutions. It is often noted that this question had been downplayed during the process of UK accession in the 1970s, with ministers suggesting that parliamentary sovereignty would be largely unaffected (Bogdanor 2012, Norton 2011), though the extent to which this is true can be exaggerated (Saunders 2018). But such arguments became harder to sustain as the European project gradually developed.

The legislation to implement Maastricht was introduced in the House of Commons shortly after the 1992 general election, which had been narrowly won by Major's Conservatives. Labour was broadly supportive of the treaty, though unhappy that the government had negotiated a UK opt-out from the 'social chapter', which introduced new employment protections. At the second reading debate, some of the key arguments from the 1970s were replayed. Tony Benn argued that approval of the treaty should be subject to a referendum, and that the Labour leadership's refusal to support this was 'not only immoral but inexplicable'.[7] The preceding year Margaret Thatcher had argued—in contrast to her previous hostility to the device—that a referendum on the treaty was essential.[8] Major's government was determined to resist these calls.

Passage of the bill was subject to multiple rebellions. Those on the Conservative side were most important, given the government's narrow majority, but there was also resistance from MPs from the Labour left. At second reading, 58 Labour members, including Benn and others who had argued for exit in 1975, such as Jeremy Corbyn (elected to parliament in 1983), joined 23 Conservative Eurosceptics in voting against the bill. In total, there were 62 different occasions when Conservative MPs rebelled, and 50 such rebels in total (Cowley and Stuart 2012a). The demand for a referendum was debated during the Commons committee stage, when a Labour backbench amendment on the issue was fairly easily defeated. But it attracted support from Conservative Eurosceptics, including new members such as Bernard Jenkin and Iain Duncan Smith, who had entered the Commons in 1992. Once the bill had passed, ministers faced particular difficulties in a follow-up vote to bring its provisions into effect, engineered by Labour over the social chapter. This provided a last-ditch opportunity for Eurosceptics to block the legislation, and resulted in a government defeat by eight votes. Major persuaded the Commons to overturn this, but only by declaring the issue a matter of confidence (Baker, Gamble, and Ludlam 1994).

The Maastricht battles were a significant turning point. Within parliament, they inspired formation of the Fresh Start group of Conservative MPs, which gathered over 80 signatures to an early day motion (EDM) opposed to the treaty, and sought a 'fresh start' to the UK's relationship with Europe. This and the rebellions on the bill helped to harden alliances among Eurosceptics. This significantly destabilized the Major government, which at one stage stripped eight Eurosceptic rebels of the whip, though they were subsequently reinstated.

Outside parliament, these events also helped to motivate the formation of new organizations. The UK Independence Party (UKIP) was officially launched in 1993, having grown out of a prior organization created to field anti-Maastricht candidates at the 1992 general election (Ford and Goodwin 2014). In subsequent years it gradually increased in strength. More significant in the short term was formation of the Referendum Party in 1994, by wealthy businessman James Goldsmith.[9] It sought a public vote on the UK's relationship with Europe—not explicitly opposing European membership itself, but firmly arguing that the

Maastricht Treaty had gone too far (Carter et al. 1998). Goldsmith's party went on to field 547 candidates at the 1997 general election; partly in response, 284 Conservative parliamentary candidates issued Eurosceptic statements that contradicted the party's official policy (McAllister and Studlar 2000).

Europe under Blair and Brown

The 1997 election resulted in a landslide victory for Labour, and a governing party which was more unequivocally pro-European. Nonetheless, even Tony Blair was reluctant to extol the virtues of Europe, and he continued to present Britain as an EU 'outsider' (Daddow 2015). A key motivator was appealing to the press, which had moved from overwhelming support for EEC membership in the 1970s to increasingly strident Euroscepticism (Daddow 2012).

Blair's government swiftly implemented a manifesto commitment to sign up to the social chapter. In the ensuing period, the prospect of the UK joining the European single currency (the euro) became a significant topic of debate and tension, including on the Labour side. Both the Labour and Conservative 1997 manifestos had pledged that this would only happen if the public supported it in a referendum.

Labour remained in power for 13 years, during which pressure grew for referendums on various European matters, again partly in response to new treaties furthering European integration. The new Conservative leader, William Hague, cultivated a relatively Eurosceptic image, demanding that the 1997 Amsterdam Treaty should be put to a public vote, and approaching the 2001 general election with a campaign to 'save the pound'. At that election both main parties repeated their pledge that entry into the euro would require approval at a referendum, and the Conservatives went further, promising that this would apply to any further transfer of power to European level.

On the Labour side both the Amsterdam Treaty and the Nice Treaty, which followed in 2001, were relatively uncontroversial. In any case, Labour's large Commons majority assured the implementing legislation an easy passage. A key purpose of these treaties was to facilitate European enlargement, with 10 new member states joining what was by now the European Union (EU) in 2004, followed by a further two in 2007. The principle of enlargement was supported by both the Conservatives and Labour, and had even been explicitly supported in the Fresh Start EDM. But, importantly, the UK became one of just three existing member states to allow immediate free inward movement from the new accession countries, such as Poland,

Hungary, and the Czech Republic. This came to fuel increasing public anxiety about immigration.

More contentious over this period was another new treaty proposing a Constitution for Europe, initially signed in 2004. It raised significant additional concerns about sovereignty, and pressures for a referendum on the treaty's terms. Before it was signed, Blair conceded a referendum in principle, and the party's 2005 general election manifesto repeated the pledge. The Conservatives, Liberal Democrats, Scottish National Party (SNP), and Plaid Cymru all promised the same. By this point pressure from UKIP was growing—the party had won 16 per cent of the national vote and 12 of the UK's 78 seats in the European Parliament elections of 2004. Seemingly there was something approaching political consensus that a referendum would be needed.

But before the necessary legislation was approved in the UK, referendums in both France and the Netherlands rejected the Constitutional Treaty. This prompted a renegotiation, resulting in the Lisbon Treaty of 2007. The Conservatives, now under the leadership of David Cameron, retained the commitment that a referendum must be held. Liberal Democrat leader Vince Cable proposed instead that there should be an in/out referendum—making this traditionally most pro-European of the parties the first in the recent period to make such a pledge. But Labour, now led by Gordon Brown, used the switch to the Lisbon Treaty as an opportunity to drop the commitment to a risky referendum.

The implementing legislation for Lisbon was introduced in January 2008, and the absence of a referendum commitment was a central focus of parliamentary debate. At the bill's second reading in the Commons, William Hague (now Shadow Foreign Secretary) argued that the treaty was 'nearly identical' to the Constitutional Treaty, and should be subject to a public vote.[10] Labour's Gisela Stuart—a centrist backbencher who had been one of two House of Commons representatives on the European Convention, which had agreed the 2004 draft Constitution—stated that 'I cannot for the life of me understand why our side is reneging on its promise'.[11] At the end of the second reading, 18 Labour MPs voted against the bill, including left-wingers such as Jeremy Corbyn and John McDonnell, and other Eurosceptics such as Frank Field and Kate Hoey. During the subsequent committee stage, a Conservative frontbench amendment, which attracted 28 Labour rebel votes, demanded that the treaty should be subject to a referendum. The demand was raised again in the House of Lords, but proposals for a referendum were defeated in both chambers—meaning that the treaty came into effect without a public vote.

Notwithstanding these upsets, Labour was now significantly more united on European questions than it had been in the past, and significantly less divided than the Conservatives. The small group of Labour Eurosceptics was unable seriously to trouble Blair and Brown. It hence might have appeared that the turmoil of the 1970s and 1990s had been left behind. As Cowley and Stuart (2010: 140) remarked, during this period 'Europe was the dog that didn't bark'. But that was all set to change.

Pressures under the 2010–15 Coalition Government

Labour left office in 2010, to be replaced by the Conservative/Liberal Democrat coalition led by David Cameron. Cameron presented himself as a centrist modernizer (Denham and O'Hara 2007), and shortly after being elected leader in December 2005 had appealed to his party to stop 'banging on about Europe' (Cameron 2006). Nonetheless, he had given in to Eurosceptic pressure during the leadership contest by promising to remove Conservative Members of the European Parliament (MEPs) from the centre-right European People's Party, to the consternation even of his more naturally Eurosceptic opponent David Davis (Watt 2009). This balancing act of seeking to placate the party's Eurosceptic wing while pursuing a more centrist path was to plague Cameron's premiership—and indeed, that of his successor.

The 2010 Conservative manifesto repeated the commitment to a 'referendum lock' on any further treaty transferring powers to European level, and commented that the 'steady and unaccountable intrusion of the European Union into almost every aspect of our lives has gone too far' (Conservative Party 2010: 114). The Liberal Democrats, in contrast, were conventionally far more pro-European, but had a manifesto pledge to facilitate an in/out referendum before any other fundamental change was made. Interviewees put the evolution of this rather curious position down to electoral pressures, including in the party's then stronghold of south-west England, coupled with the fact that few in the party expected it to wind up in government. The coalition agreement signed after the election combined elements of both parties' positions, promising that the government would be 'a positive participant in the European Union', but that it would resist any further transfer of powers and legislate for a 'referendum lock' (HM Government 2010: 19).

This latter policy was delivered via the European Union Act 2011, which passed relatively easily through both chambers of parliament in the first session after the election. Labour did not resist the principle of a referendum lock on further treaty change. Liberal Democrat backbenchers expressed concerns that the legislation was pandering to Conservative Eurosceptics, while members of that bloc argued that it didn't go far enough. At the second reading, veteran Eurosceptic Bill Cash described it as a 'mouse of a Bill' which did little to protect parliamentary sovereignty.[12] Here, writ large, was the paradox of parliament being asked to legislate ostensibly to protect its own powers—by removing its powers to decide on future treaties and handing them to the people (Bogdanor 2019, Wellings and Vines 2016).

More significant than this was the increasing level of pressure heaped on Cameron by his own backbenchers to facilitate a referendum on the principle of EU membership—as was ultimately delivered in 2016. Conservative backbenchers used a variety of parliamentary mechanisms to keep this issue on the agenda, before and after Cameron himself had promised to act.

Early Backbench Pressures

The 2010 general election had put the Conservatives back in government for the first time in 13 years, but tempered by a strongly pro-European coalition partner. Meanwhile, continuing the trend from previous elections, the new intake of Conservative backbenchers was increasingly Eurosceptic. This provided a fertile environment in which hardliners could organize dissent targeted at the government (Lynch and Whitaker 2013).

From relatively early on, a small group of established Eurosceptics began meeting on a regular basis to plan a coordinated backbench campaign, with the aim of nurturing rebel voices and demonstrating increasing strength against the government (Whale 2021). Some key members were newly elected in 2010, including John Baron, David Nuttall, and the group's unofficial whip, Steve Baker (D'Arcy 2016). Its work was assisted by a shifting environment outside parliament, including continued electoral pressures from UKIP and the growing assertiveness of the Eurosceptic press. In an early demonstration of this in November 2010, the front-page headline in the *Daily Express* demanded that the government should 'Get Britain out of the EU', citing the recent eurozone crisis as an added reason for hostility to the bloc. The article suggested that the Lisbon Treaty had been 'disgracefully imposed upon the public without the referendum they were promised' (Daily Express 2010). Eurosceptic MPs encouraged, and sought to profit from, this external pressure.

One of their key moves took advantage of a new mechanism which became available to backbenchers from 2010, allowing them to get issues of interest onto the parliamentary agenda. Towards the end of the previous parliament the Select Committee on the Reform of the House of Commons (commonly known as the 'Wright Committee') had been established by Gordon Brown in response to the MPs' expenses crisis, to consider changes to revitalize the Commons. It recommended a series of reforms which would strengthen the hand of MPs against the party whips (Russell 2011). The best known was the introduction of elections for chairs and members of select committees, with chairs elected by all MPs on a cross-party basis. But the other significant change was the establishment of a Backbench Business Committee, run by and for backbenchers. This committee invited proposals for debates, prioritizing topics able to demonstrate cross-party support. Using this route, a group headed by David Nuttall secured a debate on an EU referendum. This followed a symbolic visit to 10 Downing Street by a collection of Eurosceptic MPs, to deliver a petition of over 100,000 signatures demanding the same, which had been gathered with the help of the *Daily Express*.

The debate on Nuttall's motion took place on 24 October 2011, and crucially ended in a vote—allowing MPs to express their views on the record. The motion was carefully constructed to maximize support, asking the government to introduce a bill providing for a referendum on three options—maintaining the status quo of EU membership, leaving the EU, or renegotiating the terms of membership. Notably, some key Conservative Eurosceptics at the time favoured the third of these options, rather than an in/out vote. Introducing the motion, Nuttall argued that 'this country, indeed this Parliament, is becoming ever more impotent as more and more decisions are taken in Brussels', while his ally John Baron argued that the 'nature of our relationship with the EU has fundamentally changed since we joined it in 1975, yet the British people have not been consulted on that change'.[13] Speaking for the government, Foreign Secretary William Hague expressed agreement that 'disillusionment with the European Union in this country is at an unprecedented level', but argued that the coalition's approach of introducing a referendum lock, coupled with efforts to repatriate responsibilities, was sufficient.[14] But this didn't satisfy restive backbenchers, and 81 Conservatives voted against the government. This was one of the largest Conservative rebellions of the post-war era, and 49 of the rebels were new MPs, drawn from the 2010 intake (Cowley and Stuart 2012a). Labour abstained, meaning that the government easily won the vote (although 19 Labour members, including the usual Eurosceptic names, such as Corbyn, McDonnell, Field, Hoey, and Stuart, supported the motion). But the political effect was nonetheless significant. Writing subsequently, David Cameron

(2019a: 332) recalled that the result 'showed the extent to which the ground was moving beneath us'.

After this, the Eurosceptic rebels sought to maintain pressure and demonstrate increasing support. In June 2012, John Baron organized a letter to the Prime Minister, demanding a referendum on the UK's relationship with the EU, which attracted almost 100 Conservative MPs as signatories (Montgomerie 2012). This resulted in a meeting with Cameron, who hinted that he might concede. When no action followed, Eurosceptics inflicted a defeat on the government on 31 October 2012 in a non-binding vote on the EU budget, with an amendment led by backbencher Mark Reckless that attracted 53 Conservative rebels.

Cameron's Referendum Pledge at Bloomberg

David Cameron finally committed to holding a referendum in a speech delivered at Bloomberg's London headquarters on 23 January 2013. By then he was facing yet further pressures. In November 2012, UKIP had taken second place in two by-elections in safe Labour seats in the north of England, forcing the Conservatives into fourth and fifth place. Those close to Cameron believed that he could soon face a leadership challenge if he didn't promise a public vote (Bale 2018, Oliver 2016). His closest allies were divided on the wisdom of making such a pledge, but increasingly it seemed inevitable. With the next European Parliament elections due in 2014, there were reasonable expectations of a further UKIP surge. One senior Conservative interviewee recalled a mood that 'if you're going to do it, then you really need to get in before the 2014 elections, otherwise you'll be seen as having it extracted from you by [UKIP leader] Nigel Farage'. Cameron (2019a: 398) himself noted that the announcement in the speech was the product of '[m]onths, even years, of thinking, arguing, listening and planning', and that he had first given serious thought to promising a referendum in early 2012—shortly after the backbench business debate.

The Bloomberg speech itself noted some of the same public frustrations that had been voiced by backbench Eurosceptics—including the numerous treaty changes made with no public vote, even when one had been promised by party leaders. Cameron (2013) was fairly frank about his motives, noting that the longer a referendum was put off, the more likely that when one came it would result in rejection of the EU; hence 'simply hoping a difficult situation will go away' was no longer an option. There was no claim that the desire for a referendum came from his own Euroscepticism, and it was clear that his preference was for continued EU membership. At the time, polling seemed to suggest that this was the likely outcome—the British Social Attitudes survey showed a narrowing but very large gap between those wishing to remain or leave, standing at 57 per cent to 35 per cent in 2014, though a substantial majority held more broadly defined Eurosceptic attitudes (Curtice and Ormston 2015). Recalling the decision to commit to a referendum in his memoirs, Cameron (2019a: 400) noted that, paradoxically, 'I believed this strategy was the most likely way to keep Britain in the EU'. In retrospect, however, his words at Bloomberg seem better to describe Gordon Brown's risky avoidance strategy over the Lisbon Treaty, while Cameron's own high-stakes gamble proved to come too late.

Cameron (2019a: 406) was later open, and unapologetic, about the extent to which he had succumbed to backbench pressure in making the Bloomberg pledge. He noted that '[i]n a parliamentary democracy, the leader of a parliamentary group has to pay attention to the views of that group. And that group was pressing for a referendum.'

Further Backbench Pressures, and the Private Members' Bills

By promising a referendum, Cameron clearly hoped to resolve a difficult situation, but even after the Bloomberg speech the tension within parliament continued growing. The following month, John Baron proposed the UK Membership of the European Union (Referendum) Bill, as a 10-minute rule bill. These are largely symbolic opportunities for MPs to bring issues to prominence on the floor of the House of Commons, but the signal from the rebels was clear—they wanted not just the promise of a referendum but the introduction of a bill to secure one.

This message was heard very plainly in May 2013, when the rebels used unusual means to draw attention to their demands and show their strength. The government had just introduced its Queen's Speech, setting out the proposed legislative programme for the coming parliamentary session. Eurosceptic backbenchers, again led by Baron, tabled an amendment to the motion approving the speech, criticizing the absence of a bill to facilitate an EU referendum. The amendment attracted over 90 signatures, the great majority of them Conservative.

As with the backbench business debate, and Baron's mass letter to the Prime Minister the year before, signatories went well beyond the 'usual suspects' of hardline Eurosceptics. Obvious supporters of such initiatives (many of whom would rise to prominence later in the Brexit debates) included Steve Baker, Graham Brady, David Davis, Bernard Jenkin, Andrea Leadsom, and Jacob Rees-Mogg. But these various schemes also drew in more centrist Conservatives, not all of them Eurosceptic, and some of whom (such as Guto Bebb, Phillip Lee, and Sarah Wollaston) subsequently found themselves on the opposite side of the debate.[15] It therefore isn't possible to take such lists as a pure indication of Eurosceptic sentiment, or indeed of a politically cohesive group. Some rebels supported these initiatives because of local electoral pressures, whereas some committed Eurosceptics who held ministerial office were unable to support them. Importantly, some proponents of a referendum shared a similar analysis to Cameron—simply seeking to bring a divisive argument within the party and the country to an end. As one supporter put it in interview, their attitude was 'let's just lance this boil…let's get that part of the party boxed into a corner where they can't legitimately bellyache about it any more.'

The Queen's Speech amendment was striking for various reasons. First, such a widely supported hostile amendment from the government's own side was unusual. But second, it was also unprecedented for such an amendment to be selected for decision. Up to that point, the norm had been for the House of Commons Speaker to select two amendments on the final day of debate on the motion approving a Queen's Speech—one from the official opposition and the other from the second opposition party. On this occasion the Speaker, John Bercow, selected three, including the Conservative back-bench rebel amendment. This caused significant controversy.

The role of Speaker Bercow was to become increasingly contested in later years over Brexit. He had been elected to the position in 2009 in the wake of the MPs' expenses crisis, on a manifesto to revitalize the chamber. In line with the Wright Committee reforms, he presented himself as a champion of backbenchers. Despite his own background, having been a Conservative MP since 1997, he was disinclined to give ministers an easy ride. And despite his later characterization as an arch-Remainer, he had begun his political career as a Eurosceptic. In one debate in the 1990s, for example, Bercow had spoken of 'the stench of the course of European federalism', arguing that 'the drift in the direction of more Community power will need to be arrested and reversed'.[16] There are various reasons, therefore, why he may have been well disposed towards the rebel amendment. Despite the precedents being pointed out to him behind the scenes by his neutral procedural advisers, the parliamentary clerks, he chose to select it for debate.[17]

In response, there were reports that the Prime Minister was considering supporting the rebel amendment in order to neutralize the argument (Syal 2013), but for the coalition government as a whole to do so would have been impossible, given the Liberal Democrats' opposition. This was the first clear sign of splits over the issue inside the coalition. Cameron was now prepared to accede to his backbenchers' demands, but there was no possibility of a government bill on a referendum. Instead, the Conservative Party pursued the highly unusual route of publishing a draft referendum bill on its own behalf. Speaking during the last day of debate on the Queen's Speech, Chancellor of the Exchequer George Osborne indicated that the party leadership had done this 'in good time' for the ballot on private members' bills—so that any backbencher could take up the bill, knowing that it had the party's blessing.[18] But without a Conservative majority in the Commons, and with limited support on the opposition side, it was always unlikely to pass. The concession proved insufficient to buy off most of the rebels, and 116 Conservatives (plus 14 others) voted for the Queen's Speech amendment on 15 May. Conservative whips had sought to minimize conflict by encouraging the party's MPs to abstain; they therefore effectively relied on opposition MPs' votes to defeat the rebel amendment.

Two iterations of the Conservative-sponsored bill were introduced, in the parliamentary sessions of 2013–14 and 2014–15. The first was sponsored by Conservative backbencher James Wharton. Its Commons second reading was on 5 July 2013, with 304 MPs voting in favour and none against. Six Labour members, including Gisela Stuart, supported the bill.[19] Although the Labour frontbench spokesperson, Douglas Alexander, argued in favour of EU membership and against a referendum, the party asked its members to abstain—as did the Liberal Democrats—not wishing to be accused of denying the public its say. The bill completed its Commons stages in November, but ran into difficulties in the Lords. Here divisions within the coalition were very clear, with the minister Baroness (Sayeeda) Warsi taking care to point out when responding to the debate that 'I am not speaking for the whole coalition. As will be obvious to the House, I am speaking on behalf of the Conservative Party.'[20] The possibility of sabotage was significantly higher in the Lords, given that the chamber attracts relatively little media attention and members are not subject to the same electoral pressures as those in the Commons. Despite dire warnings from the former Conservative Leader of the Lords, Lord (Tom) Strathclyde, that it would be quite wrong for peers to engage in 'procedural tactics' to block a bill that the Commons had approved, this is exactly what went on to happen.[21] On 31 January 2014, a Labour backbench motion, with support from the Liberal Democrats, curtailed debate and effectively killed the bill.

By the next session, pressures were further mounting on the Conservatives. In the June 2014 European Parliament elections, UKIP achieved 27 per cent of the national vote—a higher proportion than any other party, pushing the Conservatives into third place. In August, Eurosceptic rebel MP Douglas Carswell announced that he was quitting the party and joining UKIP, followed by fellow rebel Mark Reckless the next month. Both resigned as MPs in order to trigger by-elections, which they fought and won as UKIP candidates.

It was in these gloomy circumstances for Cameron's party that the second iteration of the European Union (Referendum) Bill was introduced by Conservative backbencher Bob Neill. It had its second reading in the Commons on 17 October 2014. However, this time it was blocked more directly, due to disagreements between the coalition partners, which resulted in it being denied a government-supported money resolution (required for any bill entailing spending). This prevented it from proceeding any further.

The Conservative Government of 2015

The 2015 general election was held, in line with the coalition's new Fixed-term Parliaments Act 2011, at the end of the 2010 parliament's allotted five-year period. It was by now an inevitability that the Conservative Party (2015: 30) would go to the country with a pledge to hold, in the words of the manifesto, 'a straight in-out referendum on our membership of the European Union'. The proposal, highly reminiscent of Wilson's strategy 40 years previously, was to do so after a renegotiation over the UK's terms of membership. More unexpectedly, the Conservatives won a narrow House of Commons majority at the election. Many had anticipated a further coalition, but the Liberal Democrats lost all but eight of their 57 seats, while Labour's total declined due to SNP gains in Scotland. The Conservatives made a net gain of 24 seats overall.

The Principle of Holding a Referendum

The question of whether David Cameron ever really intended to follow through on his referendum promise has been subject to much speculation. Cameron (2019a) himself has denied that he had been banking on a new deal with the Liberal Democrats to allow him to drop the pledge, though senior interviewees for this book from both parties assumed that this had been the case. In practice, the tide of opposition on the Conservative benches in parliament, and from UKIP outside, by now made avoidance difficult. The

Liberal Democrat manifesto had repeated the party's commitment to an in/ out referendum in the event of further treaty change (already enshrined in the European Union Act 2011). Labour's leader, Ed Miliband, had resisted calls to promise a referendum in the manifesto—despite some mainstream figures in the party having pressed for it in order to resist the UKIP tide. This question remains one of the many 'what-ifs' of the Brexit story, but a referendum was probably not stoppable by 2015.

Having made the promise and won the election, the new Conservative government moved immediately to introduce the European Union Referendum Bill, which had its second reading in the House of Commons on 9 June 2015. Speaking for the government, Foreign Secretary Philip Hammond used the now-familiar argument that repeated treaties had left the EU 'changed almost beyond recognition' since the 1975 referendum, with 'an entire generation of British voters…denied the chance to have a say'.[22] In contrast, he pointed out, other referendums had since been held on devolution and potential change to the voting system for the House of Commons. Leading for Labour, Shadow Foreign Secretary Hilary Benn (the son of Tony Benn, so central to the debates of previous decades) indicated that the party's position was to 'support the Bill and its passage through Parliament, but…also support Britain remaining a member of the EU', despite the imperfections of the bloc.[23] A similar position was taken by Tom Brake, speaking for the Liberal Democrats, and by Caroline Lucas, speaking for the Greens, who argued in favour of 'three yeses—yes to a referendum, yes to major [EU] reform, and ultimately yes to staying in the EU'.[24] The only party spokesperson expressing opposition to the principle of a referendum was the SNP's Alex Salmond. The SNP also provided the dissenting reasoned amendment—a procedural device commonly used at the second reading of contentious bills, which states reasons why the bill should be opposed. The amendment pointed out that 16- and 17-year-olds, and EU nationals living in the UK, would be excluded from the franchise, and argued that there should be a 'double majority provision', requiring support for exit in every part of the UK.[25]

By this point, therefore, support for the principle of a referendum on EU membership was virtual parliamentary orthodoxy. The main UK-wide opposition parties may not have relished such a vote, but felt unable to resist one, particularly after its endorsement in the governing party's manifesto. Labour also had been immediately thrown into turmoil after the election, following Ed Miliband's resignation as party leader (which resulted, as discussed in the next chapter, in the surprise election of Jeremy Corbyn as leader). As one Labour interviewee emphasized, 'people were shellshocked' after the election defeat. Another senior Labour interviewee said of the government's bill, 'I was of the view that we should support it because it was going to happen anyway and there's no point in opposing it, because that will be used as a stick with which to beat us in the referendum when it happens'. The bill's second reading was approved by 544 votes to 53, with Labour supporting the government.[26]

The Principle of Brexit

One remarkable feature of the 2010–15 period, given the magnitude of the question to be put in the referendum, was the total lack of parliamentary debate on the principle of the UK's EU membership. There were multiple opportunities to debate the principle of a referendum, as summarized above, but never a formal debate—in government, opposition, or backbench time—on the far more fundamental principle of whether the UK should remain in or leave the EU.

Instead, these discussions, insofar as they took place, did so within the framework of debates about a referendum. Hence Philip Hammond's speech at the second reading of the European Union Referendum Bill struck a noticeably Eurosceptic tone, putting emphasis on the flaws in the current arrangements—perhaps calculated not only to please backbenchers and the Eurosceptic public but to prepare for a sense of 'victory' in the renegotiations. The other parties used the bill to express lukewarm support for the principle of membership, while their key arguments focused on the principle of public consultation and the logistics of a referendum. Overall, 21 of the 79 speakers in the second reading debate spoke explicitly in favour of remaining in the EU, and 14 explicitly supported leaving, while various others supported the principle of renegotiation.[27] But a full 35 members avoided these topics entirely. In retrospect, parliamentarians' abdication of responsibility for formally debating this question is striking. Had MPs been invited to vote on the principle of EU membership prior to the referendum, and done so sincerely, support for it would likely have been overwhelming. The government's dominance of the Commons agenda (discussed in Chapter 8) means that such a debate would most readily and naturally have been provided in government time. But the ever more Eurosceptic drift among Conservative MPs obviously made this an awkward topic for ministers. On balance, both main parties clearly preferred to avoid it.

Examination of the parliamentary record during debate on the EU Referendum Bill also shows that remarkably little attention was given to key issues that went on to dominate debate after the referendum. During the entirety of the House of Commons debates on the bill, Article 50 (the article of the Lisbon Treaty specifying the conditions for a member state to leave the EU) was mentioned only once. Cheryl Gillan, a moderate Conservative Eurosceptic, made a plea at second reading for 'the necessary intricacies of article 50 of the Treaty on European Union to be spelt out to people', arguing that '[o]n both sides of the argument, we need to know what would govern the processes and negotiations of unilateral withdrawal'.[28] However, this call went unheeded throughout the rest of the debates—and indeed throughout the months that followed.

Likewise, the impact of Brexit on Northern Ireland became absolutely central to later debates, given its status as the only part of the UK sharing a land border with the EU. But just one member—Mark Durkan of the Northern Ireland Social Democratic and Labour Party (SDLP)—raised this question during the debates on the bill, again during second reading. There were 57 mentions of Northern Ireland in total throughout the Commons debates, but the others related to more administrative matters concerning the referendum itself—for example in the context of the SNP's 'double majority' proposal. Throughout the entire period preceding the referendum, there was just one half-hour debate, outside the main Commons chamber, again sponsored by the SDLP, on the likely impact of Brexit on Northern Ireland.[29]

Possibly both of these specific issues would have attracted further attention had there been a major parliamentary debate on the principle of Brexit itself. Instead, as discussed in the next chapter, both remained largely absent from the referendum campaign that followed. Even the House of Lords Constitution Committee (2015: 3), which reported on the EU Referendum Bill during its parliamentary passage in October 2015, commented, 'We do not intend to comment on the Bill in detail. Although the referendum it institutes will be of the utmost constitutional importance, the Bill itself simply provides for the holding of a referendum.' The fact that the bill 'simply' provided for a referendum on EU membership—and that the prospect of a vote to leave was never really taken seriously—enabled parliament to avoid ever airing its collective view on the substance of the issue to be put before the public.

The Detailed Arguments over the European Union Referendum Bill

The debates on the government's bill facilitating the referendum thus largely focused on the detail of how it should be implemented. While the UK has some standing arrangements for the holding of referendums, set out in the

Political Parties, Elections and Referendums Act 2000 (PPERA), details for each specific referendum must be legislated for separately, and there have frequently been departures from the basics in PPERA on a case-by-case basis.

Three main topics about referendum organization attracted particular attention during the parliamentary debates: the so-called 'purdah' provisions, the government's proposal for the franchise, and the specific question to be put to the public. While other issues such as timing, the 'double majority', and details of campaign regulation received attention, there was no change and limited resistance to the government's proposals in these areas. Notably, on all three of the key topics parliament's ultimate decision came down in favour of provisions likely to benefit those campaigning to leave the EU.

The Purdah Provisions

In UK politics, 'purdah' is a prescribed period immediately before an election or referendum vote when the government and other public bodies must avoid controversy and activities likely to influence the result, such as making major new policy announcements. For referendums, section 125 of PPERA prescribed a 28-day purdah period.

The government's initial proposal in the European Union Referendum Bill was that section 125 should be disapplied. At second reading, Philip Hammond argued that following the usual provisions would be 'unworkable and inappropriate'.[30] Unworkable because they would impede the government's day-to-day business of dealing with the European Union, and inappropriate because the government intended to renegotiate the UK's membership terms, after which it believed it would be justified to advocate these new terms to the British people. Hilary Benn was inclined to agree. However, this provision concerned many MPs, particularly Eurosceptics—who feared that the government would try to influence the vote—and it became a key focus of their objections to the bill. Even Dominic Grieve, the former Conservative Attorney General, who would later become a leading opponent of the parliamentary Brexiteers, claimed that the proposal 'could convey an impression that the Government will come in and try to load the dice, and that must be avoided'.[31]

At the Commons committee stage in mid-June 2015, the government faced a rebel amendment signed by Conservative Eurosceptics, alongside Labour's Kate Hoey and members of the DUP, to apply the usual section 125 provisions. The amendment was defeated by 288 votes to 97 (mainly comprising these groups, plus the SNP)—with Labour choosing to abstain. But this put the government in potential trouble. In the ensuing weeks, before the bill reached its report stage, the House of Commons Public Administration and Constitutional Affairs Committee, chaired by Eurosceptic Bernard Jenkin, announced an inquiry into the bill. Having taken evidence, it submitted a letter to the government arguing that section 125 should not be disapplied, and that the proposal to do so had 'cast a shadow of doubt over the propriety of the process' (Jenkin 2015). At report stage, on 7 September, the government brought forward a compromise amendment which failed to satisfy the Eurosceptics. By this time Labour had spotted an opportunity to inflict defeat, so joined forces with the rebels, causing the government's own amendment to fail by 312 votes to 285.[32] Immediately afterwards, an opposition amendment which removed the offending clause of the bill, and made the referendum subject to the usual section 125 restrictions, was agreed without a division.

In his memoirs, Cameron (2019a: 624) admits to having faced some dilemmas around the detailed provisions for the referendum, including the possibility of expanding the franchise (discussed below). But he had feared the impression of 'an establishment stitch-up, tipping the balance in favour of remaining'. He indicates that, having considered the various options, 'I saved my firepower for trying to make sure that the government could operate effectively as close to referendum day as possible' (Cameron 2019a: 626). The Eurosceptics had frustrated his plan, facilitated by a Labour opposition that seemed to prioritize the short-term satisfaction of defeating the government over its larger, longer-term policy objectives.

The Franchise

The issue of the franchise, as Cameron's comment illustrates, was treated differently. An argument running throughout the debates on the bill was whether it was right to stick to the usual default for general elections, which excluded 16- and 17-year-olds from the vote, and also excluded EU citizens resident in the UK—who clearly had a significant stake in the outcome of the referendum. If included, both groups would, in practice, be disproportionately likely to vote in favour of remaining in the EU.

The government's decision was to maintain the standard franchise—not least because to do otherwise would have fuelled accusations of manipulation of the referendum result. Opposition parties questioned this. Hilary Benn spoke in favour of enfranchising 16- and 17-year-olds, which was now Labour Party policy for general elections, but did support the government on EU citizens. Liberal Democrat Tom Brake and the SNP's Alex Salmond proposed change on both fronts—with Salmond able to cite the fact that 16- and 17-year-olds had now been enfranchised for Scottish elections. Amendments on these points were easily defeated in the Commons as they had little Conservative support. When the bill got to the Lords, where combined opposition forces were substantially stronger, the government did suffer a defeat on extending the vote to 16- and 17-year-olds. However, this was swiftly overturned when the bill returned to the Commons, and peers did not insist on their amendment.

The Referendum Question

The third and final issue was not hugely contentious during the parliamentary debates, but did result in a change to the wording of the bill. As a referendum question, the government had initially proposed 'Should the United Kingdom remain a member of the European Union?', inviting a Yes/No response. But part of the process for referendums under PPERA is that the independent Electoral Commission must report and advise on the question. In considering the Wharton Bill, the Electoral Commission (2013) had suggested that either a Yes/No format, or an alternative of Remain/Leave, could be acceptable. The latter could be considered more neutral, due to the positive connotations of 'Yes', but would be a departure from previous practice. The original formulation of the government's bill hence complied with this advice.

But in the context of the new bill the Electoral Commission (2015) conducted a fresh assessment, based on testing alternative question formats with voters and conducting a public consultation. This time, the Commission came down more firmly in favour of a Leave/Remain referendum question, which asked 'Should the United Kingdom remain a member of the European Union or leave the European Union?' Appropriately, given the Commission's independent status, the government immediately accepted this recommendation, and the bill was amended to this effect during its passage through parliament.

Looking back on these events, some experts suggested that the Commission's recommendation may have been influenced by very effective lobbying by supporters of leaving the EU (Renwick and Hazell 2015). In general, Yes/No questions have not been considered biased—indeed, of 264 referendums held in independent democratic states between 1990 and 2015, only six had diverged from this format. Meanwhile, many submissions from UKIP supporters had argued against it. Arron Banks (2016: 41–2), a major UKIP donor and co-founder of the campaign group Leave.EU, reported that when he and Nigel Farage received the news of the question change there was some frustration because '[a]ll our branding [would] have to be binned', but that 'secretly I was pleased. Nigel's also happy. He thinks it's the best question we could get.'

With the changed question, and the re-established purdah rules in place, the European Union Referendum Act received royal assent on 17 December 2015.

Conclusion

It is often assumed that backbenchers in the UK House of Commons have little real influence. During the fallout from the 2016 referendum, it was also sometimes implied that party dissent was some kind of freak event. Undoubtedly, as discussed in later chapters, the extent to which the parties (and the Conservatives in particular) were divided over Brexit was unprecedented—and was fuelled by other unique factors, including the public mandate from the referendum and the advent of minority government in 2017. But large-scale parliamentary party dissent on Europe was very far from new. As this chapter has traced, the main parties were seriously divided right from the very start regarding the UK's membership of what became the EU. This division inspired action, through a multitude of parliamentary channels, to put pressure on party leaders to change policy, with significant effect. Internal divisions in Labour led to the 1975 referendum, and persistent divisions among Conservative MPs drove David Cameron towards conceding the referendum that facilitated Brexit. While there were undoubtedly other external pressures—particularly the rising electoral popularity of UKIP—parliamentary pressures played a very significant role in this decision.

Amid the internal party arguments about the UK's relationship with Europe, discussions about referendums were never far away. With every new treaty, there were new calls for the public to be consulted directly on changes to the balance of power between the UK and European institutions. Somewhat paradoxically, these were often couched in terms of defending the power of parliament. As John Major (2000: 375) has written, reflecting on the Maastricht period, there was an irony that 'the rebels, always the first to speak in reverent tones about parliamentary sovereignty, were quick to seek means to bypass the will of the House of Commons when this sovereignty clashed with their own beliefs'. There is a conundrum here, that parliamentary sovereignty was a key argument for those wanting to loosen the UK's ties to the European institutions, and yet the mechanism proposed—the referendum—removed decision-making power from parliament. This apparent conflict is a major theme throughout the book.

Such pressures became particularly acute over the Maastricht Treaty (helping lead to the foundation of UKIP), and again over the Lisbon Treaty. In the second case these were fuelled by the promises made by all of the main parties to put the Constitutional Treaty to a referendum, which were widely seen as having been reneged upon with respect to Lisbon. Another recurring theme in the book is the various 'what-ifs', in terms of turning points that might have changed the course of Brexit. An obvious early example is what might have happened if a referendum on the Lisbon Treaty had been held. As one senior Conservative interviewee put it, 'I do very strongly believe that, if you're tracing the history of the earthquake of 2016, that with hindsight...the failure to have referendums after Maastricht, Nice, Amsterdam, Lisbon—Lisbon in particular—was a mistake'. Had such a referendum been held, the treaty might well have been defeated, but the focus would have been on renegotiating the relationship, not on a UK exit from the bloc.

The events recalled in this chapter demonstrate clearly how much could be achieved by a cohesive and determined group of Eurosceptic government backbenchers in the House of Commons. They presage in some ways what Conservative rebels were able to achieve after the 2016 referendum. But one interesting feature of these early debates is that the proponents of a referendum were not uniformly Eurosceptic. Some joined the backbench campaigns against the government because they had already come to the conclusion which David Cameron would eventually reach—that holding a referendum was a means of 'lancing the boil' of Euroscepticism. As one such interviewee commented, 'there were those who thought it would just clear the air', and 'there was a very widespread assumption that it would be a Yes vote, that it would be a Remain vote'. This complacency about the referendum outcome helps to explain the otherwise puzzling phenomenon that there was never, throughout the whole of the Cameron years, a major debate in the House of Commons on the merits or otherwise of leaving the EU. Among many in the party, and in parliament more widely, the prospect was never really taken seriously—which also explains why there was no serious provision made, in the EU Referendum Bill, or by government more widely, for what should hap-pen in the event of a Leave vote. As a senior Labour interviewee described,

> I remember I had lots of conversations with Tories who were backing Brexit and they went along the lines of saying to them 'you don't believe this nonsense do you?' and they said 'no, of course I don't, I've just got to keep the constituency association happy. You guys win the referendum and then politics can return to normal'.

But clearly this is not how things turned out.

Notes

1. This total fluctuates slightly as a result of periodic boundary reviews, but the principle of the electoral system remains the same.
2. One factor here has been the use of proportional systems for other UK elections, where there are greater incentives for voters to support smaller parties, which has contributed to old party loyalties breaking down (Dunleavy 2005). Aside from such systems applying at the devolved level, in Scotland, Wales, and Northern Ireland, the whole UK moved from the use of first past the post to a proportional system for elections to the European Parliament from 1999. Ironically, this created an increasingly effective platform for the Eurosceptic UK Independence Party (UKIP) to demonstrate national support—as indicated later in the chapter.
3. These were Belgium, France, Italy, Luxembourg, the Netherlands, and West Germany. The same countries had previously come together under the Treaty of Paris in 1951 to create the European Coal and Steel Community.
4. House of Commons Hansard, 31 July 1961, column 931.
5. Two abstained and 39 voted against the government.
6. Case C-213/89 *The Queen v Secretary of State for Transport ex parte Factortame Ltd and others (No. 1)* [1990] ECR I-2433; *R v Secretary of State for Transport ex parte Factortame Ltd (No 2)* [1991] 1 AC 603 (House of Lords).
7. House of Commons Hansard, 20 May 1992, column 319.
8. Ibid., 20 November 1991, column 298.
9. Notably Priti Patel, who was later Boris Johnson's Home Secretary, was employed as the party's press officer.
10. House of Commons Hansard, 21 January 2008, column 1263.
11. Ibid., column 1278.
12. House of Commons Hansard, 7 December 2010, column 224.
13. Ibid., 24 October 2011, columns 46, 106.
14. Ibid., 24 October 2011, column 52.
15. These names combine voters for David Nuttall's backbench motion in 2011 and signatories to the Queen's Speech amendment (the signatories to Baron's letter were not made public). Baker, Brady, Leadsom, and Rees-Mogg voted for the Nuttall motion but were not signatories to the amendment; Bebb and Lee were signatories to the amendment but did not vote for the motion; Davis, Jenkin, and Wollaston supported both.
16. House of Commons Hansard, 19 January 1998, columns 716, 720.
17. The rules governing this were in House of Commons Standing Order no. 33, which at that time stated that, following proceedings on the first amendment, 'a further amendment selected by the Speaker may thereupon be moved'. The novelty in Bercow's approach was to read this as allowing more than one subsequent amendment to be selected. Later, in line with the precedent set by Bercow, Standing Order no. 33 was amended to allow selection of up to four amendments to the Queen's Speech motion, including three on the final day of debate.
18. House of Commons Hansard, 15 May 2013, column 673.
19. The others were Roger Godsiff, Kate Hoey, Kelvin Hopkins, Dennis Skinner, and Graham Stringer.
20. House of Lords Hansard, 10 January 2014, column 1832.

21. Ibid., column 1743.
22. House of Commons Hansard, 9 June 2015, columns 1047–8.
23. Ibid., column 1056.
24. Ibid., column 1141.
25. Ibid., column 1067.
26. In addition, seven of the eight Liberal Democrat MPs supported the second reading motion, as did the Northern Ireland DUP and Ulster Unionist Party (UUP), Caroline Lucas for the Greens, and Douglas Carswell for UKIP (Mark Reckless having lost his seat in the recent election). The only votes against the second reading were from the SNP.
27. Those speaking in favour of remaining included 11 Labour MPs and three Conservatives, while three Labour and 11 Conservatives spoke in support of leaving.
28. House of Commons Hansard, 9 June 2015, column 1082.
29. This debate took place on 16 March 2016 in Westminster Hall.
30. House of Commons Hansard, 9 June 2015, column 1055.
31. Ibid.
32. There were 37 rebel Conservatives, including Bernard Jenkin and chair of the party's backbench 1922 Committee Graham Brady.

3

The Referendum

Parliament had voted for a referendum, but with little expectation and only limited desire among parliamentarians that it would result in the UK's departure from the European Union. The subsequent vote for Leave was unexpected, and unprepared for on all sides. The Prime Minister's clear aspiration was that the UK would remain in the EU, which was what most parliamentarians wanted. Leave campaigners themselves did not set out a clear prospectus for the UK's future outside the EU, and the government did little serious thinking about the process of what became known as 'Brexit', or how a new relationship with the EU might work. Instead, the referendum was held on a broad point of principle, with no specific action set out for the government in the event of a vote for change. As described in later chapters of the book, this left parliament to oversee the next stages of a process whose exact destination was undefined, which drew the institution into increasing controversy.

This chapter begins with a discussion of the role of referendums in British politics, addressing both how they are conducted and how they interact with other aspects of the constitution, particularly the role of parliament. The chapter then briefly traces David Cameron's renegotiation with the EU prior to the referendum, before going on to discuss the campaign, the result, and the immediate aftermath of the vote. The referendum result sparked a period of significant upheaval and infighting in both main political parties. The Conservatives chose a new leader following Cameron's immediate resignation as Prime Minister. Meanwhile, Labour MPs tried, unsuccessfully, to unseat their party leader, Jeremy Corbyn—the former Eurosceptic rebel who had been unexpectedly elected by the wider Labour membership in 2015.

Referendums in British Politics

The Brexit vote of 23 June 2016 was only the third ever UK-wide referendum. As seen in the previous chapter, the first had been on essentially the same question in 1975. The second had taken place in 2011, on a relatively narrow question about changing the voting system for the House of

Commons (from 'first past the post' to the 'alternative vote'). A further 10 large-scale referendums had been held, all on devolution-related questions, including in Scotland, Wales, Northern Ireland, London, and the north-east of England—three of these in the 1970s, and the others from 1997 onwards; various other referendums had taken place at local level (Independent Commission on Referendums 2018). But despite having become relatively more common by the time of the Brexit vote, referendums remained fairly unusual events.

Notably, three of the UK's 13 major referendums took place during David Cameron's premiership. The 2011 vote resulted from the coalition deal with the Liberal Democrats; the minor coalition partner favoured electoral reform, but the Conservatives did not, and it was agreed to put the matter to the public. The proposal for change was overwhelmingly defeated, by 68 per cent to 32 per cent (Curtice 2013). In 2014, a far more contentious and closely fought referendum was held on the question of Scottish independence, under pressure from Scotland's SNP government. Again, Cameron's side of the argument prevailed, though this time by a much narrower margin of 55 per cent to 45 per cent (McEwen and Keating 2017). Despite widespread criticisms of the UK government's so-called 'project fear' approach in Scotland, and a last-minute rush to pledge greater devolved powers in order to quell a separatist surge, by 2016 Cameron might well have felt that he had a knack for securing referendum victories.

Various aspects of the UK's use of referendums are notable, particularly when contrasted with other countries. First, all non-local referendums to date have been on questions that are broadly 'constitutional'. This in itself is not unusual—in many countries referendums form an essential step in processes of constitutional reform. This reflects a principle that changes to the fundamental framework of government should have wide public support. But the UK's absence of a formal written constitution means that there is no clear definition of when the principle should apply. In contrast, constitutional referendums in countries that have such a document take the shape of public votes on amendments to it. This makes it clear not only when a referendum must take place, but also what form the change will take if it secures public support.

In addition, constitutional referendums in other countries are generally part of a multistage process (Independent Commission on Referendums 2018). This also fits with the principle that support for fundamental change should be broad-based. So the country's parliament will often have voted for the change proposed before a referendum takes place—meaning that both parliamentarians and the public have a veto. In contrast (as noted in the last chapter), the UK parliament never actually voted on the principle of Brexit—instead simply agreeing to hold a referendum, and leaving the public to make the decision.

In practice referendums in the UK have often been used pragmatically by the political parties to avoid decisions on questions where they are internally split. This was clearly the case in 1975, as seen in Chapter 2. It also applied to the two referendums that took place in Scotland and Wales in the late 1970s—both of which rejected devolution (Bogdanor 1999). In 2011, the two governing parties were each fairly united on the question of changing the voting system, but the coalition itself was split. In that instance, partly due to distrust between the coalition partners, the nature of the change that was offered to the public was closely specified in legislation before the referendum took place. Thus a 'Yes' vote would have triggered the immediate implementation of a pre-existing statute. This provided both clarity and certainty to the public, and came as close as is possible in the UK system to being formally binding on political leaders.

In 2016, some anti-Brexit campaigners argued that the referendum had been merely advisory. Under the UK's central constitutional doctrine of parliamentary sovereignty, parliament always retains the final say on domestic matters, so in formal legal terms this was true. But it would be highly controversial for parliament to reject a referendum result. The power of referendums in the UK lies in their political, not legal, force.

The fact that the 2016 referendum offered no clear blueprint for change has been much noted (e.g. Grey 2021, Independent Commission on Referendums 2018, Menon and Wager 2021), and clearly fed the subsequent difficulties in parliament. Blame has often been levelled at campaigners, but the government's own role was also key. The House of Commons Public Administration and Constitutional Affairs Committee (2017: 12), despite being chaired by a leading Brexiteer, strongly criticized ministers after the vote for having staged a 'bluff-call' referendum—meaning that the government had put a proposal to the voters that it didn't support, 'with the aim of using a negative result to shut down the debate'. The government did little detailed work to explore—or to inform voters about—what Brexit would look like if it occurred. This was starkly different to the alternative vote referendum, and the kind of constitutional referendums generally conducted in other countries.

Other criticisms frequently levelled at referendums, well beyond the one on Brexit, are that they by necessity simplify complex questions, and in the process tend to polarize voters around two opposing views. There is generally little opportunity for deliberation and compromise within this context.

Because referendums take decisions away from political leaders, and from the parliaments where such deliberation normally takes place, they can also serve as anti-elite devices which are therefore associated with populism (Mudde 2007, Norris and Inglehart 2019). While having the benefit of involving the public directly in the decision-making process, they may result in a significant lack of nuance, and leave a divided electorate in their wake.

By their nature, referendums also challenge the core assumption in British politics—that parliament is the highest decision-making authority. Although this principle of parliamentary sovereignty has been much questioned (e.g. Barber 2011, Bogdanor 2012, Gordon 2016, 2019), it has long been viewed as central to the UK's constitutional arrangements. In particular, the lack of a constitutional document with the status of higher law has meant that judges conventionally have a limited role in constitutional interpretation. But following the 2016 referendum the various aspects, and indeed the meaning, of parliamentary sovereignty were brought increasingly into dispute. Arguably, parliament is only sovereign because it represents the voters, who always in practice remain the highest authority—so perceiving a conflict between 'direct' democracy (via referendums) and 'representative' democracy (via parliament) could be misplaced. But, as already seen in Chapter 2, there were apparent ironies in the debates about Europe—in which Eurosceptics argued their case on the basis of a need to return sovereignty to parliament, while not trusting parliament to take the decision to do so for itself. These were particularly exposed over the coalition's European Union Act 2011—which sought to prevent parliament from ceding further powers to the EU without a public vote (Bogdanor 2019, Wellings and Vines 2016). But this demonstrated how (as discussed particularly in Chapter 11) conflicting meanings can be attached to the term 'parliamentary sovereignty' for different purposes. Subsequent chapters show that arguments of this kind would gradually become more extensive and heated as politicians battled over the interpretation of the Brexit referendum result.

Renegotiation to Referendum

David Cameron laid out his reform objectives in a speech at Chatham House in November 2015, shortly after the EU Referendum Act had passed. Clearly hoping to replicate Harold Wilson's successful renegotiation and referendum, Cameron (2015b) framed his objectives not purely as a renegotiation 'to fix the problems in Britain's relationship with the European Union', but as a reshaping of the bloc itself, designed to address challenges 'vital to the success of the European Union'. His list of objectives—set out that day in more detail in a letter to European Council President Donald Tusk (Cameron 2015a)—were familiar from the previous decades of Eurosceptic arguments. They included targets for reducing 'red tape', restrictions on EU migrants' ability to access social security benefits, and a UK exemption from the foundational principle of 'ever closer union', as articulated in the 1957 Treaty of Rome.

By early February 2016, Cameron had reached agreement on draft terms. These were formally signed off by the European Council at a summit that month, and the Prime Minister declared the negotiation a triumph (Cameron 2016). He announced the referendum date—23 June 2016—and confirmed that he would be campaigning for Remain.

Cameron (2019a: 645) himself later described his negotiation as 'a significant achievement', but one which could not meet the level of expectations that he had set—an assessment with which some expert commentators concurred (e.g. Glynn and Menon 2018). Judged against the aims previously articulated, the renegotiation was at least partly successful, with Cameron's achievements including restrictions on benefits for EU migrants, and a promise that a UK opt-out from ever closer union would be included in the next treaty (Menon 2016). However, Cameron had claimed that this would be an opportunity to achieve fundamental change to the UK's relationship with the EU, when in reality its extensive existing opt-outs had left relatively little scope for this to occur. But more importantly, once an in/out referendum had been conceded, Eurosceptics were not measuring the renegotiation against the status quo, but against an imagined 'out'.

It is hence unlikely that the Eurosceptics in Cameron's party and in the press would ever have greeted his renegotiation as a success. With the referendum confirmed, the clear incentive was to paint the renegotiation as a failure, and to use that message to stir up further support for leaving the EU. The *Daily Mail* front page accordingly splashed the headline 'Call that a deal, Dave?' (Slack and Stephens 2016), and editorials in the *Daily Telegraph* (2016) and *Times* (2016) respectively criticized Cameron's deal as 'paltry' and 'thin gruel'. Conservative Eurosceptic backbenchers were equally damning; on the day that the draft terms were published, Steve Baker colourfully accused Europe Minister David Lidington, who was putting the government's case in the Commons, of 'polishing poo'.[1] In a parliamentary debate shortly after the terms were signed off, Jacob Rees-Mogg likewise lamented that 'for so much labour [Cameron] has achieved so little'.[2] This debate demonstrated the limited impact of the renegotiation on what had become an in/out argument: of the 108 MPs who spoke, 63 either were ambivalent about the new terms, or ignored them entirely; just 18 expressed support for the new terms, while 27 (mostly Conservatives) opposed them.

At this stage, Cameron faced significant—and previously underestimated—splits within his Cabinet. When announcing the referendum date, he also indicated that collective responsibility would be suspended for the campaign, meaning that ministers would be free to campaign on either side. That same day, a group of ministers held a photo opportunity at the headquarters of the recently formed Vote Leave campaign. This so-called 'gang of six' included four Secretaries of State, among them Michael Gove and Iain Duncan Smith; Leader of the House of Commons Chris Grayling; and junior minister Priti Patel. Other Conservative MPs also began to declare. Most notably, the then Mayor of London Boris Johnson (2016) used a column in the *Telegraph* to announce that he would campaign for Leave. Johnson, who had previously been MP for Henley and returned to the Commons representing Uxbridge and South Ruislip in 2015, enjoyed significant popularity among the Conservative grassroots. Cameron (2019a) had been hopeful of his support for Remain, claiming that Johnson had regularly sent him messages saying he was undecided. Johnson was widely reported as torn, and later admitted that he had written two versions of his *Telegraph* column, one for Leave, and one for Remain, with the experience convincing him that Leave had the stronger argument (Bower 2020). Before entering parliament, Johnson had built his reputation as the *Telegraph* Brussels correspondent on eye-catching copy that lambasted EU bureaucracy, often with a tenuous basis in fact (Oborne 2021, Rankin and Waterson 2019). This had helped nurture a Eurosceptic mood, in and beyond the press, but many believed that he was at heart a pro-European.

In contrast to the Conservatives, Labour was far less divided, and the party leadership had committed to campaigning for Remain even before the renegotiation began (Wintour 2015). However, the parliamentary party did contain a small handful of committed Labour Eurosceptics, as identified in Chapter 2. At least historically, they had included Jeremy Corbyn—the man who (as described later in the chapter) had unexpectedly been elevated to the party leadership in autumn 2015—and John McDonnell, whom he had appointed as his Shadow Chancellor.

The Campaign and the Result

Despite the divisions in the Cabinet, the government's official position was to back Remain. This led to various attacks from Eurosceptics, even before the campaign officially began on 15 April—when purdah and campaign spending limits kicked in. One concerned the role of the civil service, which had been forbidden from carrying out referendum-related work for Leave-supporting ministers. The second related to a leaflet setting out the Remain argument, which was mailed to every UK household by the government in early April at a reported cost of £9.3 million.[3] Leave supporters took both of these actions as confirmation that ministers intended to abuse their position to advance the Remain cause. In a debate about the government leaflet, senior Conservative backbencher Cheryl Gillan accused the government of 'blatantly trying to load the dice'.[4] The leaflet itself contained a number of contestable claims about the likely economic consequences of leaving the EU; one expert called it 'a mixture of facts, fair points, some dubious assertions and straw men' (UK in a Changing Europe 2016). Notably, it also contained a firm commitment: 'This is your decision. The government will implement what you decide' (HM Government 2016b), firmly underscoring the politically binding nature of the referendum.

The Electoral Commission was responsible for designating one official campaign group for each side in the referendum, which would then receive access to public funding, the right to campaign broadcasts, and other benefits. Only one Remain organization—Britain Stronger in Europe—applied for designation. But two key Leave groups did so. Vote Leave, which ultimately won, was dominated by Conservatives, with its campaign committee including heavyweight backbenchers such as Bernard Jenkin and Iain Duncan Smith, alongside Michael Gove, and Boris Johnson, who finished his term as Mayor of London during the campaign. The group was chaired by Labour MP Gisela Stuart. As Campaign Director, it hired Dominic Cummings, a controversial former adviser to Gove, who had previously worked on the successful campaign to defeat the Labour government's devolution proposals in the 2004 North-East England referendum. He aimed to develop a message that would reach beyond the UKIP base (Clarke, Goodwin, and Whiteley 2017). The other group to apply for designation was Leave. EU, which had strong UKIP links, having been founded by party supporter and donor Arron Banks, and Richard Tice, a Eurosceptic Conservative donor. Despite not winning designation, it campaigned actively throughout the referendum period.

The vast majority of MPs—an estimated 479 of 637—publicly backed the Remain campaign (Clarke, Goodwin, and Whiteley 2017).[5] But there was cross-party support for both campaigns, reflecting the long-standing divides over Europe within the main parties. Leave won support from 45 per cent of Conservative MPs—more than double the number that Downing Street had anticipated (Glynn and Menon 2018). By contrast, 96 per cent of Labour MPs backed Remain (Curtice 2017b). The Liberal Democrats, SNP, Plaid Cymru, and Greens also supported Remain, as did all but one of the main parties in Northern Ireland. The exception was the Democratic Unionist Party (DUP), which campaigned for Leave (Murphy and Evershed 2020).

The cross-party nature of the campaigns caused complications on both sides, but these were particularly keenly felt by Remain. Among Conservatives, attacking opponents in the campaign meant attacking members of one's own party, threatening longer-term party unity. David Cameron (2019a) was extremely reluctant to engage in such 'blue-on-blue' attacks, and claims to have vetoed Remain posters which would have shown Boris Johnson in UKIP leader Nigel Farage's pocket. But members of the Leave campaign, including Johnson, did not share the same reticence (Wheeler 2016). Polling found Johnson to be the single most trusted politician on the question of Brexit (Curtice 2017b), and he was a prominent figure throughout the campaign, including in the televised debates.

Distinctly lower profile was Jeremy Corbyn. He was accused not only of failing to engage constructively with the Remain campaign but of actively seeking to sabotage it (Shipman 2017a). His team was criticized for not focusing on the referendum until after the May local elections, cutting pro-EU lines from his speeches, and refusing to have him share platforms either with David Cameron or with former Labour leaders (Evans and Menon 2017). Corbyn's own support for Remain also appeared lukewarm: just a few days before the vote, he was asked to rate his enthusiasm for staying in the EU out of 10, and his response—'seven, seven and a half' (BBC News 2016b)—was widely viewed as uninspiring. Partly in consequence, Labour lacked a clear message: one poll found that only 52 per cent of voters believed that Labour MPs predominantly backed Remain (Curtice 2017b). The fact that Vote Leave had painted its battle bus in traditional Labour red may well have exacerbated the confusion.

Crucially, there was no clear manifesto offered during the campaign for what Brexit might look like. One Brexit-supporting interviewee reflected that within the Leave campaign itself 'there were big arguments about what Leave meant'. There were some efforts on the Remain side to highlight this (Oliver 2016), but it was not a prominent attack line. Overall, rather than focusing on specific models for change, both campaigns highlighted broad issues, of which three were dominant: the economy, immigration, and sovereignty (Clarke, Goodwin, and Whiteley 2017, Curtice 2017b).

The Remain campaign repeatedly emphasized the economic risks of leaving the EU. The Leave campaign's economic message was instead summed up on the side of its battle bus: 'We send the EU £350 million per week; let's fund our NHS instead'. This figure, which ignored the UK's rebate, was hotly disputed, and criticized as 'at best misleading' (Glynn and Menon 2018: 26). But the Remain campaign's attempts to discredit it seemed to backfire, by guaranteeing it more airtime. Immigration was initially the focus of Leave. EU, but Vote Leave focused increasingly on the issue during the final stages of the campaign (Clarke, Goodwin, and Whiteley 2017). Some campaign materials attracted accusations of outright racism—most notably UKIP's 'Breaking Point' poster, showing a line of predominantly male, non-white individuals apparently queueing at a border (Morrison 2016). The Vote Leave campaign's economic and immigration arguments were summed up by its slogan authored by Dominic Cummings—'Vote Leave: Take Back Control'. This also played to the third general theme, of regaining sovereignty.

The sovereignty debate at times featured implicit or explicit calls for greater power for the Westminster parliament. Boris Johnson's (2016) *Telegraph* column, subsequently quoted in Vote Leave literature, called parliamentary democracy 'the most valuable British export...the one that is now increasingly in question' as a result of EU membership. Similarly, UKIP (2016) complained that 'most of our laws are now made by the European Union, not by our own Parliament and Government in Westminster'. One *Telegraph* columnist went so far as to argue that 'the Brexit vote is about the sovereignty of Parliament. All else is noise' (Evans-Pritchard 2016). But in keeping with the general lack of focus on precisely what would happen after a vote against EU membership, no real attention was given to the role that parliament might play in what happened next. One notable exception was a speech by Michael Gove on 19 April, which made a rare reference to Article 50 of the Treaty on European Union—the provision setting out the process for a member state to leave. Once triggered, this would begin a period of exit negotiations lasting a maximum of two years. Gove (2016) predicted that 'in the days after a vote to leave, the PM would discuss the way ahead with the Cabinet, and consult parliament, before taking any significant step'. He added that no 'responsible government would hit the start button on a two-year legal process without preparing appropriately. Nor would it be in anyone's interest to hurry parliamentary processes.'

Just as Article 50 was barely mentioned during the campaign, the other issue which was to dominate debate over subsequent years—the potential impact of leaving the EU on Northern Ireland—was conspicuously absent. The Belfast/Good Friday Agreement of 1998, which had been crucial to securing peace in the province, had been agreed in the context of EU membership, including its framework of common standards that guaranteed free movement of both people and goods between the UK and Republic of Ireland. Brexit raised the prospect of introducing a hard border between the two, and fears of a return to sectarian conflict. These topics were prominent in the referendum campaign in Northern Ireland itself, with pro-Remain parties citing the need to safeguard the peace process (Berberi 2017). But in Great Britain they were little discussed, and a joint visit to Northern Ireland by former Prime Ministers Tony Blair and John Major, with the express purpose of raising the profile of the topic, had little impact on the established campaign narratives. Nigel Dodds, deputy leader of the pro-Brexit DUP, dismissed their warnings as 'irresponsible nonsense' and 'scaremongering' (McKeown 2016).

The darkest moment of the campaign was the murder of Labour MP Jo Cox in her constituency by a right-wing extremist one week before the vote, on 16 June. Campaigning was temporarily suspended, and the House of Commons was recalled for tributes. These featured many calls for unity, with repeated quotations of Cox's own words, that 'we are far more united and have far more in common than that which divides us'.[6] But they took place in a political environment that had become increasingly fractured by the referendum.

The subsequent week's referendum result surprised many. As seen in Chapter 2, polling had long suggested public support for continued EU membership. The gap between Remain and Leave had significantly tightened as the referendum approached, but most polls during the campaign suggested that Remain would clinch a narrow win (Curtice 2016a). On the day of the vote, YouGov (2016b) still predicted a 4-point Remain victory, and, as voting ended, Nigel Farage appeared to concede defeat (Cooper and Forster 2016). But hints of Leave's success emerged with some of the earliest areas to declare. First, Newcastle voted for Remain by a far narrower margin than the campaign had hoped; then Leave won a larger majority in Sunderland than expected (Shipman 2017a). As the local results mounted and it became clear that Leave would win, the extent of the parties' unpreparedness for such a result became clear. One Labour interviewee who attended the counting of votes in their local area recalled that the party had not even issued any lines for its MPs to take in the event of a Leave victory. The vagueness of the Leave campaign, meanwhile, meant that the victors were similarly unprepared, and had no clear, unified plans.

As is by now familiar, the national result was 48.1 per cent for Remain and 51.9 per cent for Leave, on a turnout of 72.2 per cent (Electoral Commission 2016). It exposed multiple deep fault lines in UK politics, including in the Union itself. The majority in both England and Wales voted to leave, while majorities in Scotland and Northern Ireland voted to remain. But the result also revealed demographic and more localized geographic splits, based on urban and rural locations, age, income levels, and, most markedly, education (Clarke, Goodwin, and Whiteley 2017, Glynn and Menon 2018); these made visible divisions that had been developing for some time (Ford and Sobolewska 2020). Likewise, in Northern Ireland there was a clear divide between nationalist (pro-Remain) and unionist (pro-Leave) voters (Murphy and Evershed 2022). These various complex divisions, within and between communities and political parties, would have significant repercussions in the years to come.

The Aftermath

The Immediate Response

In the early morning of 24 June, the Brexit-supporting press issued jubilant early editions. The *Daily Mail*'s front page featured a beaming Nigel Farage with the headline 'We're out!: After 43 years UK freed from shackles of EU' (Slack, Martin, and Groves 2016). The front page of the *Sun* joyfully quipped 'See EU Later!' (Newton Dunn 2016). But the Leave campaign's victory created a less happy situation for the leaderships of both main political parties.

The result left David Cameron in an undeniably difficult position: his flagship policy had been defeated, after a referendum campaign which had bitterly divided his party, leaving him looking 'more like the leader of the Opposition than the Prime Minister' (Curtice 2016b). Nonetheless, many members of the Leave campaign had urged him to stay in post whatever the referendum outcome. The night before the vote, 84 Leave-supporting Conservative MPs sent him an open letter, claiming that he had 'both a mandate and a duty to continue leading the nation' whatever the result (Syms 2016). The morning after the referendum, 1922 Committee Chair Graham Brady, himself a committed Leave supporter, gave several media interviews expressing the importance of the Prime Minister staying on to provide stability—only to be interrupted by the news of Cameron's resignation in a Downing Street statement shortly after 8 a.m.

The Labour leadership was also thrown into turmoil in the immediate aftermath of the referendum. In an interview early on the morning of 24 June, Jeremy Corbyn called for the immediate triggering of Article 50 (Pine 2016).[7] Although he would later claim to have misspoken (BBC

News 2016c), he was widely criticized for suggesting the start of a time-limited negotiating process when the UK hadn't established its negotiating position and the Prime Minister was about to step down. Later the same morning there was a troubled meeting of the Shadow Cabinet, at which most members were exhausted and angry. One recalled in interview that there were tears, and 'a sense of emptiness'; another that this marked 'the collapse of the Corbyn Shadow Cabinet'.

The Following Weeks

The result left the government with the task of developing a detailed prospectus for Brexit. The then Foreign Secretary Philip Hammond (2020) recalled the mood inside government as being one of 'complete disarray and disbelief'. The disappointment felt by many was exacerbated by the lack of a clear plan from Leave campaigners. This uncertainty was worsened by Cameron's decision before the referendum to forbid the civil service from carrying out contingency planning for a Leave result. Cameron (2019a: 686) claimed to have been concerned that drawing up such plans would have been a distraction, and could have been politically 'disastrous' had they leaked. But the consequence was that, at the time of the result, no preparatory policy work existed. The then most senior official at the Department for Environment, Food and Rural Affairs (one of the departments likely to be most affected by Brexit) recalled that 'it was only on the day of the referendum that any kind of discussions had started about what might happen if the answer was a no' (Moriarty 2021).

In his final weeks as Prime Minister, Cameron set up a Brexit unit within the Cabinet Office, which was headed by civil servant Olly Robbins and represented in Cabinet by Oliver Letwin. They sought to carry out early scoping work on the options available to the next Prime Minister. As discussed further in the next chapter, Letwin proposed early on that a cross-party approach was needed. After this conclusion was rejected by Cameron's successor, he went on to play an increasingly active role from the backbenches.

Another unknown was the part that parliament would play in the Brexit process (as discussed more fully in Chapter 4). When the Commons met on the Monday immediately following the referendum, MPs raised questions about parliament's role in triggering Article 50, and the structures that the Commons would need to scrutinize the Brexit process.[8] Cameron confirmed that 'the British Government will not be triggering article 50 at this stage', adding that '[b]efore we do that, we need to determine the kind of relationship we want with the EU, and that is rightly something for the next Prime Minister and their Cabinet to decide'.[9]

Demands for a further referendum also emerged immediately. Such proposals had already been made before the referendum—typically coming from Leave supporters. At the time of Cameron's renegotiation, Dominic Cummings (2015) had advocated a two-referendum process—with suggestions that a vote for exit in the first referendum could encourage the EU to offer a better membership deal, which the UK might then accept in a second vote. The media reported Boris Johnson arguing for this same view (Shipman 2015). A starker suggestion, that the in/out referendum should instead simply be rerun in pursuit of a different outcome, had come from Nigel Farage during the campaign. In an interview on 16 May he claimed— predicting an outcome exactly the reverse of what occurred—that '[i]n a 52–48 referendum this would be unfinished business by a long way' (Maguire 2016). That same month, a parliamentary petition had been set up by a Leave supporter, apparently designed to press for the referendum to be repeated in the event of a narrow Remain victory (Cockburn 2016). It called for a rerun unless either Leave or Remain won with at least 60 per cent of the vote, on a turnout of at least 75 per cent. Immediately following the referendum, Remain supporters flocked to the petition; it had gathered 2.5 million signatures by 25 June, and over 4 million by 8 July, when the government rejected it on the basis that 'the [23 June] decision must be respected' (UK Government and Parliament 2016). Among the political parties, the Liberal Democrats quickly backed a second referendum (Walker, Stewart, and Elgot 2016); Labour, as explored in subsequent chapters, was far more cautious; the Conservatives mostly remained firmly opposed throughout.

The Conservative Leadership Contest

Cameron's resignation triggered a leadership contest in the Conservative Party, to identify not just a new party leader but a new Prime Minister. The process for Conservative leadership contests begins with candidates seeking nominations from the party's MPs, who hold a series of knock-out ballots, eliminating the least popular candidates until only two remain. After this the wider membership is balloted to make the final choice between the two. This method—unlike the Labour system, described below—ensures that a candidate can become leader only if a supported by a significant number of MPs, as well as the wider party.

Despite the shock of the referendum result, the nomination period ended just one week later, on 30 June. At this point, the main story was not the candidates who had been nominated, but the one who had not (Gimson 2016). Boris Johnson had been widely expected to run, with Michael Gove taking a senior role in his government. But on the day that Johnson was due to confirm his candidacy, Gove instead announced his own run at the top job. Moreover, he stated that he had decided to enter the race because 'Boris cannot provide the leadership or build the team for the task ahead'. 'Sources close to Gove' told at least one journalist that he had been alarmed by the chaotic nature of Johnson's campaign and concluded that he was not fit to be Prime Minister (Sparrow 2016). Johnson then used the very event which had been expected to be his campaign launch to announce that he would not run after all.

This left five candidates in contention. Former Defence Secretary Liam Fox was eliminated on the first ballot, after which Work and Pensions Secretary Stephen Crabb dropped out. Michael Gove was eliminated at the next round on 7 July, with just 46 votes. While seeking to capitalize on his Leave background, he had alienated supporters by his betrayal of Johnson. By 8 July, therefore, two final candidates remained potentially to go forward to the member ballot: Andrea Leadsom on 84 votes, and Theresa May on 199.

Theresa May had been Home Secretary since 2010, winning admiration for her staying power in what is often considered a particularly difficult role. An interviewee close to her reported that allies had pressed her to consider a leadership bid during the referendum campaign, anticipating that Cameron might stand down in the event of a Leave vote. She presented herself as the candidate of expertise and experience, able to bring both the fractured Conservative Party and the country back together. Although by her own admission 'not a showy politician' (May 2016d), she promised the party stability, including a pledge that there would be no general election before 2020. However, May had been a Remain supporter—albeit a quiet one, having made just a single major speech during the campaign (Shipman 2017a). She therefore clearly felt the need to prove her commitment to delivering the referendum result; her famous phrase 'Brexit means Brexit', later much cited, first dates to her campaign launch. More substantively, she claimed in the same speech that '[t]here must be no attempts to remain inside the EU, no attempts to rejoin it through the backdoor, and no second referendum' (May 2016d). Andrea Leadsom's political career was far less distinguished than Theresa May's: she had entered the Commons in 2010 and spent just two years as a junior minister. But she was a committed Leaver, having represented the campaign in the televised Brexit debates.

Ultimately, no member ballot took place, and the campaign reached a far quicker resolution than expected. During a newspaper interview on 9 July, Leadsom made a number of comments about the direct stake that her children gave her in the UK's future (Sylvester 2016). This was widely interpreted as a cruel dig at May, who had spoken publicly about her own regret at being unable to have children. The ensuing backlash forced Leadsom to drop out of the contest two days later. Theresa May thus became leader by default.

Such a resolution to a Conservative leadership contest was not unknown. In 2003, Michael Howard had been the only candidate nominated. But the speed of the contest perhaps created a misleading impression of the extent to which the party was coalescing around May. She had achieved majorities in both rounds of MPs' voting, winning 50.2 per cent of votes in the first round and 60.5 per cent in the second. But she lacked support from Leave MPs, many of whom had instead backed Gove or Leadsom (Jeffery et al. 2018). Even among Remainers, May's level of support did not necessarily reflect real enthusiasm. Dominic Grieve (2020) described an immediate rallying around her by Remain-voting MPs once a contest became inevitable, driven primarily by 'a general view that whatever happened, Boris Johnson must not become leader'. After Johnson and Gove dropped out, Amber Rudd (2021)—formerly May's deputy at the Home Office—felt that their 'mutual destruction' had shocked and unsettled the party so much that it had chosen her 'like holding onto nurse's hand'. Meanwhile, the lack of a member ballot meant that she was untested in the wider party.

Theresa May became Prime Minister on 13 July. Making her first speech outside Downing Street, she promised that 'as we leave the European Union, we will forge a bold new positive role for ourselves in the world' (May 2016b). But, strikingly, much of her speech was dedicated to laying out a domestic agenda focused on social injustice. At this stage, it appeared that May had not realized how all-consuming Brexit was to become.

The Labour Leadership Contest

May perhaps lacked the enthusiastic backing of her MPs, but Labour's Jeremy Corbyn held onto his position after the referendum in the face of his MPs' outright opposition. A long-standing member of Labour's left wing, and a serial rebel on European and other matters, Corbyn had been elected after Labour's loss in the 2015 general election—becoming the first UK party leader in history to win his post with virtually no support from his parliamentary party. The roots of such a remarkable feat lay in the change in rules for Labour leadership contests introduced by his predecessor, Ed Miliband (Dorey and Denham 2016). The new system required candidates to gain nominations from just 15 per cent of MPs and MEPs to get onto the leadership ballot, after which MPs' special influence over the process would end.[10] At the second stage the leader was elected from among the nominated candidates in a vote of all members—including in 2015 a new category of 'registered supporters', who received full voting rights for only £3 per year. Corbyn struggled to gain enough MP nominations to get onto the ballot, but swept to victory on a tide of grassroots support. Perhaps unsurprisingly, his subsequent relationship with the parliamentary party proved very difficult (Diamond 2016, Watts and Bale 2019).

This situation significantly worsened following Corbyn's poor performance during the referendum campaign. Three days after the vote, Shadow Health Secretary Heidi Alexander wrote him an open letter resigning her post, citing her lack of confidence in his leadership. The same day, the *Observer* claimed that Shadow Foreign Secretary Hilary Benn was organizing support within the Shadow Cabinet for a leadership coup. Corbyn promptly fired Benn, precipitating a wave of resignations: 19 Shadow Cabinet members and a further 18 junior shadow ministers quit their posts (Syal, Perraudin, and Slawson 2016).

On 28 June, Labour MPs voted no confidence in Corbyn by 172 votes to 40.[11] But this overwhelming rejection of the leader by the parliamentary party had no formal force under Labour's rules. Corbyn chose simply to disregard the political logic which suggested that he couldn't credibly lead a group which had so resoundingly spurned him. Instead, he released a statement claiming that the ballot had 'no constitutional legitimacy' and that he would not 'betray' Labour members by resigning (Pope 2016)—clearly believing that his authority stemmed not from MPs but from the party's grassroots.

Corbyn's opponents were thus left with the option either of accepting his leadership or of mounting a formal contest—which he openly challenged them to do. Two more centrist figures, recently resigned shadow ministers Angela Eagle and Owen Smith, launched leadership campaigns. Eagle then quickly withdrew in favour of Smith. Corbyn was unlikely to garner the required MP nominations, but in July Labour's ruling National Executive Committee (NEC), itself dominated by Corbynites, ruled this unnecessary in the case of an incumbent leader. Smith won nominations from 162 Labour MPs (70 per cent of the total), and attempted to capitalize on Corbyn's poor referendum performance and to appeal to Labour's Remain-supporting base—including by proposing a second referendum. But the grassroots remained loyal to Corbyn, who secured 61.8 per cent of the vote. The bitter campaign had dragged on all the way through to late September, deepening Labour's internal divisions and distracting its politicians from Brexit. It ended with re-election of a leader whose alienation from his parliamentary party was now clearer than ever before.

Conclusion

Referendums occupy a less clear place in the UK's constitution than in many other states. There is no formal definition of when a referendum is required, and they can be seen as sitting uncomfortably alongside the traditional doctrine of parliamentary sovereignty, which upholds parliament as the ultimate decision-maker. Historically, the use of referendums has often been highly politically pragmatic, and the Brexit vote was a particularly striking case. The long history of backbench pressure described in the previous chapter led Prime Minister David Cameron to call one primarily as a means to quell Conservative dissent. Parliament had not expressed its view on the central question; Cameron's hope that his renegotiation would pull people together behind a new vision of the UK in Europe proved hopelessly optimistic; and the poll lead for remaining in the EU gradually crumbled. His Eurosceptic opponents had no interest in compromising, and found simple but convincing messages that cut through with the public. In contrast, the Remain campaign underperformed, aided by the ambivalent attitude of Labour's new leader Jeremy Corbyn, himself a former Eurosceptic rebel.

Leave supporters did not put forward a clear proposal during the campaign for the form that Brexit should take, championing an unspecified vision of 'taking back control'. Meanwhile, there was no official preparation for a Leave result. The referendum itself, while a moment of huge political significance, was by necessity only the first stage in a process—whose completion now lay in the hands of the government and parliament. This included defining, negotiating, and implementing Brexit, and dealing with complex problems which had achieved no more than passing attention during the campaign, including dealing with the post-Brexit status of Northern Ireland, and navigating the Article 50 process. The uncertainties surrounding these questions, but the need for parliament to oversee them, risked parliamentarians appearing to come into conflict with the 'will of the people'.

Though by definition, given the doctrine of parliamentary sovereignty, the referendum was not formally legally binding, its political force was clear. Despite not having supported change or having fully thought through its consequences, Cameron had repeatedly promised that the result would be respected. But after a divisive campaign which stirred up increasing bitterness both in his own party and the country, the Prime Minister quickly departed the scene, leaving others to deal with the result. Resolving the multiple dilemmas thrown up by the referendum thus became the job of his successor as Prime Minister, Theresa May.

Despite the enormity of the policy questions lying ahead, the political parties were in shock following the referendum result, and had little immediate capacity to respond. Both the Conservatives and Labour were plunged immediately into leadership contests. The Conservative process ran smoothly and finished quickly, but Theresa May became Prime Minister without facing detailed scrutiny on her Brexit position, and without a mandate from the party grassroots. The surprise wrecking of Boris Johnson's campaign by Michael Gove left the party unsettled, and there was limited positive enthusiasm for May among Leave supporters. Labour's bitter contest, meanwhile, lasted through the summer, and left Jeremy Corbyn in place despite the clear opposition of his own MPs. This followed, in a sense, the same logic as the referendum itself—with Westminster politicians left to manage the unwelcome result of a grassroots ballot. As seen in later chapters, Corbyn's continued presence caused multiple problems, which might have been significantly lessened if he had stepped aside. Even the pro-European Liberal Democrats, who at least remained united, were, in the words of one interviewee, 'really depressed' and 'demoralized' by the referendum result. Hence none of the main UK-wide parties were immediately focused on the crucial questions of how it might be interpreted and implemented, or what the political process for doing so might be.

It was in this context, and this climate of shell shock and widespread disappointment, that parliament was left to oversee the implementation of the result.

Notes

1. House of Commons Hansard, 2 February 2016, column 784.
2. Ibid., 22 February 2016, column 47.
3. Ibid., 11 April 2016, column 72.
4. Ibid., 11 April 2016, columns 80–1.
5. The figure of 637 MPs excludes the Speaker and Deputy Speakers, and Sinn Féin.
6. House of Commons Hansard, 20 June 2016, columns 1884 (Jeremy Corbyn), 1886 (David Cameron), 1890 (Stuart Andrew) and 1896 (Alison McGovern).
7. Corbyn was not the first party leader to have made this suggestion. Cameron, speaking in February in the House of Commons, had said that in the event of a vote to leave Article

50 would need to be triggered and the 'British people would rightly expect that to start straight away' (House of Commons Hansard, 22 February 2016, column 24), although this position changed after the result.

8. See, for example, comments by Mike Gapes (House of Commons Hansard, 27 June 2016, column 40) and Yvette Cooper (ibid., column 34).

9. Ibid., column 24.

10. Previously, the party used an 'electoral college' system, whereby trade unions and MPs also played a large part in the final vote on who should be leader.

11. A further 17 MPs either abstained or spoiled their ballots.

4

Theresa May and the Triggering of Article 50

The enormous challenge of delivering Brexit demanded a swift end to the instability created by the referendum result. Theresa May, as the new Prime Minister, needed to assemble a Cabinet and begin work on a Brexit strategy. But the absence of a blueprint, and the lack of certainty about the government's direction, generated arguments about parliament's oversight role. Parliament is the key public forum to which the government is accountable, and it was natural for both members and external observers to argue for its full involvement in the uncertain steps ahead. However, parliament was also known to be dominated by former advocates of remaining in the EU, making Leave supporters fearful that its involvement could provide opportunities to undermine the referendum result.

This chapter begins with a discussion of MPs' local representative roles, which played an important part in the debates about Brexit, as many parliamentarians faced dilemmas over how to prioritize between local constituency opinion, the national referendum result, and their own personal views. It then moves to consider Theresa May's characteristics as an incoming Prime Minister, and how these helped to set the tone for the subsequent debates. Following this, the chapter focuses on the early arguments about the place of parliament in the Brexit process. These fell into three key areas: parliament's role in triggering the two-year negotiating period provided by Article 50, its subsequent role in overseeing the negotiations with the EU, and its role in approving the final Brexit deal.

The first of these was the most urgent question and, in the face of government resistance to involving parliament in the trigger, a legal case reached the Supreme Court, which ruled in favour of parliamentary involvement. This generated controversy about the role not only of parliament but of the courts. While Theresa May began to sketch out her strategy for Brexit, which initially pleased hardline Brexiteers and alarmed more moderate Conservatives, parliament moved on to legislating to approve the trigger. This resulted in some agonized debates where MPs grappled with their conflicting representative roles. It also provided a vehicle for debate about the government's negotiating objectives and parliament's role in the next steps. By the end of this initial period it was clear that May was going to struggle to resolve the rifts within the Conservative Party, and that parliament's place in the Brexit process would be highly contested.

The Constituency Link and MPs' Representative Roles

As touched upon in Chapter 2, a defining feature of the UK parliamentary system is the strong local link between each MP and their constituency. The 'first-past-the-post' electoral system means that each local area elects a single MP, which creates a strong bond of accountability. Local MPs generally make great efforts to remain in contact with their constituents, for example through newsletters, the local media, doorstep campaigning, and constituency 'advice surgeries' (Gay 2005). Many constituents attend such surgeries, or write to their MPs, to ask them to take up grievances on their behalf, or simply to express their views on matters of policy. These links, which are replicated in various other countries that use single-member districts, such as Canada and the US, are far deeper and better developed than in the many countries where MPs are elected in multi-member districts (Bogdanor 1985, Thomassen and Esaiasson 2006).

The strength of local links and accountabilities can create representational dilemmas for MPs. This was most famously articulated by the eighteenth-century political thinker and MP Edmund Burke, who drew a distinction between MPs acting as 'delegates', who seek to follow the wishes of their constituents in parliament, and 'trustees', who apply their own judgement in what they consider to be the national interest. Burke (2000 [1774]) came down on the side of the trustee, believing that the national interest could not be served by a House of Commons full of members pursuing disparate local interests, and that reaching conclusions through open-minded parliamentary deliberation was crucial. In contemporary times, these tensions remain present, but a third factor has become at least as important—the MP's responsibility to their political party. Occasionally, any of these three things may be in conflict—the party may ask the MP to pursue a policy that they personally disagree with, or that conflicts with the interests of their constituents. Likewise, constituents may pressure an MP to support a policy that conflicts with party policy, or with their own beliefs.

Usually, such conflicts can be fairly easily smoothed over. As Chapter 2 demonstrated, Westminster MPs have significant freedom to speak out against their parties, and if the level of backbench dissent becomes high, the party itself may change course. Meanwhile, much of what goes on in parliament is not scrutinized closely by constituents, and MPs have no reliable measure of constituency opinion on policy, so can usually only guess at what their voters would want them to do. Where party policy very clearly conflicts with local opinion (for example, on a new railway line), whips will often tolerate abstention, or even votes against the party line. But the Brexit referendum created far bigger problems. This was a high-profile issue, where the nation's mood was known through the referendum result, and there were high levels of awareness about how each local area had voted. Meanwhile, many MPs had strong opinions—potentially in conflict with the views either of their constituents or of the nation as a whole.

As noted in the previous chapter, there were some clear geographical factors in the referendum result. Most obviously, a majority of voters in Scotland, Northern Ireland, and London voted for Remain, while a majority in Wales and the other regions of England voted for Leave. In addition, there was significant local variation, which often cut across party lines. Although the referendum vote was not counted by constituency, detailed estimates indicate that majorities in 409 seats voted Leave, while 241 voted Remain (Dempsey 2017).[1] These same estimates suggest that Conservative seats were split 249 to 85 in favour of Leave, and Labour seats were likewise split 149 to 83. Hence a lot of MPs in both parties would be potentially at odds with their constituents—though clearly not with the country as a whole—if they supported Brexit. In pure electoral terms, the dilemma was perhaps not quite as grave as these figures might suggest: many of those voting Leave in Labour areas would be Conservatives, while many Remain voters in Conservative constituencies would be supporters of other parties. But in some Labour areas in particular it was quite clear which way the party's own voters had tilted. For example, in areas of London such as Hackney and Islington, towns such as Brighton and Cambridge, and parts of Liverpool and Manchester, the Remain vote was estimated at 70–80 per cent. Meanwhile, in other Labour areas such as Doncaster and Barnsley, the estimated Leave vote was close to 70 per cent.

Local considerations therefore played a significant part in MPs' reactions to the referendum result. Many would naturally want to respect their constituents' wishes and broader interests, while some clearly feared the electoral consequences of straying from the constituency view. This applied most crudely to the question of Leave/Remain, as addressed in this chapter. But it also applied to considerations about the form that Brexit should take—for example, where MPs' constituencies were very dependent on certain industries, as touched upon in Chapter 6.

When considering MPs' local pressures, a further factor was also important. MPs depend not only on the support of their electorate but also on that of their local parties. Party members campaign for MPs at election times, and can serve as important champions in the local community. They hold MPs accountable, particularly through local party meetings. Grassroots members tend by their nature to be highly political, watching politics more closely, and often holding stronger views, than the electorate at large (Bale, Webb, and Poletti 2019). Meanwhile, crucially, this group plays a major part in the selection of parliamentary candidates, and can potentially press for an MP's deselection. These internal party relationships also played a major role in the dynamics over Brexit, particularly at the later stages. Labour MPs needed to placate their members, a large proportion of whom (particularly in urban areas) were opposed to Brexit. Conservative MPs, meanwhile, often faced local associations dominated by hardline Brexiteers. This last factor had helped to play a part in forcing the referendum; it would also prove significant in how the subsequent battles in parliament developed.

The Theresa May Government

The woman who took up office in 10 Downing Street on 13 July 2016 faced a unique challenge: to implement an unexpected referendum result on a hugely complex question, with no detailed policy blueprint and a deeply divided party. This would have been a daunting task for any person, and ultimately proved impossible for Theresa May.

During the leadership campaign, May had presented herself as an experienced pair of hands able to bring the party together and deliver Brexit. As indicated in the previous chapter, she hadn't been strongly associated with either side of the referendum campaign. Her long background at the Home Office inspired hardline attitudes on immigration, and Seldon and Newell (2019: 29) describe her as 'the most pro-Brexit of all those in Cabinet who came out for Remain'. Or, as one commentator more colourfully put it, she had 'sat on the fence with a lukewarm endorsement of Remain and a wink at Leave' (O'Toole 2020: 52). In some respects, such demonstrable ambivalence created opportunities to heal the Brexit divide that had stricken both the country and parliament. A senior Brexiteer suggested in interview that her positioning 'felt helpful: it seemed like she was almost the embodiment of a will to heal the argument and to make sure that the democratic mandate was followed'—in a less divisive manner than might have been possible for a leader who had been a committed Leave supporter. On the other hand, in a polarized environment, there was a risk that she would struggle to maintain the trust of either side.

There were also key aspects of May's personal and political style that made her an unlikely candidate to navigate such difficult political waters. In existing accounts, and the testimony of interviewees, two traits are repeatedly mentioned. First, as Liberal Democrat David Laws (2016: 276)—who served with her in government during the coalition—suggested, she was 'instinctively secretive and very rigid'; or, in the words of a senior civil servant interviewed by Shipman (2017a: 531), '[s]he's totally inflexible...that's both the strength and the weakness'. Of all the adjectives attached to Theresa May by interviewees for this book, 'rigid' occurred particularly frequently. Second, a specific manifestation of rigidity was her total commitment to her party and its survival. Dominic Grieve (2020) has described her as 'absolutely rooted in the Conservative Party'; two interviewees who had sat in her Cabinet described her respectively as 'tribal' and 'blood and bone a party woman', while another senior Conservative called her 'very much a party animal'. Consequently, one close observer commented that 'throughout the period of coalition Theresa had been very uncomfortable doing business with the Liberal Democrats'—an observation also made by Laws (2016: 275).

May arrived from the Home Office with two of her most trusted former advisers, Nick Timothy and Fiona Hill, who became her Downing Street Joint Chiefs of Staff. They had been instrumental in encouraging May to stand for the leadership (Seldon and Newell 2019), and were hugely influential on her as Prime Minister—at least until their departure in 2017. Timothy was a committed Brexiteer, and worked closely with May on her positioning and key speeches on the topic. In the words of her former Number 10 Director of Strategy, Chris Wilkins (2020), 'Nick was probably the most prominent voice in the whole debate and decision-making process'. He helped to ensure that the Prime Minister maintained good communications with Brexit-supporting MPs, and Wilkins reports that, early in May's premiership, 'Bernard Jenkin, John Redwood, Iain Duncan Smith, people like this...I would quite often see trooping into meetings in Number 10'. Not unreasonably, May perhaps anticipated that those who had campaigned passionately for the UK's departure from the EU could help develop workable solutions regarding what should happen next. One interviewee who served in Downing Street suggested that, initially, members of the hardline Eurosceptic ERG (European Research Group, described in Chapter 6) 'were relatively supportive' and 'seen as being broadly helpful and pushing in a direction that the government wanted them to push it'. This was to change fundamentally later on.

Meanwhile, in line with her character, May put no effort at all into building support from other parties. Nick Timothy himself told Seldon and Newell (2019: 122) that 'reaching out just wasn't her. It was not in her nature.' As Chapter 3 indicated, Cabinet minister Oliver Letwin was initially tasked by David Cameron with drawing up plans for Brexit. His assumption was that this would depend on building cross-party alliances, given the tensions within the Conservative Party and its narrow Commons majority of 16 seats. As Letwin (2020) saw things, a wholly Conservative-centric approach would leave the Prime Minister vulnerable to two opposing groupings in the party: 'very hard Brexiteers' and 'ultra Remainers'. Hence, in his words, the 'only way to keep those two groupings under control was to have a solid phalanx of 400-plus members of parliament' who were joined in a single pursuit'. At least theoretically, there was a clear initial opportunity for May to neutralize both her own hardliners and the official opposition by inviting Labour into helping deliver on the referendum result. This proposition would have made many Labour members uncomfortable, but might have been difficult to refuse. As a key insider suggested in interview, 'a bold and generous offer, so to speak, at the beginning would have been hugely advantageous'.

This kind of more open approach could have been extended to the public—through consultation about the form that Brexit should take, given that the referendum had not gone beyond the principle itself. But instead, on arrival in Downing Street, the new Prime Minister's inclination was to keep decision-making narrow, and firmly within her party. Letwin's approach of tentative discussions with key Labour figures was abruptly dropped—his comfort with cross-party working during the coalition years was directly mirrored by May's discomfort. Remarkably, one key figure reported that 'there was absolutely no handover whatsoever' on Brexit between May's team and either Cameron or Letwin. In terms of co-opting Labour, an additional deterrent was, of course, the nature of the party's leader, Jeremy Corbyn. He was not only seen as extreme, but plainly lacked support from his own parliamentary party—making him both an unattractive and risky potential partner. As a senior Labour backbencher commented in interview, Theresa May 'was absolutely in a strong enough position straight after her election' to make a bold offer to the opposition, but 'the tragedy was about us kind of not having the right individuals in place to be able to do it'.

Upon taking up office, one of May's immediate tasks was to appoint her Cabinet. In direct response to the referendum result she established two new government departments—the Department for Exiting the European Union (DExEU), and the Department for International Trade (DIT). Creating the latter appeared to signal that May planned a 'hard' Brexit, allowing the UK to do its own trade deals—but it is not actually clear that the decision was that thought-through. DExEU's creation was criticized by many insiders—Philip Hammond (2020), who was appointed May's Chancellor of the Exchequer, later referred to it as 'absolutely ludicrous' and 'a stupid idea'. The alternative was to keep the function close at hand within the Cabinet Office, and this was pressed on the government by, among others, the House of Commons Public Administration and Constitutional Affairs Committee (2016) (chaired by Bernard Jenkin). But creation of the new department was symbolic.

May conspicuously sought to balance the Cabinet between the different wings of her party. Thus, senior Brexiteers David Davis and Liam Fox joined to head up DExEU and DIT respectively. May also appointed Boris Johnson as Foreign Secretary, and former leadership rival Andrea Leadsom as Secretary of State for Environment, Food and Rural Affairs. Former Remainer David Lidington, meanwhile, became Leader of the House of Commons, while Amber Rudd moved within the Cabinet to replace May as Home Secretary. Many prominent figures from the coalition years, including Letwin, former Chancellor of the Exchequer George Osborne, and Michael Gove, departed.

Shortly afterwards, as a matter of course, Commons select committees were established to shadow the new departments, and Labour's Hilary Benn—recently sacked by Corbyn as Shadow Foreign Secretary—was elected to chair the Exiting the European Union (ExEU) Committee.

Parliament's Role in the Next Steps

As should already be clear, the government, the parties, and parliament were all unprepared for the referendum outcome. There was a widespread appreciation that the public mandate must be respected, but glaring gaps regarding how this should be achieved. The most obvious concerned the form that Brexit should take, which was the dominant preoccupation of the next three years. But there was also a total lack of clarity regarding what the process should be. As very few people had expected a vote for Leave, the respective roles of government and parliament in implementing Brexit had received practically no consideration.

A key Eurosceptic objective over the preceding decades, up to and including the referendum campaign, had been to restore 'parliamentary sovereignty'. But, as discussed in previous chapters, this was potentially contradicted by empowering the public directly in a referendum. Given that most MPs had supported Remain, parliament's role in the next steps was not only unclear but also contested. In addition, proposals for parliamentary involvement bumped up against the executive's role, and in particular the historically wide discretion given to governments to use royal prerogative powers in the field of foreign affairs (discussed in more detail in Chapter 6). These three claims regarding who should have a decisive role—the public, parliament, or government—were also to dominate debates in the years ahead. Very soon, as discussed below, the courts were drawn in to adjudicate.

While parliament normally sits at the heart of political decision-making, there were hence various sources of resistance to such involvement. Theresa May's own style also played a significant part; when Home Secretary, she had tended to resist compromise with parliament (Russell and Gover 2017). To some extent, that can be seen as a typical executive mindset, which extends to civil servants at least as much as to ministers (who, being members, are indeed often more alert to parliament's needs). One former Cabinet minister said in interview that 'the truth is the government is never that keen on parliament having a big role in anything', while a senior official commented that as a 'sort of rule of thumb throughout all this, the less done with parliament, the better'. The knee-jerk response to the unexpected Brexit outcome was thus a kind of battening down in government, particularly given the known tensions in the Conservative parliamentary party. The referendum mandate—however non-specific—plus its foreign affairs focus, provided ministers with convenient pretexts for excluding parliament. However, there were clear differences of emphasis within the executive; Brexit Secretary David Davis had been an activist backbencher and tended towards relative parliamentary openness. In his first formal statement to the Commons he suggested that '[t]he referendum result was a clear sign that the majority of the British people want to see Parliament's sovereignty strengthened, and so throughout the process Parliament will be regularly informed, updated and engaged'.[2] The instinct in Theresa May's Number 10 tended to the reverse.

Meanwhile, many in parliament—and indeed outside—were eager that the arguments both about the form and process of Brexit should be fully aired and examined. A Labour frontbench interviewee recalled thinking, 'we can't have an unclear referendum and then give the executive power on all of this'. A backbencher likewise said, 'mine wasn't so much of a constitutional concern. It was more that I didn't think the government really knew what it wanted to do'—making parliamentary oversight essential. However, even at an early stage there were differences over this question along Brexit lines. A senior Eurosceptic reflected that, given the Prime Minister's initial Brexit stance, 'I don't think many of us felt there was a great need to keep an eye on her at that point', and there were clearly concerns that Brexit could be derailed by a parliament dominated by members who had voted Remain.

In terms of how parliament might be involved, there were three key questions: its potential role in the triggering of Article 50, in oversight of the government's negotiating objectives and negotiations with EU partners, and in the approval of any final Brexit deal. Each of these was raised very quickly after the referendum, and each became the subject of considerable disagreement.

The Triggering of Article 50

As already noted, the question of authorization for the triggering of Article 50, and thereby beginning the formal two-year legal process towards exit, emerged almost immediately after the referendum. At David Cameron's initial statement to the Commons four days later, Labour backbencher Mike Gapes had asked for assurance that 'we will have a vote in this House before article 50 is triggered'.[3] Cameron had responded that this would be a question for his successor. Responding to a similar question in the Lords on the same day, Leader of the House Baroness (Tina) Stowell suggested opaquely that 'it is very important that Parliament has a role in this process, but at this time I am not able to specify what that role is'.[4]

The most substantive early discussion of this question occurred in the House of Commons on 11 July—the day that Andrea Leadsom's forced withdrawal left Theresa May the winner of the Conservative leadership contest. Helen Goodman, a former Labour frontbencher, asked an urgent question on 'whether the Government will seek parliamentary approval before triggering article 50'.[5] The response from John Penrose, a Cabinet Office minister, was that 'Government lawyers believe that it is a royal prerogative issue. Nonetheless, I hope that everyone here will agree that democratic principles should out rank legal formalities.'[6] This implied, prior to installation of the new Prime Minister, that parliament would be given a vote—and concurs with the analysis of many interviewees that parliamentary involvement (at all three stages discussed here) was in truth a political inevitability. Goodman argued that a failure to consult parliament would 'be a clear breach of the promises made to the public by the Brexiters during the referendum campaign that they would "take back control" and "restore parliamentary sovereignty"'.[7] The Labour frontbencher present, Louise Haigh, expressed a view that would soon become central to the opposition's line—that there should be no trigger 'until there is a clear plan in place about what the UK will be negotiating for and how it will be achieved'.[8]

This did highlight a difficulty for the Prime Minister: that a vote on the trigger would offer parliament leverage on the form that Brexit should take—which remained undetermined. It also raised concerns for Leave supporters that parliament would use that leverage to water down, or perhaps even block, Brexit. Nonetheless, some Brexit supporters saw a vote on the trigger as reasonable. One such government insider said in interview that the idea of invoking the prerogative 'never ever seemed to me to be a runner, frankly', because 'the referendum did amount to some authority, but, nonetheless, you would need the authority of parliament'. The House of Lords Constitution Committee (2016: 8) agreed, issuing a report in September 2016 suggesting that it 'would be constitutionally inappropriate, not to mention setting a disturbing precedent' for the government to act on the referendum result without parliamentary approval. However, this point was resisted by the May government, and ended up—as discussed below—being resolved in the Supreme Court.

Oversight of the Negotiations

The referendum was clearly going to instigate a process of negotiations between the UK and its then EU partners, which had previously been given extremely little thought. How parliament was to be involved in this process—and how the UK's opening objectives in those negotiations were to be agreed in terms of the form of Brexit—were further obvious questions that arose very quickly after the result.

One suggestion that never gained much traction was for establishment of some kind of bespoke cross-party committee or commission to oversee the process. Senior Labour backbencher Yvette Cooper (a former leadership contender, and chair of the Commons Home Affairs Committee) suggested this at Cameron's first statement on 27 June. On 5 July two Labour backbenchers, Seema Malhotra and Stephen Kinnock (2016), published an article suggesting how this might work—through a body that would include not only parliamentarians but local and regional leaders, business and trade union representatives. Key protagonists discussed the idea with Oliver Letwin, and saw it partly as a way of navigating the Corbyn problem. It could also have been a potential mechanism for drawing a wider public, or at least key 'stakeholders', into the Brexit discussions. But it never got off the ground, and the two authors instead became members of the ExEU Committee—which went on to perform a scrutiny function of a more standard kind.

David Davis commented at his first statement on 5 September that, when it came to oversight of the negotiations, 'we should be as open with Parliament as possible'.[9] However, the government position on parliament's role in setting the objectives was more hardline. There was repeated pressure on this latter point, particularly from Labour. On 12 October, after Theresa May's party conference speech (discussed below) had pointed towards a 'hard' Brexit, Labour dedicated one of its opposition day debates to a motion arguing that Article 50 should not be triggered until the Commons had been able properly to scrutinize the plans for leaving the EU. This proposal attracted sufficient support from concerned Conservative backbenchers that the government was forced largely to fall in behind it. But this in turn attracted some concern from hardline Brexiteers: Jacob Rees-Mogg claimed that 'the sovereignty of Parliament is delegated by the British people', who had expressed their clear wish through the referendum.[10] Rather than seeking to control the negotiations, he argued, the Commons always reserved the power to vote no confidence in the government if it was unhappy with the direction of travel.

Theresa May appeared uncomfortable with subjecting her negotiating stance to oversight, and resisted making even the general commitments that Davis had done. Her preferred mantra became 'no running commentary'— which she deployed repeatedly, for example when appearing in front of the Commons Liaison Committee on 20 December 2016, to the clear frustration of its Conservative chair, Andrew Tyrie.

Approval of the Final Deal

The third question was whether parliament would be asked to approve the deal ultimately negotiated with the EU. This was on the face of it less contentious—government interviewees recognized that implementing a deal would require primary legislation, and that parliamentary approval of international treaties was also formally required. On the question of the vote on the final deal, a senior Conservative interviewee said, 'frankly, unless we're turning into a tyranny, that almost certainly had to happen'. The House of Lords Constitution Committee (2016: 9) unsurprisingly agreed that, as well as approving the Article 50 trigger, and having a 'central role...in the subsequent negotiation process', parliament should be involved in 'approving or otherwise the final terms under which the UK leaves the EU'.

But even on this most central and obvious point, Theresa May was initially resistant to commit. In her December appearance at the Liaison Committee, she manifestly avoided answering questions about whether there would be a final parliamentary vote on the deal. The headline in the *Daily Express* the following day gleefully reported 'why MPs won't be able to block Brexit' (Hall 2016), and the other papers (presumably briefed by Number 10 sources) also took this as her meaning. As on the other points above, May's refusal to concede at an early stage that parliament's involvement in these key decisions was in line with precedent angered MPs, and enabled a media narrative to develop about opponents in parliament (and elsewhere) allegedly seeking to obstruct Brexit. In January 2017, the Exiting the European Union Committee (2017b)—which included both diehard Brexiteers and former Remainers—unanimously recommended in its first report that parliament should have a vote on the final deal.

The First Miller Case

The first of these three questions—parliament's role in the triggering of Article 50—was ultimately decided not politically, but through the courts. It was a final decision of the Supreme Court in late January 2017 that forced the government to concede the point, and to introduce a bill to provide for parliament's authorization. The court case generated long-drawn-out and bitter arguments, which fed further angry headlines from the Brexit-supporting press. Whether the responsibility lay with the government or with those who pursued the case—or with some combination of the two—is debatable. But the result was undeniably to heighten polarization around the Brexit process, including over the role of both parliament and the courts.

Origins of the Case

The opportunity for the legal case was created by the structure of the European Union Referendum Act 2015. As indicated in earlier chapters, this authorized a referendum—nothing more, nothing less. During its parliamentary passage there was essentially no discussion of the process that would follow a Leave vote, and notably only one mention of the term

'Article 50' during the Commons stages—which went unanswered by the government. In theory, as with the bill authorizing the 2011 referendum on the electoral system (see Chapter 3), it would have been perfectly possible to spell out more clearly what the government should do in the event of a vote for change; in this case, through a clause authorizing ministers to trigger Article 50. But the government had not chosen to do this.

Almost immediately after the referendum, on 27 June, three legal academics (one also a practising barrister) published a blog arguing that parliament's approval was legally required for the trigger (Barber, Hickman, and King 2016). This was followed three days later by an article in the *Times* by prominent constitutional QC (and member of the House of Lords) David Pannick (2016), which supported their case.

The blogpost authors argued that, since parliamentarians would wish to respect the referendum result, seeking parliamentary approval might prove 'a mere formality'. But, '[a]s a matter of constitutional law, Parliament is not bound to follow the results of the Brexit referendum'. Both they and Pannick emphasized that it was well established in law that the executive's prerogative powers cannot be used to override an Act of parliament, and that since the inevitable consequence of the trigger would be reversal of the European Communities Act 1972, a new Act of parliament would be required (Barber, Hickman, and King 2018). These were not uncontroversial views, and various other commentators weighed in subsequently to suggest that the arguments might not hold up; but many nonetheless agreed that there were strong democratic arguments for a parliamentary vote (e.g. Elliott 2016, Millett 2016, Renwick 2016).

Gina Miller (2019a) was a businesswoman who had been involved in the Remain campaign. The daughter of a former Attorney General of Guyana (though a UK resident since childhood), she developed concerns about the legal and parliamentary consequences of a Leave vote during the campaign. On the same day that the blogpost was published, she was speaking at an event organized by law firm Mishcon de Reya, and fell into conversation about these matters with one of the firm's partners. She was told that they were working with clients to take a legal case against the government to force it to seek parliamentary approval for the triggering of Article 50, and agreed to join the group. Subsequently, these other litigants dropped out, and she became the sole client. A pre-action letter was sent on her behalf to the government on 1 July, and the matter became public shortly afterwards. A separate but similar case brought by Deir Dos Santos was subsequently joined to Miller's case.

Government and Parliamentary Views

Miller and her legal team anticipated that the case would create pressure for a parliamentary vote, thereby encouraging the question to be resolved politically. Perhaps counter-intuitively, they were not actually working with MPs, and the response from parliamentarians was mixed. Some valued this pressure, whereas some, in the words of an interviewee closely involved, 'were actually very angry…they felt it was the place of parliament to resolve this and not the courts'. One key parliamentarian interviewed described the case as 'a bit of a sideshow', while a Labour frontbencher suggested that 'it was a battle we should have been fighting through parliament'. But the existence of the court case meant that the government was under not only typical parliamentary pressures but legal pressures as well.

Rather than conceding, as Miller had anticipated, the government chose to fight the case. This was notwithstanding various key figures internally feeling that it was the wrong course. David Davis (2021) himself subsequently described the decision as 'ethically wrong, democratically wrong, tactically unwise'. His preferred option had been for government to propose a short bill to parliament authorizing the trigger—but Number 10 decided differently. Several ministers in closely related positions agreed with Davis, while the Prime Minister's own Director of Strategy reported, 'I kept saying, "why are we doing this"…I always thought this was a waste of time and a strange thing to be fighting' (Wilkins 2020). A key Labour backbencher recalled in interview being 'gobsmacked', saying 'I was incredulous that they fought the case. I just thought it was astonishing.'

So why did the government choose not only to do so but to go on to fight an appeal? Interviewees suggested various contributory factors. First, in the words of a government insider, 'there was actually quite a strong push from officialdom, as it were, to fight the case just to lay down a marker about prerogative powers and not be fettered in the future'. Oliver Letwin (2020) reported that when initially holding the Brexit brief he received 'unusually categorical advice' from the government's chief lawyer that the matter fell within such powers. Another ministerial figure said that 'the whole senior civil service instinct is to defend the power of the prerogative'. So there were clearly official voices encouraging the Prime Minister to resist the case.

But Theresa May's political calculations—or those of her senior advisers— were also important. One pro-Brexit government insider suggested that 'there was a political impetus from some at the top of Number 10 to want to fight this case and make a point about it', detecting 'some political desire to set up the narrative of the Remainers trying to undermine the result, and all that'. This was a framing which the Prime Minister appeared happily to embrace. In her speech to the Conservative Party conference on 2 October, May (2016c) suggested that 'those people who argue that Article 50 can only be triggered after agreement in both Houses of Parliament are not standing up for democracy, they're trying to subvert it. They're not trying to get Brexit right, they're trying to kill it.'

Such political tactics were far away from the unifying message that May had presented on taking over the party leadership. They risked fuelling divides, when public opinion was already deeply polarized after the referendum result. A poll conducted just over a week after the speech asked 'who should have the final say on activating Article 50?'; 83 per cent of Leave voters thought this power should lie with the Prime Minister and only 7 per cent with parliament, but among Remain voters 31 per cent supported the Prime Minister and 57 per cent supported parliament. A divide about parliament's role was increasingly being set up between the two, with at least tacit encouragement from the Prime Minister.

The High Court and the Supreme Court

Within days of this poll, the *Miller* case's hearing in the High Court began—in front of a panel of three senior judges, comprising the Lord Chief Justice Lord Thomas, the Master of the Rolls Sir Terence Etherton, and Lord Justice Sales (Elliott, Williams, and Young 2018). Miller's legal team was led by Lord Pannick. Central to his case was the idea that notification of withdrawal under Article 50 was equivalent to firing a gun: once the trigger is pulled, the bullet will inevitably reach its target.[11] As that target was withdrawal from the EU, it implied a statutory change, which fell outside the scope of prerogative power. In contrast, the government's case was based on more political arguments: that parliament's passing of the legislation to facilitate the referendum implied its permission for ministers to give effect to the outcome. It suggested that the claimants' position was that 'it would be constitutionally appropriate for the British people to vote to leave, and for the Government and/or Parliament then to decline to give effect to that vote', declaring this to be 'a surprising submission in a modern democratic society'.[12] Nonetheless, in an attempt to ward off the need for legislation to authorize the trigger, the government's lawyer did concede that there was 'very likely' to be a parliamentary vote on the final agreement with the EU. But this could potentially see parliament consulted very late in the day, and leave Brexit to occur by default without any parliamentary authorization—even if parliamentarians voted against the deal.

The court's judgment, on 3 November, concluded that the government's case was 'flawed' at a 'basic level'.[13] On use of prerogative powers, it cited the conclusion of a case from over 50 years before, which already stated that '[t]he prerogative is really a relic of a past age, not lost by disuse, but only available for a case not covered by statute'.[14] The judges agreed that '[a]n important aspect of the fundamental principle of Parliamentary sovereignty is that primary legislation is not subject to displacement by the Crown through the exercise of its prerogative powers'.[15] Hence, supporting the claimants' views that statute would be required, the court found against the government.

This sparked a furious, and distinctly alarming, response by the Brexit-supporting media. The following day the *Daily Mail* front page carried pictures of the three judges with a banner headline, 'Enemies of the People' (Slack 2016); the *Daily Telegraph* presented an only slightly more muted front-page headline, 'The judges versus the people' (Dominiczak, Hope, and McCann 2016). The *Sun* ran with 'Who do EU think you are?', with a subtitle 'Loaded foreign elite defy will of Brit voters' alongside a smiling picture of Gina Miller (Reilly and Newton Dunn 2016). The official government response was that it was 'disappointed' by the outcome in the High Court, and intended to appeal (HM Government 2016a). But some Brexit-supporting politicians echoed the media rhetoric, which sought to undermine the legitimacy of the court decision in the eyes of the public—and cast doubt on the propriety of parliament becoming involved. On the evening of the verdict—therefore before these headlines—Cabinet minister Sajid Javid suggested on BBC *Question Time* that the judges had made 'an attempt to frustrate the will of the British people' (quoted in Shipman 2017a: 51). Lord Chancellor Liz Truss was widely criticized for failing to carry out her statutory duty to defend the independence of the judiciary by being slow to comment, and failing to condemn the media attacks on the judges (Rozenberg 2020).

The government's appeal was fast-tracked to the Supreme Court, where it was heard on 5–8 December—for the first time ever, in front of the maximum panel of 11 justices. On 7 December Labour again used one of its Commons opposition days to demand greater clarity, with another motion calling on the Prime Minister to publish her plans for Brexit before triggering Article 50. Again, the government faced threats that up to 40 Conservative MPs might vote with the opposition (Swinford 2016). To neutralize the rebellion, but also achieve wider political objectives, the government proposed an amendment to the opposition's motion, inserting the words 'and further calls on the Government to invoke Article 50 by 31 March 2017'. This challenged MPs of all parties—for the first time—to support the principle of the trigger. As a reluctant trade for the government's agreement to provide further detail, and not wanting to appear resistant to the principle of Brexit, most Labour and Conservative MPs voted for the government's amendment and then the amended motion. The *Daily Express* headline the following day proclaimed 'Hooray! MPs say yes to EU exit' (Maddox 2021).

Some in government might have hoped that this would make the Supreme Court case go away. It had been demonstrated—as it potentially could have been much earlier—that the trigger had the Commons' political support. But the legal proceedings were now well advanced, and the core principle remained that of the prerogative versus statute law. Although the court's ruling, on 24 January 2017, acknowledged the outcome of the opposition day debate, it noted that 'if, as we have concluded, ministers cannot give Notice by the exercise of prerogative powers, only legislation which is embodied in statute will do. A resolution of the House of Commons is not legislation.'[16] By a majority of eight justices to three, the court found against the government, meaning that a statute would be required (Craig 2017, Elliott 2017c).

The court also ruled—this time unanimously—on an issue regarding devolution. The standard expectation under the Sewel convention was that a bill passing through Westminster which would affect the powers of the devolved administrations in Scotland, Wales, and Northern Ireland required a 'legislative consent' motion from the respective devolved legislature(s). This expectation had existed since the 1990s, and was written into the Scotland Act 2016 and Wales Act 2017, which stated that devolved consent was 'normally' required. A group of cases originating in Northern Ireland sought to argue that these provisions should be binding upon the government over Brexit. They reached the Supreme Court alongside the *Miller* case, but it confirmed that the term 'normally' meant that the devolved institutions' consent would not be necessary for the triggering of Article 50.

The Political Response

The media response to the Supreme Court ruling was somewhat more muted than had been the case for the High Court (McNeil 2017). Nonetheless, the previously jubilant *Daily Express* warned on its front page that 'MPs must not stop EU exit' (Hall 2017a), and the *Daily Mail* suggested that 'Remoaner' MPs might seek to fight a 'rearguard action' against the bill (Tapsfield,

Sculthorpe, and Dathan 2017). In a statement to the Commons on the day of the judgment, David Davis announced that the government would shortly be bringing forward legislation to approve the triggering of Article 50. His response to the court case was calm and emollient, commenting that 'the Court was asked a question, a proper, thorough and independent process was gone through, and it has given its answer in law'; the UK was 'a law-abiding nation', so of course the government would comply.[17] His Labour shadow, Keir Starmer, broadly welcomed the ruling, calling it a 'good day for parliamentary sovereignty', and signalled that the opposition planned to table amendments to the government's bill to 'ensure proper scrutiny and accountability throughout the process' ahead, and to ensure a 'meaningful vote' on the final deal.[18] Brexiteer voices were generally muted, largely encouraging the government to keep the promised bill short and simple.

With hindsight, the *Miller* case may be judged quite differently to how it was at the time. It was not, as many may have assumed, an attempt by parliament to push back against the Brexit result—Gina Miller and her team appear to have had relatively little active backing from within parliament itself. In addition, Brexit-supporting MPs—notwithstanding the anger of the newspapers on that side of the debate—ultimately came to view it as a useful intervention. In interviews, two senior Brexiteers independently referred to the case as a 'godsend', which, in the words of one, 'meant we had to have a bill, and we got the bill through and it gave absolutely cast-iron cover for the triggering of Article 50'. The other suggested that 'Miller 1 sort of solidified the Brexit ground, because Theresa May could always have withdrawn the Article 50 notification if she'd been left to do it for herself. But that simply wasn't possible once it had been passed into law.'

The Brexit Options and May's Red Lines

With the new Prime Minister in place, attention turned increasingly to the shape of Brexit. No clear blueprint existed, either inside government or in terms of proposals set out by the Vote Leave campaign—which had focused on the perceived benefits of Brexit, but not on how these could realistically be achieved. At this point it became increasingly clear that the options available involved a fundamental trade-off: the UK could either minimize economic disruption or maximize its autonomy—it would not be able to do both (Grey 2021, Menon and Wager 2021).

The various options, and their implications, are summarized in Table 4.1. At one end of the spectrum lay the possibility of continued Single Market

Table 4.1 The Brexit options

	Soft Brexit			Hard Brexit	
	Single Market and Customs Union	EEA	Customs Union only	Canada model	No-deal Brexit
End freedom of movement	No	No	Yes	Yes	Yes
Independent trade policy	No	Mostly	Limited	Yes	Yes
Freedom to diverge from EU regulations	No	No	Partial	Yes*	Yes
Single Market access for services	Yes	Yes	No	Limited	No
Tariff-free trade in goods with the EU	Yes	Yes	Yes	Yes	No
Frictionless border with the EU	Yes	Partial	Partial	No	No

* with some mutual recognition of standards

Note: many of the entries in this table are, inevitably, simplifications. Based on Institute for Government (2017).

membership. The EU Single Market is based on the 'four freedoms': free movement of goods, services, capital and people, all underpinned by common regulations. Continued membership—which would also require membership of the Customs Union, discussed below—would allow tariff-free, quota-free trade within the EU, and avoid non-tariff barriers, which could particularly threaten the UK's sizable services industry.[19] In return, the UK would need to continue following EU standards, and in doing so become a 'rule-taker': bound by regulations that it no longer had any role in deciding. It would be required to remain subject to the jurisdiction of the European Court of Justice (ECJ). And crucially, it would need to continue to allow free movement of people between its territory and the EU to live and work.

Another option—possible either in tandem with Single Market membership, or independently—was membership of the Customs Union, the EU-wide agreement that applies consistent tariffs to goods entering the bloc, and removes tariffs on those produced internally, allowing them then to be freely shipped within the EU. Continued Customs Union membership would offer little help to the services sector, but had some significant potential advantages to goods producers—particularly manufacturing businesses reliant on frequent shipping of components back and forth within the EU. There were again trade-offs in terms of autonomy: the requirement for shared tariffs would limit the UK's ability to negotiate its own trade deals, which became an increasing focus for Brexiteers, and the ECJ would retain a role in settling trade disputes.[20]

A third related option was membership of the European Economic Area (EEA)—often referred to as the 'Norway model'. The EEA had been created by an agreement between the EU and the member states of the European Free Trade Association (EFTA).[21] This granted the participating EFTA states a similar level of Single Market access to full members, allowing free trade in services, as well as tariff-free trade on most goods (Emmerson, Johnson, and Mitchell 2016).[22] In return, they accepted the 'four freedoms'. The model would require the UK to accept continuing freedom of movement, and 'rule-taker' status on regulation, but largely allow it to strike its own trade deals. A version of this model was often espoused by those who wanted to retain Single Market access, without Customs Union membership.

These options—which, despite their differences, all involved sacrificing some autonomy in order to minimize disruption—would come after the referendum to be known as forms of 'soft' Brexit. As discussed further in Chapter 6, their desirability became closely entangled with the question of how to avoid a hard border on the island of Ireland. The alternative, in which autonomy was prized above continuity, came to be dubbed 'hard' Brexit. Its proponents often spoke of a 'Canada model'—an EU trade deal which would allow tariff-free trade in most goods without the requirement to comply with EU regulations, though would likely require so-called 'mutual recognition' of standards in some areas. Such a model would give the UK freedom to control immigration, and to strike other trade deals. But increased customs checks would create more friction for goods moving between the UK and EU than the 'soft' Brexit options, and there would be only limited EU trade access for services.

The hardest Brexit of all would be 'no deal'. In this scenario, the UK would simply not reach a trade agreement with the EU, falling back instead on the basic rules imposed on both parties by their World Trade Organization (WTO) membership (Barnard and Menon 2018). This would give the UK maximum freedom to strike trade deals and to diverge from EU regulations; but it would also mean import duties and controls on trade with the EU, plus goods quotas which risked severely limiting trade in some sectors. Expert analysis suggested that its economic costs to the UK would be high, with inflation rising and manufacturers likely to close their UK factories (UK in a Changing Europe 2018a). It also warned of the potential for major disruption, with goods checks causing lengthy queues at ports, potentially impacting supplies of fresh food and medicines; sudden restrictions on UK airlines; and uncertainties about the legal status of UK and EU citizens resident in the other jurisdiction. Advocates of a no-deal Brexit suggested that these impacts could be constrained through more limited agreements, but it was far from sure that these were achievable. Perhaps most worryingly, a no-deal outcome would result in a 'hard' border—requiring physical infrastructure—on the island of Ireland, a concern more fully discussed in Chapter 6.

Theresa May announced in a speech to the Conservative Party conference in October 2016 that Article 50 would be triggered by the end of March 2017. This would start the clock on the two-year negotiating period, after which the UK would leave the EU with or without a deal unless both sides agreed to extend the negotiations. The announcement left only six months to develop a negotiating strategy, and to resolve the inherent trade-offs, before the Article 50 period began. Having been tight-lipped during the leadership campaign, May (2016c) used her conference speech to hint at her likely approach, outlining her ambition for a bespoke relationship with the EU which would borrow elements from existing models without conforming exactly to any one of them. Although she explicitly rejected the labels of 'soft' or 'hard' Brexit, the speech suggested that she planned to pursue the latter. In particular, her ultimatums that '[w]e are not leaving the European Union only to give up control of immigration again. And we are not leaving only to return to the jurisdiction of the European Court of Justice' appeared to signal that she was ruling out membership of the Single Market or Customs Union.

Eurosceptic voices welcomed the speech as confirmation that the former Remainer could be trusted to deliver Brexit. The *Sun* (2016a) claimed that 'Any doubt about Theresa May's commitment to Brexit has been quashed—May is the capable PM we can be proud of'. A senior Leave-supporting inter- viewee who had not backed May for the leadership recalled that, at this point, 'she said all the right things from a Brexiteer point of view'. Former Conservative Remainers, though, were horrified. One recalled in interview that 'the alarm bells started to ring' at this point. Not only was May failing to engage the public on the options for Brexit; she was excluding members of her own Cabinet. Then Chancellor of the Exchequer Philip Hammond (2020) recalled being 'completely stunned' and considered the speech 'almost a coup: a definition of Brexit without any proper Cabinet consultation at all'. Worse was to come. In a second conference speech, May (2016a) included the distinctly nationalistic line, 'if you believe you're a citizen of the world, you're a citizen of nowhere'. Rather than pursuing her leadership campaign promise to reunite the party and country, she now appeared to be siding with the hard Brexiteers.

MPs, as well as attempting to secure an in-principle role for parliament in the negotiating process (as described above), were keen to press May for details of her proposed strategy before the formal negotiations began. The first report from the Commons Exiting the European Union Committee (2017b: 31) mapped the areas where agreement would need to be found in a Brexit deal, noting that 'there will be an enormous amount of ground to be covered'. It urged the government to avoid a return to tariffs or regulatory barriers between the UK and EU, and to ensure that stability in Northern Ireland was not endangered by Brexit. It also recommended—by a narrow vote, indicating the divisions within the committee on Brexit (see Chapter 6)—that the government should seek a 'transition' or 'implementation' period, during which the UK would temporarily continue following EU rules post exit, to allow time for businesses and others to adjust.

On 17 January 2017, a few days after the committee's report was published and a week before the Supreme Court decision, the Prime Minister gave a major speech on Brexit at Lancaster House. This repeated themes from the party conference. It was here that May (2017a) first used the words 'no deal for Britain is better than a bad deal for Britain', which legitimized the idea of a no-deal Brexit. The speech set out 12 so-called Brexit objectives—later often dubbed May's 'red lines'—including control over UK laws and immigration, and the ability to make free trade agreements, reinforcing the impression that the UK would leave the Single Market and Customs Union. Again, Brexiteers were delighted. In interview, one called this 'an excellent speech [that] could have been written by any member of the [hardline] ERG'. But the text did contain some commitments welcomed by other parliamentarians, by proposing a transition period and conceding for the first time that parliament would be given a vote on the final Brexit deal.

In the Commons the day after the Lancaster House speech, multiple backbenchers pressed the government to produce a White Paper setting out its plans. This demand had appeared in the report from the Exiting the European Union Committee (2017b), and had the potential to spark rebellions on the EU (Notification of Withdrawal) Bill (discussed below) if not conceded. On 25 January, May confirmed that such a document would be forthcoming, and it was published the following week (HM Government 2017). Although perhaps looking like a concession to parliament, the White Paper essentially just repeated what the Lancaster House speech had said.

As a former Remainer, May was initially under suspicion from her pro-Brexit colleagues. These early speeches must be seen partly as an attempt to establish her Brexit credentials—in the words of her Chief Whip Julian Smith (2020), 'to prove that she was one of them'. But this hardline stance, which was obviously influenced by lobbying from Brexiteer MPs, boxed her in to a position that was irreconcilable with some of her other objectives. Shortly after the Lancaster House speech, David Davis told the House of Commons that the government aspired to a Brexit deal that would deliver 'the exact same benefits' as membership of the Single Market and Customs Union—words which would later be repeatedly quoted back at ministers.[23] But May herself had ruled out the obligations that such benefits entailed. Philip Hammond (2020) was among those who suggested that the Prime Minister's early commitments were the result of her not really understanding their full implications (see also Rogers 2020, Wilkins 2020). Likewise, her words that 'no deal for Britain is better than a bad deal for Britain' were later described by May's close aide Fiona Hill as 'just a tactic', which she suggested the writer of the speech, Nick Timothy, may have believed, but May never did (Seldon and Newell 2019: 140). Hill thought that the Prime Minister 'had made the calculation that we would never end up with the threat of no deal'.

As it turned out, by borrowing the language of the hard Brexiteers May had heightened their expectations, alarmed more moderate Conservatives, and limited her own room for manoeuvre. In good faith, she may have believed that they had a plan. But the challenges set by her red lines, and the threat of no deal, went on to reverberate through much of the next three years, as described in subsequent chapters.

The EU (Notification of Withdrawal) Bill

As Keir Starmer had indicated immediately after the *Miller* case, the need for the government to introduce a bill opened up possibilities for parliamentary resolution on all three key questions identified earlier—not just the triggering of Article 50, but the extent to which parliament should be involved in the oversight of the negotiations and in approving the final deal. In contrast, the government was determined to stick solely to the question of the trigger. Its European Union (Notification of Withdrawal) Bill was extremely short and simple, comprising just two clauses—together amounting to 66 words. The main clause stated that 'The Prime Minister may notify, under Article 50(2) of the Treaty on European Union, the United Kingdom's intention to withdraw from the EU'. The government seems not to have prepared any kind of 'concession strategy' to respond to parliamentary pressure—as ministers commonly do (Russell and Gover 2017)—instead being set on getting its bill through unamended.

A few days before the bill's introduction, the left-leaning *Guardian* newspaper noted that 'there is not a large appetite in either the Commons or the Lords to actively block the process', though it predicted pressure (including from Conservatives) for greater detail on the next steps (Bowcott, Mason, and Asthana 2017). In contrast, the Brexit-supporting media again warned of parliamentary ambush—in the *Daily Express* Leo McKinstry (2017) suggested that '[t]he Remoaners prattle about democratic accountability in the wake of the Supreme Court verdict yet they are seeking to overthrow the democratic will of British voters', while in the *Daily Telegraph* Philip Johnston (2017) claimed that 'May will need a kamikaze squad to get Brexit Bill through the Lords'. The idea here was that the House of Lords, where the Conservatives were not only seriously outnumbered but where the party's own representatives were more 'old-school' and pro-European, might need to be 'flooded' with new Brexit-supporting peers in order to overwhelm resistance. This recalled the tactic last threatened by Asquith's Liberals in 1911 against the Conservative-dominated chamber (Jenkins 1999).

Notwithstanding such doom-laden predictions, an official close to the process recalled that the government never really anticipated major problems with the bill, as parliament had by now accepted the public mandate for Brexit. And these expectations proved correct. As a Brexit-supporting government insider put it, 'I didn't have any concerns about getting it through...ultimately, there was barely a whimper of opposition'.

The Principle of Brexit and MPs' Representative Roles

The bill's second reading—which took place in the Commons over two days on 31 January and 1 February 2017—provided an opportunity to debate the rights and wrongs of Brexit. This was, as highlighted in Chapter 2, essentially the first time that MPs had been asked by the government to debate this question—though by now, clearly, the public had already spoken.

Some outside parliament hoped that the bill might provide an opportunity to block Brexit altogether. Commentator Chris Grey (2021: 66) has pointed out that 'it would be naïve to suppose that remainers did not hope that, were there to be a parliamentary vote, it might have the effect of stymying Brexit', and certainly some parliamentarians reported being under public pressure. As one former Remainer recounted:

We were getting lots of correspondence pressing us to use it as an opportunity to block Brexit. All the arguments about misinformation, and it should have had a supermajority, and it was a bad referendum and all that stuff, so you need to press the 'reset' button. But we never seriously considered that.

These external hopes misread the attitude of MPs. Interviewees uniformly indicated that there was no realistic expectation that parliament would use the bill to reverse the public's decision. As a senior Labour figure said, 'there was never a chance of parliament voting to ignore the referendum result, ever'. In introducing the second reading debate, David Davis summed the mood up by saying that the bill's purpose was to authorize ministers 'to implement a decision already made—a point of no return already passed'.[24]

The attention of frontbench speakers had already begun to shift beyond the trigger, to questions of implementation, and parliament's role in overseeing the negotiations—as further discussed below. Keir Starmer emphasized that the bill mustn't 'give the Prime Minister a blank cheque' to determine the form of Brexit.[25] Liberal Democrat leader Tim Farron proposed avoiding this by putting the final deal to the public for approval in a second referendum. Ministers expressed resistance to parliament being too closely engaged in oversight of the negotiating process—David Davis emphasized that 'to disclose all the details as we negotiate is not in the best interests of this country', while his junior DExEU colleague David Jones suggested that the bill 'is positively not a vehicle for determining the terms of the broader negotiations that will follow'.[26]

Over the two-day second reading debate there were 189 speeches, many of them impassioned and agonized. More than in any other debate in living memory, MPs articulated classic Burkean dilemmas of whether they should be following local opinion, national opinion, or their own personal beliefs. In a public survey conducted immediately after the Supreme Court decision, 43 per cent of respondents had felt that MPs should vote in line with the referendum result, while 17 per cent thought they should follow constituency opinion, and 23 per cent believed that they should 'vote in line with what they think is best for the country' (YouGov 2017b). The full range of possible behaviours was displayed in the debate when it took place.

Those MPs who faced no representational dilemmas, because they had supported Leave and their constituencies had done the same, clearly had the easiest task. Hence Conservative Tom Pursglove indicated that he was happy to support the bill, as 'I used my judgment in advocating that my constituents and people across this great country vote to leave'.[27] Those who regretted their constituents' or the country's decision were presented with more difficult choices. Labour's Emma Reynolds was a former Shadow Europe Minister and a passionate pro-European, but argued that 'those of us on the remain side might not like the result, but we have to accept it'.[28] Likewise, Conservative Anna Soubry commented that '[i]t is with a heavy heart, and against my long-held belief that the interests of this country are better served by our being a member of the European Union, that I shall support the Bill.[29] Dominic Grieve commented that 'at no time did I have any doubt that being a member of the European Union was in our national interest', but that if MPs had a primary responsibility to protect the national interest, this wouldn't be served 'if we tried to obstruct the decision that the electorate so clearly made.'[30]

For those MPs whose constituents had voted Remain, the dilemma was whether to follow constituency or national opinion. Labour's Stephen Doughty stated that 'my constituents voted overwhelmingly to remain. Because of my constituents, because of my conscience and because of the facts that I see before me, I shall vote against the triggering of article 50.'[31] In contrast, Kate Hoey—a long-time Labour Eurosceptic rebel—commented, 'I accept that Lambeth voted overwhelmingly for remain but, as I have made it very, very clear, this was a United Kingdom referendum, not a constituency or borough-based referendum'; hence she would be 'wholeheartedly voting to trigger article 50.'[32] Fellow Labour member Chris Bryant faced a different predicament (and had different firmly held beliefs), so chose to vote against the trigger, notwithstanding his own constituency having voted Leave; he argued that 'I am a democrat, but I believe in a form of democracy that never silences minorities.'[33]

Labour did not table a reasoned amendment to the bill's second reading, so the Speaker instead selected one from the SNP, which focused on the government's lack of consultation with the devolved administrations and the general lack of clarity about the form of Brexit.[34] This was heavily defeated, and the second reading was overwhelmingly approved, by 498 votes to 114. The largest block of opponents were the SNP's 50 MPs, but 44 Labour members also voted, in defiance of a three-line whip, to oppose the bill. Among them, 40 represented constituencies that estimates suggested had voted to remain, while the others (like Bryant) represented constituencies that had voted to leave. Just one Conservative, the veteran pro-European Ken Clarke, who had held various Cabinet roles from the 1980s to the 2010s, voted against the trigger. His primary justification was that he had always opposed referendums, and indeed he had abstained on the EU Referendum Bill in 2015. Overall, an analysis of the second reading debate shows that 34 Conservative MPs and 22 Labour MPs explicitly stated that they were voting for the trigger only reluctantly. At the bill's third reading on 8 February the number of Labour opponents had risen to 52. Among the new names, Clive Lewis had resigned from the Shadow Cabinet to vote against, on the basis that he could not support an unamended version of the bill.

Despite the anguished debates, the bill essentially had an easy passage through the Commons, and debates in the Lords were if anything even more focused on the next stages, rather than the principle of Brexit itself. Theresa May pointedly went to the chamber to watch the initial day of the second reading debate, on 20 February, seemingly to warn peers that they should not cause trouble. But there was even less threat in that chamber—which by convention does not seek to block government bills in their entirety, and does not normally vote at second or third reading (Russell 2013). Winding up the second reading debate for the opposition, Baroness (Dianne) Hayter of Kentish Town stated that '[n]o matter how much I regret the choice of the British people, I respect and accept it', and the second reading was approved unopposed.[35] This did not prevent the usual negative headlines, with the *Sun* screaming, 'If Lords hold up Brexit...they'll be next fur [*sic*] the chop' (Parsons 2017).

Debate on the Subsequent Stages of the Brexit Process

Aside from the principle of Brexit, the bill provided an opportunity for members in both chambers to discuss the appropriate management and objectives of the next steps. This included the second and third questions identified above: of parliament's role during the negotiations, and in approving the final deal. Both were matters on which the government had been reluctant to make firm commitments, although the Lancaster House speech had moved things on to some extent on the latter. Had the government been willing from an earlier stage to commit to the kind of parliamentary oversight which many (even ministers) considered ultimately inescapable, some bitter arguments might usefully have been avoided.

The emphasis on next steps at the Commons second reading was indicated above. Similar points were made later in the Lords. Labour's leader in the chamber, Baroness (Angela) Smith of Basildon, suggested that while 'the [referendum] question was simple and straightforward, the simplicity ended there'; hence it 'would be irresponsible to merrily wave the Government off to negotiate a future without parliamentary engagement or accountability'.[36] This argument was echoed by various others, including former Conservative Lord (Tim) Boswell of Aynho, chair of the chamber's European Union Committee.[37] On parliament's role in the negotiations, he suggested that '[i]t is not enough that Parliament will get a vote at the end of the day in early 2019, presented with a "take it or leave it" offer...Consent must be earned over time and by dialogue, so the Government need to embrace scrutiny'.[38]

In both chambers, a need for clarity on the detail of Brexit was a key debating point on the bill. Labour's continuing refrain, supported by other opposition parties and some Conservatives, was that there should be 'no blank cheque' for ministers. Parliamentary pressure had encouraged the government to finally publish its Brexit White Paper on 2 February, between the bill's Commons second reading and committee stage. But new clauses proposed by the Labour frontbench at committee stage sought to create statutory objectives for the Prime Minister during the negotiations, and to prevent her from triggering Article 50 until she had promised to report to parliament on progress at least every two months. Both of these proposals were defeated, though the minister, David Jones, insisted that 'the Government will keep parliament well informed'.[39] Labour returned to these questions in the Lords—including through an amendment requiring at least quarterly parliamentary reporting to parliament. Ministers resisted amending the bill but emphasized that there would be a report to parliament after every meeting of the European Council, which would be at least quarterly. On this basis Labour withdrew the amendment, and a potential defeat of the government was avoided.

Various more detailed points were also discussed during the bill's passage concerning the preparations for Brexit, and the form that it might take. Opposition proposals in the Commons included requirements to publish impact assessments, to include the devolved administrations in the process, and to respect the provisions of the Belfast/Good Friday Agreement. A cross-party clause from members of the Joint Committee on Human Rights proposed that EU citizens resident in the UK at the time of the referendum should retain their residency rights post Brexit. All of these proposals were voted down. In the Lords, many similar points were made, and the government was defeated over the citizens' rights proposal.

A key question, which at this stage gained little traction, concerned the prospect of a further referendum to agree the terms of the Brexit deal. The Liberal Democrats proposed this during debate in both chambers. A Commons amendment was heavily defeated, but exposed some divisions on the Labour side, with 19 Labour members supporting it (and six opposing), despite the party whipping to abstain. Labour's discomfort continued in the Lords, when 22 of the party's peers—including senior figures such as former Leader of the Lords Baroness (Jan) Royal of Blaisdon and former Lord Chancellor Lord (Derry) Irvine of Lairg—voted for a similar Liberal Democrat amendment, which was heavily defeated. An unconventional reasoned amendment from the Liberal Democrats followed at the bill's third reading. This proposed outright rejection of the bill, on the basis that no referendum was planned—Labour's Baroness Smith denounced the amendment as 'irresponsible', and it was heavily defeated.[40] As a symbolic stance by an anti-Brexit party this move perhaps made sense, but it risked unnecessarily fuelling hostile headlines.

The biggest point of contention regarding parliament's involvement in the next stages concerned its right to a final say over whether to accept the Brexit deal. By this point, Theresa May (2017a) had made her Lancaster House promise that the deal would be put to 'both Houses of Parliament' for approval. In response to a proposed new clause from the Labour frontbench in the Commons, David Jones confirmed that this would 'cover not only the withdrawal arrangements but also the future relationship with the European Union', which Keir Starmer greeted as 'a huge and very important concession'.[41] However, doubts remained about parliament's role in decision-making if the government failed to reach a deal—a point raised in the chamber by Anna Soubry.

In the Lords, there were concerted attempts to insert a statutory requirement for a 'meaningful' vote on the deal, and to give parliament a vote on any proposals to end the negotiations without a deal. An amendment to this effect was proposed by the Labour frontbench, jointly with Lord (David) Pannick and others, including Conservative Viscount Hailsham (the former Cabinet minister Douglas Hogg). Hailsham argued that it was 'Parliament and not the Executive which should be the final arbiter of our country's future', claiming affinity 'with the campaigners for Brexit who wanted Parliament to recover control over policy and legislation'.[42] But pro-Brexit senior Conservative Lord (Michael) Forsyth of Drumlean denounced this as 'a clever lawyer's confection' designed to reverse the referendum result.[43] The minister Lord (George) Bridges of Headley suggested that the argument 'really comes down to a judgement about whether Ministers and the Government can be trusted'.[44] The Lords decided that the government shouldn't be given the benefit of the doubt, and passed the amendment by 366 votes to 268, with support from 13 rebel Conservatives.

On the bill's return to the Commons both Lords defeats—on the 'meaningful vote' and on citizens' rights—were readily overturned. Labour supported both, but there were just two Conservative rebels on citizens' rights, and—despite some journalists' predictions—none at all on the meaningful vote. In rejecting the meaningful vote amendment, David Davis argued that the government 'must have the freedom to walk away' from the negotiations.[45] This echoed May's previous words on no deal, and a comment from Foreign Secretary Boris Johnson the preceding day, that Britain would be 'perfectly OK' without a deal on Brexit (Rayner 2017). Notwithstanding these threats of no deal, Conservative MPs, unlike some of their counterparts in the Lords, were still at this point prepared to put their trust in the Prime Minister. Without support from the Commons, the Lords backed down.

Hence the EU (Notification of Withdrawal) Bill completed its passage, as the government had insisted, unamended. But the arguments about the meaningful vote and the risk of a no-deal exit were not over; they would significantly escalate later, as discussed in Chapter 7.

The bill received royal assent on 16 March 2017. On 29 March a letter was delivered from Theresa May to the European Council President, Donald Tusk, authorizing the trigger of Article 50. This marked the beginning of the formal two-year negotiating period.

Conclusion

Theresa May was dealt an incredibly difficult hand when taking over as Prime Minister. The referendum outcome was unprepared for, her party was deeply divided, and she inherited a parliamentary majority of just 16. Both instinctively and due to this inauspicious parliamentary arithmetic, her priority was to keep her party together. But actions during the early months of her premiership, in retrospect, sowed the seeds of some of the key problems that developed later.

May was a former Remainer now tasked with delivering Brexit, for which no blueprint was available—including from those who had been its strongest advocates. In the absence of a plan, her instinctive party tribalism, and desire to build trust among members of the hardline ERG, saw May look to them for guidance. Their demands influenced her initial 'red lines', set out in her party conference speech of autumn 2016 and Lancaster House speech of early 2017. But this positioning moved her away from the unifying ambitions that she had articulated when campaigning to be party leader, and raised increasing concerns among more moderate Conservative MPs. As discussed more fully in the next chapter, the alternative of pursuing an explicitly cross-party approach to Brexit—which would be necessary without the support of the hardliners, given her narrow Commons majority—would always have been difficult. But a greater openness with the public about the challenges of Brexit at an early stage might have enabled May to establish a more broad-based appeal, strengthening her hand against the hardline Eurosceptics. Instead, by embracing their objectives, and even raising the prospect of a no-deal Brexit, May boxed herself in to commitments that would create problems at subsequent stages—including in reaching agreement with the EU and finding majority parliamentary support.

May's instinctively closed and non-consultative style extended to parliament's role in the Brexit process. This was encouraged by several other factors: her slender Commons majority; the Whitehall mindset, which tends towards excluding parliament where possible; traditions of using the prerogative in the field of foreign affairs (further discussed in Chapter 6); the government's severe uncertainties about its own policy direction; and concerns on the Leave side that parliamentarians dismayed by the result might seek to undermine or overturn it. Nonetheless, even committed Brexit supporters inside government acknowledged that parliament could (and indeed should) not be shut out of the process completely. The reluctance by Number 10 to engage with parliamentarians generated suspicion and frustration. It also fuelled a developing media narrative that presented parliament as an enemy of Brexit. The UK tradition of parliamentary sovereignty, previously celebrated by Brexiteers, faced challenges from the new imperative of popular sovereignty as a result of the referendum, which had a potential to pit parliament against 'the people'. May's team did little to discourage this narrative, and indeed exploited it to justify its own lack of openness with parliament.

These tensions soon resulted in the involvement of the courts, through the *Miller* case regarding the triggering of Article 50. Ultimately, this clarified core relationships in the constitution: reinforcing that the executive cannot use prerogative powers to overturn statute. But in other respects, the recourse to the courts was unfortunate. Had the 2016 vote been better planned for, the EU Referendum Bill could have provided legal certainty by including formal authorization for the trigger, making the case unnecessary. In the absence of that certainty, the government could have responded through introduction of a short bill to authorize the trigger, as Brexit Secretary David Davis proposed. Instead, Number 10 responded to the court case by hunkering down further, and even used it to further feed resentment against parliamentary 'remoaners' (despite Miller having acted independently, with very little parliamentary support). The judgment against the government secured parliament's role in the process, but further fuelled the developing media narrative, resulting in vitriolic headlines against not just parliament but the courts. Rather than seeking to ease these tensions, May's team unfortunately tended to stoke them.

The consequence of the *Miller* case was the EU (Notification of Withdrawal) Bill. Passage of this bill, when it came, faced only limited parliamentary resistance—though many members spoke in debate of their regret about Brexit. By this time, concerns about May's closed style and increasingly hardline Brexit stance led opposition parliamentarians, with some support from Conservative backbenchers, particularly in the Lords, to use the bill to influence her negotiating objectives and seek guarantees of future parliamentary involvement. The government's line remained one of resistance. Hence the vehicle facilitated by Gina Miller was not used to win any further powers for parliament at the subsequent stages—Miller later declared herself disappointed that MPs had not made better use of the opportunity presented to them (Roberts 2017). At root, two key parliamentary dynamics could be seen in operation here. First, parliament was—as ever—very mindful of the public mood. Had opinion moved against Brexit, many MPs might willingly have put up greater resistance to May's plans. But the so-called 'Remainer' parliament, while saddened, was highly respectful of the referendum result, and polls showed no evidence of a subsequent public backlash (YouGov 2022a). Second, at least for now, Conservative MPs were willing to maintain the standard position of giving their leader the benefit of the doubt, and supporting her position. This relative harmony was not to last.

Notes

1. Unlike the rest of the UK, in Northern Ireland results were released at constituency level. Dempsey (2017) draws together data on Great Britain from Chris Hanretty (2016, 2017), who produced the first constituency-level estimates, and the BBC, which later produced results for some constituencies using ward-level data obtained from local authorities (Rosenbaum 2017).
2. House of Commons Hansard, 5 September 2016, column 40.
3. Ibid., 27 June 2016, column 40.
4. Ibid., 27 June 2016, column 1396.
5. Ibid., 11 July 2016, column 23.
6. Ibid., 11 July 2016, column 23.
7. Ibid., 11 July 2016, column 23.
8. Ibid., 11 July 2016, column 25.
9. Ibid., 5 September 2016, column 50.
10. Ibid., 12 October 2016, column 371.
11. The European Court of Justice would later conclude that Article 50 could be revoked, in its judgment on the *Wightman* case (see Chapter 8). Nonetheless, the government stressed at the time of the *Miller* hearings that, even if revocation were possible, it would not become government policy.
12. 'Skeleton Argument of the Secretary of State for Exiting the European Union', in *R (Miller and Dos Santos) v. Secretary of State for Exiting the European Union* CO/3809/2016; CO/3281/2016 at [20(1)], https://www.bindmans.com/uploads/files/documents/Miller_v_SSExEU_-_Skeleton_Argument_of_the_Secretary_of_State_300916.pdf.

13. *R (Miller and Dos Santos) v. Secretary of State for Exiting the European Union* [2016] EWHC 2768 (Admin), at [85].

14. Ibid., at [24], quoting *Burmah Oil Co (Burma Trading) Ltd v Lord Advocate* [1965] AC 75 at [101].

15. Ibid., at [25].

16. *R (Miller and another) v. Secretary of State for Exiting the European Union*, [2017] UKSC 5, at [12].

17. House of Commons Hansard, 24 January 2017, column 162.

18. Ibid., column 163.

19. Non-tariff barriers are any barriers to trade other than customs tariffs. They include, for example, non-recognition of overseas professional qualifications.

20. Customs Union membership would prevent the UK from striking independent trade deals affecting goods covered by the Customs Union, but would allow it to agree deals covering areas such as services, procurement, and data. Supporters of this option variously referred to 'the Customs Union' and 'a customs union', implying a more bespoke settlement. Their language is reproduced throughout the book, but the distinction was little more than a matter of political semantics—third-party status would have required some tweaks to the country's customs union with the EU, but the fundamental benefits and obligations would largely have been the same.

21. Three of EFTA's four member states participate in the EEA: Norway, Iceland, and Liechtenstein. The fourth, Switzerland, instead trades with the EU via a series of bilateral agreements.

22. EEA members also do not participate in the Customs Union, meaning that goods face customs checks at the EU border.

23. House of Commons Hansard, 24 January 2017, column 169.

24. Ibid., 31 January 2017, column 818.

25. Ibid., 31 January 2017, column 826.

26. Ibid., 31 January 2017, column 822; 1 February 2017, column 1129.

27. Ibid., 31 January 2017, column 891.

28. Ibid., 31 January 2017, column 876.

29. Ibid., 31 January 2017, column 849.

30. Ibid., 31 January 2017, column 861.

31. Ibid., 1 February 2017, column 1116.

32. Ibid., 31 January 2017, column 851.

33. Ibid., 1 February 2017, column 1076.

34. There were various others, not selected for decision, including one from a group of pro-European Labour backbenchers (including Heidi Alexander, Ben Bradshaw, Chris Bryant, Peter Kyle, and Owen Smith), demanding that parliament or the electorate should be given the chance to decide whether the UK should stay in the Single Market, and one from the Liberal Democrats calling for a referendum on the final Brexit deal.

35. House of Lords Hansard, 21 February 2017, column 318.

36. Ibid., 20 February 2017, column 17.

37. Boswell was a former minister, and only a 'former' Conservative due to the convention that the chamber's Senior Deputy Speaker (a position that he then held) renounces party affiliation.

38. House of Lords Hansard, 20 February 2017, column 57.

39. House of Commons Hansard, 6 February 2017, column 119.

40. House of Lords Hansard, 7 March 2017, column 1342.
41. House of Commons Hansard, 7 February 2017, column 264. For the distinction between these elements, see Chapter 6.
42. House of Lords Hansard, 7 March 2017, column 1267.
43. Ibid., column 1260.
44. Ibid., column 1296.
45. House of Commons Hansard, 13 March 2017, column 41.

5

Seeking, but Losing, a Majority: The 2017 General Election

Theresa May had won the Conservative leadership contest in 2016 on a promise to steady the party, and to deploy her considerable political experience to deliver Brexit. She also explicitly pledged that she would do so without calling a potentially destabilizing early general election. However, as the reality of implementing Brexit sank in, and with the new Prime Minister riding high in the polls, she was persuaded to break that pledge. But rather than increasing May's majority, and strengthening her hand in parliament, the June 2017 election resulted in the loss of the Conservative majority, and she spent the remainder of her premiership as head of a minority government. This was a governing form relatively unfamiliar at Westminster, which required both skills and strategies inaccessible to May.

This chapter begins with some brief reflections on the UK and international experience of minority government, and what it requires to succeed. It then goes on to discuss the background behind the calling of the 2017 general election, the campaign, the results, and the political fallout. The outcome of the election severely dented May's credibility, and there were immediate questions about whether she could and should be unseated; but she went on to form a confidence and supply arrangement with the Northern Ireland DUP, and to redouble her commitment to deliver Brexit. However, the new parliamentary arithmetic made this even more challenging than previously. May had hoped that the general election would be a pivot point, liberating her from the constraints of a small parliamentary majority and enabling her to govern more boldly. When that strategy failed, many people inside and outside her party called for an alternative pivot, to bring senior Labour figures on board to deliver a softer Brexit. But this presented both a risky and a deeply uncomfortable route for the Prime Minister. Using words from the election campaign, her response was instead largely to continue as if 'nothing had changed'—when in fact many things had changed fundamentally.

Minority Government

A fundamental feature of the UK political system, as in any 'parliamentary' (rather than presidential) democracy, is that the government must be able to maintain the confidence of parliament. MPs ultimately have the power to remove the government from office via a vote of no confidence, making it important that, at least on key issues, the government enjoys majority Commons support.

Throughout most of the post-war period this has been straightforward, as the electoral system has resulted in single-party majority governments. For example, the Conservatives held comfortable majorities under Thatcher and Major, from 1979 to 1992, and the same was true for the Labour governments of Blair and Brown from 1997 to 2010. Generally, in comparative terms, the UK is characterized as a 'majoritarian' democracy, where a ruling party is relatively unconstrained (Lijphart 1999). The extent to which this is true can be exaggerated, particularly following reforms during the Labour years (Flinders 2005, Hazell 2008), but it is generally accepted that there is a 'majoritarian' mindset in Whitehall and Westminster—particularly compared to the greater spirit of cooperation between political parties that may exist in what Lijphart called 'consensus' democracies.

There have clearly been exceptions to the rule of Westminster single-party majority government. The most obvious was the Conservative/Liberal Democrat coalition of 2010–15. That involved close cooperation between the two parties, which between them enjoyed a comfortable Commons majority and significant support in the Lords. The coalition was relatively stable, running to its full five-year term. In contrast, minority governments at UK level have tended to be short-lived. The only post-war examples prior to 2017 were the Wilson Labour government of February 1974, which governed briefly before staging a second election that October which resulted in a Labour majority, and the gradual attrition of small majorities under the Callaghan government of the late 1970s and the Major government of the 1990s. Both were unstable, and the Callaghan government ultimately fell following a Commons no-confidence vote.

But minority governments do not need to be short-lived and insecure. They are relatively common internationally, and there have also been recent examples of this model working fairly smoothly at the devolved level in the UK. The SNP governed as a single-party minority in Scotland 2007–11, and again post 2016, while in Wales Labour has governed in the same way several times. But successful minority government requires different approaches to the standard single-party majority model familiar at Westminster.

These factors were reviewed in anticipation of the UK's hung parliament of 2010, in a report jointly produced by the Constitution Unit and Institute for Government (IfG). It concluded that a 'key lesson' from historical and international practice was:

> that when minority prime ministers seek to govern as if they had a majority the result is instability, partisanship...and likely failure. By contrast, minority administrations which adopt a more consensual approach, negotiating and making concessions with opponents...are more likely to remain in office.
>
> **(Hazell et al. 2009: 7)**

The comparative academic literature likewise emphasizes the importance of cross-party bargaining and concessions (Strøm 1990). This may involve negotiating with different parties on different policies, so that majority alliances shift on a case-by-case basis. But if such majority support on an issue can't be found, governments need to be pragmatic. Ultimately, minority governments normally seek to avoid controversial policies on which a majority cannot be built. But this kind of avoidance was not available post 2017 on Brexit, given the acceptance that the referendum mandate must be honoured. By the time of the 2017 election the Prime Minister had also laid down various Brexit 'red lines', which would prove difficult to reverse.

The authors of the Constitution Unit/IfG report also concluded that the most important lesson for a Prime Minister under minority government is that their 'personality and leadership style help to set the tone for how parliament will function'. A Prime Minister 'who respects political and parliamentary realities, and the need to seek cooperation from the opposition parties...[will have] the best chance of having success as a minority government', whereas one who is 'obdurate' and adopts a 'confrontational style' is likely to undermine such success (Hazell et al. 2009: 70). Theresa May's inflexible style and party tribalism (as discussed in the previous chapter) did not bode well in this regard.

Minority government can present challenges for the opposition as well as for the governing party. An opposition that uses its full strength to block the government in parliament can appear petulant and attract public censure. Thus the Conservatives worked actively not to appear 'obstructionist' under the newly elected Wilson government of February 1974 (Peacock 2018: 70). But in 1979 the party keenly seized opportunities to inflict defeats upon the ailing Callaghan government, and ultimately to bring it down (Ball 2003).

The literature on minority governments focuses largely on the need to build parliamentary cooperation with other parties. The standard expectation, as explored in Chapter 2, is that parliamentary parties are relatively cohesive, and that deals can be agreed between stable party blocs. But post 2017, this was very much not the case. It would not be enough for Theresa May to bring on board an additional pro-Brexit party, and thereby guarantee a narrow but stable majority. The deep divide on her own party benches was a significant threat to any such majority—putting her government in an even weaker position than it appeared. The arrival of minority government attracted much attention. But the bigger ongoing problem was the divisions in the Conservative Party, making formal minority status, in some ways, just the icing on the cake.

The Decision to Hold the Election

One of Theresa May's (2016d) first pledges when launching her leadership campaign was that '[t]here should be no general election until 2020'—the year that one was due under the Fixed-term Parliaments Act. Given the government's small parliamentary majority, and the Prime Minister's high popularity compared with Jeremy Corbyn and his Labour Party, the idea of holding an early election was put to May repeatedly in the early months of her premiership. But she consistently rejected it. For example, on the BBC's *Andrew Marr Show* in September 2016 she insisted, 'I'm not going to be calling a snap election' (Samuelson 2017). The following month, talking to Tim Shipman (2016) of the *Sunday Times*, she made this a point of principle—suggesting that an election would create 'instability', and that it 'isn't about political games, it's about what is right for the country'.

A key moment came in February 2017, when the Conservatives won a by-election in the Cumbrian seat of Copeland—which had been held by Labour since its creation in 1983. From early in the year national opinion polls consistently showed strong support for Theresa May and her party, in contrast to Corbyn's Labour. In late March, YouGov (2017c) gave the Conservatives an 18 per cent lead, at 43 per cent against Labour's 25 per cent. Consequently, May came under growing pressure from figures in her party to seek a snap election, and this argument became increasingly difficult to resist.

In and of itself the proposal looked very tempting. But the Brexit timetable gave these arguments greater weight. With the Article 50 trigger on 29 March, negotiations were due to end two years later, and a spring 2020 election would most likely then fall during any Brexit transition period. Those close to May have argued that this was a serious consideration—negotiating with an election looming, and then fighting that election before Brexit was fully 'done' could have had significant disadvantages for the Prime Minister (Hammond 2020, Wilkins 2020). Crucially, as Wilkins argued, an early election would also give May a personal mandate that could strengthen her position in the party.

There were also parliamentary considerations regarding the next stages of Brexit. In her 2016 party conference speech May had promised that a 'Great Repeal Bill'—significantly more complex, and potentially more controversial, than the EU (Notification of Withdrawal) Bill—would soon be introduced to parliament. Number 10 insiders, including the Prime Minister's Deputy Chief of Staff (Penn 2020) and her Special Adviser on Europe (Davidson 2020), have stated publicly that the experience of getting the initial bill through made them realize how things would be easier with an increased parliamentary majority. Seldon and Newell's (2019: 144) Number 10 interviewees claimed that they had been 'exhausted by the effort of getting Article 50 through Parliament'. This perhaps suggests a certain naivety—as described in the previous chapter, that bill had sailed through both chambers rapidly and without amendment, with virtually no rebellion on the Conservative side. But rebellions had been threatened, and Cowley and Kavanagh (2018: 14) suggested that the lack of dissent 'masked the [enormous] effort that had been involved' on the part of the party whips. As recounted in the last chapter, it was already becoming clear that it would be difficult to hold the party together once the question shifted beyond the principle of Brexit, to the precise details of a Brexit plan.

Increasingly, May came under public as well as private pressure for an early election from within her party. Cowley and Kavanagh (2018: 410) report that those arguing in favour included 'all of her key aides, the Chancellor, the Brexit Secretary' and others. Philip Hammond and David Davis were clearly working together to encourage the Prime Minister to change her position. Ross and McTague (2017: 87) summarize Davis's pitch as 'Call a snap election, thump Corbyn's Labour Party, and then thump the EU in the Brexit talks'. In early March, former party leader William Hague (2017b) made the case for an election in an article for the *Daily Telegraph*. He argued that 'a large and decisive majority in the Commons' would strengthen the government on Brexit, and also 'catch the Labour Party in its worst condition since the early Thirties, and with its least credible leader ever'. This looked like an almost irresistible opportunity.

The difficulties in seizing the opportunity were twofold. First, Theresa May's repeated protestations that calling a general election would be the wrong thing to do. Second, the public's view. Polls showed significant hostility to an early election, and May reportedly received a memo from her campaign adviser Lynton Crosby warning that 'there is clearly a lot of risk involved...and there is a real need to nail down the "why" for doing so now' (quoted in Ross and McTague 2017: 91). Seldon and Newell (2019: 201) suggest that May was very concerned about how a U-turn on this issue would look, and so focus groups were run on how the argument for such a change of heart could be framed. This led to a conclusion that 'the only workable basis for calling an early general election was to get a stronger majority to secure the best deal out of the EU'.

The Prime Minister's shock announcement was made in a statement outside 10 Downing Street on 18 April, immediately after the Easter weekend. This firmly laid the blame for her change of heart at parliament's door. May (2017f) suggested that '[a]t this moment of enormous national significance there should be unity here in Westminster, but instead there is division. The country is coming together, but Westminster is not.' She accused Labour of threatening to vote against the final Brexit deal, and the Liberal Democrats of wanting 'to grind the business of government to a standstill', while suggesting that 'unelected members of the House of Lords have vowed to fight us every step of the way'. All of this, she argued, 'weakens the government's negotiating position in Europe', making a general election necessary to end the 'political game-playing'.

Some of these claims clearly bore only a tenuous connection to reality. It was particularly ironic that May now accused others of playing political games, having earlier used that term to refute the idea of calling an early election. Nonetheless, her message was warmly embraced by the Brexit-supporting media. Most notable was the *Daily Mail* front page, given over to a fierce-looking close-up of May, alongside a banner headline, 'Crush the Saboteurs'. This strongly echoed an editorial from the *Sun* (2016b) several months before, which had urged May to consider calling an election, and suggested that the 'Brexit saboteurs of the Commons and Lords must be faced down and crushed'. That same newspaper greeted the election announcement enthusiastically, suggesting that 'all the...knife-edge Parliament votes' over Article 50 had demonstrated a determination by MPs and peers to 'defy the referendum', so what was needed was a 'thumping Tory victory—and surely few can imagine any other result' (Sun 2017a). This prediction of the outcome, of course, subsequently proved only about as accurate as the paper's description of parliamentary events to date. Various other outlets acknowledged that there had been little parliamentary resistance so far, and several published lists of the various occasions when May had stated that an election would not be called.

The Fixed-term Parliaments Act meant that the Prime Minister needed the approval of a two-thirds majority in the House of Commons to hold an early election. Hence a debate was held the day after the Downing Street statement. Immediately beforehand the matter was also raised at Prime Minister's Questions. Labour's Yvette Cooper, who was a long-time adversary of May's, having served as Shadow Home Secretary 2011–15, raised a direct challenge to her allegations. She commented that the Prime Minister 'yesterday said that she was calling a general election because Parliament was blocking Brexit, but three quarters of MPs and two thirds of the Lords voted for article 50, so that is not true, is it?'[1] Jeremy Corbyn was more mocking, pointing out that parliament had voted to respect the Brexit mandate, 'but instead of getting on with the job, she is painting herself as a prisoner of the Lib Dems, who have apparently threatened to grind government to a standstill. There are nine of them.'[2] May gave no substantive response on either point. Referencing the headlines, the SNP's Westminster leader Angus Robertson invited the Prime Minister to 'agree that political opponents are not "saboteurs"'.[3] Again, the Prime Minister simply avoided comment. Many MPs were clearly perturbed both by May's statement and its media representations. Labour's Stella Creasy (2017) referred to the tone as 'chilling', while a senior Brexit-supporting interviewee described it as 'a very demagogic act'.

Of course, the reasons given by the Prime Minister did not tell the whole story. Insofar as May had concerns regarding the parliamentary dynamics, they were as much about her party as the opposition parties. Given the divisions between Conservative hardline Brexiteers and former Remainers, and the slender majority, the risk of rebellion on either side creating major difficulties was high. A larger majority would have given May greater room for manoeuvre within her own party, and the ability to sideline either camp. On the question of whether she would have sidelined the pro-Europeans or the Eurosceptic hardliners in this scenario, an interviewee from the former group said 'I think most of us thought that it was more likely that she would use a big majority to face down the [hardline] ERG, because she knew the ERG were really a serious nuisance'. A senior Brexiteer agreed, saying, 'I was quite concerned privately that if she had got a huge majority this wouldn't have been great for Eurosceptics. I was nervous of a big Theresa May majority'. In reality, of course, it is not normal for a Prime Minister to rely on opposition parties to deliver their policy—this is the task of government backbenchers. But May found it easier to round on the opposition parties instead. An interviewee close to her said:

I think privately she felt, given the numbers in parliament, 'I've got no chance of passing a deal. Because it's going to be hard to get opposition support and whatever deal I do is going to be too hard for some of my colleagues, or too soft for others'. But it was quite difficult to explain that to the electorate…because you're kind of saying 'well some of my MPs aren't really trustworthy to deliver the thing that we're trying to do'.

Consequently the blame was placed on parliament, and her political opponents outside the party. This again fuelled negative headlines and public resentment.

Given Labour's weak position in the polls, it might have been expected that the party would vote to block an early election. Some have suggested that May's proposed election date—nearly two months later, on 8 June—was tailored to allow for delay created by Labour resistance (Ross and McTague 2017).[4] Ultimately, however, though many Labour MPs feared that the party faced annihilation, it was politically difficult to resist an election, and Corbyn whipped them to support the government's motion (Mason and Elgot 2017). MPs approved this on 19 April by 522 votes to 13, with just nine Labour members voting against, and the SNP choosing to abstain. As a result, the UK was now on course for its second general election in little more than two years.

The Campaign and the Result

May's (2017g) first speech of the election campaign, delivered in Bolton on 19 April, summed up her central pitch to the voters: 'a choice between strong and stable leadership under the Conservatives, or [a] weak and unstable coalition of chaos led by Jeremy Corbyn'. This message—with clear echoes of David Cameron's (2015c) warning of 'stability and strong Government with me, or chaos with Ed Miliband'—would be repeated ad nauseam throughout the following weeks.

May's team was, unsurprisingly, keen to present this as a Brexit election, and themselves as the only ones able to deliver on the referendum result. Her approach demonstrated continued willingness to stoke polarization over Brexit—in Bolton she described herself as 'utterly determined to deliver the democratic will of the British people', while accusing other parties of 'lining up' to help Corbyn frustrate the negotiations. She also drew in other perceived adversaries—on the day that parliament dissolved for the election, making a speech outside Downing Street suggesting that the European Commission might seek to influence the election result (CNN 2017). Yet the Conservative manifesto contained no chapter dedicated to Brexit, and little new about the party's proposed approach. Instead it referred to pre-existing statements in the Lancaster House speech, the White Paper, and May's letter invoking Article 50. It repeated that the UK would no longer belong to the Single Market or Customs Union, but promised to seek 'a deep and special partnership including a comprehensive free trade and customs agreement' (Conservative Party 2017: 36). The manifesto also repeated May's Lancaster House promise of a parliamentary vote on the final deal. But much of it focused on other matters entirely, well beyond Brexit.

Labour's main campaign messages were also on other things. But the party's manifesto contained a chapter on Brexit, focusing on the negotiating priorities. It pledged to rule out a no-deal exit, and to negotiate to retain the benefits of the Single Market and Customs Union. It also promised legislation to guarantee parliament a 'truly meaningful vote' on the final deal, and 'a meaningful role' throughout the negotiations (Labour Party 2017: 24, 27).[5] The Liberal Democrats (2017) likewise expressed opposition to a 'hard Brexit', and repeated the commitment to a second referendum. The most detailed set of Brexit demands came in the Democratic Unionist Party (2017) manifesto, which featured 30 negotiating priorities, including a frictionless border with the Republic of Ireland, a proportionate regulatory regime tailored to local needs, and strengthened relationships across the UK Union.

The unusually long seven-week campaign provided ample time for the Conservative lead to unravel. The campaign ran into trouble on various fronts, with the most dramatic being the disastrous launch of the manifesto. Uproar from the right-leaning press and voters forced May into a humiliating U-turn on a flagship policy for funding social care after only a few days. When asked about this, she simply claimed that '[n]othing has changed' (May 2017c). This tin-eared response highlighted a broader problem with the party's approach. Particularly in the early weeks, it ran a presidential-style campaign, focusing strongly on May—notably referring to local candidates as 'standing with Theresa May' in election literature (Cowley and Kavanagh 2018: 293). But this was ill-suited to the Prime Minister's personality and style: as the same authors note, 'she came across as wooden and over-scripted, robotically mouthing soundbites' (Cowley and Kavanagh 2018: 433). Such a campaign served to spotlight May's weaknesses, particularly when she refused to attend televised debates—on one occasion sending Home Secretary Amber Rudd in her place. Blame for running a campaign so unsuited to the candidate was often ascribed to campaign adviser Lynton Crosby—but also to May's personal team (Shipman 2017b).

The Labour campaign, by contrast, was unexpectedly strong. Although Jeremy Corbyn began with abysmal poll ratings, the party was organizationally better prepared to fight an election (Ross and McTague 2017), and Corbyn himself proved an energetic campaigner. Despite a muddled Brexit message, the party was able to offer some reassurance to Leave voters by pointing to its support for triggering Article 50. In some respects Labour also benefited from being the underdog—with so much talk of a Conservative landslide the fear of Corbyn as Prime Minister seemed remote, potentially allowing voters who were sceptical of his leadership still safely to support the party, including to avoid May winning by too great a margin (Cowley and Kavanagh 2018).

In the final week of the campaign, the Conservatives emphasized the importance of being returned with a majority—David Davis warned of 'five days to save Brexit' (quoted in Wheeler 2017). The Brexit-supporting press firmly backed May; the *Daily Express* (2017), for example, urged its readers to 'Vote May or we face disaster'.

Instead, the disaster proved to be May's. Rather than winning the enhanced majority that she had hoped for, the Conservatives lost 13 seats—of which nine belonged to ministers (Bate et al. 2019). In addition, Amber Rudd faced a recount in her Hastings and Rye constituency and clung on by a mere 346 votes. Even greater losses were averted only by the Conservatives' strong performance in Scotland, where the party gained 12 seats and doubled its vote share—a performance typically ascribed to the campaigning of Scottish Conservative leader Ruth Davidson (Bale and Webb 2018), who had been prominent in the 2016 Remain campaign. Although the overall Conservative vote share increased compared to 2015—from 36.8 per cent to 42.3 per cent—this failed to translate into seats. Labour, meanwhile, performed better than expected, making a net gain of 30 constituencies and increasing its vote share by 9.2 percentage points, to 40 per cent. The final result left the Conservatives as the largest single party, on 317 seats, and Labour on 262, meaning that both fell short of a Commons majority. The SNP lost 21 of its previous 56 constituencies, and the Liberal Democrats made a small gain, from nine to 12. UKIP's support, meanwhile, collapsed: the party lost 85 per cent of its 2015 voters, and its vote share fell from 12.6 per cent to just 1.8 per cent. A majority of these voters switched to the Conservatives (Mellon et al. 2018), but this had little impact in terms of seats.

While much of the parties' focus was away from Brexit, survey data showed this to be by far the most important issue in the election identified by voters themselves (Ashcroft 2017, Fieldhouse and Prosser 2017)—though significantly more so for Conservative than Labour supporters. There were sufficient parallels between the pattern of the Brexit vote and the outcome of the election for one scholar to dub it the 'revenge of the Remainers' (Denver 2018: 22). In general terms, the Conservatives underperformed in Remain-voting seats, and Labour performed strongly. Meanwhile, in a precursor to what would occur in 2019, various safe Labour seats in the North of England which had voted decisively for Leave saw significant swings to the Conservatives, while still remaining Labour-held at this election (Cowley and Kavanagh 2018). The British Election Study found that the Conservatives had made significant gains among Brexit supporters, but also lost votes among those who had previously supported Remain; in contrast, Labour managed to gain new votes from both groups (Ford and Sobolewska 2020).

Not all of the Brexit-related realignment going on was visible through seats changing hands at this election. But the Conservatives lost the constituencies of Kensington and Canterbury to Labour, at the same time as taking Stoke-on-Trent South, Southport, and North East Derbyshire from the party. Demographics played an important part—polls suggested that 49 per cent of graduates had voted Labour, up 15 percentage points on 2015, while the Conservatives won 55 per cent of votes from among those educated no further than GCSE level, up 17 points (Curtice 2017a). Meanwhile, around 60 per cent of voters aged over 65 backed the Conservatives, but Labour enjoyed a similar degree of support amongst voters in their twenties and thirties. These differentials strongly echoed the 2016 Brexit divide.

Despite May's hopes of capitalizing on a Brexit realignment in British politics, her attempt to gain a majority had unquestionably failed. Instead of the strong position that she had hoped for, she was now required to deliver Brexit with her parliamentary majority gone, and her personal authority severely damaged.

The Post-election Fallout

On the morning of the result, the *Financial Times* noted that 'Mrs May's weak election performance has thrown Brexit into confusion, including whether the prime minister's restive party, demoralised by a poor election campaign, will even allow her to lead the country into the negotiations' (Parker, Barker, and Beesley 2017). There were immediate questions regarding whether Theresa May would stay on, and how a government could be formed that would command the confidence of the House of Commons. Beyond this lay the dilemma of how a parliamentary strategy could realistically be developed for delivering Brexit.

The Immediate Aftermath and Leadership Threats

The result was a shock for almost all concerned, and the consequences for Brexit were close to the front of many people's minds on both sides of the divide. Number 10 insider Chris Wilkins (2020) recalled that on election night 'a senior pro-Brexit person in the party looked at me and said, "Oh my God, I think we might just have screwed Brexit"'. On the other side, a Labour Remain-supporting interviewee recalled texting their partner that night to say, 'this means Brexit can be stopped', and remembered 'a sort of sense of new optimism' in the air.

The most immediate question concerned the Prime Minister's own future. Having gambled and lost her parliamentary majority, there was a real possibility that she could step down—either voluntarily or under duress. Overnight, some Conservative MPs briefed journalists that she should 'consider her position' (Rigby 2017). Graham Brady, the chair of the party's backbench 1922 Committee (who had unsuccessfully sought to persuade Cameron to stay the previous year), urged May not to do anything rash. Nonetheless, there was much behind-the-scenes discussion. In particular, it was reported that Boris Johnson was 'already on manoeuvres', and that others—including the former Vote Leave Campaign Director Dominic Cummings—were phoning round to gauge levels of support for him (Shipman 2017b: 430). On the weekend immediately after the election, the *Mail on Sunday* reported that 'Boris Johnson is preparing a new bid to become prime minister' (Owen and Carlin 2017), while the *Sunday Times* claimed that he had the support of five Cabinet ministers (Shipman 2017c). Meanwhile, other ministers were desperate to find an alternative candidate to block him.

One key factor was that the result was so unanticipated, even compared to Cameron's departure in 2016, that little thought had been put into preparing for a possible leadership election. Without preparation, both the hardline Brexiteers and their opponents feared that a contest could favour the other side. Plus, the prospect of taking over as Prime Minister in a minority government situation, and with a hugely complex and controversial policy to deliver, was hardly an attractive one. May (2017e) made a widely criticized statement outside Downing Street on the morning after the vote, which barely acknowledged the painful predicament of many Conservative MPs who had lost their seats; but she nonetheless wasn't forced out. Johnson allegedly responded to the *Mail on Sunday* report by sending a WhatsApp message around MPs urging them to support her, though some claimed that he did so because he realized that he lacked adequate parliamentary support

(Shipman 2017b). At a meeting of the 1922 Committee on 12 June, May reportedly demonstrated appropriate contrition; with what was to become her typically steely commitment to public service in the face of adversity, she stated, 'I got us into this mess, and I'm going to get us out of it' (quoted in Asthana and Elgot 2017). The immediate victims were, instead, her joint Chiefs of Staff, Nick Timothy and Fiona Hill, who were widely blamed for the campaign's errors, and had long been unpopular among Conservative MPs. In their place, Gavin Barwell, one of the ministers to have just lost their seats at the election, was appointed Chief of Staff. A key priority for him, endorsed by May, was to rebuild relations with the parliamentary party. Number 10 also set up a new legislative affairs team, headed by Nikki da Costa.

On the Labour side the position was almost the reverse. Corbyn had lost the election, but significantly outperformed against initial expectations. Meanwhile, many Labour MPs had been anticipating catastrophe and pre-paring to demand that the leader finally depart—but their plans were scup-pered by the party's unexpectedly strong result. The sum total, therefore, was that both parties were left with unpopular leaders, whom they already feared incapable of the task ahead. May's political capital was greatly diminished, and her hold on the leadership extremely fragile, while Corbyn still lacked the confidence of his parliamentary party, but was more secure than ever before.

Constructing a New Government

An additional barrier to changing the Conservative leader, of course, was that the party urgently needed to navigate how to secure the House of Commons' confidence, given its lack of a single-party majority. There was no immediate prospect of doing a deal with most of the smaller parties, given their hostility to Brexit. The Liberal Democrat manifesto had ruled out a coalition with the Conservatives, while an arrangement with the SNP would have been very difficult indeed. The Prime Minister instead turned to the DUP, which had won 10 seats at the general election. Unlike other Northern Ireland parties, it had strongly supported Leave in 2016, while its 2017 mani-festo had set out a clear set of demands.

Talk of an arrangement with the DUP began almost immediately, with Theresa May's (2017e) Downing Street statement of 9 June proposing to work together as 'friends and allies' and claiming that the two parties had 'enjoyed a strong relationship for many years'. The DUP leader, Arlene Foster, made a statement that same day confirming that they were entering talks (McDonald and Syal 2017). The arrangement reached between the parties, following lengthy negotiations, was not a formal coalition but a confidence and supply agreement, through which the smaller party agreed to support the government on key decisions, including motions of confidence, the Queen's Speech, budget and other financial matters, 'legislation pertaining to the United Kingdom's exit from the European Union', plus limited other items.

Although this gave the Prime Minister the House of Commons majority that she needed, that majority was very slim—just 13. This clearly placed her numerically in a weaker position than in the previous parliament, with its slender Conservative majority of 16. The situation was very fragile, given the need to accommodate the minor party, and particularly given the huge sensitivities caused by Brexit for Northern Ireland. Indeed, the arrangement itself caused significant concerns in the province, which had voted strongly to remain in the EU. The Belfast/Good Friday Agreement gave the UK government a formal responsibility to act with 'rigorous impartiality' between the different political traditions in Northern Ireland, and some questioned whether this was consistent with coming to such an arrangement (Tonge 2017).[6] In January 2017, the Northern Ireland power-sharing Executive established under the terms of the Agreement had collapsed.[7] At the general election the DUP then became the only Northern Ireland party to take Commons seats, putting it in a distinctly privileged position.[8] But clearly government insiders felt that there was little choice; in interview one of them recalled that 'there was a real smack of desperation in the air'. Consequently, the DUP was able to extract commitments to a reported £1 billion of spending in Northern Ireland over two years (Tonge and Evans 2018)—as well as policy concessions on pensions, benefits, and grammar schools. The final agreement was published on 26 June, after the Queen's Speech (discussed below) had taken place, but before the crucial votes on it. Forecasting what lay ahead, Irish commentator Fintan O'Toole (2017: 73) predicted that '[t]he Tories will endure the DUP while they must and betray it when they can'.

The other immediate question facing Theresa May was the construction of her ministerial team. She was too weak to oust the senior Brexiteers, but the election result generated calls for greater inclusivity, including from within her own party. Paul Goodman (2017), the respected commentator and editor of news website ConservativeHome, suggested that May 'now need[ed] to broaden her Cabinet in a way that she wouldn't have considered previously'. Specific suggestions included inviting Michael Gove back into government, and making Dominic Grieve Justice Secretary, on the basis that 'the Prime Minister could do without having [him] tearing into the Great Repeal Bill'.

These suggestions were to prove prescient, in different respects. May did reappoint Gove, as Secretary of State for Environment, Food and Rural Affairs, while Grieve—who was not appointed—indeed went on to cause significant trouble, as discussed in subsequent chapters. Brexit supporter Andrea Leadsom was demoted within the Cabinet to become Leader of the House of Commons, while David Lidington was promoted from that role to Justice Secretary, and other former Remainers David Gauke and Damian Green also received promotions. The *Sunday Telegraph* referred to these changes as the 'march of the Remainers' (Riley-Smith 2017). On the flip side, however, May appointed arch Brexiteer Steve Baker to a junior position at DExEU—albeit replacing fellow Brexiteer David Jones. Various interviewees suggested that this was, in the words of one, a sign that she wanted to 'bind in the ERG and that wing of the party into the Brexit approach'.

There were hence clearly attempts to please both sides of the party as much as possible, unsurprisingly given the delicate parliamentary balance. But this was inherently difficult. The result was, in the words of another well-qualified government insider, that 'no doubt, Mrs May's Cabinet was far more divided than the coalition cabinet' over which David Cameron presided from 2010 to 2015. It also had a substantially smaller government majority, and an unusually difficult central policy promise to deliver.

Options for a New Approach to Parliament

While the immediate focus was on existential questions of how to retain a Prime Minister, and secure a Commons majority, there were big longer-term questions about how to navigate Brexit in this now more difficult political environment.

One concern, which essentially came to nothing, was whether the government would face new challenges from the House of Lords. May had (without much justification) cited threats from the second chamber in her statement announcing that she wanted an early election, and one benefit of restating her Brexit objectives in the party manifesto was potentially to neutralize the chamber. Under the Salisbury Convention the Lords does not block measures set out in the governing party's manifesto—but questions were raised about whether it would hold in the circumstances of minority government (Elliott 2017a, Newson 2017). However, notwithstanding lurid claims in the *Daily Express* that the Lords planned to 'plunge Brexit into chaos' (Hunt 2017), the chamber rarely challenges government policies head-on, and would feel constrained to respect both the House of Commons' decision and the referendum mandate. The far bigger question was how the government was going to manage the House of Commons.

The election result sparked new speculation, and numerous suggestions, that the Prime Minister should now seek a broader cross-party agreement to deliver Brexit, and that to achieve this she would need to soften her 'red lines'. This was entirely consistent with the normal expectations of minority government, as discussed earlier in the chapter. It looked particularly necessary in circumstances where the Prime Minister could not use the typical minority government strategy of shelving her most controversial policy commitment, and where her own party was deeply split. This seemingly inexorable logic was reflected in analyses from parts of the quality media: the previously mentioned *Financial Times* piece published the morning after the election predicted that there would now need to be a 'softer' Brexit. A few days later, the BBC's Political Editor, Laura Kuenssberg (2017), predicted that there would have to be 'a change in tone, a more overtly consensual approach', with 'the reality of the parliamentary numbers' meaning that May would be 'forced to take other opinions into consideration'.

Voices from across the political spectrum began urging the Prime Minister, publicly and privately, to make this kind of shift towards a cross-party alliance on Brexit—drawing in individuals from Labour. Many such voices came from within her own party. Hence Scottish party leader Ruth Davidson suggested immediately after the election that '[w]hat's really clear is that the Conservative Party, having failed to win a majority, now needs to work with others'; this was echoed by well-respected former minister Alistair Burt, who suggested that broadening beyond the Conservative Party would strengthen May's hand in negotiations with the EU (both quoted in Johnson and Hughes 2017). Former party leader William Hague (2017a), who had argued so strongly for the election to take place, now suggested in the *Daily Telegraph* that she would need to 'call in…the leaders of all the opposition parties— yes, even Corbyn—leading MPs of all parties, and say: "If you are willing to discuss how to make this work within these parameters, come in and we will be open to your views"'. This was precisely the strategy that Oliver Letwin had advocated—and May had rejected—immediately after the referendum. Recalling the election fallout, Letwin (2020) said that 'I assumed she would reverse her position and accept that it was necessary to have a bipartisan approach…My level of anxiety about the lack of bipartisan governance of the matter increased from considerable to extreme at that point.'

From the Labour side, senior backbencher Yvette Cooper (2017) strongly advocated a cross-party arrangement in an article for the *Guardian*. Gently mocking May's election slogan, she suggested that '[t]here is neither strength nor stability in a narrow, bunkered one-party approach...so we should set up a small cross-party commission to conduct the negotiations'. This, she acknowledged, would require flexibility: 'Everyone will have to compromise. But in the national interest we all have a responsibility to work in a grown-up way'. The various advocates of such an approach across the parties were talking to each other, and to other key figures in the Commons. Rumours reached the *Sun* newspaper that 'some senior Tories' were 'pushing Mrs May to invite Labour to join an extraordinary cross-party Brexit war cabinet', and had calculated that there would be a 44-seat majority in the Commons for a soft Brexit. This did not meet with the paper's approval, and was presented as threatening 'a fresh Tory civil war' (Dathan and Clark 2017). But such an approach was popular with the public. A poll conducted immediately after the election found that 51 per cent of respondents would 'prefer Brexit to be negotiated by a cross-party team', as against 30 per cent who would 'prefer Brexit to be negotiated by the Conservatives alone' (YouGov 2017a).

One notable feature of those calling for such a cross-party pivot was that all had previously been Remain supporters.[9] While they may have appeared to be following an inexorable logic of parliamentary arithmetic, their arguments could easily be seen as self-serving by hardline Brexiteers. As the *Sunday Telegraph* reported, the latter group was in a mood of 'little disguised fury...for what the election result has done to their EU exit' (Riley-Smith 2017). In the few days after the election, before the new parliament assembled, the hardliners did everything they could to hold May to her previous promises, exploiting Labour's manifesto to claim that, far from being a setback for Brexit, the election provided an overwhelming mandate for it. Bernard Jenkin (2017) suggested in a column in the *Mail on Sunday* three days after the election that '[b]oth Labour and the Conservatives stood on Brexit manifestos...[while] pro-Remain parties received a total of 11 per cent of the vote'. Jacob Rees-Mogg echoed this in the *Sunday Telegraph*, claiming that the 'election was therefore a tacit endorsement of Mrs May's Brexit strategy'. A few days later, Steve Baker, speaking in his new ministerial capacity, denied that there would be any change of course (Hall 2017b). Around the same time, Boris Johnson reportedly challenged May in a Cabinet committee meeting to confirm that she stood by the commitments in the Lancaster House speech, including leaving the Customs Union and Single Market—and her response was 'absolutely' (Shipman 2017b: 483).

In important respects, the logic was on the side of those arguing for a change of direction—May's majority even with the DUP was perilously small, and her fractious party seemed increasingly unlikely to hold together. However, there were important factors standing in the way of such a pivot.

Some should already be obvious, and were present when such proposals were previously made in 2016. Cross-party working was not in Theresa May's nature, and Jeremy Corbyn was an extremely unpalatable ally. Furthermore, May had just spent seven weeks arguing publicly that he was unfit to deliver Brexit. And her own leadership was now hanging by a thread.

The people urging a cross-party approach perhaps did not appreciate how readily this could have galvanized May's critics to try to unseat her. As an interviewee close to her put it, 'there's a lot of talk now about, "it was obvious that you should have tried to build a cross-party consensus post the 2017 election": if she had done that quickly after the election, she would have been gone straightaway, so it wasn't really a credible path'. Another close ally likewise said, 'I think it would have been terminal for her leadership of the Tory party had she tried'. The difficulty didn't just concern the principle of working with Corbyn's Labour; moves in that direction would also have required compromising on Brexit itself. Recalling this period, Denzil Davidson (2020), May's Special Adviser on Europe, has indicated that 'we were fairly clear early on that [the] parliamentary arithmetic had changed profoundly', and that it might be easier in principle to build a majority around a softer version of Brexit. But explaining why formal overtures were not made to Labour, he said, 'bear in mind, you're trying to stop the Conservative Party from exploding underneath you'. A senior Brexiteer confirmed that, 'had she simply abandoned the Lancaster House prospectus, then I think she almost certainly would have faced a confidence vote'. Of course, her opponents might not have found sufficient support to remove her in such a vote (as seen in Chapter 7, attempts of this kind can fail even when critics claim to have the numbers), but it was certainly very risky. Facing down the hardliners in her party might have been a chance worth taking—as in truth May's leadership was otherwise doomed to fail. But disillusionment with her in the party was not confined to this group; plus there were further significant factors which militated against such a move.

Key among these was Labour's attitude, and the calculations facing the party. As a source close to May said, 'whatever incentive there was on Corbyn to play ball in 2016, that incentive had been significantly weakened by the election'. With Labour having made gains, and the government looking so fragile, Corbyn had his eye on the bigger prize of unseating May. In any case, as David Gauke (2020) has put it, '[n]o opposition is necessarily going to come to the government's rescue after a general election just like that'. Labour was facing its own internal splits on Brexit, so sitting on the sidelines watching the Conservative government unravel was both more tempting to senior figures, and far less risky, than helping the government out. This was articulated bluntly by Barry Gardiner, Labour's Shadow Secretary of State for International Trade, in a media comment six days after the election. He suggested that '[w]hen Governments are in a fix they say…"we need to consult other parties about this". What that means is "shit, we don't know what to do, so let's rope others into this so they can share the blame"' (quoted in Watts 2017).

While some senior Labour figures, including on the frontbench, undoubtedly believed that it was in the national interest to try working with the government on achieving a softer Brexit, there were hence also strong counterarguments. At the same moment that cross-party working appeared more necessary, it had become more difficult both for both sides. Notably, while former Labour Remain supporters had tended previously to accept that a soft Brexit would be the least worst option, and would likely have been forced into this acceptance had May won her landslide, the election had engendered new hope among many that Brexit could be reversed. In the months ahead, Labour would increasingly face its own internal arguments on this question, particularly regarding a possible second referendum.

With hindsight it may appear obvious that May should have adopted a new strategy at this point. But in the immediate aftermath of the election she was distracted by the need to do a deal with the DUP to secure a majority (and by the need to respond to the national tragedy of the Grenfell fire, which happened just six days after the election).[10] Instead, she found herself increasingly boxed in by the Brexit hardliners in her own party, while Labour looked even less likely than previously to want to rescue her.

The Queen's Speech

The Queen's Speech setting out the new government's legislative programme for the period ahead was held on 21 June, after a short delay to allow for talks with the DUP. Votes on the speech would be the first test of Theresa May's ability to command a parliamentary majority—and a failure to do so would likely have toppled her government. The DUP deal included its guaranteed support, and, to stave off the need to repeat the exercise, the government announced that the new parliamentary session would last two years rather than the usual one. This allowed a clear period for Brexit legislation in the run-up to the planned exit day of 29 March 2019. As with other aspects of the parliamentary timetable (discussed particularly in Chapter 8), the government had sole control over the length of the session.

The speech was shorn of some policies that might otherwise have been included, in order to maintain DUP support, but unsurprisingly Brexit was a central focus. The words at this point were relatively conciliatory, suggesting that ministers would 'build the widest possible consensus on the country's future outside the European Union'—a pledge repeated by Theresa May herself when she addressed the Commons later that day.[11] The legislative plans set out in the speech included the previously promised 'Great Repeal Bill', plus Brexit-related bills on trade, immigration, agriculture, and fisheries. In the debate, Dominic Grieve was among those who emphasized the need to build broad-based support, suggesting that 'particularly in the view of the inconclusive results of the election, the totality of opinion in this House will start to matter very much'.[12]

The Speaker selected two reasoned amendments to the speech. The first came from the Labour frontbench, essentially regretting the omission of its own manifesto policies, including on Brexit—demanding that (in line with the previous promise from David Davis) the government 'negotiate an outcome that prioritises jobs and the economy, [and] delivers the exact same benefits the UK has as a member of the Single Market and the Customs Union'.[13] But there was also a second Labour-led amendment. This was proposed by a 67-strong group headed by Streatham MP Chuka Umunna, and signed by 45 Labour backbenchers. It went beyond the party's policy to demand that the government should negotiate a deal to remain within the Customs Union and Single Market. This exposed splits in both main parties. No Conservatives rebelled in the vote on Umunna's amendment, though former Cabinet minister Nicky Morgan pointedly stated that she was 'tempted' by it—highlighting a potential threat from the party's former Remainers. A total of 49 Labour MPs defied a three-line whip to vote for it, including three frontbenchers who were sacked by Corbyn. Nonetheless, both amendments were defeated, and the Queen's Speech passed by 323 votes to 309.

Reflecting on the new parliamentary dynamics on the day after the speech, one respected news outlet suggested that:

> Such is the scale of the challenge that Brexit poses, it is also the issue which could see May removed from power at any moment. This forces her to stick to her hard Brexit vision but also find compromise with soft Brexit colleagues who she'll need in order to pass the legislation to successfully navigate Britain's departure.
>
> (McTague 2017)

Unfortunately, these two imperatives were essentially incompatible—as would become increasingly clear.

Conclusion

The story in this book invites many 'what-ifs', and some of the biggest concern the 2017 general election. Three particularly obvious questions arise: what if Theresa May had not called the early election; what if she had won the landslide victory that many had anticipated; and what if—having failed to do so—she had pursued a compromise deal with Labour? In addition it might be asked, what would have happened if May had resigned, or been challenged for the leadership in June 2017? Could her opponents have forced her out, and how might an alternative leader, perhaps Boris Johnson, have handled the months ahead?

These questions are by their nature impossible to answer with certainty. On the first, May had not yet (despite her claims when calling the election) faced significant parliamentary resistance on Brexit. Had the election not occurred, her opponents in the Commons might have stayed more quiescent.[14] Her majority prior to the election was undoubtedly narrow, and might well have disintegrated once the outcome of the EU negotiations became clear. But in the words of May's former Chief Whip Julian Smith (2020), on the wisdom of calling the election, '[y]ou could see why there was a case for trying to get a bigger [majority], but in retrospect it looks heavenly to have those [pre-election] numbers'. Nonetheless, the biggest blow from the election in terms of party management was not to the arithmetic in parliament but to the Prime Minister's authority.

Had May won the large majority that was predicted, she would have gained greater flexibility to sideline critics inside her parliamentary party—though the question remains of which group she would have shut out: the former Remainers, or the hardline Brexiteers. Since May was firmly pledged to respect the referendum result, and parliament had voted overwhelmingly for the triggering of Article 50, an enhanced majority would never have resulted in a turning away from Brexit. But the months ahead, as seen in subsequent chapters, demonstrated some of the uncomfortable trade-offs involved in delivering Brexit, particularly with respect to Northern Ireland. Once the negotiations had begun, a strengthened May would likely have retained support from the more pragmatic Conservative moderates, but been better able to face down her hardliners.

In the event, the Conservatives' dismal election performance saw May's credibility drain away—particularly in the eyes of her own party. Although she was not removed as leader, and key figures urged her not to resign, her leadership was hugely undermined. From that point on she was, in the cruel words of former Chancellor George Osborne, a 'dead woman walking'

(Elgot 2017). In interviews, even her allies agreed on this point. One senior Conservative suggested that 'in a way, from the moment the election result came in, she was dead. It was just how long it would take for it all to unravel.'

Whether May's critics could in practice have removed her is uncertain, as is the identity of the person with whom she might have been replaced. But whoever that was, they would have faced a difficult challenge, and significant pragmatism would have been required. Meanwhile, the election result had, ironically, dealt a blow to those in the Labour Party who had hoped that a poor result would allow them to remove Jeremy Corbyn. A stronger Conservative performance might well have led to a more pragmatic, and possibly more cohesive, Labour opposition.

These dynamics are connected to the question of whether, having lost her majority, May could have pivoted towards a cross-party arrangement to deliver a softer form of Brexit—the same choice she had faced upon becoming Prime Minister in 2016. Although the worsened parliamentary arithmetic appeared to demand this, such a strategy had become far riskier to adopt: it might well have seen May unseated by her hardline critics, while the reasons for Labour not to cooperate had strengthened. Attempting this approach could have caused major difficulties inside both parties, and on both sides of the Brexit divide. May's own hardliners, as well as those originally opposed to Brexit, had become increasingly irreconcilable. As one Brexiteer MP recalled in interview, prior to the election 'it seemed more like the people who had been disappointed by the outcome of the referendum were being genuine when they said "we accept the outcome and will go along with it"—which really shifted after the election'.

In hindsight, this was a moment which held great risks, but perhaps demanded really bold and imaginative thinking. Looking back at the period, a senior government interviewee said:

> I think…there was an opportunity to say 'the electorate has not delivered the results I hoped for. We now have to respect the electorate's decision and by sending us back with no overall majority they are asking us to find a way to work together and try to compromise, and that's what I am now seeking to do'. And I think if she'd set that out firmly – she had a chance.

As in 2016, the best opportunity for May probably lay in appealing directly to the public, rather than moving straight to a cross-party approach in parliament. This was a moment when she could have levelled with voters about the difficulty of the task ahead—presenting herself as a pragmatist and her opponents as irreconcilable ideologues of one or another kind. A public consultation could have highlighted, and sought views on how to balance, the tricky Brexit trade-offs. Notably, a citizens' assembly on the form that Brexit should take, convened by the University College London Constitution Unit a few months after the election, in autumn 2017, concluded by compromising around a 'soft' Brexit (Renwick et al. 2017, 2018).[15] Pragmatic public voices might thus have helped May isolate the hardliners, and perhaps even have persuaded Labour figures into support. This would have been consistent with the opinion poll evidence showing backing for a cross-party approach.

But none of this was Theresa May's style, and her overriding instinct remained to try and hold her divided Conservative Party together, while painting opposition parties as the villains. Julian Smith recalled to Seldon and Newell (2019: 299) that, 'instead of saying "Let's look at this again", we made the red lines even redder. Instead of opening it out, we held to the same approach, even though we didn't have the majority for it. No one was thinking long-term.' Likewise, a Conservative interviewee who strongly favoured a cross-party approach lamented that 'the car was heading straight for a large brick wall. And it is not rational under those circumstances to just keep driving. You have to either brake or turn.'

Yet May continued, in the words of another Conservative interviewee, to behave 'as if she had a majority, and then expressed speechless surprise and anger when the House wouldn't do what she wanted'. As the opening of this chapter indicated, this was precisely the wrong attitude when heading a minority government; plus, the divisions in her party made that situation far worse than it looked. As Philip Cowley (2017), a leading academic expert on parliamentary party management, wrote shortly after the election, the prospects for maintaining party cohesion were bleak. He highlighted eight factors which help leaders to contain party rebellion, including prime ministerial authority, sticking to policies of low political salience, and the threat of an impending election—all eight of which were now inaccessible to May. As if these major worries with her own party were not enough, she now also needed to worry about maintaining her relationship with the DUP.

Hence a key Downing Street interviewee suggested that the election result 'actually hurt her in the negotiations as well, because the EU was never sure she was going to be able to pass whatever she agreed...I think if they'd have been more confident that she could actually deliver it, they would have probably met her a little more halfway than they did.' Nonetheless, within just a few days of the election those negotiations were now set to begin.

Notes

1. House of Commons Hansard, 19 April 2017, column 673.
2. Ibid., column 688.
3. Ibid., column 688.
4. There were various potential means of seeking to avoid the two-thirds majority set out in the Fixed-term Parliaments Act. These same authors suggest that the government might have sought to engineer a vote of no confidence in itself, which requires only a simple Commons majority. An alternative was a short bill to authorize an election, as subsequently deployed by Boris Johnson in 2019 (see Chapter 10).
5. The demand for a 'meaningful vote' was central to a tactical voting campaign put together by Gina Miller. When asked about her own definition of 'meaningful', Miller specified that she had in mind a choice between remaining in the EU, accepting the negotiated deal, and leaving without a deal (Roberts 2017).
6. Former Green Party candidate Ciaran McClean led a crowdfunded legal challenge to the confidence and supply agreement, alleging that it contravened the Belfast/Good Friday Agreement and the Bribery Act, but his attempt failed after judges refused permission to bring a judicial review (Guardian 2017).
7. The power-sharing system seeks to ensure cross-community (i.e. both nationalist and unionist) consent for the governance of Northern Ireland. Provisions include multiparty, cross-community power-sharing within the executive, including across the posts of First Minister and deputy First Minister, and mechanisms in the Northern Ireland Assembly that require cross-community support for many decisions (Coakley and Todd 2020).
8. An additional seat was won by Lady Sylvia Hermon, an independent MP who had in the past sat for the more moderate Ulster Unionist Party (UUP). The UUP had lost its two seats, and the Social Democratic and Labour Party (SDLP) had likewise lost all three of its seats. The other seven constituencies were won by Sinn Féin, which does not take seats at Westminster.
9. Others included David Gauke, George Osborne, and former Prime Minister John Major.
10. The fire at Grenfell Tower, a housing block in West London, resulted in the deaths of over 70 people.
11. House of Lords Hansard, 21 June 2017, column 5; House of Commons Hansard, 21 June 2017, column 61.
12. House of Commons Hansard, 21 June 2017, column 91.
13. Ibid., 29 June 2017, column 776.
14. The prospect of May threatening an election later to pull the parliamentary party into line might also have remained more credible, which (as discussed in Chapter 10) it really wasn't after this point.
15. This was a demographically representative group of randomly selected citizens, presented with evidence by experts and proponents of different Brexit outcomes and asked to deliberate on the options over two weekends.

6

Determining the Form of Brexit

With the big milestones of the Article 50 trigger and the June 2017 general election out of the way, the task ahead was to negotiate the UK's exit from, and future relationship with, the EU. This required extensive talks between Theresa May's team and the EU negotiators, under the watching eyes of both Cabinet and parliament. Approval of the principle of Brexit, both through the referendum and the EU (Notification of Withdrawal) Bill, had already been high-profile and polarizing. This next stage, which required confronting the trade-offs entailed in any Brexit deal, was set to be even more so. May battled constantly to hold her party together and keep her DUP partners onside, and Labour also struggled to maintain a party line. Meanwhile, various intra- and cross-party parliamentary groups were emerging, each with its own preferred Brexit outcome. Such groups sought to scrutinize the negotiations and to promote their own objectives through numerous parliamentary mechanisms. One route was the promised 'Great Repeal Bill' (formally named the European Union (Withdrawal) Bill), amendments to which offered legislative opportunities to enterprising backbenchers. But MPs' attempts to capitalize on these were hampered by the splits within the two largest parties.

The chapter begins with a brief consideration of parliament's role in foreign affairs. While negotiations and treaty-making have historically been the preserve of the executive, MPs and peers resisted being sidelined over Brexit, seeking influence beyond parliament's usually limited role. The chapter then describes the first stages of the exit negotiations between the UK government and the EU, and the Conservative and DUP response to May's strategy, before providing a parallel summary of Labour's own internal arguments. Next, it moves beyond the parties themselves, to consider the various parliamentary groupings developing on Brexit—inside the Conservative Party, inside the Labour Party, and across party lines. The remaining sections discuss parliament's influence as an open forum for debate, and its attempts to shape the Brexit negotiations—first through various non-legislative scrutiny mechanisms, and then through scrutiny of the EU (Withdrawal) Bill. This bill's use as a vehicle to guarantee a 'meaningful vote' for parliament on the final Brexit deal is then further discussed in Chapter 7.

Parliament's Role in Foreign Affairs

The UK's constitution has traditionally put foreign affairs largely in the hands of the executive. This reflects a historical view that, despite the central principle of parliamentary sovereignty, there are some policy areas in which executive room for manoeuvre remains justified. Ministers instead make policy in these areas using the royal prerogative—a category of powers exercised on behalf of the monarch. These have included powers such as the management of the civil service and the granting of honours and passports—as well as core foreign affairs activities such as treaty-making, and decisions to declare war and deploy troops (Hazell and Foot 2022). Governments may nonetheless seek explicit parliamentary endorsement of their policies in such areas. Chapter 2 emphasized Prime Minister Harold Macmillan's commitment in the early 1960s to parliamentary involvement in decisions over joining the EEC, and the actions of his successor Edward Heath in the 1970s to do so. But parliamentary votes on the principle of membership—as opposed to those on the implementing legislation—resulted primarily from political considerations, rather than being legally required.

Recent decades have seen increasing pressure for parliamentary oversight and control of prerogative powers. For example, legislation in the 1980s and 1990s put these on a statutory footing with respect to national security (Public Administration Select Committee 2004), while the Constitutional Reform and Governance Act 2010 (commonly known as 'CRAG') did the same with respect to key aspects of the civil service. In the field of foreign affairs, there has been particular pressure on the prerogative power to deploy military force. In 2003, Tony Blair granted parliament a vote on his plans for military action in Iraq, which many regarded as creating a new convention under which the Commons is asked to approve the use of force—though the 'convention' hasn't always held (Mello 2017, Strong 2022).

This long-running debate about the limits of the prerogative and the appropriate role of parliament was intensified by the extraordinary circumstances of Brexit, and its high political salience. In particular, Brexit engaged questions about the proper extent of the prerogative power over treaties: first to begin the process of withdrawing from an existing treaty, through triggering Article 50; and then to negotiate the Withdrawal Agreement and new trade deal with the EU. As discussed in Chapter 4, the dispute about parliament's role in the Article 50 trigger was ultimately resolved by the Supreme Court, which concluded that Brexit's domestic legal impact made prerogative powers alone insufficient, and primary legislation essential. But the debate about what role parliament should have in scrutinizing the negoti-ations and approving the final deal continued.

Two key schools of thought exist in the academic foreign affairs literature with respect to treaty-making (McLachlan 2014, Mendez 2017, 2020, Smith, Bjorge, and Lang 2020). The first argues pragmatically that government con-trol allows negotiators to present a united front without being distracted by parliamentary squabbling, and affords governments the flexibility to adapt their negotiating stance as necessary. This argument would often be used by Theresa May's ministers, who claimed that parliament should not be allowed to tie the negotiators' hands.[1] The other position argues for far greater parlia-mentary involvement, on the basis that shutting elected representatives out of treaty-making risks creating a democratic deficit. Such scholars point par-ticularly to the changing nature of treaties over recent decades, suggesting that parliamentary involvement has become increasingly necessary as trea-ties have expanded in scope and topic, moving from high-level international politics to affect matters with clear domestic impact, such as standards for environmental and consumer protection. The Brexit negotiations, with their potentially profound impact on everything from the Belfast/Good Friday Agreement to workers' rights and pollution rules, certainly fitted this charac-terization. Hence many MPs argued that it would be wrong for the govern-ment to sideline parliament. Crucially for the parliamentary dynamics of Brexit, academics have also argued that the apparent negotiating strength offered by government control of treaty-making is illusory—as it is not underpinned by scrutiny, so does not guarantee parliament's support (Smith, Bjorge, and Lang 2020).

By the time the Brexit period was reached, parliament's formal involve-ment in treaty-making took two main forms. The first was the need for gov-ernments to pass implementing legislation. This requirement does not apply to all treaties, but given the wide domestic implications of any Brexit agree-ment, it was generally assumed (as discussed in previous chapters) that some form of legislation would be necessary to give it effect. As the fierce debates over the Maastricht Treaty showed (see Chapter 2), parliamentarians can put governments under significant pressure on such legislation. The second form of parliamentary involvement came through provisions in CRAG.[2] These formalized a longer-standing convention on the publication of some treaties, and gave the House of Commons a new theoretical power to delay ratifica-tion. But CRAG's short timescales for parliamentary action, combined with government's control of the Commons agenda (see Chapter 8), meant that these provisions were considered fairly toothless (Mendez 2020, Smith, Bjorge, and Lang 2020).[3]

Notably, both of these forms of oversight come only at the end of the treaty-making process, too late for parliament to influence or amend a treaty's content. Ministers could potentially develop negotiating objectives, hold talks, and even sign treaties without parliamentary oversight—a degree of control that many parliamentarians were unwilling to accept when it came to Brexit. The UK parliament's limited power over treaty-making stood in stark contrast to the powers of the European Parliament, which has a legal right to be informed of the negotiating mandate and receive regular updates throughout the talks; a majority vote in the European Parliament is also required for treaty ratification.[4] Some other states go even further; for example, the US Congress sets out the mandate for trade negotiations in primary legislation (Jones and Sands 2020).

MPs' concerns about parliament's limited formal role over Brexit were exacerbated by the time-limited nature of the negotiations. The logic of 'anticipated reactions' normally suggests that governments will only negotiate major treaties that parliament is likely to find acceptable. But the deadline imposed by Article 50 raised concerns among parliamentarians that they would face a last-minute choice between an unsatisfactory deal and a no-deal exit. Consequently, they sought to influence the negotiations from an early stage. As the next two chapters will show, these efforts by MPs took two key forms. The first, covered in this chapter, consisted of multiple attempts to influence the government's negotiating objectives, with competing groups within the Commons all using a plethora of parliamentary mechanisms to advance their preferred Brexit outcomes. In addition, as the next chapter discusses, MPs sought to guarantee a parliamentary role in approval of the deal—through defining and expanding the government's offer of a meaningful vote.

The Government's Negotiations

Less than a fortnight after the general election, the UK's negotiations with the EU began. As already seen, the triggering of Article 50 had started a two-year negotiating period within which the UK and EU would need both to reach and to ratify an agreement, if a no-deal exit was to be avoided. Despite the UK government's distractions, this time-limited period had begun in late March.

The UK negotiating team was led by Brexit Secretary David Davis, and on the official side by Olly Robbins, who was initially DExEU Permanent

Secretary, but moved to become the Prime Minister's Europe Adviser in September 2017. The two men had a famously dysfunctional relationship (Ruparel 2020). From the EU side, the negotiations were led by the French politician and former European Commissioner Michel Barnier. Though not formally part of the negotiating team, European Council President Donald Tusk and the European Parliament's Brexit Coordinator Guy Verhofstadt were also key figures.

The negotiators were tasked with reaching agreement on two topics: how the UK should be disentangled from the EU, and the post-exit relationship. For each, agreement would first be sought on the high-level principles of a deal, before talks over the detailed drafting of a formal treaty took place. The EU was adamant that the exit and future relationship negotiations should be addressed sequentially, rather than jointly; this was quickly agreed, despite objections from Davis (Menon and Wager 2021). The ultimate result was a staggered timetable, divided into three stages—with two taking place pre exit, and the third one afterwards. In phase one, the high-level principles of the Withdrawal Agreement—citizens' rights, a financial settlement, and the Northern Ireland border—would be the focus. When 'sufficient progress' had been achieved, the talks would move on to phase two, in which the text of the Withdrawal Agreement would be finalized. At this stage the broad principles of the future relationship would also be agreed and set down in a 'Political Declaration'. Post exit, a third phase of talks would take place to translate the Political Declaration into a future relationship treaty.

After the distraction of the general election, the government's policy on both the exit terms and the future relationship was sketchy; Raoul Ruparel (2020), then adviser to Davis, recalled that at the beginning of talks the government 'still didn't have a particularly clear policy on anything'. Thus, even during the talks with the EU, the UK was still deciding and refining its negotiating objectives, particularly regarding the future relationship arrangements. As Theresa May went about this, she would come into increasing conflict both with Brexit hardliners on her own benches and her confidence and supply partners the DUP, as further discussed below. Her relationship with the latter became increasingly strained due to the Northern Ireland border steadily emerging as the most significant dilemma in the negotiations. These domestic difficulties reached a high point in summer 2018 over what became known as the Chequers proposals (discussed in the next chapter). The current chapter focuses on parliamentary attempts to influence the negotiating objectives up to that point.

The Northern Ireland Problem

As the site of the UK's only land border with the rest of the EU, Northern Ireland was a key location for goods to move back and forth between the two.[5] This generated highly technical questions of customs and regulatory policy. But crucially, any solutions would engage the deeply sensitive topic of identity—making the subject extremely contentious both in Northern Ireland and at Westminster. Resolving the tensions and trade-offs generated by Brexit regarding the treatment of the Northern Ireland border would lie at the heart of the government's struggles over the coming years.

At the core of the problem lay three incompatible Brexit objectives articulated by Theresa May, which became known as the 'Irish trilemma': leaving the Single Market and Customs Union, delivering a Brexit agreement which treated all of the UK equally, and avoiding a hard border on the island of Ireland. Delivering any two of these goals ruled out the third. Leaving the Single Market and Customs Union would mean customs and regulatory divergence between the UK and EU, necessitating border checks. If these applied to goods moving between Northern Ireland and the Republic of Ireland, a hard border would be created—which was unacceptable to nationalists in the province and was incompatible with the Belfast/Good Friday Agreement (Murphy and Evershed 2022). An alternative would be for Northern Ireland to remain more closely aligned to the EU, but this would necessitate checks on goods moving between Northern Ireland and Great Britain at a so-called 'border down the Irish Sea', thereby treating Northern Ireland differently to the rest of the UK, which was unacceptable to the unionist community. The only way to avoid any form of contentious border would be for the whole country to stay in the Single Market and Customs Union—which was unacceptable to hardline Brexiteers.

These questions concerned the nature of the post-Brexit UK–EU relationship, which would be agreed in principle during phase two and finalized post exit. But the Northern Ireland border was tackled in the phase one talks—partly at the UK's behest, in an attempt to start discussions on the future trading relationship as early as possible (Ruparel 2020). Consequently, these talks began considering how to avoid a hard border on the island of Ireland. Such an outcome was considered highly undesirable by both the UK and the EU, and particularly concerned the Irish government—but would be required in the event that a hard Brexit was agreed, or that there was no future relationship deal at all. The negotiators' solution was hence to write an insurance policy (or 'backstop') into the Withdrawal Agreement. The two key options for this essentially mirrored the imperfect solutions to the Irish trilemma laid out above. An 'all-UK backstop' would require the whole of the UK to maintain an agreed level of convergence with EU customs and regulatory policy, thus continuing to apply the same environmental, labour, and product standards, state aid rules and tariffs as the EU. In contrast, a 'Northern Ireland-only backstop' would require this in Northern Ireland only, allowing the rest of the UK to diverge. These models could potentially be varied or combined—for example, by converging at UK level on customs policy and at Northern Ireland level on regulatory policy, or vice versa. However, such solutions raised political problems; although the DUP supported a hard Brexit, it considered any form of Northern Ireland-only arrangement unacceptable, while Conservative hardliners opposed continuing alignment in general.

Insiders have given differing accounts of precisely when the government realized how thorny a problem the Northern Ireland border would be. As discussed in Chapter 3, the question had barely featured in the referendum debate outside Northern Ireland itself, and its complexities had been downplayed by the Leave campaign, Boris Johnson having claimed that Irish border arrangements would remain 'absolutely unchanged' by Brexit (BBC News 2016a).

Some clear warnings about Brexit's risk to the border were soon given, including in a joint letter to the Prime Minister in summer 2016 from the Northern Ireland First Minister and deputy First Minister. May's response in October 2016 confirmed that the future of the border was 'an important priority' (quoted in Murphy and Evershed 2022: 25). Her March 2017 letter to Donald Tusk triggering Article 50 then explicitly ruled out a hard border (May 2017b). But during this period ministers faced numerous distractions, including the *Miller* case and the general election, and little real progress on the topic was made (Davidson 2020). May's Chief of Staff Gavin Barwell (2020) later claimed that the government had recognized that Northern Ireland would be the 'Gordian knot' of the negotiations by the time talks began. At this stage, the recent general election had placed the DUP in the pivotal position of May's confidence and supply partner, and moreover left it as the only Northern Ireland party represented at Westminster. This, along with the absence of a functioning Northern Ireland Executive, freed the party from the need to face awkward compromises with other local representatives on Brexit, and left it able to retain an unequivocally hardline stance (Barwell 2021).

Difficulties in reaching a UK–EU agreement on Northern Ireland were a major factor in delaying the end of the first phase of negotiations. In December 2017 a draft phase one agreement was leaked, which suggested that Northern Ireland could end up with some form of differentiated status. The DUP claimed to have been unaware of the government's plans (BBC News 2017), and its furious response forced further discussions and revised wording in the final phase one agreement (Negotiators of the European Union and the United Kingdom Government 2017). But much remained unclear regarding what type of future relationship might prove acceptable, leading one expert to describe it as 'a textbook example of kicking the can down the road' (Menon 2017). As the negotiations moved on from the principles of withdrawal to the details of an agreement, the conundrum emerged again. In February 2018 the EU published its proposed Withdrawal Agreement text, containing Barnier's preferred solution of a Northern Ireland-only arrangement, favoured by the EU because it avoided providing British companies with preferential access to the European market (Menon and Wager 2021). May, concerned about the risk of a border down the Irish Sea, responded that 'no UK Prime Minister could ever agree' to such a proposal.[6] Disagreements between the UK and EU about the form that any backstop should take then continued over the following months. Throughout this period a failure truly to face up to the inevitable trade-offs meant that even by summer 2018 the problem of the Northern Ireland border had still not been resolved.

Cabinet and Party Management

The talks with the EU began just as Theresa May's authority within her party had been badly weakened by the general election result. The reality of the negotiations, and in particular the growing appreciation of the complexity of the Northern Ireland border problem, demanded pragmatism and a willingness to compromise on the substance of Brexit. But the general election made the Prime Minister, who had publicly embraced the objectives of the ERG, even more dependent on them than previously for her survival. The hardliners meanwhile tended to dismiss the need for compromise, citing the perceived exceptional significance of the UK market as a reason to demand concessions from the EU (Glencross 2022, Martill and Staiger 2021). This made it difficult for May to shift to a more pragmatic position that acknowledged the trade-offs, without threatening her parliamentary majority.

These handling problems extended all the way up to May's Cabinet, which was split between Leavers and former Remainers. One member recalled in interview that any substantive proposition risked splitting the Cabinet into 'armed camps'. This period also saw a distinct toughening of attitudes within the parliamentary party as a whole, including a growing proportion of back-benchers preferring a hard Brexit. Notably, a survey of Conservative MPs in December 2016 found that 44 per cent believed staying in the Single Market would not be fully consistent with the referendum result; but by January 2018 this figure had risen to 76 per cent (Mile End Institute 2018). May's own early rhetoric had, of course, tended to encourage such views.

The Prime Minister's difficulties with her hardline Brexiteers became evident over her first major post-election Brexit strategy announcement. This came via a speech in Florence in late September 2017, after the start of negotiations but before the phase one agreement had been reached (May 2017d). Though she repeated her previous red lines of an independent trade policy and an end to the jurisdiction of the European Court of Justice (ECJ), May's concession that the UK would continue to be bound by EU rules during any transition period led hardliners to fear that she was weakening her stance. Senior Brexiteer Jacob Rees-Mogg demanded that free movement should end immediately upon the UK's exit in 2019, and Foreign Secretary Boris Johnson insisted that the transition period should last no longer than two years (Shipman 2017b). The following month's Conservative Party conference reinforced her vulnerability. Days beforehand, Johnson (2017) published a lengthy column on his vision for post-Brexit Britain which went well beyond his brief, and was widely interpreted as a veiled leadership bid (Shipman 2017b). May's conference speech was then marred by a series of disasters; and former party chairman Grant Shapps admitted to coordinating a leadership plot against her (Seldon and Newell 2019).

The Prime Minister's next major Brexit speech, delivered at Mansion House the following March and looking ahead to the second phase of the talks, temporarily reassured her hardliners (May 2018a). She argued for a bespoke deal to continue free trade in goods, allow the UK to choose where it would follow or diverge from EU regulations, and retain membership of some EU agencies. This was hailed as 'a sensible, pragmatic and generous approach' by Rees-Mogg (2018a), and a 'clear and convincing vision' by Johnson (Rothwell and Bennett 2018). But the EU reaction was less positive, with Guy Verhofstadt concluding that the speech had reiterated the UK's existing red lines, but failed to provide any workable suggestions for the future.[7] Academic commentators noted that May's strategy had been 'directed more at a UK than a European audience' (Menon and Portes 2018)—underlining how she was encountering difficulties in balancing the two.

Meanwhile, May's typically closed style meant that she tended to be tight-lipped, rather than publicly admitting the dilemmas. Her approach to both her Cabinet and her confidence-and-supply partners also largely mirrored her general attitude to party and parliamentary management (as discussed in Chapter 4). Philip Hammond (2020) claimed that Cabinet members were largely kept in the dark about negotiations, given only fragmentary information, and then presented with full drafts of complex agreements on a take-it-or-leave-it basis at the last possible minute. Amber Rudd (2021), likewise, recalled May's failure to consult her Cabinet. The Prime Minister was also subject to similar complaints by the DUP. This was clearly driven in part by a determination to maintain cohesion, as also seen in her dealings with backbenchers. A senior Leave-supporting MP suggested in interview that 'you never got positive assent to what you were saying, [but] you didn't get dissent. So you got the impression that she didn't disagree with you, and, obviously she did that to everybody.' A more pro-European backbencher agreed: 'the trouble was that she was pretending to agree with both sides. So she would be meeting with us and saying "yes, yes, yes, I think that there's definitely merit"…But then she'd be meeting with the other side and trying to agree with them as well.' The overall effect was that May consistently failed to explain to her party—or to parliament, or the country—the true extent of the difficult choices entailed by Brexit, and the impossibility of pleasing everybody.

Labour's Brexit Journey

As seen in previous chapters, Brexit also posed major challenges for Labour. The party's representatives were far less ideologically divided than the Conservatives, though prior to the referendum its parliamentarians included a handful of Eurosceptics. Party members, likewise, had overwhelmingly supported Remain (YouGov 2016a). But the referendum result divided the party's voters, with many Labour-held constituencies strongly supporting Leave.

This presented serious positioning problems, and a risk of party splits. Publicly, the frontbench had initially accepted the national referendum mandate, albeit regretfully, and pledged to fight for an outcome that would minimize damage to the party's supporters—for example, through protecting key industries and employment rights—which implied a 'soft' Brexit. But the 2017 election opened up new challenges. The advent of minority government made it harder for Labour simply to wash its hands of Brexit and leave the matter to the Conservatives. Meanwhile, Remain supporters—both inside and outside parliament—increasingly hoped that the referendum result could be reversed, and this included many on the Labour benches.

Others, in seats that had strongly voted for Leave, were worried about the electoral consequences of such a possibility. The post-2017 period therefore saw Brexit fought out painfully within the party, as well as among Conservatives (Pogrund and Maguire 2020).

Labour's formal structures of decision-making in opposition include the leader, the Shadow Cabinet, and the party conference. Within the Shadow Cabinet, the DExEU team was led by Keir Starmer, but a special 'Brexit sub-committee' was also created, comprising various figures including Corbyn. Arguments were played out between all of these different groups, as well as in the wider Parliamentary Labour Party (PLP). The Brexit subcommittee was variously described by interviewees as 'dysfunctional' and 'not serious', with a moving cast of characters designed to keep the leader in control. Corbyn himself had a distinctly ambiguous position on EU membership, having previously been a Eurosceptic rebel, and then having been challenged over his poor performance in the referendum campaign. Some close to him, such as his Strategy and Communications Director Seamus Milne, were seen as having strong Eurosceptic leanings in line with the party's traditional left. Starmer, Shadow Foreign Secretary Emily Thornberry, and indeed Corbyn himself, all held inner London seats which had voted strongly for Remain, while other key figures such as party Chair Ian Lavery represented strongly pro-Leave constituencies. Many of Corbyn's own supporters in the party, particularly through the grassroots organization Momentum, were instinct-ively pro-European, as were most in the PLP. This created ample opportun-ities for conflict.

Over the summer of 2017 Corbyn was under increasing pressure in his party to set out a firmer Brexit position—at least in favour of a soft Brexit, if not for a referendum on the final deal. Statements from the leader and his allies appeared to reject proposals to remain formally in the Customs Union or Single Market (summarized in Shipman 2017b). At the first post-election party conference, Corbyn (2017) maintained the more ambiguous manifesto line from three months earlier, accepting the referendum result, but arguing for a Brexit deal that 'guarantees unimpeded access to the single market' and 'delivers jobs, rights and decent living standards'. This implied a significant degree of future alignment with the EU, but remained unclear. Unease among activists was dealt with through careful procedural manoeuvring by the leader's team to ensure that there were no conference votes on Brexit.

A reported turning point came in a speech by the leader in Coventry in February 2018. Corbyn (2018) committed the party for the first time to 'a new comprehensive UK-EU customs union', in order to prevent tariffs with Europe and a hard border in Northern Ireland. With regard to the Single

Market, he repeated his previous vague wording, promising only to 'maintain the benefits' of membership. The difficult behind-the-scenes arguments preceding this speech have been described elsewhere (Pogrund and Maguire 2020). One interviewee closely involved recalled 'tortuous negotiations' and 'bitter discussion' between the party leader's office and Starmer's team, who had been pushing in a 'softer' Brexit direction. But for all of these agonies, it is important to note (as discussed in the next chapter) that the opposition's primary function is usually to expose shortcomings in the government's own policy, rather than necessarily to come up with a coherent policy of its own. This allowed Corbyn to maintain a vague position, whose actual difference from May's proposals was sometimes distinctly unclear. But he also had to manage pressures from his own backbenchers, and faced moments when the delicate Commons arithmetic presented opportunities to team up with moderate Conservatives and force policy change. At times backbenchers such as Chuka Umunna (see Queen's Speech amendment in Chapter 5), and Chris Leslie (discussed below) used parliamentary mechanisms to try and force the leadership into positions on which cross-party agreement might be achieved. But there was another angle to these dynamics, with Corbyn and his allies suspecting such internal critics (almost certainly correctly) of deliberately exploiting Brexit divisions to undermine his leadership.

But many Labour figures saw a soft Brexit as an undesirable compromise (e.g. Blair 2018), and the bigger prize pursued by former Remainers was getting the leadership to back a second referendum. In March 2018, Corbyn's past leadership adversary Owen Smith was sacked from the frontbench for publicly advocating such a vote. This argument ran on throughout 2018, and came to a head at that year's party conference, when local parties submitted hundreds of motions in favour of a referendum. Starmer—who was clearly more drawn to the idea than his leader—negotiated a form of words with delegates whereby 'Labour must support all options remaining on the table, including campaigning for a public vote' (Labour List 2018). Speaking to the conference in favour of this motion, Starmer (2018) went beyond the text agreed with the leader's office, to suggest that 'nobody is ruling out remain as an option'. This came just a day after Shadow Chancellor (and Corbyn ally) John McDonnell had seemed to do exactly that (Walker, Stewart, and Elgot 2018). While the motion and Starmer's speech were greeted rapturously by most delegates, and by many Remain supporters outside the conference hall, they raised concerns about alienating Labour Leave supporters. One such activist described them as 'a P45 to our MPs in the Midlands and Wales' (quoted in Stewart and O'Carroll 2018), while former Vote Leave chair and

Labour MP Gisela Stuart (2018) argued in print that Labour was 'turning against its traditional voters'.

As Pogrund and Maguire (2020: 196) have noted, within the party '[c]alamity awaited Corbyn no matter which direction he jumped in': the party stood to lose seats in its traditional heartlands if it was seen to be blocking Brexit, but faced similar threats in areas such as London if it supported Brexit. Corbyn's natural reflex was to run from the issue, leaving his own position constantly ambiguous. As these same authors suggest, 'to Remainers, Corbyn was a Brexiteer. To Brexiteers, he had been corrupted by Remainers' (Pogrund and Maguire (2020: 192). On this most polarizing of issues, he ducked from alienating either side. Here, as in various other ways, there was a striking resemblance between Corbyn's approach and that of his opponent Theresa May.

The Various Parliamentary Groupings over Brexit

With both main parties in significant disarray, the aftermath of the referendum saw a gradual blossoming of various parliamentary groupings. Such groups developed both within parties and also, increasingly, between them. They largely reflected the Leave/Remain divide, but also debated and promoted alternative visions of Brexit. As time went on, and the hardline Conservative ERG was drawn towards a no-deal outcome, other groups coalesced to avoid its potential economic costs, disruption, and impact on Northern Ireland.

Intra-party and cross-party groups are not unusual within Westminster—both main parties contain various informal ideological factions as well as blocs of MPs with particular policy interests. Meanwhile, MPs frequently work together informally on matters of common interest across party lines, most obviously through All-Party Parliamentary Groups (APPGs). But the fragmentation over Brexit took these forms of activity to a new high. With neither party leader able to keep their MPs together, MPs themselves sought increasingly to try and build a majority to resolve the impasse.

Conservative Groups

The most prominent grouping of all, which gained significant public visibility, was the European Research Group (ERG)—made up of hardline Conservative Brexiteers.

The ERG had a long history, having formed in the 1990s in the wake of the Maastricht Treaty, to promote a looser relationship with Europe. From its outset the group held discussion meetings, and briefed members on European issues coming to the UK parliament for decision. Its first researcher was Daniel Hannan, who later became a leading voice in Conservative Euroscepticism, serving as a Member of the European Parliament from 2009 to 2020. Initially, the ERG included relative moderates, some of whom, like David Gauke and Oliver Letwin, eventually ended up on the other side of the parliamentary arguments over Brexit.

Key ERG members—such as Bernard Jenkin, Jacob Rees-Mogg, and Steve Baker—were instrumental in campaigning for a referendum to be held, and then active in Vote Leave. After the result, the ERG became increasingly energetic in lobbying within the party for a hard Brexit, arguing that only this constituted a 'real' Brexit. Baker chaired the group from 2016, until being appointed as a junior DExEU minister after the 2017 general election, when he was replaced by Suella Braverman. She was subsequently appointed a DExEU minister herself, and the group was then chaired by Jacob Rees-Mogg for the remainder of May's premiership. Baker resumed the chair in 2019, when Rees-Mogg entered government.

The ERG was always secretive about the number and identity of its members. In early 2018, the BBC reported that Cabinet ministers who had declared financial contributions to the group in the immediately preceding years included David Davis, Liam Fox, Michael Gove, Chris Grayling, and Andrea Leadsom—all high-profile Brexiteers (Doherty 2018). Some report that Boris Johnson regularly attended its meetings (Bower 2020), but insiders deny that he was a member (Francois 2021). After the referendum there was regular speculation about the group's size, and therefore the number of votes that it could potentially control—with one report estimating this at 69 (Spence 2018). An ERG interviewee said that the group's size was 'the one thing we've never divulged', going on to recall that there 'was a saying about Rolls-Royce motors that when you asked them what the horsepower of a Rolls-Royce car was the answer would be "enough"'. The ERG certainly had 'enough' members to exercise significant influence through this period, even before Theresa May lost her parliamentary majority.

As already indicated, ERG members had close access to Number 10 from an early stage after the referendum. At this point, another member said in interview, the group was 'basically thinking that our job is to support the Prime Minister in doing what she has said she intends to do'. But as her approach began to shift, the group's position became more of a threat. The same member recalled that after May's September 2017 Florence speech there was a feeling 'that she's watering down...so, we go from being the people who really want to support her, to people who are reminding her of why we're supporting her—that it's not unconditional support'. As noted in Chapter 5, key ERG members had been among those suggesting that the Prime Minister might be removed immediately after the 2017 election.

In comparison to the other parliamentary groupings, the ERG had formidable organization and discipline, benefiting from both its longevity and its ideological cohesion. It held weekly plenary meetings and steering group meetings, ran a WhatsApp operation, and had its own internal whipping system. Whips, known as 'buddies' in part to avoid detection, also met frequently to compare notes on members' views—led by their chief, Mark Francois (2021). One ERG interviewee boasted that they had 'a better whipping operation than the government's'. This may or may not have been true—but the group often held together very effectively. This meant that, notwithstanding its disagreements with the government, it was a potentially reliable negotiating partner—as it could control a relatively predictable number of votes. This in itself gave the group influence, and made it challenging for Number 10 to cross.

On the other side of the argument were the more pro-European Conservatives. They had long been represented, for example, by the Conservative Group for Europe which was originally formed in the 1960s under the name European Forum, in support of EEC membership. MPs from this wing of the party also began to organize more vigorously after the referendum result. For the key period when MPs were wrangling over Brexit, they met weekly, convened by Stephen Hammond. Prominent attendees included Dominic Grieve, Nicky Morgan, Ken Clarke, and Anna Soubry. One interviewee who frequented the group's meetings described how it 'started out as a psychotherapy session and then it gradually [began asking]—what are we going to do about this?' It grew increasingly assertive following the 2017 election, seeking explicitly to counter the ERG's activities. Asked what united members of the group, the same interviewee said 'a desire for a soft Brexit; a deepening concern about the future of the party and the power of the ERG; a desire to support Theresa...and a sense that, if we didn't stand up for what I would call liberal Conservatism, we were just going to be bulldozed out of the way'.

The more pro-European grouping appeared to have some clear advantages. It contained many senior figures, and at the time of the referendum the number of Conservative MPs supporting Remain had outnumbered those supporting Leave. However, its concerted parliamentary organization started later, and was less aggressive. The group was also less ideologically coherent;

some members, such as Grieve and Soubry, came out quite early on in favour of a second referendum and opposed a soft Brexit, while others, including Hammond, supported soft Brexit and were strongly opposed to a referendum. All of these views crucially left the group vulnerable to accusations from the ERG and others that it was anti-Brexit, and was seeking to undermine the referendum result.

Both the ERG and its opponents organized largely at backbench level, but both communicated with, and were mirrored by, groups of sympathetic ministers. The 'pizza club' comprised pro-Brexit ministers, and was coordinated by Andrea Leadsom.[8] It attracted Cabinet members who had campaigned for Leave, such as Liam Fox, Chris Grayling, Penny Mordaunt, and Michael Gove, plus others that had come firmly round to Brexit after the result, such as Sajid Javid. There was clearly a strong line of informal communication between these members and the backbench ERG, and also between the ERG and DExEU ministers who had been drawn from it, such as Steve Baker.

The equivalent ministerial group on the opposing side of the argument was convened by Chancellor of the Exchequer Philip Hammond, and included other former Remain supporters, such as Amber Rudd, David Lidington, David Gauke, Greg Clark, Karen Bradley, and Rory Stewart. As matters became more tense, this group also began meeting weekly, and it retained open lines of communication with Stephen Hammond's backbench group. According to interviewees, its members were loyal to Theresa May but 'very worried' about where she would end up under the ERG's influence. One suggested that 'we did become more cohesive and organised in response to the success of the hardliners', but that 'the hardliners were better at organising, better at lobbying for their cause, better at projecting their arguments than we were throughout'.

Labour Groups

There are some clear parallels within Labour, although the number of committed Brexiteers was very limited. The primary organization took place on the pro-European side, with a focus on both beating the arguments of Conservative Brexiteers and bringing Jeremy Corbyn round to supporting a soft Brexit or further referendum.

Immediately after the referendum, a group of pro-European Labour MPs (some of whom had just quit the frontbench) began meeting regularly. As with its Conservative counterpart, this group was described by one of the interviewees involved as partly 'a kind of support network'. In the early stages, in particular, it was clearly difficult to disentangle members' concerns about the referendum result from their frustrations with Corbyn. This made the leader's office suspicious of the group, threatening to impede its influence. It also helped to spark initiatives such as the 'Love Socialism, Hate Brexit' grassroots campaign, supported by more overtly Corbynite MPs such as Clive Lewis—to demonstrate that a dislike of Brexit did not automatically signal a rejection of the party leader.

Labour MPs' dilemma over the EU (Notification of Withdrawal) Bill, as described in Chapter 4, helped to solidify the broad pro-European group. As members weighed whether to vote for the Article 50 trigger or not, an informal whipping operation developed, encouraging pro-Europeans to vote against the bill. This allowed organizers to gather intelligence and encourage members to coordinate their behaviour. The 52 Labour MPs who had voted against the third reading—who included Ben Bradshaw, Chris Bryant, Stephen Doughty, Peter Kyle, and Alison McGovern—then formed an obvious core for the group, which went on to refer to itself as 'Beyond Article 50'. One interviewee who was closely involved claimed that there were eventually over 240 Labour MPs on its list of supporters, which fell only around 20 short of the whole PLP. But while numerous Labour MPs may have shared pro-European sentiments, it was far more difficult to coordinate how those sentiments should be translated into policy goals. A Labour frontbench interviewee recalled that 'it was very hard for us to get a read on what [the group] ultimately wanted'. As with their Conservative counterparts, the pro-Europeans were divided on strategy; some were reluctantly prepared to embrace a soft Brexit, while others wished to pursue a second referendum. As time went on, support gradually shifted toward the second of these objectives.

Labour MPs were involved in several more narrowly focused cross-party groups pursuing certain soft Brexit options, as described below. In addition, particularly during 2019, there was some organization by Labour MPs in Leave-supporting seats who felt firmly that the referendum result must be respected—even, if necessary, by supporting a Conservative Brexit deal. Caroline Flint, who was herself a former Europe minister, and had campaigned for Remain, was one of the coordinators of this group. While (as discussed in subsequent chapters) it failed to secure many Commons votes, it numbered 20–30 members, and at key moments had direct access to Number 10.

Cross-party Groups

There were then numerous cross-party groups. These held multiple, often overlapping, goals; the same MP might be at the core of one group and more peripherally associated with several others. Some cross-party groupings were linked to groups outside parliament, which also became increasingly organized from the 2017 election onwards. Most also connected to groups within the parties.

The key external groups were pro-European, and primarily focused on lobbying for a referendum on the final Brexit deal. The People's Vote campaign was formally launched in April 2018, by a cross-party panel of parliamentarians—Conservative Anna Soubry, Labour's Chuka Umunna, Liberal Democrat Layla Moran, and Caroline Lucas of the Greens (BBC News 2018). It was a largely extra-parliamentary organization, but worked with sympathetic parliamentarians to try and build support at Westminster for a further Brexit referendum. Corbyn's allies generally considered it hostile to his leadership—those involved included various of the Labour MPs listed above, plus key Blairite figures such as Peter Mandelson and Alastair Campbell (Pogrund and Maguire 2020). The organization faced dilemmas regarding its positioning. It never presented itself as explicitly pro-Remain, instead focusing tactically on the 'People's Vote' as a process question. But its supporters were overwhelmingly drawn from the Remain side of the argument. There were also internal tensions regarding when was the right moment to press the referendum question inside parliament—with the Liberal Democrats always keen to lay down challenges to Labour, but Labour figures concerned that forcing Corbyn's hand too soon would be counterproductive (Campbell 2021, Cherry 2020). The campaign's most notable success was the organization of mass public demonstrations, the first of which, on the second anniversary of the referendum in June 2018, reportedly attracted around 100,000 protesters (ITV News 2018a). A subsequent demonstration in October 2018 then attracted around half a million (Full Fact 2018). Beyond the People's Vote, there was a complex and overlapping set of other external pro-European groups, many of them working with parliamentarians.

Within parliament, cross-party organization in favour of a hard Brexit was essentially limited to the quite close working relationship between the DUP and ERG. In contrast, pro-European cross-party organization ran significantly wider. An APPG on EU Relations was formed in July 2017, jointly chaired by Chuka Umunna and Anna Soubry, and with support from various minor parties. It was focused on securing a close future relationship with the EU, and initially organized around the EU (Withdrawal) Bill (Mason 2017).

Later on, in autumn 2018, an influential group that called itself 'Trains and Buses' began to meet, pulling together key figures from the pro-European groups on the Labour and Conservative benches, alongside representatives of other parties. The group's name came from the fact that several central figures, including Conservatives Justine Greening and Jo Johnson, and Labour's Lord (Andrew) Adonis, had previously been transport ministers. Meanwhile, its innocuousness allowed members to exchange WhatsApp messages in the Commons chamber, or discuss meetings, without broadcasting the nature of their association. By this point (as discussed in the next chapter) Theresa May's Brexit deal seemed increasingly unlikely to secure Commons support, creating a renewed sense of urgency and a desire by members across parties to find some kind of stable resolution. As an interviewee commented, 'we had an autumn where it became clearer and clearer that we were heading for a massive political crisis, and that was the point in anticipation of the deal coming back to the House of Commons that the cross-party working really started in earnest'.

Participants in this group included many of those previously mentioned—for example, Ben Bradshaw, Chris Bryant, Chris Leslie, Alison McGovern, and Chuka Umunna from Labour, Dominic Grieve and others such as Guto Bebb, Phillip Lee and Sarah Wollaston from the Conservatives, plus frontbenchers Jo Swinson of the Liberal Democrats, Caroline Lucas of the Greens, Joanna Cherry of the SNP, and Liz Saville-Roberts of Plaid Cymru. In both main parties those participating enjoyed good relationships with supportive frontbenchers, maintaining communication with them and with the wider groups within their parties. The forum exchanged information, and sought to coordinate action and develop cross-party strategy.

Shortly afterwards, a smaller, more senior grouping began meeting. This took primary responsibility for cross-party decisions, coordinating between the other groups. Several interviewees called this grouping, which included various former senior ministers, 'the grandees'. Several members of this group later put their names to key motions, amendments, and bills, including Margaret Beckett, Hilary Benn, and Yvette Cooper from Labour, and Nick Boles, Dominic Grieve, Oliver Letwin, and Caroline Spelman from the Conservatives. These members, effectively, began seeking the kind of cross-party compromise that Theresa May had instinctively been reluctant to pursue. Later on, in mid-2019, the group expanded to include some who had departed the Conservative frontbench. Letwin (2020) later noted that it was 'more or less happenstance' who was named on some of the key initiatives, because 'we just worked out who would do the next bit'. The group was united around the position of 'no to no deal', and otherwise not focused on a specific outcome (some of its members, for example, being opposed to a second referendum). One member said that it 'consisted of folk who ranged from those who would abandon the whole [Brexit] thing if they got the chance—second referendum supporters—to people like Oliver, who was very frank in saying "the moment something comes along I'm voting for it. But the one thing I'm resolutely opposed to is no deal".'

In addition to these broad alignments, there were various more narrowly focused groups agitating for particular versions of Brexit. Their membership reflected MPs' preferred models, and also sometimes constituency interests—as different models entailed different economic outcomes for particular sectors, as well as differing immigration rules (see Chapter 4). One interviewee described how MPs holding urban seats, perhaps containing many financial services workers, might conclude that 'we want Single Market access, we don't mind free movement'. They might join the 'Norway plus'/'Common Market 2.0' group, which formed quite early on—driven by members such as Labour's Stephen Kinnock and Conservative Nick Boles. Its solution envisaged the UK joining the European Free Trade Association (EFTA) and European Economic Area (EEA) after the transition period, preserving near-full membership of the Single Market. This group aspired to remain only temporarily in a customs union with the EU, while negotiating unspecified longer-term arrangements to avoid a hard Northern Ireland border. Boles (2018) claimed that this would ensure the backstop never needed to come into force. Conservative backers included Robert Halfon, Oliver Letwin, Nicky Morgan, and Nicholas Soames, while Lucy Powell was a key organizer on the Labour benches. In contrast, MPs concerned about free movement of people, but representing seats dependent on manufacturing, would be more likely to join another group, which focused on remaining in a permanent customs union, without Single Market membership. They included Labour's Yvette Cooper, Jack Dromey, and Helen Goodman, and senior Conservative Damian Green. Groupings such as these became particularly important at the later stages, when parliamentarians were exploring the alternatives to Theresa May's failed deal, and the options that they championed were among those voted upon in the 'indicative votes' of 2019 (described in Chapter 8).

Parliament was a hive of activity in this period, with innumerable conversations going on between members within and across parties to seek solutions on Brexit. On one side there was brute cohesion—in the form of the hardline ERG. On the more pro-European side, there were potentially many more votes available; but the plethora of groups, the inability to coalesce around any specific solution, and the risk of being branded as anti-Brexit (and thus of resisting the referendum result) were all to prove a significant weakness.

Holding the Government to Account on the Floor and in Committees

By the post-election period, May's 'no running commentary' approach (described in Chapter 4) was already well established. But parliamentarians remained unwilling to be sidelined. Parliament's core role as a public forum for debate and accountability was exploited by the various groups now coalescing, to press the government on its Brexit strategy. MPs used government statements and parliamentary questions to advance their preferred Brexit outcome on the floor of the Commons chamber, while select committees pursued inquiries which allowed them to explore the detail of the negotiations and their consequences. MPs' attempts to get access to information on the government's strategy, meanwhile, culminated in the opposition's revival of the humble address procedure—an innovation which would go on to be repeatedly used. These mechanisms allowed MPs to put the government under pressure, and flushed out many of the difficult Brexit trade-offs. But their use also often revealed the extent of splits, including among Conservative backbenchers, and the continuing breakdown of their relationship with the government.

Government Statements and Parliamentary Questions

Government statements are made at ministers' instigation, and allow them to set out their stall and then be questioned by parliamentarians of all parties on the floor of either chamber.

Nine Brexit-focused statements were delivered in the Commons between June 2017 and July 2018, totalling over 13 hours of debating time. These followed key negotiating sessions, European Council meetings, or domestic speeches—and offered MPs from competing groups a chance to quiz ministers on the detail, and to champion their preferred Brexit outcomes. For example, in a nearly two-hour session on a statement reporting the October 2017 European Council, as the end of the phase one talks approached, Conservatives such as Ken Clarke and Anna Soubry argued for a softer Brexit, while others, such as Owen Paterson, supported a bullish approach to trading on WTO terms.[9] Similarly, in a March 2018 statement following the

Mansion House speech, May spent an hour and 40 minutes answering questions from all sides. Veteran Brexiteer John Redwood asked her to confirm that the UK would leave the EU on 29 March 2019, with or without a deal, while fellow Conservatives Sarah Wollaston and Bob Neill, chairs respectively of the select committees on health and justice, pressed her to retain close cooperation in those policy areas.[10] At the same session, Labour's Ben Bradshaw challenged the wisdom of leaving the Single Market, while Yvette Cooper raised concerns about the Northern Ireland border unless the UK remained in a customs union with the EU.[11]

The negotiations were understandably the single most common topic in DExEU departmental questions during this period. Like questioning to other departments, these took place every few weeks, with MPs able to enter a ballot to participate. They were used by MPs from the various groups described above as an opportunity to press the government on the shape of the negotiations or to raise particular constituency interests. Urgent questions— which are granted to MPs by the Speaker, and must be answered by a minister in the Commons on the day they are asked—offered another opportunity to interrogate the government at points of particular tension, when ministers might not have come to the Commons of their own accord. In early December 2017, for example, as May struggled to finalize the phase one agreement, an urgent question from Keir Starmer allowed MPs to cross-examine David Davis for an hour on progress. By contrast, Jeremy Corbyn's continued ambivalence on Brexit meant that he raised the topic at just 10 of 35 sessions of Prime Minister's Questions over this period, mostly in the run-up to Chequers.

Select Committees

Commons select committees are designed to encompass the breadth of opinion in the chamber, with seats shared proportionately between the parties. Since the Wright reforms of 2010, the chairs of most such committees have been elected on a cross-party basis, by all MPs (Russell 2011). This benefits candidates who command cross-party support, and has provided an alternative route to influence for respected backbenchers, including those out of favour with their party leaderships. As already seen, former Shadow Foreign Secretary Hilary Benn became chair of the Exiting the European Union Committee; another key Labour backbench voice on Brexit was Yvette Cooper, who chaired the Home Affairs Committee. On the Conservative side, Nicky Morgan succeeded Andrew Tyrie as chair of the Treasury

Committee after the 2017 election, while Brexit critic Sarah Wollaston replaced him as chair of the influential Liaison Committee. The duties of this committee, which comprises chairs of all other select committees, include regular questioning of the Prime Minister.

Brexit was the single most dominant theme for select committees in the 2017–19 parliament, during which every departmental committee held at least one Brexit-related inquiry (Marshall et al. 2020). In the post-referendum period almost all committees included a mix of former Remainers and Leavers, which—much like the standard split between parties—chairs had to navigate as far as possible to maintain the committees' norm of working by consensus. With a few exceptions, this was achieved (Lynch and Whitaker 2019). The International Trade Committee (2017), for example, published a unanimous report which was highly critical of the government's approach to rolling over trade deals with non-EU countries, pointing out multiple flaws and omissions in its planning. The Northern Ireland Affairs Committee (2018: 31), likewise, unanimously agreed regarding potential for technology to solve the border dilemma that 'we have had no visibility of any technical solutions, anywhere in the world, beyond the aspirational, that would remove the need for physical infrastructure at the border'.

However, the Exiting the European Union Committee was an outlier. As the select committee overseeing the Whitehall department bringing together all strands of Brexit planning, it was—more than any other—forced to confront the inherent trade-offs. It was unusually large—at 21 members rather than the more standard 11—in order to encompass a diverse range of voices. Its membership also included key players from all sides of the Brexit divide, such as Jacob Rees-Mogg, Stephen Kinnock, and the SNP's Joanna Cherry. Seven of its members had backed Leave, while 14 had backed Remain—with both represented among members on the Conservative side. In this context, the chair abandoned the norm of working by consensus soon after the committee's formation, feeling that this would make it impossible for it to reach conclusions (Benn 2021). The committee recorded an unprecedented number of divisions (i.e. formal votes), including on 13 of its 14 reports between January 2017 and March 2019 (Lynch and Whitaker 2019).

Select committees have various means of achieving influence, only one of which is for the government to accede to recommendations in their reports (Benton and Russell 2013). They can gather information and put it on the public record, and their oral evidence sessions—often reported by the media—provide a challenging environment for questioning of ministers, civil servants, and other witnesses. Throughout this period, the ExEU Committee and the Liaison Committee saw some dramatic questioning of ministers and the Prime Minister, respectively, much of it focused on teasing out the government's position. Philip Rycroft (2020), the former Permanent Secretary of DExEU, noted that Benn's committee 'rather effectively' put pressure of this kind on his department. Its regular reports also often informed parliamentary debates, by providing information and analysis. Many of these covered the negotiations, setting out the areas of progress and those where agreement was still needed, while others set out options and evidence—for example on possible models for the future trading relationship with the EU (Exiting the European Union Committee 2018a, 2018b, 2018c).

Opposition Days and the Humble Address

In addition to the preceding commonly used forms of scrutiny, MPs began in this period to innovate. In particular, they revived a procedure known as the humble address. The spur for this—as it would be for future instances of procedural innovation, particularly those discussed in Chapter 8—was Theresa May's tendency to shut parliament out of the Brexit process. The legislative affairs team in Number 10, at the admission of its former Director, was focused on 'protecting the ability of the government to do things where they don't have to go to parliament' (da Costa 2021). This partly stemmed from fears that pro-Remain parliamentarians might seek to stand in the way of Brexit.

One manifestation of the government's resistance to parliament was its increasing refusal to engage with opposition day motions. Opposition days give non-government parties occasional opportunities to determine the topic for a full- or half-day debate, followed by a vote. Ordinarily, any motion agreed at the end of such a debate would have some political force—despite not being legally binding. But when the government enjoys a majority, such motions are routinely defeated. Following the 2017 general election result, the risk of defeat was clearly heightened. In response, the government began whipping its MPs to abstain in votes on opposition days. The official justification from Leader of the House Andrea Leadsom was that 'we will not necessarily always choose to take part in party political games'.[12] But the presumed intent was to take the sting out of defeat, by partially delegitimizing MPs' decisions—giving the government an excuse to ignore the motions that were agreed. The Public Administration and Constitutional Affairs Committee (2018b: 3), chaired by Conservative Brexiteer Bernard Jenkin, would later criticize this tactic, accusing ministers of showing a 'lack of respect for the House'.

Labour felt compelled to seek new means of influence, and turned to the House of Commons clerks for advice on how a binding opposition day motion might be constructed. The clerks are parliament's procedural specialists, and willingly advise parliamentarians of any party or group on which parliamentary procedures would best enable them to achieve their aims. Although the clerks would later come under fire from the Brexit-backing press for providing procedural advice to rebellious MPs (see Chapter 8), this betrayed a fundamental misunderstanding of their role. It is their duty to advise members, of all political persuasions, on the available procedural mechanisms.

The immediate question concerned the release of government information. David Davis had claimed on multiple occasions—including in his first Commons statement as Brexit Secretary, and again when questioned by the ExEU Committee—that DExEU was carrying out 50–60 sectoral analyses or impact assessments on Brexit. Labour sought to have these released to parliamentarians, arguing that proper scrutiny by MPs depended on access to information. The solution suggested by the clerks was the humble address: in formal terms, a message from parliament to the monarch. Although this mechanism was still used for ceremonial purposes, it had otherwise largely fallen out of use since the mid-nineteenth century (Erskine May 2019: 7.31). But one earlier use had been petitioning the monarch, and therefore the government, for release of information. Crucially, such a motion, once agreed, was generally considered binding.

Thus Labour used an opposition day in November 2017 to move a motion for a humble address, requiring the Brexit impact assessments to be disclosed to the ExEU Committee. The government, as was now its habit, whipped Conservative MPs to abstain on the motion, which duly passed without a vote. Andrea Leadsom accepted that the motion was 'binding and that the information [would] be forthcoming'.[13] But ministers subsequently released only more limited sectoral analyses to the ExEU Committee, claiming that this was all that was available. Later, in January 2018, Labour repeated the humble address procedure, calling for the government's full analysis to be released. The published document predicted a slowdown in UK economic growth under all of the Brexit scenarios that it considered, offering ammunition to pro-Remain MPs.

A third attempt at using the humble address—this time to request Cabinet papers on the government's preferred arrangements for the future relationship—was voted down in May 2018. But by this point the procedure was well established. Its use, in the words of Chief Whip Julian Smith (2020), 'was just showing how far trust had broken down'. But it was an early indication that, in the face of a government prepared to bend norms to shut parliament out of Brexit debates, MPs were willing to use procedural innovation to push back. As the Public Administration and Constitutional Affairs Committee (2018b) report concluded, the behaviour of May's minority government had started a game of tit for tat.

The EU (Withdrawal) Bill and the Form of Brexit

Announced with great fanfare at Conservative Party conference in October 2016, and originally nicknamed the 'Great Repeal Bill', the European Union (Withdrawal) Bill was designed to repeal the European Communities Act 1972, which enshrined the UK's EU membership in domestic law. For Brexiteers, it was thus a vehicle to restore British sovereignty. But the bill also provided an opportunity for competing sets of MPs to seek to bind the government into particular negotiating positions. The debates during its parliamentary passage between autumn 2017 and summer 2018 were hence a key forum for discussion of the form that Brexit should take.

This section first introduces the bill itself, and the debates over its original content, which was primarily domestic and constitutional. In some technical areas, parliamentarians secured changes. It then considers the bill's use as a vehicle for debates about the form of Brexit, which were extensive but resulted in very little change, due to the internal splits in both main parties. The next chapter then discusses the parliamentary battles which took place on it specifically over the so-called 'meaningful vote', and the role that parliamentarians should have in approving the final Brexit deal.

Debates on the Topics Originally Covered by the Bill

Clause 1 of the EU (Withdrawal) Bill announced that 'The European Communities Act 1972 is repealed on exit day'—to implement domestically the UK's departure from the EU. But after over 40 years of membership, departing in an orderly fashion was a far from simple task. The remaining 61 pages set out proposals for how this would be legally achieved. Disentangling EU law from the UK statute book was a gargantuan task, and one which risked leaving gaps or incoherence unless it was carefully tackled. Far from repealing, therefore, in the short term the bill provided for a large volume of EU law to be moved into domestic law, and enabled ministers to amend it as needed in readiness for exit day.

This exercise not only entailed a wealth of detail but also engaged some fundamental questions about the relationships between the UK's different constitutional actors. Three key constitutional topics—the extent to which parliament should delegate powers to ministers pre-Brexit, the status of retained EU law post-Brexit, and the respective roles played by the devolved nations and Westminster in defining policy—recurred throughout the bill's nine-month passage. Each touched on existing constitutional tensions regarding the powers of the UK government, and each continued to resonate long after Brexit had occurred.

First, there were anxieties about the powers that the bill would grant to ministers before exit day, to modify legislation without facing full parliamentary oversight. The growing scale and scope of such 'delegated legislation' had been of concern to parliamentarians for years (Fox and Blackwell 2014), but Brexit threatened a further step change in this direction. It was clear early on that the sheer volume of detailed legislative revision needed for Brexit would necessitate significant delegated powers—for example, to amend statute to remove the names of European regulators and replace them with UK bodies (Constitution Committee 2017b). But powers too broad could allow ministers to go beyond necessary technical revision and enact more fundamental policy changes without oversight by parliament. The extent of discretion sought by ministers shocked many, with the Lords Constitution Committee (2017a: 13–14) identifying 'an unprecedented and extraordinary portmanteau of effectively unlimited powers'. This led to some changes, including tightening up the bill's wording over when powers delegated to ministers could be used, though these remained very extensive. Amendments also introduced a somewhat greater degree of oversight, creating a 'sifting' mechanism in both chambers for legislation made using the powers delegated in the bill; this idea had been supported to varying extents by key parliamentary committees (Constitution Committee 2017b, Delegated Powers and Regulatory Reform Committee 2018, Procedure Committee 2018b).

As well as this, the process of transposing EU legislation onto the UK statute book raised some fundamental rule of law issues. In particular, the translation of EU law into domestic legal categories raised questions about the extent of long-term ministerial control over this legislation—including whether it should have the status of primary or delegated legislation. Questions also arose over how the courts should treat EU case law. These highly technical matters became the subject of significant attention by parliamentarians, parliamentary committees, and external experts (Constitution Committee 2017a, 2018, Craig 2018, Elliott 2017b), and led to multiple changes to the bill. For example, it was agreed that UK courts could continue to take future European Court of Justice (ECJ) decisions into account in their decisions. But the thorny question of the status of retained EU law was to resurface later (see Chapter 11).

A third key area of constitutional dispute was devolution. Brexit would involve substantial repatriation of powers to the UK, but many of these powers would be in policy areas that had been devolved to Scotland, Wales, and Northern Ireland since the 1990s, such as agriculture and environmental protection. Questions therefore arose over whether such repatriated powers would go to Westminster or to the devolved institutions. Devolution had taken place in the context of an EU framework which limited the scope for policy divergence within the UK, protecting its common market (Bogdanor 2019). But some argued that if Westminster took over this role post-Brexit it would represent a disruption of the post-devolution status quo (Rawlings 2017). The initial government proposals in the bill would have automatically reserved all such powers to Westminster, unless the UK government proactively released them to the devolved nations. This provoked a furious response from the Scottish and Welsh First Ministers, who condemned it as a 'naked power grab' (Jones and Sturgeon 2017).[14] Experts noted that this demonstrated the lack of trust between Westminster and the devolved administrations (Paun 2017). Discussions took place with the devolved governments, and when the bill was in the Lords, ministers introduced amendments to reverse the original position—with powers returned to the devolved nations by default, unless specifically reserved to Westminster. On this basis, the then Welsh Assembly (now Parliament) gave its legislative consent to the bill, but the Scottish Parliament did not.[15] Nonetheless, as the Supreme Court had confirmed in early 2017 (see Chapter 4), such consent was not legally necessary for Westminster to agree the proposals.

Attempts in the Bill to Shape the Timing and Form of Brexit

While there were heated arguments about the technicalities of the post-Brexit legal arrangements, the bigger political questions for many parliamentarians concerned the form of the future UK–EU relationship. The bill became a vehicle for amendments supported both by hardline Brexiteers and by proponents of a softer form of Brexit, plus those who wanted the final agreement reached with the EU to be subject to a further referendum. However, the various splits in parliament meant that very little change resulted.

Exit Day

One of the earliest topics introduced was that of exit day—the date on which the UK would leave the EU. The debate on this was initiated by the government, with Theresa May announcing in November 2017 that the government would bring forward amendments to specify exit day as 29 March 2019. This was an attempt to placate ERG members, after the Florence speech a few weeks earlier had raised their suspicions that May was softening her position. A government interviewee indicated that the decision to put exit day into the bill 'was entirely driven by the whips' office, and by trying to keep the Brexiteers and the ERG onside', while another noted that civil servants had strongly advised against the plan. More pro-European MPs, meanwhile, were immediately concerned by the new proposal—believing that it would weaken the UK's hand in the negotiations, while creating a legal cliff edge that increased the risk of a no-deal exit.

This row quickly demonstrated the levels of vitriol which were coming to characterize the Brexit debates, including within the Conservative Party. With a rebellion by pro-European Conservatives clearly likely, the government brought forward its amendments for discussion but did not push them to a vote. The following day, the front page of the *Telegraph* named the 15 Tory 'Brexit mutineers' believed likely to rebel, with a quote from Bernard Jenkin claiming that such MPs were 'open to the charge that they do not actually want us to leave the European Union' (Swinford 2017). The 'mutineers', meanwhile, refused to back down; but one of them, Anna Soubry, cited abuse and threats which her office was receiving from Brexit-supporting members of the public (Groves and Doyle 2017).

A solution to this impasse was brokered by David Cameron's former right-hand man on Brexit, Oliver Letwin. It involved inserting exit day into the bill as ministers had planned, but including a mechanism which would allow the date subsequently to be changed easily via delegated legislation. The Brexiteers got to see a date for exit day included in the bill. The pro-Europeans were reassured that the UK could if necessary agree later to an Article 50 extension, to avoid 'crashing out' of the EU without a deal, without the need for parliament to approve further primary legislation. The upshot of needing to balance both competing sides of the party was ultimately that the policy more or less stood still.

Pressure for a Softer Brexit

The most overt attempts to bind the government's hands in negotiations sought to secure either a customs union or European Economic Area (EEA) membership (which, as indicated in the discussion of cross-party groups above, would entail something close to full membership of the Single Market). Soft Brexiteers in both the Commons and the Lords, particularly on the Labour side, attempted to insert these as negotiating objectives in the bill.

At least some of these advocates clearly hoped that the government might be willing to compromise on its Brexit strategy at this point. One Labour interviewee closely involved with the amendments recalled, 'I thought I would get a phone call and somebody would say "alright so is your party going to move then?", and maybe we'd get a Single Market deal and take it over the line...And, you know, that never happened.' But the Labour organizers were also using the bill to try and flush out the position of their own frontbench, and largely failed. The fate of these amendments, and the ultimate inability to agree a compromise, reflected how far not just the Conservative side but also Labour was split over the form that Brexit should take.

Labour's dilemma was evident over a raft of customs union and EEA amendments tabled by its own backbenchers at Commons committee stage. The party whipped to abstain on most of these amendments, but a sizeable number of Labour backbenchers broke the whip, mostly to support them. A customs union amendment tabled by Chris Leslie was supported, against the party whip, by 62 Labour MPs. Later, at report stage, 48 Labour MPs voted for an SNP amendment that aimed to keep the UK in the Single Market and Customs Union.

These arguments continued in the House of Lords, where Labour votes significantly contributed to two key defeats in April and May 2018 on amendments which sought to impose negotiating objectives upon the government. The first came from Crossbench peer Lord (John) Kerr of Kinlochard, a former senior diplomat who had been involved in the original drafting of Article 50, and sought to encourage continued membership of a customs union. It was carefully worded simply to require the government to report on its efforts in this area, which enabled the Labour frontbench to support it. Along with votes from 24 Conservative rebels, this led to a heavy government defeat. Nonetheless, when the bill returned to the Commons the commitment was watered down by a government amendment using the looser preferred terminology of a 'customs arrangement'. This was adequate, for now, to placate pro-European Conservatives.

The second defeat was more challenging for Labour. Sponsored by party backbencher Lord (Waheed) Alli, it sought to build on Kerr's amendment by stating that the government must adopt a negotiating objective of keeping the UK in the EEA. This caused evident difficulties for the Labour frontbench, which asked its members to abstain. But the amendment passed when 83 Labour peers broke ranks to vote for it, along with 17 Conservatives. When the bill returned to the Commons, there was potential for a government defeat had Labour supported the Lords position, and a small number of Conservatives rebelled. But the Labour frontbench again whipped to abstain. Although 74 party MPs defied the whip to vote for the pro-EEA position, including one junior shadow minister who resigned to support it (Culbertson 2018), this made it doomed to fail.[16] These events highlighted the depth of division on the Labour side, and the early failure to build a cross-party soft Brexit alliance.

The EU (Withdrawal) Bill was far from the only piece of domestic legislation necessary to ready the UK for Brexit. A raft of other bills was also needed, either making sector-specific changes or creating the frameworks and ministerial powers to, for example, establish a new tariffs regime. Rebels were conscious that this gave them multiple opportunities to try to impose their preferred negotiating objectives on the government, meaning that defeat on the EU (Withdrawal) Bill was not the end of the line. By the time the Alli amendment was overturned in the Commons, a similar EEA amendment had already been tabled to the government's Trade Bill. That bill would ultimately be so significantly amended in the Lords that ministers indefinitely paused its passage, rather than risking further defeats when it returned to the Commons.

Hence the EU (Withdrawal) Bill appears in retrospect a missed opportunity by proponents of a soft Brexit, and also a missed opportunity for Theresa May to build a majority around such a compromise. During the bill's Lords report stage the *Times* suggested that she might 'surrender' over membership of a customs union, claiming that a source close to her had said that she and her team would 'not be crying into our beer' if this were forced upon her (Shipman and Wheeler 2018). But Labour's reticence over the matter meant that there was insufficient parliamentary pressure on the Prime Minister to necessitate such a concession.

A Further Referendum

Finally, alongside these attempts to determine the form of Brexit, some parliamentarians used the EU (Withdrawal) Bill to continue agitating for a further referendum. This was another question on which Labour remained internally split, and in this case the Liberal Democrats were the primary advocates of change. As during the earlier passage of the EU (Notification of Withdrawal) Bill, discussed in Chapter 4, their best opportunities came through the House of Lords, where it is easier to get minority amendments debated, and the party could more readily benefit from the support of rebels in other parties.

One such rebel was former Labour Cabinet minister Lord Adonis, who proposed an unusual amendment at Lords second reading, regretting that the bill did not include a commitment to a referendum on the final terms of the Brexit deal. But the party's frontbench did not support him, and he withdrew the amendment rather than putting it to the vote.

At the subsequent Lords report stage, the Liberal Democrat frontbench moved another amendment calling for a referendum. Labour, once again, was split. The party whipped to abstain, with deputy leader Baroness (Dianne) Hayter of Kentish Town arguing that demanding a second referendum would 'foster more division and distrust' and that it would be seen 'simply as a device to stop Brexit rather than a serious poll on the terms negotiated'.[17] The amendment was voted down, but 51 Labour peers (and four Conservatives) rebelled to vote for it.

The proposal of a second referendum remained distinctly taboo in parliament at this stage of the Brexit debates. Only later would public pressure on the issue grow, with the first People's Vote rally taking place two months after the Lords report stage. As Labour did not embrace the idea until significantly later (and even then less than wholeheartedly), it is more difficult to see this as a missed opportunity on the bill. Instead, the question of a second referendum would reach centre stage only after Theresa May's Brexit deal had been defeated, as discussed in Chapter 8.

Conclusion

In the months following the 2017 general election the work of preparing for Brexit began in earnest. This period demonstrated early signs of the key difficulties that lay ahead.

Following the referendum, and Theresa May's early statements, there remained limited clarity about how Brexit would be implemented. Negotiations began between the UK government and the EU, but the UK failed to specify its preferred destination, beyond the previously articulated 'red lines'. The election result left the Prime Minister, more than ever, struggling to appeal simultaneously to all sides of her divided party. But now she had also to confront reality regarding the outcomes, and consequences, achievable through the negotiations. In particular, Brexit's potential impact on the Northern Ireland border became a growing preoccupation. Both the UK and EU were committed to avoiding a hard border, but the difficulties of achieving this, without either breaching May's red lines or developing a distinct status for Northern Ireland, proved intractable. This led to the idea of the 'backstop', an ostensibly temporary arrangement to maintain an open border in the absence of workable solutions emerging during the subsequent future relationship negotiations. But this implied alignment at some level with EU rules, which fuelled increasing controversy among Brexiteers.

As the reality of negotiating Brexit sank in, differing groups in parliament consolidated in support of the various possible outcomes. The most well known, and probably best organized, was the Eurosceptic ERG, which campaigned for a hard Brexit. ERG supporters had initially welcomed Theresa May's Brexit stance, as articulated at the 2016 party conference and at Lancaster House. Post election—particularly as it became clearer that the Prime Minister might be drawn to 'softer' Brexit options to resolve the Northern Ireland issue—this group grew increasingly hostile. It began more actively to hold May to her previous words, coming increasingly to see her threatened no-deal Brexit as a desirable alternative.

Other groups in parliament pursued objectives that explicitly conflicted with those of the ERG. Many Conservatives (particularly former Remainers) favoured explicit long-term commitment to a close relationship with the EU, which would prioritize frictionless trade as well as an open Northern Ireland border. Former Remainers on the Labour side argued openly for continued membership of the Single Market and/or a customs union if Brexit was to proceed. However, a growing number also began to see merit in putting any agreed Brexit deal to a further referendum (often dubbed a 'confirmatory' referendum or 'people's vote'). As time went on, all of these groups' positions became increasingly entrenched.

The Labour leadership, meanwhile, remained reluctant to come down clearly on any side of the argument, leaving the party's position ambiguous and its parliamentarians divided. As discussed in the next chapter, the opposition's role is generally to oppose rather than necessarily to construct coherent alternatives. But Labour's divisions, coupled with the fragmentation of positions by moderates on both sides of the Commons, undermined opportunities to construct a majority that could steer May away from her apparently hardline position. Chances to require the government to negotiate a 'soft' Brexit—particularly through amendments to the European Union (Withdrawal) Bill—were consequently missed. The original contents of the bill, meanwhile, raised various constitutional concerns which would remain contentious post Brexit.

Parliamentarians used a wide range of mechanisms beyond legislation to scrutinize and question the government over its Brexit policy. Theresa May was often subjected to intense grilling during statements to the House of Commons, and Brexit became a key subject for consideration by select committees. Although these mechanisms could not force decisions, parliament's status as an open public forum for accountability frequently flushed out the contradictions in the government's position, as well as the internal divisions within the parties. In this period, MPs also began to innovate procedurally in response to the government's resistance to parliamentary involvement. A key example was Labour's adoption of the humble address procedure, to extract information from the government which it was otherwise not prepared to give.

In all of these ways, the initial post-election period began to exhibit patterns which became more visible later, as relations within parliament increasingly broke down. Theresa May's approach was closed and secretive, excluding even her own Cabinet—which itself was deeply divided over Brexit. Both main party leaders stubbornly sought to downplay the difficult trade-offs involved in Brexit, and avoid decisions that would alienate groups within their divided parties. In response, backbenchers sought new means to influence the process, including increasingly by working across party lines—but were themselves too fractured to form a majority. Such trends were to intensify in the months ahead.

Notes

1. See, for example, David Davis, House of Commons Hansard, 12 June 2018, column 741.
2. Under the CRAG provisions, the government must lay signed treaties before parliament. Both chambers have 21 days to object to the treaty's contents prior to ratification. If the Commons does object, the government must put forward its case in a written statement, starting another 21-day countdown. The House of Lords can also object to the treaty but, unlike with the Commons, this does not prevent ratification. Instead, the government can simply make a statement explaining its rationale.
3. As a result of Brexit, parliament's treaty scrutiny capacity was enhanced through the creation of the House of Lords International Agreements Committee (Horne 2021). This was followed by agreements between the committee and the government about standards for the scrutiny of post-Brexit free trade agreements (Hayter 2022), though disputes over the extent of these commitments and their operation have since continued.
4. 'Mixed' treaties—those covering policy areas which are within the competence of member states—must also be ratified at national level.
5. Free movement of people between Northern Ireland and the Republic of Ireland is provided for by the Common Travel Area (CTA). The CTA predates the UK's EU membership, having existed in various forms since 1922.
6. House of Commons Hansard, 28 February 2018, column 823.

7. Speaking in the European Parliament debate on 'Guidelines on the framework of future EU–UK relations', 13 March 2018.

8. It was so named because it met over takeaway in Leadsom's office.

9. House of Commons Hansard, 23 October 2017, column 36. See columns 28 and 32 for speeches by Clarke and Soubry.

10. Ibid., 5 March 2018, columns 33, 36, 44.

11. Ibid., 5 March 2018, columns 34, 37.

12. Ibid., 10 October 2017, column 225.

13. Ibid., 2 November 2017, column 977.

14. Northern Ireland continued to lack an Assembly or Executive, following the collapse of power-sharing in January 2017.

15. Official Report of the Scottish Parliament, 15 May 2018, column 76.

16. Only three Conservatives supported it—Ken Clarke, Dominic Grieve, and Anna Soubry; however, these numbers might have been higher if Labour had been whipping in favour, as without that the proposal faced certain defeat.

17. House of Lords Hansard, 30 April 2018, column 1895.

7

The Emerging Deal and the Meaningful Vote

As the previous chapter described, the formal Brexit negotiations began immediately after the 2017 general election; but the government's objectives were vague and progress was slow. Parliamentarians, meanwhile, were divided and sought to influence the negotiations in conflicting directions. Both Theresa May and Jeremy Corbyn did their best to hedge, in order to contain the conflicts in their own parties. But the timetable for Brexit was fixed by Article 50, and this prevarication could not continue forever. Sooner or later the negotiations had to end, and a decision on the UK's future be reached.

It was only in summer 2018, at a meeting at the Prime Minister's country residence of Chequers, that the Cabinet agreed a blueprint for the UK's preferred future relationship with the EU. This triggered a serious rupture in the Conservative Party. Meanwhile, concerns among many parliamentarians about the threat of a no-deal exit—which risked severe disruption both to the economy and the Northern Ireland peace settlement—were rising. A dominant theme during the passage of the European Union (Withdrawal) Bill was the role that MPs should have in approving any final deal—and more importantly, in what would happen if no agreement could be reached. This resulted in a major showdown between government and parliament (or more specifically, between the Prime Minister and her backbenchers) over the nature of the so-called 'meaningful vote', and subsequently over the Brexit deal itself.

The chapter begins by reviewing the role of the opposition at Westminster. This was crucial in an environment of minority government, particularly since the Prime Minister could not be assured even of her own party's support. The chapter then considers the arguments over the EU (Withdrawal) Bill regarding parliament's right to a meaningful vote on the final Brexit outcome. Next, it gives an account of the emerging tensions within the Conservative Party over the Chequers proposals and the subsequent deal reached with the EU. This culminated in the first meaningful vote in January 2019, where May's government suffered the largest parliamentary defeat on record. The defeat left the Prime Minister further weakened, and both parliament and Brexit in disarray.

The Role of the Opposition

As Chapter 5 discussed, the unexpected arrival of minority government after the 2017 general election reawakened questions about whether a broad alliance, including figures from within Labour, could be formed to deliver Brexit. While there was always a strong case after the referendum for making Brexit a national endeavour that cut across party lines, the post-election numbers in parliament made this look almost a necessity. But Theresa May rejected such proposals, while at the same time criticizing Labour for not supporting her Brexit plans. From the Labour opposition's point of view, there may have been principled arguments in favour of offering to support the government's implementation of the referendum result. But various other factors always made this unlikely. Among them were the traditions of opposition at Westminster.

The notion of opposition exists in some sense in all democratic parliaments—there will almost always be parties that are excluded from the government. But cultures of opposition differ, and the system at Westminster is often seen as particularly adversarial. This flows, in large part, from the electoral system tending to deliver single-party majorities. Because coalitions and minority governments are fairly rare, there is generally little need for institutionalized party cooperation. Although the culture of cross-party working at Westminster is often underestimated (for a discussion see Russell and Gover 2017), the normal expectation is of an alternation between one of the large parties serving in government and the other serving in opposition, with limited cooperation between them over policy. In contrast, systems where minority or coalition government are frequent tend to normalize cross-party engagement.

Academic studies emphasize that a central function of opposition parties is to expose the government's weaknesses, in part in order to present themselves as a credible alternative government (Blondel 1997, Helms 2008, Johnson 1997, Kaiser 2008). This role, which is particularly institutionalized in the UK system, may exaggerate differences but can be very effective for accountability. Awkward questions from the opposition ensure that government policies are properly exposed to scrutiny. In acknowledgement of this important role, 'His Majesty's loyal opposition' has official recognition at Westminster, and is privileged in House of Commons procedures in various ways. These include the provision of opposition days, and guaranteed speaking rights for opposition frontbenchers during parliamentary question times and debates. As Norton (2008) has emphasized, there is a balance here: the opposition has a right to be heard, but the government—providing it can command a majority—ultimately has the ability to get its policies agreed.

The dynamic of opposition can present a major dilemma to parties that hold that role, which is well recognized in the academic literature. While there may be merit in supporting government policies in the national inter-est, too much support could compromise accountability, and crucially make it hard for the opposition party to present a sufficiently distinct appeal to the electorate (Prasser 2009, Punnett 1973). At the same time, opposing too fiercely could damage the opposition's electoral appeal by making it appear overly obstructive. The behaviour expected, and tolerated, by the public is in part a matter of national culture. Comparing across democracies, one scholar has suggested that Westminster demonstrates 'a standout case of negative rather than constructive oppositional politics' (Uhr 2009: 67). This allows opposition parties to focus primarily on knocking down the government's position, without necessarily having to develop fully thought-through policy alternatives of their own.

The dilemmas of opposition are well understood and articulated by Westminster politicians. For example, Jacob Rees-Mogg has publicly defended a culture where the opposition seeks actively to undermine the government, suggesting that 'you want to stymie your opponents, not help them' (Procedure Committee 2013: 16). Interviewees for this book, from across the political divide, strongly recognized such a dynamic. A senior Labour figure commented that 'trying to make life difficult for the government is always a really important part of the opposition's motivation'. Likewise, a member of May's own Cabinet conceded,

> I've been in opposition and it's very, very difficult to get over that because even if you have an instinct to do something a bit more constructive, oppositions are measured by their propensity to oppose. And if they don't, leaders of the oppos-ition get accused of being weak, useless, not doing their job, etc. So [offering sup-port] is difficult from an opposition point of view.

This standard culture was not the only thing preventing the opposition from supporting the government on Brexit. First, the divisions in the Conservative Party made such behaviour even less attractive than it might normally be. Should the government side fall apart over the Prime Minister's Brexit policy, Labour stood potentially to gain. This might even have resulted in the abandonment of Brexit—a policy that few Labour politicians had ever considered to be in the interests of the country. Second, supporting the government would require Labour to confront its own internal divisions, and to expose itself to condemnation by one side or the other of its delicate electoral coalition of Brexit-voting heartlands and Remain-supporting metropolitan seats. Throughout this period, there was a very high risk of fundamental splits in both parties over Brexit, and both prioritized trying to hold together.

King's classic account of the dynamics at Westminster characterized the dominant pattern in the House of Commons as the 'opposition mode', noting that the 'cross-party' or 'non-party' mode might be more familiar in some other democratic parliaments. But this was not presented as a problem, given that the government routinely had a Commons majority and depended primarily on its own backbenchers (as discussed in Chapter 2). As King (1976: 18) put it, the 'Government fully expects the Opposition to make hostile speeches. It does not need, or want, the Opposition's moral support... [or] votes.'

In the unusual circumstances of Brexit, particularly under minority government post 2017, ministers might instead have benefited very greatly from the opposition's votes. But Theresa May was for a long time reluctant to admit this, and did nothing initially to encourage the opposition's support. Without such appeals, and given the divisiveness of Brexit, the opposition's own first instinct was understandably to steer clear of the political risks involved in stepping in to rescue the government.

The EU (Withdrawal) Bill and the Battle for the Meaningful Vote

As Chapter 4 highlighted, MPs raised three key questions about parliament's involvement in the Brexit process almost immediately after the referendum, one of which was its role in approving the final Brexit deal. This was eventually answered through Theresa May's (2017a) promise in her Lancaster House speech that the deal would be put to 'both Houses of Parliament' for approval. The pledge was then repeated in the Conservative manifesto in 2017, while Labour's manifesto proposed that parliament should have a 'truly meaningful vote' on the final deal (Labour Party 2017).

Attempts to use the European Union (Notification of Withdrawal) Bill to secure a guaranteed vote on the deal had failed in 2017. But the argument subsequently resurfaced during the passage of the European Union (Withdrawal) Bill. This bill was substantively discussed in the previous chapter, and was used by parliamentarians to attempt to influence the Brexit negotiations. But it also became a key vehicle for debating parliament's appropriate role in approving the final deal. This resulted in the biggest overall showdown between government and parliament on the bill.

At least initially, what exactly constituted a 'meaningful vote' was ill-defined. Many instinctively believed that parliament should have a 'meaningful' role in the final decision on a Brexit deal, and that it would be highly inappropriate for the government to settle such huge questions about the country's future purely using prerogative powers. As described in Chapter 6, different arguments exist regarding the merits of executive freedom in international negotiations, with both the EU and some other countries requiring higher levels of parliamentary accountability than had traditionally been the case in the UK. But how exactly parliament could exercise such a role, particularly once Article 50 had been triggered, and the UK's departure from the EU looked both a legal and political inevitability, was unclear. Meanwhile, the May government's reluctance to make commitments about parliament's role fed suspicions.

The most obvious mechanism for parliamentary approval was through the implementing legislation for Brexit. But a vote on the legislation alone promised parliamentarians little real control, absent an earlier vote on the principle of the Brexit deal. It was less clear whether and how parliament would get this. The biggest conundrum of all, however, which came increasingly to the fore during the passage of this bill, concerned what would happen in the event that the government failed to reach an agreement with the EU, or if the deal agreed was voted down by parliament. With the UK on the two-year conveyor belt to exit set out in Article 50, either outcome could lead to 'crashing out' of the EU without a deal, which most commentators considered deeply undesirable (see Chapter 4). But as the necessary compromises to achieve a deal became gradually clearer, hardline Brexiteers grew progressively more attracted to this outcome. Theresa May, meanwhile, refused to rule it out. Hence other parliamentarians who feared the ERG's influence focused increasingly on how such an outcome could be stopped. Because MPs have limited control over which big questions get debated in the Commons (as discussed further in Chapter 8), they could not rely on trying to force parliamentary decisions on the government at later stages. The EU (Withdrawal) Bill thus presented a key opportunity to guarantee in statute that parliament would get a say.

The Grieve Amendment in the Commons

The first steps toward the meaningful vote came in the Commons. Demands at this stage focused fairly narrowly on guaranteeing parliament's right to approve primary legislation on the deal before it could be formally brought into effect. These were headed by former Conservative Attorney General Dominic Grieve, who feared that clause 9 of the bill—which delegated extensive powers to ministers for the specific purpose of enacting the Withdrawal Agreement—could be used to implement a Brexit deal without full parliamentary approval.

Whether ministers ever seriously considered this route is unclear, but their muddled responses certainly fuelled suspicions. On 7 September 2017, at the bill's second reading, ExEU Committee chair Hilary Benn asked Secretary of State David Davis to confirm that the government would not use the powers in clause 9 to implement a withdrawal agreement before parliament had voted upon it. Davis appeared unprepared for the question, and prevaricated rather than fully agreeing. The following month, answering questions from Benn's committee, Davis suggested that parliament's vote on the deal might not occur until after it had come into effect (Exiting the European Union Committee 2017a). Theresa May stated at Prime Minister's Questions later the same day that she was 'confident' MPs would get a vote before the UK left the EU; but this fell short of a cast-iron guarantee.[1] And even if parliament did get a vote shortly before Brexit day, this might give it little choice but to approve what it considered an unacceptable deal.

On 13 November, before the bill's Commons committee stage, David Davis made a parliamentary statement promising that there would be further implementing legislation for the deal—dubbed the Withdrawal Agreement and Implementation Bill (WAIB).[2] This was intended to reassure pro-European Conservative MPs. But they responded with concerns about the risks of either a no-deal exit or parliament being presented with a proposition at the last moment on a 'take it or leave it' basis.

At the bill's committee stage itself, Grieve proposed an amendment preventing the government from using the clause 9 powers to implement Brexit unless parliament had first passed a statute approving the terms of the deal. Ominously for the government, the nine lead signatories on Grieve's amendment were all Conservatives—more than enough to inflict a Commons defeat.[3] Ministers might have been expected to back down, given that they had already promised implementing legislation, but they did not. Speaking for the government, Dominic Raab argued that it was 'important that the necessary legislative mechanisms are available to us'—which implied that delegated legislation might indeed be used.[4] Avowed Brexiteers accused Grieve of an 'attempt to reverse Brexit'.[5] This seemed to be an overstatement, but there was a valid question regarding what would happen if Commons consent was withheld. Oliver Letwin inquired whether Grieve's intention was to ensure that 'if this House does not approve the terms on which we leave…we should not leave'.[6] With the Article 50 clock ticking, the fallback position would instead be a no-deal Brexit.

The government was keen to maintain freedom of manoeuvre. Number 10 insider Nikki da Costa (2021) subsequently stated that she saw the meaningful vote as 'the biggest threat' to delivering Brexit, and had sought 'to do everything possible to prevent it'. Attempting to head off Grieve's amendment, Raab promised a government amendment at the subsequent report stage. But Grieve, who had already held informal discussions with the government and been disappointed by the results, pushed it to the vote. The government was defeated by 309 to 305, with 11 Conservatives supporting Grieve's amendment.[7] This was Theresa May's first defeat in the House of Commons as Prime Minister, and the first ever rebellion by several of these MPs.

The response from the Brexit-supporting media was largely predictable, and painted the intervention as an anti-Brexit move rather than one seeking to enhance parliamentary accountability. The following day's *Daily Mail* front page pictured the rebels, with the banner headline 'Proud of Yourselves?' (Groves 2017). The *Sun* (2017b) answered this question in its editorial, suggesting that 'Tory rebels should be ashamed', and claiming that '[f]or most the real goal is to delay or halt Brexit'. The *Daily Telegraph* (2017) editorial acknowledged this, but also noted that the rebels 'blame[d] Government obduracy for placing them in this position'.

The Lords Stages

Grieve's amendment had imposed a requirement for primary legislation to implement the Brexit deal. But it had done nothing to answer the trickier question of what would happen in the event that no deal was reached or that, when a parliamentary vote took place, the deal was rejected. This became a central focus during debates on the bill in the House of Lords.

The Lords' second reading of the bill took place in January. Labour's leader in the chamber, Baroness (Angela) Smith of Basildon, was among those who welcomed the Grieve amendment, but argued that 'the Bill must set out how Parliament will play a truly meaningful role in the process, including if we face the most catastrophic of possible outcomes, that of no deal'.[8] These concerns were raised repeatedly during committee stage, by Conservative as well as opposition peers. The minister insisted that there would be a parliamentary vote as soon as negotiations concluded, but emphasized that the choice would be 'to accept the terms of the final agreement or to move forward without a deal'.[9] This understandably failed to appease peers who feared a 'take it or leave it' vote.

At the subsequent report stage, the key meaningful vote amendment came from Conservative peer Viscount Hailsham, and was co-signed by a senior Crossbencher, and representatives of the Labour and Liberal Democrat frontbenches. It set out a series of deadlines, suggesting that the Commons should approve the deal by 30 November 2018, and the statute to implement it by 28 February 2019. If either condition went unmet, or there was still no deal agreed by 31 January 2019, the House of Commons could formally instruct the government on its next steps. Notably, despite the Lancaster House promise that 'both Houses' would be required to approve the deal, peers deliberately did not attempt to impose approval by the Lords (though this would be required for the implementing legislation).

Hailsham's amendment was controversial. Brexit-supporting peers argued that it overstepped parliament's role in foreign affairs, seeking to turn parliament into the government. Former Conservative leader Lord (Michael) Howard of Lympne claimed that it could 'lead to not one but several constitutional crises'.[10] Lord (Martin) Callanan, for the government, largely concurred, suggesting that it 'would create a profound constitutional shift in terms of which branch of the state holds the prerogative to act in the international sphere'.[11] However, supporters expressed concerns that, unless the protections in the amendment were added, the UK could end up leaving the EU both without a deal and without parliament having approved such an outcome.

The amendment ultimately passed by 335 votes to 244, supported strongly by Labour, Liberal Democrats, and most Crossbenchers, alongside 19 Conservative rebel peers. The latter included some notable figures who had previously been ministers, such as Lord (Michael) Heseltine, former European Commissioner Lord (Chris) Patten of Barnes and Lord (David) Willetts.

The defeat provoked a furious response from the pro-Brexit media, with the *Daily Mail* front page headline pronouncing the Lords a 'House of Unelected Wreckers' (Stevens 2018a). Immediately before the vote David Davis (2018a) had written in the *Sun* that 'those who want to overturn the result of the Referendum have been calling for a "no Brexit option" for months, and this amendment would grant it to them'. Whether this interpretation was correct depended on whether the Article 50 trigger was reversible—which remained legally undecided at that stage[12]—as well as how the House of Commons might choose to use such a power. But the

Lords alone could not put the meaningful vote into statute; the bill's final wording would need to be endorsed by the Commons, and it now returned there.

The Drama of the Parliamentary Ping-pong

Hailsham's amendment put huge pressure on the government, given the clear anxiety among many Conservative backbenchers about a no-deal exit. In principle, if ministers are defeated on an amendment in the House of Lords, they can simply ask MPs to overturn it; but where there is sympathy for the Lords' position among government backbenchers, a compromise will often be agreed (Russell 2013). This clearly seemed necessary in the case of the Hailsham amendment. But ministers were determined not to concede on the meaningful vote, and the resultant 'ping-pong' between the two chambers became the single biggest drama over government legislation during the whole Brexit period (though plenty more drama was soon to follow on other matters).

When the EU (Withdrawal) Bill returned to the Commons on 12 June 2018, the government did propose a compromise amendment, stating that ministers could only ratify a Brexit deal if this had both been approved in principle by MPs and implementing legislation had been passed by parliament. If parliament did not approve the deal, the government would be required to provide a written statement within 28 days indicating its next steps. But the government's proposal removed the opportunity for formal instruction by the Commons as envisaged in the Hailsham amendment, and removed its deadlines. This offered little certainty to MPs concerned about a situation in which no deal with the EU had been agreed. Dominic Grieve, who had been working behind the scenes with Hailsham, therefore took up the cause of the meaningful vote again, and proposed an amendment to toughen up the government's new proposals. This required ministers to present a motion if the deal had not been approved by 30 November 2018, or if there had been no deal agreed by 15 February 2019. By default, MPs would be able to amend such a motion, and Grieve's proposal explicitly stated that in the event of no deal the government must follow the Commons' direction. On the day of the debate the tensions inside government became clear when Phillip Lee, a junior minister at the Ministry of Justice, resigned to support Grieve's amendment.

In debate, Grieve and his supporters emphasized the need for meaningful parliamentary input in the event that there was no deal agreed. But David

Davis echoed the arguments made in the Lords, that it would be 'a profound constitutional shift' for parliament to be able to direct the government in foreign affairs.[13] He also emphasized that it was 'incredibly, almost implausibly, unlikely' that the government would choose to pursue a no-deal exit.[14] This came closer than previous government utterances towards ruling out no deal; but this clearly remained the default if parliament rejected a deal—as several of his ministerial colleagues had already stressed during debates on the bill. Plus, it was by now evident that significant numbers of hardline Brexiteers were attracted to a no-deal outcome. If this remained the default, they could potentially achieve it by blocking the deal; hence they strongly opposed Grieve's amendment. One characterized it as 'the ultimate wrecking amendment…wrecking of the will of the people and democracy'.[15] The levels of anger between these two opposing groups on the Conservative backbenches (see Grieve 2020) clearly left the whips and Downing Street in a very difficult position.

Grieve was ultimately persuaded to climb down, on the promise of more talks with the government. In particular, Solicitor General Robert Buckland gave clear indications that talks would result in a toughened-up government amendment when the bill returned to the Lords. This averted a further Commons defeat. The *Guardian* reported that Theresa May had met with 14 Conservative supporters of Grieve's amendment immediately prior to the vote, and given 'personal assurances that she would agree to the broad thrust of their proposals'. The government's amendment watering down Hailsham's proposal was approved, but Grieve insisted that further talks 'must be done in good faith'.[16]

Negotiations of this kind are not unusual, though the tensions on this occasion were both very public and very high. The government rarely accepts rebel amendments in their original form, preferring to do its own redrafting (Russell and Gover 2017). But ministers found themselves trapped between demands from the two conflicting rebel groups, and continued to try and fudge the matter rather than picking sides.

Although talks took place with Grieve, ministers backtracked on the assurances that Buckland had provided. The government amendment proposed in the Lords on 18 June did not offer the promised safeguards, instead stating explicitly that any motion proposed by ministers in the event of no deal would be in 'neutral terms'. In the language of parliamentary standing orders, this signalled that it would be unamendable: MPs might be asked to note the outcome, but would not be able to propose alternatives. Grieve told the *Times* that he found the government's reversal 'incomprehensible and unacceptable' (Wright and Coates 2018), while fellow rebel Anna Soubry described it as 'unforgivable', claiming that the group felt 'badly let down' by Theresa May (Sculthorpe, Tapsfield, and Ferguson 2018).

This resulted in a furious debate in the Lords. Viscount Hailsham moved an alternative amendment, which he claimed incorporated the words agreed privately by the government (one procedural specialist commented in interview that it 'did very much have the air of a government draft'). It sought to guarantee MPs an amendable motion in the event of no deal. Hailsham argued that his purpose in proposing this was merely 'to send to the Commons the agreement which Dominic Grieve and others thought they had reached with the Prime Minister'.[17] The Lords backed the proposal by a larger margin (354 to 235) than the original Hailsham amendment, with 21 Conservatives voting against the government.

The bill now returned to the Commons again. Here the government attempted to amend Hailsham's wording, to reiterate that any motion would be in 'neutral terms'. At this point, ministers sought to convince wavering MPs with reassurances that did not really procedurally stand up. David Davis published a written statement, pointing out that 'it will be for the Speaker to determine whether a motion . . . is or is not in fact cast in neutral terms and hence whether the motion is or is not amendable'.[18] This appeared to signal to the rebels that John Bercow might be able to help their cause. But as Hilary Benn pointed out in debate, the wording of such motions is very straightforward; so, 'as long as the Government do their job in drafting the motion, the Speaker will have no choice'.[19] Nonetheless, few MPs will have followed the detail of these complex procedural arguments, so (as is often the case) the decision came down to who they were prepared to trust. Sufficient Conservative rebels were won over, leading Grieve to conclude that the fight was over. Though he had tabled a new amendment to secure an amendable motion, he backed down and—somewhat surprisingly—voted against it. Just six Conservatives voted for it, and the government prevailed. The BBC's Laura Kuenssberg (2018) concluded that the anti-no deal rebels 'weren't willing to take dramatic action in enough numbers to humiliate the PM', and questioned 'if they really have the guts'. In the Lords, where peers had fought to get Grieve the words he wanted, his U-turn left members, in the words of one interviewee, 'exasperated and fed up'.

This was, at least for the moment, the end of the argument on the meaningful vote. The final wording of section 13 of the EU (Withdrawal) Act specified that the government must put any Brexit deal to the House of Commons for approval, and also pass a bill through both chambers in order to put it into effect. In the event that MPs defeated a government motion on a deal, a government statement on next steps was required within 21 days, to be debated on a motion 'in neutral terms' within seven days of its publication. Speedier action of a similar kind was also required if no deal had been agreed by 21 January 2019. This boxed the government in significantly more than it had wanted, but still left the door open to a no deal exit without parliament's approval. As things turned out, while the meaningful vote had been secured by the moderates, the outcome strengthened the position of hardline Brexiteers.

From Chequers to the Meaningful Vote

Chequers

Up to this point Theresa May had just about kept her party together. She had done this in no small part by maintaining significant ambiguity about the shape of the final deal. Although triggering Article 50 and laying out red lines without consultation had annoyed many in her party and Cabinet, it had allowed them to get this far through the Brexit process without having to squarely confront the trade-offs inherent in negotiating a deal. But this approach also laid the ground for a major split in the party at the point when ambiguity about the final package was no longer possible. The cracks became obvious following a Cabinet meeting held at the prime ministerial country residence of Chequers on 6 July 2018.

By June, talks with the EU had stalled over the issue of the Northern Ireland border (Menon and Wager 2021). Meanwhile, two competing ideas to remove the need for a backstop had emerged within the Cabinet. May's preferred option was known as a 'facilitated customs arrangement'. Its basic premise was that the UK and EU would collect customs duties on one another's behalf on goods passing through one territory en route to the other. This would allow the UK to set different tariffs to the EU, but remove the need for customs checks between them. The arrangement would be complemented by a 'common rulebook' which would maintain shared UK–EU goods standards. These proposals had been floated informally with a handful of EU politicians to mixed response, but were far from being agreed (Barwell 2021). Commentators warned that the EU was unlikely to accept what could be seen as an attempt to be both in and out of a customs union (Grey 2021). The alternative scheme championed by Cabinet Eurosceptics was dubbed maximum facilitation (or 'max fac'), and proposed to use technology to minimize the need for border checks, removing, they argued, the need for any continued alignment. But critics pointed out that no comparable technological system yet existed anywhere in the world, and that even minimized border checks were not the same as a frictionless Northern Ireland border (Menon and Bevington 2019).

May called the Chequers meeting in order to line up Cabinet support for her facilitated customs arrangement proposal so that she could present it to the EU. But the mood was fragile. Her relationship with David Davis and the ERG had become increasingly strained throughout spring and early summer 2018, as their suspicions mounted about the direction of the negotiations. In early July, Davis reportedly accused May of developing a Brexit policy 'incompatible' with her own manifesto (quoted in Seldon and Newell 2019: 428). Boris Johnson, meanwhile, was said to have convened a group of Brexit-supporting ministers—including Davis, Michael Gove, and Andrea Leadsom—at the Foreign Office, to discuss their concerns. A series of meetings between the Prime Minister and key Cabinet Brexiteers in the run-up to Chequers was not encouraging; Barwell (2021) recalled that, while International Trade Secretary Liam Fox was relatively sanguine, Davis expressed clear frustration—not least because DExEU had separately been working up its own proposals—and Johnson was openly hostile.

By the end of the Chequers meeting the Cabinet had signed up to May's proposals, with Michael Gove instrumental in bringing the Brexiteers around to her side, according to Barwell (2021). But two days later David Davis—along with junior Brexit minister Steve Baker—resigned. In his resignation letter, Davis argued that the Prime Minister's plans, and particularly the proposed common rulebook, would result in 'illusory rather than real' UK autonomy (Sky News 2018b). Boris Johnson (2018a) then resigned the next day, claiming that the proposals for retaining EU standards would see the UK adopt 'the status of colony'. Number 10 had anticipated Davis's possible resignation (Barwell 2020, Davidson 2020). Davis (2021) himself claims to have given 12 hours' notice to Johnson of his intention to go, at which point Johnson 'wasn't enthusiastic about resigning'. Many assumed that ERG members had pressurized the pair after Chequers; Julian Smith (2020) has claimed that 'clearly, they got contacted. They got lobbied to pull back.' Bower (2020) suggests that Johnson felt compelled to resign, as he feared that Davis would become the ERG's preferred leadership candidate if he chose to stay.

Chequers marked a major turning point in the ERG's relationship with May. Its members were openly and vocally unhappy about the proposals, with one MP allegedly calling the Cabinet Brexiteers who had agreed to them 'traitors to the nation' (quoted in Malnick and Mikhailova 2018). A Brexit-supporting interviewee recalled 'I can't describe to you how traumatic the Chequers day was', and how he concluded that 'the government was not trying to deliver Brexit'. Ominously, immediately after the meeting Jacob Rees-Mogg (2018b) wrote in the *Telegraph* that the proposals 'must come before Parliament where there will be a "meaningful" vote'—a procedure that he and other Brexiteers had previously firmly resisted. A week later, the Commons report stage of the Brexit-related Taxation (Cross-Border Trade) Bill attracted amendments from ERG members that sought to prevent the government from implementing the Chequers proposals.[20] Rather than face defeat, and notwithstanding the contradiction, the government chose to support these amendments. Despite opposition from some pro-European Conservatives, they narrowly passed with Labour rebel support.

The pro-European side of the Conservative parliamentary party was alarmed by the ERG's response post Chequers, with one interviewee recalling a feeling that 'we were in really dangerous and uncharted territory'. The day after the vote just described, this group mounted a rebellion of its own on the government's Brexit-related Trade Bill. Former minister Phillip Lee proposed an amendment aiming to keep the UK in the European Medicines Agency post Brexit. This time the government resisted, and was narrowly defeated, with 12 Conservatives voting for the rebel amendment. This showed how finely balanced were the numbers in the Commons, with May's government vulnerable to defeat from either side.

Despite the political capital expended on Chequers, May's plans received a chilly reception from the EU (Barnier 2018), and were formally rejected in late September on the basis that they threatened the integrity of the Single Market (Tusk 2018). May had tried to head off the need for a backstop arrangement to protect Northern Ireland—but her attempt had failed.

May's Initial Brexit Deal

The febrile atmosphere created by the Chequers conflict provided the backdrop for the final weeks of talks, with MPs on all sides distrustful of one another and the government, and polls showing more of the public now expecting the UK to leave the EU without a deal than with one (UK in a Changing Europe 2018b). Meanwhile, tensions inside the Conservative Party were running high. At the party conference in early October, Boris Johnson publicly attacked Theresa May's Brexit proposals as an 'outrage' (Butterworth 2018). This was widely reported as a leadership challenge, and described by Barwell (2021: 196) as 'a naked attempt to provoke a confidence vote in her leadership'.

A few days later, the Brexit negotiators announced that they had entered 'the tunnel'—the final decisive weeks of talks. The deal, comprising the Withdrawal Agreement and non-binding Political Declaration on the future relationship, was agreed on 13 November. Arguments about its content, and whether it counted as a 'true' Brexit, would dominate the following months.[21] MPs' answers depended on their attitude towards the trade-off between a frictionless relationship with the EU and maximum UK autonomy. The most heated disagreement concerned the backstop, which was set out in a section of the Withdrawal Agreement named the Northern Ireland Protocol. It borrowed elements from both the all-UK and Northern Ireland-only models described in the previous chapter: an all-UK customs union and continuing UK-wide alignment with the EU's 'level playing field' provisions on state aid and labour and environmental standards, plus further Northern Ireland-only regulatory alignment in areas such as agriculture, energy, and VAT (Curtis 2018). Thus, the UK would remain a 'rule-taker' in areas covered by the level playing field provisions, while Great Britain—but not Northern Ireland—would be able to diverge from other EU regulations. While the backstop lasted, the UK would have limited ability to negotiate independent trade deals, but could continue to trade tariff-free with the EU. Crucially, these arrangements would avoid both a hard border on the island of Ireland and customs checks between Northern Ireland and Great Britain.

The backstop was presented as needing to come into force only if no alternative could be agreed during the coming future relationship negotiations. But in the absence of such alternatives it would be at least temporarily necessary, and could turn out to be permanent. The Political Declaration left various options open for the future relationship, but seemed to envisage a looser trade agreement than May's Chequers proposals had, notably referring to a 'close' rather than 'frictionless' relationship (UK Government and European Union 2018). This seemed to shut down the most obvious route for avoiding the backstop—that of permanent UK alignment with EU rules. The 26-page document acknowledged that both sides would benefit from agreeing an alternative solution to the Northern Ireland border problem; from the UK's perspective the backstop was highly controversial, and from an EU perspective it offered UK firms undesirable preferential access to the Single Market (Barwell 2021). But what such a solution might look like remained, at best, unclear.

ERG supporters, who were strongly opposed to any continued alignment, saw the risks of the backstop trapping the UK indefinitely in something that they considered tantamount to continued EU membership, but without any control of the rules. A favoured Eurosceptic expression was that this would make the UK a 'vassal state', and even some ardent Remainers went along with this view that it was the 'worst of both worlds' (Blair 2018). Before the deal was yet agreed, the ERG had thus announced its opposition (Stewart and Boffey 2018), and Boris Johnson (2018b) had called for it to be 'thrown out wholesale'. Within days, a document was in circulation setting out the case against (ERG 2018). May (2018b) did succeed in securing Cabinet support for the deal at a meeting on 14 November, after what she described as a 'long, detailed and impassioned' debate. But the price was the resignation the following day of four Eurosceptic ministers—including Dominic Raab, who had replaced David Davis as Brexit Secretary just four months earlier. Notable others, including Michael Gove and Andrea Leadsom, remained.

The DUP reaction was also openly hostile. Like the ERG, the party had been vocally critical of the direction of negotiations before the details of the deal were known, even abstaining in a vote on the government's (Brexit-related) Agriculture Bill in what members described as a 'warning shot' (Rigby 2018). Their key objection was the different treatment of Great Britain and Northern Ireland: despite the backstop including an all-UK customs union, they viewed the additional Northern Ireland-only regulatory alignment as unacceptable (Sky News 2018a). Although by now the central concerns of the two groups were beginning to diverge, a joint article by DUP Brexit spokesperson Sammy Wilson and former ERG chair Steve Baker in the *Sunday Telegraph* shortly before the deal was struck had railed against the 'humiliation' that it entailed, and its threat to 'break apart or subjugate the UK' (Baker and Wilson 2018). Later in November, the DUP abstained on opposition amendments to the Finance Bill to implement the budget, and even voted with Labour on one occasion. This demonstrated that the government's confidence and supply agreement was under strain.

The vocal criticism from Brexiteers raised fears that the UK might be heading for a no-deal exit, which not only risked economic hardship but would require a hard border on the island of Ireland. There was thus a strong counterreaction from moderate Conservatives. Foreign Office minister Alistair Burt (2018) tweeted that, if the original ERG proponents of Brexit voted against the deal that May had negotiated, Conservative MPs who had originally supported Remain might cease to accept the referendum result. They had been prepared to compromise, but it increasingly appeared that the ERG would not. Former Cabinet minister Nicky Morgan claimed that, '[i]f they tear down the agreement, a number of us will revisit having close access to the single market and long-term membership of the customs union' (quoted in Watts 2018). Existing Cabinet members warned of even graver consequences for the ERG: Amber Rudd suggesting that, if the deal was defeated, '[t]he Brexiteers may lose their Brexit', because the Commons would not accept exiting without a deal, while Liz Truss claimed that, '[i]f my colleagues don't sign up to this in parliament, we're in grave danger of not leaving at all' (both quoted in Zeffman 2018).

The party's fracturing was evident at May's first Commons statement on the deal on 15 November, the day after the Cabinet meeting. She faced a steady stream of criticism, with only 15 of the 52 Conservative speakers explicitly supporting her deal, and 21 openly hostile. Her response was to plead for compromise. In a Downing Street statement later that day she suggested ominously that 'if we do not move forward with that agreement, nobody can know for sure the consequences that will follow' (May 2018c).

The agreement of the deal galvanized the ERG, but also exposed its limitations. In a meeting directly afterwards, the group resolved to try to unseat May immediately, on the basis that, in the words of one MP, 'the only way to change the policy is to change the personnel' (quoted in Coates 2018b). To initiate a Conservative leadership challenge, 15 per cent of the parliamentary party—at that point, 48 MPs—were required to submit letters to the chair of the 1922 Committee. On the same day that the four ERG ministers resigned, the group's chair, Jacob Rees-Mogg, announced that he had submitted such a letter (Hope 2018). But despite the ERG's formidable reputation for organization and tactics, it had miscalculated; the total at this point fell short of the 48-letter threshold. May was safe for the time being, but she and the ERG were left in deadlock: openly opposed, but neither seemingly able to defeat the other.

The Inevitability of Parliamentary Failure

All of this should have made obvious that there was no majority for May's Brexit deal in the Commons, and that a 'meaningful vote' of any kind was doomed to fail. Unless opposition parties chose to support the government, only a handful of Conservative rebels was needed to inflict defeat, and it was perfectly clear that many more than this were opposed to the deal. Raoul Ruparel (2020), who had moved from being David Davis's Special Adviser to Number 10 after his boss resigned over Chequers, reflected that '[m]y view was always, actually, getting a deal of some form landed with the EU was not going to be the hard part. [It was] getting one landed we [could] get through Parliament.'

With details of the deal becoming clear in mid-October, Chief Whip Julian Smith did a ring-round of Conservative MPs, and reported to Number 10 that up to 130 out of 315 might rebel (Barwell 2021).[22] At the same time, 1922 Committee chair Graham Brady sought an urgent meeting with Theresa May, and advised her that 'there was no earthly way it would get through the Commons' (cited in Seldon and Newell 2019: 481). But there was some air of unreality in Number 10. JoJo Penn (2020), May's then Deputy Chief of Staff, recalled a hope that finally agreeing a deal would 'create some momentum towards getting the deal over the line in Parliament', though she admitted that Dominic Raab's resignation 'made that very difficult'. Meanwhile, the reaction to warnings from those senior Conservatives best attuned to the mood in the Commons approached denial. Julian Smith told Seldon and Newell (2019: 498) that when he delivered his unpalatable message, he 'was regarded as a serious irritant by the PM's team', who responded that '[t]his is the deal, your job is to deliver the votes on it'. Such comments suggest a serious misunderstanding of the role of the whips, which is to communicate difficult news upwards at least as much as communicating ministerial wishes downwards. With opposition to the government's proposals on this scale, persuasive tactics by whips would be completely inadequate to the task. As a senior government interviewee put it, 'It [was] one of Theresa's great mistakes; when your Chief Whip is telling you, "you're going to go down to a historic defeat", you withdraw, regroup and move in a different direction'. Instead, May's divided Cabinet barely even discussed the matter.

One option was to defer the Commons vote on the deal until more support could be built, which is what some allies pressed on the Prime Minister. A senior Conservative interviewee said, 'all I could urge her to do was not go over the top, with an entirely defective agreement that was bound to be rejected'. Another potential option was to bring Labour MPs on board, and there were some attempts to do this; but there were few attractions for the opposition in rescuing the Prime Minister from a humiliating defeat. By late November, reports were already circulating that the government planned to hold a second vote, in the event that the first one failed. A source told Sebastian Whale (2018) that 'No 10 is banking on the risks of no deal concentrating the minds of Remain-voting MPs while relying on the threat of no Brexit at all to win Leavers round'. That these two positions were wholly contradictory, and might have the reverse effect of encouraging MPs from both camps to vote the deal down in the hopes of something better, seemed somehow to elude the Prime Minister's team.

The Debate and First Defeat on the Deal

In the event, the Prime Minister chose to proceed with the debate on her Brexit deal in early December. It was then halted—to significant consternation—in order to head off an imminent defeat, and deferred until mid-January. At that point a huge defeat took place. This chain of events greatly heightened fears about no deal, and fuelled tensions over the government's control of the House of Commons agenda. It also triggered two confidence votes, on the Prime Minister's leadership of the Conservative Party, and the government's leadership of the country.

Pre-debate Commons Defeats

The debate on the deal began on 4 December 2018. Earlier that same day, the government suffered two House of Commons defeats on associated matters. One concerned the publication of Attorney General Geoffrey Cox's legal advice on the backstop; the other related to the meaningful vote procedure, reopening the question of what would happen if the Commons voted against the deal.

As discussed in Chapter 6, Labour had sought to use its limited number of Commons opposition days to extract information from ministers about their Brexit plans, increasingly using the humble address procedure, which was considered binding on the government. On 13 November, the Commons had passed a motion for a humble address that required the government to publish its full legal advice 'on the proposed withdrawal agreement…including the Northern Ireland backstop'.[23] Legal advice to ministers would normally remain confidential, but Labour's Keir Starmer argued that this principle should be overridden given the importance of Brexit. Notably, Conservative rebels who had on occasion sided with Labour disagreed, with Dominic Grieve—as a former Attorney General—arguing that the move was unwise. ERG members meanwhile proposed an amendment to Labour's motion, requiring a government 'position statement' on the legal situation, rather than the full legal advice. Though it was rumoured that the government was set to back this, the Speaker did not select the amendment for debate. The government whipped to abstain rather than facing down Labour's proposal—as had recently become the habit on opposition motions—and it passed without a division. After the result, the Speaker confirmed in a point of order that the motion was binding.

Subsequently, however, ministers declared that they would not publish the full legal advice. On 3 December the Attorney General made a rare Commons statement, indicating that the government was instead publishing a detailed document, similar to that previously proposed by the ERG. But ERG members were now openly critical of the government, for seeking to evade a humble address that it had failed to oppose. Opposition leaders responded by proposing an unusual joint motion the following day, granted time by the Speaker as it was on a matter of 'privilege', that ministers should be found 'in contempt' of parliament for flouting its direction. This attracted heated debate before the debate on the deal itself began, and the opposition motion was approved by 311 votes to 307. Two hardline Conservative Brexiteers voted for it, while another 20 Conservatives (including some from both rebel camps) were absent from the vote, though Dominic Grieve supported the government. Once the main debate was underway, on 5 December, Geoffrey Cox's advice was published, and made clear that, legally, the backstop could last indefinitely. This offered significant additional fuel to the government's opponents.

The second defeat occurred barely an hour after the first, and related to the procedure for the meaningful vote. The government's Business of the House motion—which set out the timetable for the debate on the deal—proposed a five-day debate, running to 11 December, culminating in a vote on the deal. But the question resurfaced of what would happen if the deal was voted down. As summarized above, section 13 of the EU (Withdrawal) Act required a government statement within 21 days, and a further motion. But any such motion would be in 'neutral terms', and therefore unamendable. With time now running very short, and given the government's default tight grip on the Commons timetable, MPs could be denied the opportunity to express a formal view about the preferred next steps. To avert this, Dominic Grieve duly tabled an amendment to the government's Business of the House motion on 4 December.

Grieve's amendment was innovative, but (unlike his subsequent intervention in January, discussed below) there were no serious questions about the Speaker's propriety in selecting it for debate. It simply stated that Commons Standing Order no. 24B—which provides that motions in 'neutral terms' are not amendable—would not apply to any subsequent motion under section 13. This was a clever trick, which took advantage of the fact that, while the words in the legislation were fixed, the House of Commons is free to vary or disapply its own standing orders. Grieve's proposal allowed MPs to revisit the outcome of the 'ping-pong' on the EU (Withdrawal) Bill earlier in the year, and to render any 'next steps' motion amendable in the event that the deal was voted down.

The signatories to the proposal were a cross-party group, including several senior Conservatives. Notable among them was Oliver Letwin, who to date had been an unofficial broker for the government, and had never rebelled before. Speaking subsequently about his decision, Letwin (2020) noted that the 'irreconcilable' position of many ERG members, and the improbability of Labour members backing May's deal, left him 'extremely worried for the first time that we really were heading towards the situation in which the choice was between no Brexit and no deal'. The government was roundly defeated on the Grieve amendment by 321 votes to 299, with 25 Conservatives rebelling. They included not only Letwin but former Cabinet ministers Justine Greening, Nicky Morgan, Michael Fallon, and Damian Green—the last two of whom had been close allies of Theresa May—and Jo Johnson (brother of Boris), who had resigned as a transport minister over Brexit the previous month.

The Initial Debate, Halted by the Government

The government approached the debate already weak, and was further weakened by these two defeats. From the outset, the chances of winning Commons support looked hopeless. Theresa May opened the proceedings with another plea for compromise, stating that politics is 'about listening to people from all sides of the debate and then doing what you believe is in our national interest'. Seemingly addressing her hardliners, she argued that 'we should not let the search for the perfect Brexit prevent a good Brexit that delivers for the British people', warning members not to 'imagine that, if we vote this down, a different deal is going to miraculously appear'. She reiterated the mutually contradictory threats of what might happen following a defeat: 'the risk that Brexit could be stopped; [and] the risk we could crash out with no deal'.[24]

Jeremy Corbyn's response was predictably critical. What mattered more was the reaction from Conservative MPs. First up was Boris Johnson, who condemned the deal as 'a democratic disaster' and 'a national humiliation that makes a mockery of Brexit'. With strongly implied criticism of May and her ministers, he suggested that 'we have not even tried properly to leave' and that '[i]t is a wonder, frankly, that any democratic politician could conceivably vote for this deal'. He claimed that continuing standards alignment with the EU would make the UK a 'de facto colony'.[25] But Johnson offered no viable alternative, and indeed presented plainly contradictory objectives: while arguing that there must be no hard border in Northern Ireland, he also suggested that the UK should be prepared to contemplate leaving without a deal.

This set the tone for the debate. On the first day 12 Conservatives spoke, six of whom were openly opposed to the deal, two expressed more muted concerns, and only four supported it. The next day, 13 of the 19 Conservative speakers were critical, and only three supportive. Conservative opponents in the debate came from both rebel perspectives—Brexiteers included former DExEU ministers David Davis and David Jones, and others such as John Redwood and Owen Paterson. Dominic Grieve, Anna Soubry, and Justine Greening were among those criticizing the deal from the opposing perspective. This all suggested that Theresa May was heading for a crushing defeat. The depth of the difficulties was demonstrated by the diversity of preferred solutions proposed by these critics, covering everything from a second referendum to a no-deal exit. To make matters worse, the DUP expressed clear hostility. Nigel Dodds accused the Prime Minister of betraying his members' trust and misjudging the mood of parliament. Appearing on ITV News (2018b) on the second day of the debate, he described the government's newly published legal advice on the backstop as 'devastating', and suggested that the DUP could vote to bring the government down if parliament voted to approve the deal.

Some senior Conservatives had cautioned against holding the debate. As soon as it had started, they were urging that it should be stopped. On day two, the *Daily Mail* reported Graham Brady calling for a delay (Tapsfield, Groves, and Moore 2018). The next day, the *Times* claimed that several Cabinet ministers were privately urging this on the Prime Minister, while Chief Whip Julian Smith was advising Number 10 that many Conservatives were 'beyond reason', and there was no hope of bringing them round (Coates 2018a). The first three days of debate took place on Tuesday, Wednesday, and Thursday, after which the Commons broke for the weekend, and Conservative MPs moved their criticism to the pages of the newspapers. On Saturday David Davis (2018b) wrote in the *Telegraph* that the Prime Minister was 'forcing Parliament to vote on a flawed prospectus', and that it must 'defeat this wretched deal'. On Sunday Boris Johnson (2018c) claimed in the same newspaper that he 'devoutly' hoped the deal would be defeated, and urged the government to 'bin the backstop'.

On Monday morning, Michael Gove appeared on the BBC's *Today* programme, to insist that the vote on the deal would not be pulled. By the afternoon, when the debate was due to resume, the government had announced a U-turn. Theresa May attended the Commons to inform assembled MPs that the debate would be interrupted, and the meaningful vote postponed. Procedurally, the government could achieve this by simply failing to move the motion at the start of the day's planned debate. The Speaker made a pointed statement that it was 'deeply discourteous' to halt the debate after 164 MPs had already contributed, but neither he nor they had any procedural means to block the decision.[26]

May's statement attracted considerable criticism, although some Conservative MPs expressed support for her promise to look again at the backstop. A subsequent statement by Leader of the House Andrea Leadsom, changing the Commons' agenda for the day, then attracted fierce attacks from all sides, with hardline Brexiteer Mark Francois describing the government's behaviour as 'shameful'.[27] The following day the Speaker granted an urgent question to Labour's Yvette Cooper, as well as an emergency debate to Jeremy Corbyn, both of which provided further vehicles for Brexiteers and pro-Europeans alike to condemn the government's action. Cooper expressed a concern that the meaningful vote could now be delayed by months while the Article 50 clock ticked down. Some MPs argued that the impending Christmas recess should be cancelled.

Anger at Theresa May was clearly visible in both main parties. Labour tabled a motion 'That this House has no confidence in the Prime Minister due to her failure to allow the House of Commons to have a meaningful vote'—but this was purely symbolic, not following the wording of a formal no-confidence vote in the government, and hence was not provided time for debate. The party presumably recognized that a formal vote would fail. Within the Conservative Party, May's critics again launched a leadership challenge, this time managing to gather the necessary 48 letters to force a vote.[28] This was held rapidly, on 12 December. May promised that if she survived the vote, she would stand down as leader before the next election, and survived by 200 votes to 117. The 1922 chair Graham Brady (2018) conceded that her decision to defer the Brexit vote had brought about the leadership challenge, but argued that 'going ahead and losing the vote by a massive margin would have had exactly the same effect'. Nonetheless, a senior Conservative figure in interview commented that the result of the leadership challenge was 'almost the worst possible outcome'; 37 per cent of the parliamentary party had now expressed no confidence in its leader. Under the rules of the 1922 Committee, the fact that the Prime Minister had won a leadership contest meant that she could not be formally challenged again for another year. Her opponents had, at least for the moment, had their chance.

The Resumption of Debate

On 9 January, the government proposed a motion to resume debate on the deal. This provided for an additional five days' debating time, starting that day and ending with a vote. It triggered one of the fiercest arguments during the period over parliamentary procedure and the role of the Speaker, when Dominic Grieve again proposed an amendment to the government's motion.

Anger was high regarding the government's behaviour in December, and had focused attention on the extent to which ministers can control the House of Commons agenda—preventing debate on matters which MPs urgently want to discuss. December's events had also further eroded trust in the government, and raised concerns about ministers 'running down the clock', with the Article 50 period due to end on 29 March. It was in this context that Grieve proposed his amendment, which would shorten the timescale for the government to table a motion on next steps in the event that the deal was defeated, from a maximum of 28 days to just three sitting days. Alongside Grieve, the cross-party amendment was signed by multiple Conservatives, including Oliver Letwin, Jo Johnson, Phillip Lee, and Sarah Wollaston.

This intervention proved so controversial due to the nature of the government's motion, which itself sought to amend December's Business of the House motion, rather than presenting the timetable in a fresh motion. The original motion has said that any such amendments would be taken 'forthwith'—in parliamentary language, meaning without debate or amendment (a further illustration of the government's agenda power). It was certainly arguable that a new, amendable Business of the House motion should have been provided—and the government probably proceeded as it did precisely to avoid further trouble. But given the strength of feeling among senior Conservatives, and the widespread criticism of the government's past behaviour, John Bercow chose to break with precedent and allow a vote on the Grieve amendment. It was then agreed by 308 votes to 297 (with supporters including 17 Conservative rebels, among them former Cabinet ministers Andrew Mitchell and Nicky Morgan). Bercow's decision was questioned by Leader of the House Andrea Leadsom, and attracted furious criticism from other Brexit supporters, and subsequently in the media, for having acted against the clerks' procedural advice (e.g. Swinford 2019a). Bercow (2020a) later admitted that he had done just this, spurred by the government's previous 'extraordinary and inexcusable treatment of the House'. Grieve (2020) himself later said that, knowing the precedents, he had not expected the Speaker to select the amendment for decision. This incident significantly fuelled negativity towards Bercow in the Brexit-supporting press, with the next day's *Sun* (2019d) headline shouting 'Speaker of the Devil', and its edi-torial suggesting that '[o]dious John Bercow's prejudices are wrecking Brexit'. Such a tone was set to continue in the months ahead.

The subsequent days of debate were relatively more balanced among con-tributors on the Conservative side, with 50 speaking for the government and 43 against (plus five unclear).[29] But it remained obvious that without oppos-ition support the deal was doomed to defeat. A Labour frontbench amend-ment (which was not moved, but indicated the party's position) rejected the withdrawal agreement for failing to provide 'a permanent UK-EU customs union and strong single market deal' and for not adequately protecting workers' and environmental rights (House of Commons 2018). Theresa May's team, despite the postponement of the vote over Christmas, had unsurprisingly failed to persuade the EU to move on the backstop. But the Prime Minister offered warm words to Conservative Brexiteer Edward Leigh, who had proposed an amendment insisting that the backstop must be tem-porary, promising to work with him and 'look at creative solutions'.[30] Leigh did not press his amendment to the vote, on the basis of this 'positive response'—providing some indication of how the next stages would develop.[31]

May closed the debate with a final plea for compromise, urging MPs to 'choose unity over division', and suggesting that '[i]f we act in the national interest and back this deal tonight, tomorrow we can begin to build [a brighter] future together'. In contrast, she warned, '[a] vote against the deal is a vote for nothing more than uncertainty, division and the very real risk of no deal or no Brexit'.[32]

The Defeat of 15 January and Its Immediate Aftermath

Unsurprisingly, MPs did not heed these warnings. The vote resulted in a historic and crushing government defeat, by 432 votes to 202. Three Labour members voted with the government, as did three independents, while the Conservatives split, with 196 in support and 118 voting against the deal—making this the largest backbench rebellion in percentage terms in modern times.[33] All others voting, including the DUP's 10 MPs, were also opposed.[34] Expert on parliamentary rebellions Philip Cowley (2019) noted that this was 'by some distance, the largest genuine government defeat in the Commons for at least 100 years', and quite possibly ever.

Before considering the aftermath, the breakdown of the Conservative vote deserves consideration. This has received relatively little attention, but reveals the dynamics within the party. Of the 196 Conservatives supporting the Brexit deal, 144 had been Remain supporters in 2016, while just 49 had supported Leave (see Table 8.3, in the next chapter).[35] Among the 118 who opposed, 90 had been Leave supporters in 2016, and 26 had supported Remain. Even among these 26, several (for example Ben Bradley, Mark Harper, and Shailesh Vara) had since come firmly round to supporting Brexit.[36] In other words, fewer than 20 of the Conservative MPs opposing Theresa May did so from a pro-EU or soft Brexit position, while two-thirds of former Leave supporters had rejected her deal.[37] Most of the former Remain-supporting backbenchers who were subsequently accused of disrupting Brexit—such as Nick Boles, Ken Clarke, Stephen Hammond, Oliver Letwin, Antoinette Sandbach, Nicholas Soames, and Caroline Spelman—had in fact voted for the deal from the outset. Leavers rejecting it included all of the key leadership figures in the ERG (plus, presumably, all or most of the group's membership), 1922 chair Graham Brady, and of course David Davis, Dominic Raab, and Boris Johnson.

This was clearly an immensely difficult and destabilizing moment for Theresa May. But showing her typical resilience, she rose calmly immediately after the result to address MPs on the next steps. In doing so, she suggested a three-stage process.[38] First, that clarity was needed on whether the government still enjoyed the confidence of the House of Commons—so the government would provide parliamentary time to debate a motion of no confidence if Labour sought one. Second, that if such a vote demonstrated confidence in the government, she would lead discussions among ministers, with the DUP, and involving 'senior parliamentarians from across the House', to find support for a Brexit plan—approaching this 'in a constructive spirit'. Third, that any agreed proposals would then be put to the EU. Finally, she claimed that the government was not seeking 'to run down the clock', emphasizing that '[e]very day that passes without this issue being resolved means more uncertainty, more bitterness and more rancour'. Responding for Labour, Jeremy Corbyn criticized May for 'only attempting to reach out now to try to keep her failed process and deal alive after it has been so roundly rejected', and insisted that 'no deal must be taken off the table'.[39] He confirmed that he had submitted a no-confidence motion. Yvette Cooper then pointed out that there were barely 70 days left until the Article 50 deadline, and urged the Prime Minister to seek an extension to the timetable.

The Brexit-supporting press reacted with dismay, but was split on the question of who should be blamed. The *Daily Express* (2019a) and *Sun* (2019a) both considered May's deal unacceptable, but also expressed clear suspicion of parliament, with the former accusing 'Remainers in Britain' of emboldening the EU to offer a bad deal, and the latter speculating that a

'Remainer-dominated' parliament would now seek a soft Brexit. The *Daily Mail* (2019c), meanwhile, exasperatedly claimed that MPs had 'spurned the only viable Brexit deal on offer' and called on 'purists on all sides' to compromise.

Labour's no-confidence motion was debated the following day. Under the Fixed-term Parliaments Act 2011 a government defeat would have triggered a 14-day period during which either a new government could be formed or the existing government could regain the Commons' confidence. Failing this, a general election would be held. After six hours of debate, the vote split straight down party lines, with all Conservatives and the DUP supporting the government, and all opposition members voting against. Despite the group's behaviour the previous day, Mark Francois assured the Prime Minister during the debate that 'when the bells ring the whole European Research Group will walk through the Lobby with her to vote this nonsense down'.[40]

As to the Prime Minister's suggestion of finding a cross-party solution, Philip Hammond (2020) has complained that '[s]he said it, she walked out of the chamber, and she never came back to that thought, really'. This seems unduly harsh, particularly given Jeremy Corbyn's continued refusal to join talks unless the Prime Minister ruled out no deal, which she was not prepared to do (Sabbagh 2019). As explored in the next chapter, informal cross-party contacts of various kinds were pursued at around this time, but ultimately could not resolve the impasse.

Conclusion

Theresa May was always in a difficult position. She became Conservative leader when the central task was to implement a referendum decision that had deeply divided the party. She gambled on enhancing her parliamentary majority by calling the 2017 general election, and failed. She went into the negotiations with the EU already weakened, and the compromises needed in those negotiations to respect the referendum result while minimizing risks of instability in Northern Ireland were difficult, and unacceptable to many of her own pro-Brexit MPs. By late 2018 the cracks could no longer be papered over, and this combined set of circumstances led politics to fracture in a very serious way.

From the outset, as discussed in previous chapters, May had been disinclined to let parliament in to decision-making about Brexit. This was perhaps instinctively rational, given her lack of a parliamentary majority. But it aggravated parliamentarians, and caused concerns that she might be captured by the hardline Brexiteers of the ERG and persuaded, or even tricked, into facilitating a damaging no-deal Brexit. Throughout this period, she increasingly alarmed moderates in her party by refusing to rule out leaving without a deal. Many hardliners came to embrace this as a solution, while becoming increasingly angered by May's preparedness to compromise on continued alignment with EU rules. During the period she suffered significant defeats at the hands of both groups, each of which increased its effort in opposition to the other. Moderates helped enforce (step by step) the requirement for a parliamentary 'meaningful vote' on the Brexit outcome, in part to guard against a no-deal exit; then committed Brexiteers, for the most part, used that same mechanism to vote down her deal.

'What-ifs' at this stage are very difficult, with the Prime Minister increasingly boxed in; but some aspects of her government's behaviour undoubtedly raise questions. After Chequers, when David Davis, Boris Johnson, and others resigned as ministers, it already seemed obvious that her Brexit plans would not find Conservative support. The subsequent agreement with the EU triggered a second spate of resignations, including that of her second Brexit Secretary in just four months. Yet—against the advice of her own Chief Whip, and the chair of the 1922 Committee—the Prime Minister chose to press ahead with the vote on her deal. To many, this might appear inexplicable; the delicate parliamentary arithmetic meant that she could barely afford to lose the support of a single Conservative MP, yet the loss of 10 ministers from her government between Chequers and the end of November failed to persuade her to change course.[41] This seeming irrationality is traceable at least in part to May's own attitude to her party. One interviewee close to her suggested that, as an absolute loyalist who prioritized party unity above almost all else, she could simply not conceive that other Conservative MPs would behave in the way that they did. Having listened, and tried hard to broker what she believed was the best and only real Brexit deal available, she expected her MPs ultimately to fall in behind her.

The 'what-if' here concerns what would have happened if she had been less optimistic about her fellow Conservatives' commitment to pragmatism and party unity. It might have helped had she, as previously suggested, been more open with the public—who might, perhaps, have supported her own pragmatic search for compromise. Not having done so, the only real place that she could have turned to within parliament was Labour. As explored in Chapter 5, and in the opening of this chapter, that was always going to be difficult. Even setting aside Labour's complicated internal dynamics, opposition parties will rarely come to the rescue of a struggling government. The longer that time went on, the worse the prospects became of brokering this kind of agreement.

Another 'what-if' concerns parliamentarians' behaviour. Dominic Grieve and other moderates or Brexit-sceptics fought hard to get a meaningful vote, and yet once they had done so, it was primarily their opponents—the hard Brexiteers—who used this to inflict a historically crushing defeat on the government. As detailed above, only a relatively small number of Conservative MPs joined in the defeat from an anti-Brexit direction. So, does this suggest an error on the part of these Brexit-sceptics? Might a softer deal than was ultimately secured have been agreed if Theresa May had been able (as was her instinct) to proceed using prerogative powers, with minimal parliamentary input? Some interviewees believed this to be the case. One hardline Brexiteer suggested that the meaningful vote 'was ultimately enormously beneficial to the Eurosceptics', and that without it Grieve and his allies 'would have got Theresa May's deal which they probably would have been a lot happier with'. One on the other side of the argument likewise commented that proceeding without parliamentary approval 'would have been good, because we would have ended up with Mrs May's deal', though suggesting that 'it would have been horrendous to have a deal by Royal prerogative'. Crucially, key government insiders pointed out that implementing legislation would still have been needed, allowing opponents potentially to have scuppered things later instead. Had the mechanisms created by Grieve and his allies not existed, the ERG could still theoretically have sought to use this blocking mechanism. This would have created a high-stakes situation, placing potentially enormous pressure on the opposition to either fall in behind the government or stand by and facilitate a last-minute no-deal exit.

It was the growing fear of a no-deal situation—inadvertently fuelled by the Prime Minister's earlier rhetoric—that initially mobilized many moderates on the Conservative side, as well as opposition parliamentarians, to support the meaningful vote procedures. Once the deal had been defeated, primarily due to blocking by Brexiteers, these MPs stepped up their attempts to prevent no deal, and to find alternative solutions, as explored in the next chapter.

Notes

1. House of Commons Hansard, 25 October 2017, column 297.
2. The implementing legislation would ultimately have a slightly different name: the European Union (Withdrawal Agreement) Bill (see Chapter 10).

3. Along with Dominic Grieve, the top signatories were Ken Clarke, Nicky Morgan, Anna Soubry, Antoinette Sandbach, Stephen Hammond, Sarah Wollaston, Jeremy Lefroy, and Bob Neill.

4. House of Commons Hansard, 13 December 2017, column 475. Raab was at this point a junior minister at the Ministry of Justice.

5. Bernard Jenkin, ibid., column 419.

6. Ibid., column 438.

7. These comprised the lead signatories indicated above minus Jeremy Lefroy, alongside Heidi Allen, Jonathan Djanogly, Oliver Heald, and John Stevenson.

8. House of Lords Hansard, 30 January 2018, column 1381.

9. Lord Callanan, ibid., 14 March 2018, column 1651.

10. Ibid., 30 April 2018, column 1852.

11. Ibid., 30 April 2018, column 1866.

12. The question was later resolved by the European Court of Justice's decision in the *Wightman* case (see Chapter 8); the court found that Article 50 could be unilaterally revoked by the UK.

13. House of Commons Hansard, 12 June 2018, column 740.

14. Ibid.

15. Edward Leigh, House of Commons Hansard, 12 June 2018, column 762.

16. Ibid., column 766.

17. House of Lords Hansard, 18 June 2018, columns 1886, 1899.

18. House of Commons Hansard, 21 June 2018, columns 13WS–14WS.

19. Ibid., 20 June 2018, column 376. Labour's Chris Bryant, a known procedural specialist, added that, 'if a Speaker were to decide that a neutral motion was suddenly, somehow or other, not neutral and could be amended, we should remove him from the Chair' (ibid., 20 June 2018, column 382).

20. There were four amendments in total, sponsored respectively by Priti Patel, Laurence Robertson, Bernard Jenkin, and Craig Mackinlay.

21. At around this time ERG figures coined the dismissive term 'BRINO' or 'Brexit in name only', to describe proposals which required continued adherence to EU rules.

22. A total of 315 because two Conservative MPs elected in 2017 had been suspended from the party over sexual misconduct allegations.

23. House of Commons Hansard, 13 November 2018, column 189.

24. Ibid., 4 December 2018, columns 763–4.

25. Ibid., 4 December 2018, columns 775–8.

26. Ibid., 10 December 2018, column 27.

27. Ibid., 10 December 2018, column 75.

28. Barwell (2021) suggests that some letters may have come from Theresa May's supporters, in the belief that she would win, thereby securing her position for another year.

29. For completeness, on the third day of debate there had been 17 Conservative critics, 13 supporters, and two unclear.

30. House of Commons Hansard, 15 January 2019, column 1113.

31. Ibid., column 1116.

32. Ibid., column 1115.

33. Cowley (2019) notes that the 139-member rebellion against Tony Blair on the Iraq War in 2003 was numerically larger, but his parliamentary party contained 100 more MPs than Theresa May's.

34. The three Labour supporters were Ian Austin, Kevin Barron, and John Mann. The three independents were Lady Sylvia Hermon of Northern Ireland, who was elected as such, alongside former Labour member Frank Field and former Liberal Democrat Stephen Lloyd.
35. The referendum position of the remaining three was unclear, as was the position of two who voted against the deal. Analysis conducted using data on MPs' referendum positions made available by Cygan, Lynch and Whitaker (2019).
36. Based on analysis of their public statements at the time (including in the Commons chamber, in the press, and on their websites).
37. They included Heidi Allen, Guto Bebb, Justine Greening, Dominic Grieve, Sam Gyimah, Jo Johnson, Phillip Lee, Anna Soubry, and Sarah Wollaston.
38. House of Commons Hansard, 15 January 2019, column 1126.
39. Ibid., 15 January 2019, column 1127.
40. Ibid., 16 January 2019, column 1179.
41. These were Steve Baker, Guto Bebb, Suella Braverman, David Davis, Sam Gyimah, Boris Johnson, Jo Johnson, Esther McVey, Dominic Raab, and Shailesh Vara.

8

Backbenchers 'Seize Control'

The defeat of Theresa May's deal in the first meaningful vote sparked an increasingly bitter political period, during which divisions within both main parties deepened. With the Prime Minister unable to bring her own MPs round to her deal, parliament became a forum in which a majority might be sought for some alternative Brexit outcome. As government leadership was lacking, MPs increasingly took matters into their own hands, seeking innovative procedural mechanisms through which cross-party agreements could be reached. May's deal was defeated twice more, while numerous other votes forced outcomes on a reluctant government. This placed parliament centre stage, but proved highly controversial, raising fundamental questions about its role—with respect both to the executive and the referendum result. It also presented severe challenges to parliament, given both the conflicts and the complexities of Brexit. MPs commonly take their cues from party leaders and whips, but as this system broke down, voting became fragmented and unpredictable. They repeatedly rejected the idea of a no-deal Brexit, but could find no majority in favour of anything else except delay. Theresa May twice secured extensions to the Article 50 period, but was ultimately forced from office without having delivered Brexit.

The chapter begins with a discussion of agenda control in the House of Commons. Normally, this lies largely with the government, which became increasingly untenable given May's inability to muster a majority. The chapter then moves on to consider the immediate aftermath of the first meaningful vote, and the options available. The first major debate on these took place on the statutory 'next steps' motion required following the initial defeat on the deal, in late January 2019. MPs expressed clear opposition to a no-deal exit, but also backed a doomed attempt to send the government back to the negotiating table. Meanwhile, support was growing for parliamentary 'indicative votes' on the options, and for an extension to the Article 50 period.

There were multiple further stages, as described in consecutive sections of the chapter and summarized in Table 8.1. These included a failed second meaningful vote, and an initial short extension to Article 50, followed by MPs gaining control of the agenda to—unsuccessfully—seek agreement via indicative votes. Subsequently, there was a third failed vote on the deal, and a second unsuccessful round of indicative votes. MPs' only success was in

Table 8.1 Key Brexit decisions in the House of Commons, 15 January–3 April 2019

Date	Decision	Initiated by*
15 January	• First defeat of May's deal	G
29 January	• Next steps motion following defeat of 15 January. Amendments on alternative arrangements to the backstop (Brady), and opposing no deal (Spelman), pass. Labour amendment seeking indicative votes, and backbench attempts to take control of Commons agenda, defeated.	G(B)
14 February	• May asks MPs to reaffirm support for her deal, with alternative arrangements for the backstop. Motion defeated.	G
27 February	• Government motion amended by MPs to demand an Article 50 extension if the deal is defeated again, and if MPs reject no deal.	G(B)
12 March	• Second defeat of May's deal.	G
13 March	• Government motion rejecting no-deal Brexit is amended by MPs to toughen up that commitment.	G(B)
14 March	• MPs vote for May to seek an extension to Article 50.	G
25 March	• Next steps motion following defeat of 12 March. • MPs take control of Commons agenda for 27 March.	G(B)
27 March	• First round of indicative votes. All options rejected. • MPs take control of Commons agenda for 1 April.	B
29 March	• Third defeat of May's deal.	G
1 April	• Second round of indicative votes. All options rejected. • MPs take control of Commons agenda for 3 April.	B
3 April	• Cooper–Letwin Bill passes its Commons stages. • Attempt to take control of Commons agenda for 8 April to hold third round of indicative votes is defeated.	B

* G = government initiative; B = backbench initiative; G(B) = government initiative, amended by backbenchers.

forcing the Prime Minister to seek timetable extensions, including through the highly unusual passage of a private member's bill against the government's wishes. At the end of this period Theresa May finally did what some had long called for, and entered formal talks with Labour, in a last-ditch attempt to resolve the deadlock. But this proved the final straw for her party. The Conservatives were trounced in European Parliament elections that the government had never wanted to hold, and in late May 2019 the Prime Minister announced her resignation.

Agenda Control in the House of Commons

Previous chapters have already demonstrated the extent to which the government controls agenda time in the House of Commons. This was starkly seen over the first meaningful vote. First, in December 2018, ministers post-poned the vote days after the debate had started—to the widespread conster-nation of MPs. Then they restarted the debate in January 2019 without moving a new business motion—sparking Dominic Grieve's amendment on timing of the next steps motion, and the Speaker's controversial decision to allow it, notwithstanding that the government's proposal was due to be taken 'forthwith'. The very fact that MPs had pursued a meaningful vote on the deal through amendments to the EU (Withdrawal) Bill was, in itself, partly because of their relative lack of control of the Commons agenda. Only by guaranteeing such a vote in statute could they be certain that it would hap-pen, as they had no automatic means to initiate it themselves—because the Commons weekly business for debate is proposed by the government.

The clearest single source of the government's control of time is House of Commons Standing Order no. 14 on the 'Arrangement of public business', which states that, 'Save as provided in this order, government business shall have precedence at every sitting' (House of Commons 2021). These words are followed by various exceptions, including 20 days per session set aside for opposition debates, 27 days per session in the main chamber for back-bench business debates, and 13 Fridays per session for private members' bills.[1] The net effect is that the government decides the topic of debate on the great majority of sitting days. Crucially, the government also chooses when opposition and backbench days are given, and their number is guaranteed per session, rather than per year. After the 2017 general election Theresa May decided that there would be a two-year session to maximize the time available for Brexit legislation (another choice that is at ministers' discretion, without needing MPs' approval), effectively halving the guaranteed propor-tion of non-government time. As previous chapters have demonstrated, opposition debates in particular became a nuisance to the government over Brexit, and it first sought to minimize their effect by asking Conservative MPs to abstain in any associated votes. But eventually ministers began sim-ply to withhold opposition days. None at all were granted for the five and a half months between mid-November 2018 and late April 2019 (Russell and Gover 2021). This greatly curtailed MPs' ability to bring matters forward for decision that the government preferred to avoid. Potentially, backbench debates could have been used for this purpose, but ministers might then have chosen to block these as well.

The government's degree of control over the House of Commons agenda is fairly unusual internationally (Döring 2001, Russell and Paun 2007). In other parliaments there is often a formal cross-party body which draws up the weekly agenda. The difference at Westminster is at least partly a product of the electoral system, and the resultant norm of single-party majority govern-ment. This can in practice make government control seem almost synonym-ous with majority control, and allow decisions to be largely delegated to the governing party. Historically, Standing Order no. 14 entrenched an arrange-ment that had previously been ad hoc: through temporary 'sessional orders' being agreed which set aside certain days for government business. Rather than repeatedly agreeing such orders, government control was eventually writ-ten into standing orders in 1902 (Seaward 2019). In theory, this did not entirely remove MPs' control—as the House of Commons remains free to decide its standing orders by majority vote. But in fact it created a potential trap, because without the ability to get items onto the agenda for decision, MPs would find it difficult to secure time to debate such standing order changes.

Even before Brexit, this situation had been seen as problematic. The Select Committee on the Reform of the House of Commons (2009), colloquially known as the 'Wright Committee', recommended that the government's grip on the agenda should be loosened, in two ways. First, that a cross-party 'House Business Committee' should be created, along the lines used in vari-ous other parliaments, to draw up the weekly agenda. Second, and crucially, that this agenda should be formally put to the House of Commons for approval (instead of the existing practice of simply being announced by the Leader of the House). This mechanism, as the committee noted, was used in other legislatures, including the Scottish Parliament, without major prob-lems. Under normal circumstances of majority government, ministers would easily be able to secure majority support for their proposed agenda; but such a system would ensure that this majority was tested. It would particularly empower the government's own backbenchers, who might on occasion vote with the opposition to allocate time to matters which the government pre-ferred not to discuss.

The Wright Committee did not foresee the circumstances of minority gov-ernment; but these very clearly brought into question the appropriateness of automatic government control. Post 2017, with ministers frequently unable to command a Commons majority, significant tensions arose about what should be debated and when. Eventually, MPs found both the mechanisms and the cross-party political will to temporarily set aside Standing Order no. 14 on several occasions.

The Aftermath of the First Meaningful Vote

Having just survived a historic defeat on the Brexit deal, and a parliamentary vote of no confidence, the Prime Minister and her Cabinet clearly needed to consider their options. Numerous suggestions had been made during the lengthy debates on the deal, but these pointed in often contradictory directions. The options can broadly be divided into policy and procedural—i.e. where to get in terms of Brexit, and how to get there—although the line is somewhat blurry between the two. This section briefly delineates the different options open to government and parliament in such categories. All of these options went on to feature repeatedly in the febrile debates that followed.

The Policy Options

An interviewee from Downing Street recounted that immediately after the defeat the Prime Minister's staff strongly advised her that there were three basic routes available: pursuing a softer form of Brexit in order to bring parliamentarians on board from beyond her own party; proposing a referendum on the deal; or pursuing a no-deal exit. A fourth option, reportedly not considered credible by most Number 10 staffers, was to return to the negotiating table.

A Softer Brexit and a Deal with Labour

Perhaps the most obvious route, mooted at various earlier stages as recounted in previous chapters, was to broaden the parliamentary support for Brexit by agreeing to pursue a closer relationship with the EU, most obviously through a permanent customs union and/or continued Single Market membership. But this would involve revisiting the Prime Minister's 'red lines', and undoubtedly spark fury among Conservative hardline Brexiteers.

Theresa May's statement immediately after the defeat had proposed to work with 'senior parliamentarians from across the House', and this promise was not completely hollow.[2] In late January 2019, a wide range of parliamentarians from other parties were invited to meet with key figures at the heart of the administration, including David Lidington, Gavin Barwell, and Michael Gove. Officially, Jeremy Corbyn had refused to participate in discussions unless a no-deal Brexit was taken off the table (Sabbagh 2019), and he ordered other Labour parliamentarians not to talk to the government. But clearly many disobeyed—including key representatives of the various backbench groups pressing for different Brexit outcomes, as identified in Chapter 6. Senior Labour figures involved in the talks included Yvette Cooper, Hilary Benn, and Margaret Beckett, and there were separate meetings with Labour MPs from Leave constituencies. Talks also took place with others pushing for soft forms of Brexit or a referendum—among them representatives of the Liberal Democrats, SNP, Plaid Cymru, and Greens. At the same time discussions were taking place with soft Brexit or Remain supporters on the Conservative side.

An interviewee involved in these informal cross-party talks for the government recalled that 'we increasingly couldn't see how this would be carried on Conservative or Conservative and DUP votes alone, and that we needed to find a way to identify what options stood the greatest chance of getting sufficient Labour members on board'. But now, more than ever, the challenges for Labour were huge. A senior interviewee from that side said that the moment for cross-party agreement had essentially been lost; that 'at the beginning, if Theresa May had said right, we're going to stay in the Single Market and the Customs Union, [many Labour members] would have taken it like a shot'; but that later, as 'the trauma went on…people thought, you know what, there's a possibility we can stop the whole caboodle'. Another senior Labour figure suggested that doing a deal with the government 'would have been a disaster' given the party's support base among Remainers.

A Further Referendum

A related route, which might have brought some of the same groups of parliamentarians onside, was the possibility of making approval of the Brexit deal subject to a 'confirmatory referendum'. As recounted in Chapter 6, pressure for a further referendum had been growing outside parliament ever since 2016, with the 'People's Vote' campaign attracting increasing numbers of supporters to its rallies, and Labour agreeing at its conference in autumn 2018 to 'support all options remaining on the table', including a referendum. This was already the firm policy of other parties, including the Liberal Democrats and Greens, while the SNP had declared that it would vote in favour of referendum amendments if they were tabled.

Many factors pointed towards a referendum as a tactical compromise. The unexpected vote for Brexit in 2016 had not been based on a particular prospectus, and indeed some Brexiteers—including Dominic Cummings (2015) and Boris Johnson (Shipman 2015)—had originally proposed a two-referendum process. Such a vote was not in itself an alternative to Brexit. But Labour backbenchers Peter Kyle and Phil Wilson, in particular, championed this as a route out of the impasse—that MPs would vote for a Brexit deal on the condition that it was put to a referendum. Most Labour MPs would likely have agreed to this, and many Conservatives might have reluctantly done so if whipped in favour. An interviewee involved in these cross-party discussions from the government side said that key figures had concluded 'by the early months of 2019 that if this is going to get through it all, our last best hope was probably through biting the bullet and accepting a second referendum, however unpalatable that would be'.

But there were also strong arguments against this route. The first referendum had been deeply divisive, and staging a second one would be quickly denounced by Brexiteers as a betrayal. Theresa May was sympathetic to this view, and also concerned about the precedent that this would set with respect to Scotland—where the SNP was demanding a rerun of the 2014 vote on independence. More prosaically, there were many potential complications in holding a referendum (Sargeant, Renwick, and Russell 2018). The shortest likely timetable was around five months, which would extend beyond the date of the next European Parliament elections, probably requiring the UK to take part in those elections despite having voted for Brexit. In addition, there was no agreement even among pro-referendum campaigners about what the question should be. The likeliest version would pit the deal against remaining in the EU; but this would infuriate hard Brexiteers, who might demand a 'no-deal' option. And since a referendum required legislation, a parliamentary majority would need to be found not just for the principle but on all of these kinds of details. With both parties conflicted on the whole idea of a referendum, this looked extremely difficult.

A No-deal Exit

The third option that May needed to contemplate was a no-deal exit. She had insisted on keeping this on the table during the negotiations, and that such an outcome was 'better than a bad deal', much to the delight of her hardline Brexiteers. But economic modelling demonstrated that the consequences could be grave (HM Government 2019, UK in a Changing Europe 2018a), and this outcome would also have necessitated a hard border on the island of Ireland. The prospect horrified many, including in the business community and in parliament.

In anticipation of the first meaningful vote, forces had come together to express their concern about a no-deal exit, given its attraction among hardliners and the risks that such an outcome could occur by default if no UK political agreement was reached on a deal. Former Conservative Cabinet minister and party loyalist Caroline Spelman worked with her Labour constituency neighbour Jack Dromey to pull together an impressive coalition of MPs and business leaders in opposition to no deal. Both Spelman and Dromey represented Midlands constituencies highly dependent on employment by Jaguar Land Rover, which exported a high proportion of its goods to the EU. Many other MPs had similar concerns. On 17 December 2018 an open letter was sent to the Prime Minister emphasizing the risks of a no-deal exit to UK manufacturing, urging ministers 'to agree a mechanism that would ensure a "No Deal" Brexit could not take place' (Dromey and Spelman 2018). It was signed by over 200 MPs, including at least 22 Conservatives (Islam 2019). This was a clear signal that the Commons was unlikely to support exit without a deal.

Further confirmation came on 8 January, when Labour's Yvette Cooper proposed an amendment to the Finance Bill jointly with Conservative Treasury Select Committee chair Nicky Morgan. This would allow provisions in the bill designed to prepare for a no-deal Brexit to come into force only if the Commons had endorsed an exit on these terms. The amendment was approved by 303 votes to 296, with 20 Conservatives breaking the whip to support it.

These initiatives demonstrated not only the parliamentary strength of feeling against a no-deal exit but also that senior MPs were becoming increasingly organized across party lines. As described in Chapter 6, Spelman and Dromey were key figures in the group of 'grandees' which became more active in the months ahead in seeking to resolve the Brexit deadlock.

Renegotiating the Backstop

The fourth conceivable option was to try and renegotiate the deal itself to remove the elements deemed unacceptable by Conservative Brexiteers—particularly the backstop. At the close of the debate on the deal, the Prime Minister had responded to Edward Leigh's amendment demanding that the backstop should be temporary by saying that the government would seek alternative solutions. Hardline Brexiteers came together, with some moderate Conservatives such as Nicky Morgan, to develop such solutions. A particularly prominent initiative was dubbed the 'Malthouse compromise' after junior minister Kit Malthouse. Like previous proposals, it focused on finding technological ways around the Northern Ireland border problem, but also demanded that the EU honour the transition period even in the case of a no-deal Brexit. However, the EU had indicated that it would not reopen the deal, that the backstop was needed in order to prevent a hard border on the island of Ireland at least until concrete alternative arrangements could be found, and that the transition period was conditional on a Withdrawal Agreement. The dominant view on the staff side in Number 10 was therefore that these proposals were 'unicorns'—fantasy ideas that could never realistically be brought into effect—though some serious figures clearly believed that there was leeway to get the EU to offer more. This approach would not really represent a change of direction so much as pursuit of the same strategy that Theresa May had already steadfastly tried. With some senior MPs championing such outcomes, others perhaps unfamiliar with the detail but craving a solution were tempted to support them. Writing about the Malthouse compromise later, Gavin Barwell (2021: 327) commented that '[i]t was depressing that sensible people were prepared to entertain such nonsense'.

The Procedural Options

The four routes above offered potential choices to the Prime Minister's team in terms of the Brexit destination of travel—though the referendum was in truth more a matter of process than an outcome in itself. How to reach any chosen solution procedurally was a different question, and MPs—including ministers—had been considering this for some time.

House of Commons Indicative Votes

Given the breadth of choices on offer, and the fragmented nature of parliamentary opinion within both main parties, some suggested that the House of Commons should hold 'indicative votes' on the different Brexit options. Generally the Commons votes only yes or no on a single proposition at a time. This proposal would instead invite members to choose simultaneously from a range of options, and perhaps thereby demonstrate which way forward on Brexit had the greatest parliamentary support, enabling a majority to be formed.

There were precedents for this kind of parliamentary decision-making, albeit relatively few and far between. These were summed up at the time by Fox and Baston (2019) for the Hansard Society. Successful examples included votes on legislation, most recently on abortion time limits. But the freshest example in most parliamentarians' minds was a less happy one, of voting on a series of motions on House of Lords reform in 2003 and 2007. In 2003 all options had been rejected, due to a combination of confusion and procedural tactics by some members—notably a group that voted against all of the options in order to scupper the process (McLean, Spirling, and Russell 2003). In 2007 a majority was reached, but the decision was never implemented.

Nonetheless, suggestions that indicative votes should be held, perhaps via an improved process, gained ground from late 2018 onwards as it became increasingly clear that the government's deal would not pass. In November, the House of Commons Procedure Committee (2018a) noted that such a mechanism could be incorporated in the initial decision-making on the deal, following proposals from Dominic Grieve and Oliver Letwin—though it did not explicitly recommend this. In December, after the vote on the deal had been postponed, the *Telegraph* reported that Cabinet ministers including Damian Hinds and Liam Fox were encouraging Theresa May to provide parliamentary time for such a procedure (Maidment 2018). But when publicly pressed on this by Conservative backbencher Jonathan Djanogly, the Prime Minister responded 'I have no plans for indicative votes'.[3] Pressure also came from Labour's Hilary Benn (2018), who called for such votes 'as a matter of urgency' in December, echoed by a report from his committee immediately after the deal had been defeated (Exiting the European Union Committee 2019). Asked about indicative votes in early January, Brexit Secretary Steve Barclay had commented that 'if the deal does not go ahead, we will be in uncharted water and we as a Government will need to look at that'.[4]

There was clearly intense discussion at Cabinet level about this option. One interviewee referred to it as 'the war for Theresa's ear'; however, 'the Prime Minister's instinct was always very sceptical of indicative votes and she would always refer back to what had happened with House of Lords reform'. Some saw this as a means of moving towards a softer Brexit or a referendum. Others thought it could help rally support behind the deal. One government interviewee said 'my view was, "you go through this process, parliament will prove it can't agree on anything, and that gives us the best platform to then try and get our deal through"'. But such votes risked a chaotic outcome, and could lead to uncomfortable conclusions. As another close insider commented, 'whenever you discussed them in Cabinet, you couldn't get enough people saying "we will abide by the result"'. These political risks became clearer later.

Extending the Article 50 Period

As soon as it became evident that the Commons would likely reject the Brexit deal, the prospect of extending the Article 50 period began to be discussed. With the Brexit clock ticking down to 29 March 2019, anxiety increased as the meaningful vote was first postponed and then resulted in defeat. Without an extension, the default would be a no-deal 'crash out' on the pre-appointed exit day. An extension was not achievable by the UK unilaterally; it would need to be agreed with the EU. In order to provide time for more discussion and resolution of the Brexit question, MPs opposed to a no-deal exit therefore began to seek routes to persuade the government to request such an extension in good time if this was needed.

An important manifestation of this was a succession of private members' bills proposed by key members of the 'grandees' and 'Trains and Buses' groups (see Chapter 6) from mid-January 2019 onwards. The first of these was headed by Conservative Nick Boles, and several subsequent iterations by Labour's Yvette Cooper.[5] Other initial signatories included Hilary Benn, Oliver Letwin, Nicky Morgan, Labour's Liz Kendall, and Liberal Democrat Norman Lamb. Later versions attracted further signatures, including Caroline Spelman, Jack Dromey, and Dominic Grieve. All of these bills were slightly different, but all had a central aim of requiring the government to request an extension.

MPs Taking Control

The standard parliamentary dynamic is for members, when they want to influence the government's direction, to put pressure on ministers to make policy concessions. However, with the Cabinet divided, an apparently intransigent Prime Minister, and a finite period in which to resolve the Brexit impasse, MPs increasingly considered options for taking matters into their own hands.

An early exemplar of this was the Boles bill, which—as well as pressing for an extension—sought to hand power to the House of Commons Liaison Committee to prepare an action plan if the government's deal had not been approved by mid-February. This would have come close to creating an alternative cross-party government comprised of senior parliamentarians, accountable to the House of Commons. Although Benn, Cooper, Lamb, and Morgan were all members of the Liaison Committee, other key members firmly opposed the idea. So, in the words of one interviewee involved, 'it wasn't a runner'.

Rather than creating an alternative government, most of MPs' energy was focused on gaining control of the parliamentary agenda—initially in order to facilitate indicative votes if the government failed to do so. This was a potential threat hanging over the government if it refused to act. Discussion of the options available to MPs to achieve such an outcome also began around the time of the first failed meaningful vote. Key 'grandees', including Dominic Grieve and Oliver Letwin, sought advice from parliamentary clerks regarding the procedural options available. These approaches were provoked in part by the fact that other standard routes—in particular opposition days—had been largely shut down by the government. On 19–20 January, two news outlets reported that a cross-party group was seeking to facilitate a vote against a no-deal Brexit by temporarily suspending Standing Order no. 14 (Shipman 2019b, Wickham 2019). The *Sunday Times* specifically named Grieve and a senior clerk, Colin Lee. This brought the clerks temporarily into controversy, but was an example of fairly standard practice—official advice to MPs from neutral procedural specialists, in response to requests about how to achieve their aims. As the government lacked a stable majority, the options available were clearly wider than they would normally be. Notably, as one journalist pointed out, and as seen in Chapter 2, Conservative Eurosceptics had benefited greatly over the years from the clerks' advice about possible procedural tactics (Cameron 2019b).

The Government's Response

Returning to the questions facing the government, as posed to the Prime Minister by her staff in January 2019, there was no easy route out of the difficulties. Softening Brexit, or promising a referendum, in order to bring Labour MPs onside, would have led to bitter splits on the Conservative benches and possible retaliation by the Brexiteers. Pursuing a no-deal exit would clearly have alienated centrist Conservatives, and seemed very unlikely to secure parliamentary support. Even indicative votes were fraught with peril. Downing Street insiders advised the Prime Minister that now was the time to take some risks: to choose a new direction and muster all of the forces available in order to get agreement. But confronted with these difficult choices, an insider said in interview, 'her response was "let's just keep doing what we're doing"'. This maximized the short-term ability to keep her fragile Cabinet and parliamentary party together, but even many on her own staff thought it was ultimately doomed to fail.

The Initial Parliamentary Response

The 29 January Next Steps Motion

The first main opportunity for parliament to act following the defeat on the deal came two weeks later. As described in the previous chapter, Section 13 of the EU (Withdrawal) Act 2018 required a defeat on the deal to be followed by a government statement on the proposed next steps; and, following Dominic Grieve's amendment of December 2018, the associated government motion would be amendable. This meant that MPs could use the occasion to promote their own alternatives for what should happen next.

The debate took place on 29 January 2019, and multiple amendments were tabled, of which two were agreed, five were rejected, and various others were not selected by the Speaker. The most important amendments were those which were approved, one of which was proposed by the 1922 Committee chair Graham Brady, and the other by Caroline Spelman.

The Brady Amendment

The Brady amendment picked up essentially where the earlier amendment from Edward Leigh had left off. The government's motion was in 'neutral terms', simply stating that the House had considered earlier statements. Brady's amendment added the words 'and requires the Northern Ireland backstop to be replaced with alternative arrangements to avoid a hard border; supports leaving the European Union with a deal and would therefore support the Withdrawal Agreement subject to this change'.[6]

Notwithstanding that this amendment contradicted the government's previous position, and the deal that she had negotiated, the Prime Minister announced before the vote that the Cabinet would be supporting it. Conservative whips therefore urged MPs to do the same. Indeed, it is clear that, following the trauma of the first defeat, Number 10 and the whips' office had been central to the drafting of the amendment (Barwell 2021). In debate, Brady argued that it provided a way for parliament to 'send the Prime Minister back to Brussels to negotiate, having strengthened her hand'.[7] The idea was that parliament, by signalling conditional support for the deal, would incentivize the EU to meet those conditions. On this basis, key Conservative Brexiteers, and the DUP, spoke strongly in favour. The amendment was passed by 317 votes to 301, with seven Labour rebels in favour, and eight Conservative rebels against. There was clearly relief that something the Prime Minister had put her name to had finally gained parliamentary support, and that the party had largely coalesced.

The small band of Conservative rebels were drawn from those opposing a hard Brexit, including Dominic Grieve and Ken Clarke. Grieve (2020) subsequently said that 'the Brady amendment was a mere act of symbolism, which was why people like Ken and I didn't vote for it', suggesting that parliamentarians were 'living in fantasy land, and given how deep this crisis [was], pandering to fantasy [was] not going to solve your problem'. Jean-Claude Juncker had reportedly spoken to Theresa May on the day of the vote and emphasized that the EU would not reopen the negotiations (Barwell 2021). The recognition of this problem was widespread. David Gauke (2020), then a member of the Cabinet, has said that the 'Brady amendment was a unicorn, I voted for it as we were all required to do but it was never going to go anywhere'. A different Cabinet interviewee commented, 'I always thought it was nuts'. A senior official said that 'like the Malthouse stuff it was, you know, "why are you entertaining this?", because it is fantasy, there is no set of alternative arrangements'. But backbenchers were getting signals from their leaders that there might be an easy way out.

Writing in the *Spectator* after the vote, Isabel Hardman (2019) concluded that 'the Brady amendment gives Theresa May the strength to kick the can down the road'. The idea that it strengthened her hand in Brussels was, meanwhile, distinctly questionable. One close to the negotiations reported in interview how a European counterpart had observed:

> What we have learned from Brady is that there's a load of people in the Tory party that want a more distant relationship. And what that tells us is that if Theresa May is replaced, she's going to be replaced by someone that wants a more distant relationship. And therefore it's more important than ever that we have a backstop. So actually what we have learned from Brady is we must keep the backstop.

The Spelman Amendment

While the Brady amendment offered solace to hardline Brexiteers, the Spelman amendment did the reverse, by seeking to rule out a no-deal Brexit. It added at the end of the government's motion 'and rejects the United Kingdom leaving the European Union without a Withdrawal Agreement and a Framework for the Future Relationship'.[8]

Spelman had voted for May's deal, and emphasized that her amendment was offered in constructive spirit, using words that could almost have come from the Prime Minister herself: 'The public…want us to come together in the national interest, and we can do that by agreeing that no to no deal means that there has to be a deal.'[9] May's response to the amendment was that she 'appreciated the spirit', but that the only way to avoid a no-deal exit was to vote for a deal.[10] This clearly represented a tactical dilemma for the Prime Minister. By reversing her position and ruling out a no-deal exit, she could potentially have boxed in her hardliners to support the deal, leaving the only viable alternative on the table as 'no Brexit'. But this would have been seen as a major U-turn, and would have caused huge anger among that group. One Cabinet interviewee said, '[i]f you'd done that, I think you would then have had a putsch against her'. It would also have taken pressure off Brexit-sceptics on the Conservative benches, perhaps encouraging them to abandon the deal. Opposition MPs, meanwhile, would have sniffed new opportunities to end the whole Brexit process.

Hardliners argued against Spelman's amendment, on the (rather dubious) basis that removing the option of no deal would release pressure on the EU to make a better offer. The government whipped against the proposal. Nonetheless it passed, by 318 votes to 310, with 17 Conservatives voting in favour (and three Labour MPs voting against). Spelman had demonstrated for the second time in three weeks that there was no Commons majority for a no-deal exit, which some inside government considered helpful. But the Prime Minister was reluctant publicly to concede.

Failed Amendments: Indicative Votes and Suspension of Standing Order no. 14

Various further amendments to the government motion failed, but indicated the other competing pressures on ministers. The Labour frontbench proposed that there should be indicative votes on the Brexit options, as did several backbench amendments which were not selected for debate. It is always difficult to bring government backbenchers round to support an opposition frontbench proposal, and the idea was at this stage defeated. Dominic Grieve made the first attempt to suspend Standing Order no. 14 for future days, to free up debating time to discuss the options. This attracted 15 Conservative rebels, but failed due to inadequate Labour support. An amendment from Yvette Cooper and Nick Boles likewise sought to take control of the agenda for a day specifically to discuss a bill requiring the government to seek an Article 50 extension. Again, there were 17 Conservative rebels but insufficient Labour support. Further amendments, respectively from Labour's Rachel Reeves (chair of the Business, Energy and Industrial Strategy Select Committee) and the SNP's Ian Blackford, to move straight to an extension were also voted down. A proposal from Labour's Stella Creasy that there should be a citizens' assembly on the Brexit options was among those not selected by the Speaker.

Overall, conflicting markers had been laid down for the Prime Minister. The backstop was not acceptable, but neither was exiting the EU without a deal. Other options, for a softer Brexit or a referendum, had not been presented, and MPs were not yet ready to force indicative votes or an Article 50 extension on the government. But their patience was not to last.

Follow-up by Government and Parliament

Immediately after these votes, European Council President Donald Tusk issued a public comment that 'the backstop is part of the Withdrawal Agreement, and the Withdrawal Agreement is not open for renegotiation' (quoted in Baczynska 2019). The government nonetheless turned to the EU in search of some kind of compromise. Efforts focused on seeking one of three things: changes to the backstop, a time limit on the backstop, or a unilateral exit mechanism from it for the UK; Barwell (2021: 331) later noted that 'on the face of it, all three were unnegotiable'. Opponents demanded that a new arrangement must be legally enforceable—possibly in a side letter, rather than through reopening the Withdrawal Agreement itself. For the government, some kind of symbolic victory might normally have been enough to signal to backbenchers that it was time to back down. But whatever emerged would need to survive scrutiny, and possible counter-briefings, from the ERG.

On 12 February, Theresa May reported this strategy to the Commons, and also emphasized—in an attempt to attract Labour supporters—that the government was seeking means to guarantee no regression of workers' or environmental rights post Brexit. Further, she announced that a new amendable motion—beyond those statutorily required by the EU (Withdrawal) Act—would be brought forward two days later. This would allow MPs to affirm their support for the policy being pursued. It provided another opportunity for different groups to express views and propose alternatives, and amendments were tabled demanding indicative votes, a further referendum, an Article 50 extension, or the complete revocation of Article 50. All of these were either not selected by the Speaker or not passed. But the government's motion itself was also voted down, after five Conservative MPs opposed it and a further 66 were absent from the vote. Most were hardline Brexiteers, but some were also Brexit sceptics. An attempt to demonstrate unity had resulted in another show of division.

Notwithstanding the failure of Yvette Cooper's 29 January amendment to secure parliamentary time for a bill mandating an Article 50 extension, work on this proposal continued. Indeed, Barwell (2021) has indicated that Conservative support for Cooper's proposition had only been temporarily bought off through the uneasy harmony created by the Brady amendment. On 13 February a further bill was published sponsored by Cooper, on behalf of the same cross-party group.[11] This proposed that the deadline for the Commons to approve a deal should be 13 March, after which MPs should be asked whether they supported leaving the EU without a deal. If they didn't, the Prime Minister would seek their approval to request an extension. Barwell notes that several Cabinet ministers, including Amber Rudd, David Gauke, and Philip Hammond, threatened to resign in order to support Cooper's initiative. This created very serious pressure on the Prime Minister.

On 26 February Theresa May made another Commons statement, claiming that discussions were continuing, to 'develop alternative arrangements to ensure the absence of a hard border in Northern Ireland'.[12] She also set out plans largely identical to those in the latest Cooper bill: promising that there would be a second meaningful vote no later than 12 March, and that if this failed the government would bring forward a motion the next day allowing

MPs to vote on the principle of leaving without a deal. If consent was not forthcoming, the government would then ask MPs to support requesting an extension to Article 50. This indicated that the internal government pressure had worked, and signalled to ERG opponents that a further rejection of the deal would result in a delay to Brexit.

The next day the government presented another non-statutory amendable Brexit motion, which underlined this message by providing an opportunity for MPs to back the plan. The key amendment came from Cooper, demanding an Article 50 extension if the Commons rejected both the deal and a no-deal exit. This was in line with her bill, and with the Prime Minister's promises of the previous day, so Brexit Secretary Steve Barclay indicated that the government was happy to accept it. Finally, there were some signs of cooperation across the party divide. Some hardline Brexiteers opposed Cooper's amendment, so it was pushed to the vote, but passed by an overwhelming 502 to 20 votes. This clarified that a no-deal Brexit was off the table at least in the short term, and that parliament would demand an Article 50 extension in the absence of support for the deal. Although forced on the Prime Minister, it required hardline Brexiteers to confront the potential consequences of voting down the deal.

Party Splits: Birth of The Independent Group

A final key development ahead of the second meaningful vote was a much-delayed formal split in the main parties. Despite the evident difficulties on the Conservative side, it was Labour MPs who jumped first. On 18 February seven of them—Luciana Berger, Ann Coffey, Mike Gapes, Chris Leslie, Chuka Umunna, Angela Smith, and Gavin Shuker—held a press conference to announce that they were leaving the party to form a coalition of independent MPs, which became known as The Independent Group (TIG). Another Labour MP, Joan Ryan, joined them the following day. All of the breakaway MPs were strongly pro-European (though Brexit was not the only reason for the split), and Leslie and Umunna in particular had played visible parliamentary roles in seeking to nudge Theresa May and Jeremy Corbyn towards a soft Brexit position or a referendum. The group's founding statement argued that Labour had 'failed to take a lead in addressing the challenge of Brexit and to provide a strong and coherent alternative to the Conservatives' approach' (quoted in McNab 2021: v).

On 20 February, three Conservative MPs—Heidi Allen, Anna Soubry, and Sarah Wollaston—held their own press conference to announce that they too were breaking away, to join forces with the new group. In an open letter to

Theresa May they argued that 'Brexit has re-defined the Conservative Party—undoing all the efforts to modernise it', and that '[f]ollowing the EU referendum of 2016, no genuine effort was made to build a cross party, let alone a national consensus to deliver Brexit'. They lamented 'a dismal failure to stand up to the hard line ERG which operates openly as a party within a party' (Soubry, Wollaston, and Allen 2019). At the group's press conference, Soubry argued that 'the hard-line anti-EU awkward squad that have destroyed every leader for the last 40 years are now running the Conservative Party from top to toe' (BBC News 2019j).

The actions of the two sides seemed relatively uncoordinated, though as seen in Chapter 6, several of these members had been working closely together on cross-party Brexit initiatives. On the Labour side, at least, discussions about a possible split had been fermenting for months (Pogrund and Maguire 2020). The breakaway was delayed by the postponement of the first meaningful vote, but since Berger was heavily pregnant and about to go on maternity leave, could wait no longer (McNab 2021). Initially there were expectations that more Labour MPs might follow, but party deputy leader Tom Watson sought to shore up support within the party, and the defections were rapidly followed by a change of policy. A week after the split, on 25 February, Jeremy Corbyn announced that if the deal didn't pass on the second attempt Labour would move to supporting a further referendum (BBC News 2019k). Labour MP Jess Phillips (2020)—who was rumoured to have been considering joining the breakaway group—has commented that their actions 'definitely made the Labour Party shift, without question'.

So while Theresa May was trapped by her Brexiteers, both leaders were also being held hostage by their pro-European MPs, with very limited room for manoeuvre.

The Second Meaningful Vote and its Aftermath

The Meaningful Vote of 12 March

As Theresa May had promised, a repeat meaningful vote was scheduled for 12 March. This gave MPs an opportunity to reconsider the deal, in the light of the discussions at European level following the Brady amendment. In preparation for news from Brussels, the ERG had set up a rather audaciously named 'star chamber', chaired by veteran Eurosceptic MP Bill Cash, to consider the legal ramifications of whatever was agreed. Amid expectations that no legally binding alternative to the backstop would be achievable, it seemed very likely that the group would again instruct its members to reject the deal. Hence some senior Conservatives reportedly counselled the Prime Minister to postpone the vote (Wright and Waterfield 2019).

An agreement with the EU was announced only on the evening of 11 March. In an unusual Commons statement at 10 p.m., David Lidington advised MPs that since they had been 'clear on the need for legally binding changes to the backstop. Today we have secured those changes'.[13] There had, as widely expected, been no amendment to the Withdrawal Agreement itself. Instead, two new documents had been produced—a legally binding instrument committing the UK and EU to work to replace the backstop, and a joint political statement outlining commitments on both sides to expedite the future relationship negotiations. The next day Attorney General Geoffrey Cox (2019) published a legal opinion which nonetheless admitted that, in terms of the UK being caught in the backstop, 'the legal risk remains unchanged'. Unsurprisingly, the ERG's 'star chamber' then advised MPs against supporting the deal (BrexitCentral 2019).

Introducing the debate on 12 March, Theresa May's tone was somewhat changed, with less emphasis on the threat of a no-deal exit—which MPs had by now done their best to rule out. Instead, she suggested that 'those who want genuinely to deliver Brexit need to recognise that if this deal does not go through tonight, the House risks no Brexit at all'.[14] Again, she emphasized the need for unity, pointedly suggesting that 'democracy comes before party, faction or personal ambition'.[15] Opponents raised now-familiar objections to the backstop, with ERG members, and Sammy Wilson of the DUP, emphasizing that it would keep the whole of the UK too closely aligned with the EU. Boris Johnson spoke, objecting that it 'ties our hands for the future and sets us on a path to a subordinate relationship with the EU that is still…clearly based on the customs union and on large parts of the single market'.[16] But in terms of practical alternatives, his only suggestion was that a no-deal exit would be preferable to this deal. Some other Conservatives who had previously opposed the deal were more emollient, arguing that now was the time to back the government. Brexiteer Edward Leigh suggested that 'the fairly small risk of our being trapped in the backstop forever' was preferable to completely losing Brexit.[17] For Labour, Jeremy Corbyn maintained a typical opposition stance of picking holes in the government's position, to justify his party voting against it.

The vote, when it took place, was another resounding defeat for Theresa May—albeit slightly less crushing than before. Only 242 MPs supported the deal, while 391—including 75 Conservatives—voted against it (see Table 8.3, below). The DUP was opposed, while just three Labour members voted with the government. The number of Conservative opponents had dropped, from 118 in January, but was still formidable; and they were again primarily Leave supporters. Just 12 of the rebels were former Remainers (down from the previous 26), while various well-known Brexiteers including Boris Johnson, Dominic Raab, and Jacob Rees-Mogg rejected the deal for a second time.[18] Others now more prepared to be pragmatic included Graham Brady himself, who shifted position to fall in behind the government, as did David Davis. In total, 28 former Leave supporters (based on their declared 2016 vote) switched from opposition to support, while 62 continued to oppose the government.

The newspapers now highlighted the irony of Brexiteers' opposition to the deal—to a far greater extent than they had done following the previous meaningful vote. The *Sun* denounced 'a catastrophic failure by a Parliament of pygmies', complaining that 'Tory Brexiteers who rejected the deal have lost the plot' (Gye, Clark, and Dathan 2019). Likewise, the *Daily Mail* (2019e) argued that 'these Tory wreckers will not be forgiven', pointing out that the second defeat could result in the abandonment of Brexit, in which case 'the ERG will be directly responsible'. The *Daily Express* (2019b) likewise warned that the Brexiteers voting against the deal may have 'killed off the last chance' for Brexit. These contemporary views from the Brexit-supporting press contrast starkly with how the parliamentary blame game played out later. Though the *Daily Express* did simultaneously argue that a 'Remainer parliament ha[d] sought to thwart the will of the majority', which was to become an increasingly familiar line.

Ruling Out No Deal

While this was clearly a further significant blow for the Prime Minister, arrangements had largely already been made to deal with an anticipated defeat. The cogs of what had previously been promised therefore clicked into action.

The first step was a government motion the following day, 13 March, to allow MPs a vote on leaving the EU without a deal. The previously agreed 'exit day' was only 16 days away, so the choices were between this and an Article 50 extension—which would be proposed next, if a no-deal exit was rejected. The government's motion was strangely worded, almost certainly as a result of the rifts within the Cabinet, stating 'That this House declines to approve leaving the European Union without a Withdrawal Agreement and a Framework for the Future Relationship on 29 March 2019; and notes that leaving without a deal remains the default in UK and EU law unless this House and the EU ratify an agreement'.[19]

This wording—seeking to rule out no deal while stating that it remained the default—attracted criticism from MPs opposed to that outcome, and an amendment was led by Caroline Spelman which would simplify it, essentially to remove the second part. The usual topics of a further referendum or the revocation of Article 50 were proposed in other amendments, which were not selected for debate. The only other selected amendment proposed a return to the 'Malthouse compromise'. In a further indication of the government's internal divisions Conservatives were given a free vote on this, allegedly to avoid resignations by Brexiteer ministers who wanted to support it (Tominey 2019a).

The Malthouse compromise amendment was heavily defeated by 374 votes to 164.[20] The Spelman amendment, meanwhile, created a major upset. Spelman herself spoke strongly against a no-deal exit, but indicated that she wished her amendment to be withdrawn rather than voted upon—presumably following pressure from government whips. But other MPs pushed it to a vote, and it resulted in a narrow government defeat (by 312 to 308, with nine Conservatives in support). This meant that the government's motion had been amended in line with Spelman's words, so that when the main motion was put to the vote it was not immediately clear how Conservative members (and particularly ministers) should respond. Government whips issued rapid instructions to vote against the now-amended motion, but 46 Conservative MPs either supported it or did not vote, among them several ministers. Sarah Newton, who had voted in favour, resigned her ministerial position. But four members of the Cabinet—Greg Clark, David Gauke, David Mundell, and Amber Rudd—and some other ministers abstained. This sparked a furious response from Chief Whip Julian Smith, who reportedly wanted it to result in sackings (Rudd 2021). But to allow the motion to fall would have left the position unclear. With the amended motion approved by 321 votes to 278, the Commons had again unarguably voted against no deal. But the government's position was shambolic, and consequently the motion had passed with support from just 17 Conservative MPs.

The First Article 50 Extension

It therefore remained for MPs to consider the question of an Article 50 extension. In line with the Prime Minister's previous promises, a government motion was presented on 14 March to seek authorization for this from the Commons. It was in many ways a deeply uncomfortable development. Not only had Theresa May pledged repeatedly that the UK would leave the EU by 29 March 2019, but continued membership would also soon run up against the European Parliament elections, due to take place in May. The Brexit vote had implied that the UK would not participate in these elections, and that its MEPs would shortly be departing the parliament. Indeed, plans had already been made for the UK's seats to be redistributed among other member states. Remaining in the bloc for more than a few weeks would require these arrangements to be unpicked, and UK parties to fight elections to a body that the referendum had set the country on a course to leave.

The government's motion emphasized these anomalies, noting that 'it is highly likely that…any extension beyond 30 June 2019 would require the United Kingdom to hold European Parliament elections'. This was a bitter pill for Brexiteers, in particular, to swallow. Hence ministers' proposed solution was a short extension to 30 June. However, the UK would not get to dictate the term of any extension, as this would require negotiation with other EU partners.

This debate once again provided an opportunity for various amendments to be tabled suggesting alternative ways forward, as well as for approval of the motion itself. The most important proposal came from a large cross-party group headed by Hilary Benn, Oliver Letwin, and Yvette Cooper, recommending that Standing Order no. 14 should be suspended on 20 March to allow indicative votes to be held on the Brexit options. Speaking for the government, David Lidington indicated that ministers would 'facilitate a process…to allow the House to seek a majority on the way forward' in the coming weeks.[21] The amendment was only very narrowly defeated, by 314 votes to 312, with 15 Conservatives rebelling. Clearly MPs' patience was wearing thin, but some may have been persuaded by Lidington's assurances. Another key cross-party amendment was headed by Sarah Wollaston, with signatories including other members of The Independent Group, plus the SNP and Liberal Democrats. This called for an extension to be used to facilitate a referendum. Notwithstanding Labour's recent change of policy on this question, the party whipped its MPs to abstain on the amendment—on the basis that the time was not right, and this distracted from the straightforward question of the Article 50 extension. Nonetheless, 25 Labour MPs voted in favour, including key referendum advocates such as David Lammy and Owen Smith. More strikingly, 18 Labour MPs broke the whip to cast a symbolic vote against the amendment, four of whom resigned as frontbenchers to do so. This public display of division on the opposition benches signalled that a referendum offered no easy route out of the situation. The amendment was heavily defeated, by 334 votes to 85.

The government's motion in favour of an Article 50 extension was convincingly supported by 412 votes to 202. But the breakdown of votes indicated major difficulties on the Conservative side. Just 112 Tory MPs had voted for the extension, while 188 had voted against. Theresa May had secured approval from the Commons, but largely built on opposition votes. Those opposing the motion included seven Cabinet ministers.[22] This had officially been made a free vote, so unlike on the previous day there were no suggestions of sackings; but the situation again demonstrated the extreme weakness of May's position.

The next day a statement was published confirming that the government would now seek to negotiate an extension. Consequently, it noted, ministers would use the powers delegated to them to amend 'exit day' in the EU (Withdrawal) Act to accommodate the extension agreed.[23]

May Turns on Parliament

On 20 March Theresa May wrote to Donald Tusk as authorized, to request the first extension to the Article 50 period. Her stated justification was the need for more time to secure parliamentary approval for the Brexit deal. By now tensions were running very high, and some extremely ill-tempered exchanges occurred on the day that the letter was sent.

First, at Prime Minister's Questions, May responded angrily to a suggestion from Jeremy Corbyn that she had failed to compromise, or to take a no-deal exit definitively off the table. Lashing out at MPs, with reference to the various votes on amendments in preceding weeks, she argued that:

> this House has voted on and rejected a second referendum; it has voted on and rejected no deal; it has voted on and rejected Labour's deal; it has voted on and rejected a customs union; and it has voted on and supported leaving with a deal. It is time that this Parliament faced the consequences.[24]

Growing increasingly angry, she then suggested that '[t]he House has indulged itself on Europe for too long', and accused Corbyn of seeking 'to disrespect democracy by holding a second referendum'.[25] In turn, one of the hardline Brexiteers accused her of 'betraying the British people' in applying for an Article 50 extension, pointing out that this outcome had been rejected by two thirds of Conservative MPs.[26]

To add to the pressure, Labour had been granted an emergency debate that afternoon to discuss the length and purpose of the Article 50 extension. A notable contribution to the debate came from Dominic Grieve, who referred to his long-standing 'personal friendship' with May.[27] But reflecting on the PMQ exchanges he claimed that this:

> was the worst moment I have experienced since I came into the House of Commons. I have never felt more ashamed to be a Member of the Conservative party or to be asked to lend her support. She spent most of her time castigating the House for its misconduct. At no stage did she pause to consider whether it is, in fact, the way that she is leading this Government that might be contributing to this situation.[28]

These various exchanges were undoubtedly bruising for the Prime Minister, and must have contributed to her decision later that day to make a further vitriolic attack on parliament, in a televised statement from Downing Street—subsequently described by her then Chief of Staff as 'one of the worst mistakes we made' (Barwell 2020). Addressing the nation about the request for a Brexit extension, May (2019b) stated:

> This delay is a matter of great personal regret for me. And of this I am absolutely sure: you the public have had enough. You are tired of the infighting. You are tired of the political games and the arcane procedural rows. Tired of MPs talking about nothing else but Brexit when you have real concerns about our children's schools, our National Health Service, and knife crime. You want this stage of the Brexit process to be over and done with. I agree. I am on your side…[but] Parliament has done everything possible to avoid making a choice.

As further discussed in Chapter 9, May's rhetoric was a textbook case of populism (Müller 2016), painting parliamentarians as an out-of-touch elite, and herself as a champion of a righteous people. The statement sidestepped fundamental truths, that the Prime Minister herself was drawn from this elite, that her own job depended on its support, and that she had not facilitated the kind of debate on alternative options that many even in her own party had called for. Crucially, she failed to identify that the main responsibility for the gridlock lay with her own backbench Brexiteers. This appears to have been a serious missed opportunity, once again, to have got the public—and crucially the Brexit-supporting media—'on her side', and to isolate the hardliners.

The response to the statement from parliamentarians was one of disbelief and fury. Labour's Wes Streeting (2019) called it 'incendiary and irresponsible' at a time when MPs were already receiving death threats; his colleague Lisa Nandy (2019) likewise suggested that '[p]itting Parliament against the people in the current environment is dangerous and reckless'. Many Conservative MPs were equally upset; May's own Chief Whip Julian Smith was reported to have called the statement 'appalling' (Elliott, Zeffman, and Webber 2019). It was certainly counterproductive, given that any resolution of Brexit would require MPs' cooperation, and that Labour members such as Nandy were exactly some of those whom the whips had hoped to bring onside. Boris Johnson (2019g) memorably took to the pages of the *Telegraph* to denounce the Prime Minister's words, suggesting that 'It is wrong in every sense to blame MPs for blocking Brexit. It is both shameful, and inaccurate'.[29] This too is an important intervention to recall, given his own later rhetoric, as discussed in Chapter 9. Elements of the Brexit-supporting press, however, received May's statement more positively. The *Daily Mail* (2019b) applauded the Prime Minister's decision to go 'over the heads of incompetent MPs and hard Brexit zealots', and urged Brexiteers once more to 'stand up and be counted', while the *Sun* splashed, 'I'm on YOUR side…not warring MPs' (Newton Dunn 2019).

This new low in relations between government and parliament was followed two days later by the granting of an extension, which the EU had agreed to with a twist. Rather than approving the Prime Minister's proposed 30 June end date, the extension was granted only to 22 May, the day before the European Parliament elections—and only if parliament had approved the Withdrawal Agreement by the original exit day of 29 March. Should it fail to do so, the extension would expire on 12 April, with an invitation for the UK government to make new proposals. This increased the pressure on all sides, and opened up immediate discussion of the potential need for a further extension.

The 'Same Question' Rule

The EU's terms immediately raised the question of whether the deal could be presented to parliament for yet another vote before 29 March. There had already been speculation about this on the day of the second meaningful vote, given the obvious likelihood that the deal would be rejected. A cross-party amendment to the government's motion from Labour's Chris Bryant had noted that the parliamentary procedural guide Erskine May precluded by convention a motion or amendment being voted upon that had already been decided within the same parliamentary session. Bryant's amendment hence demanded that this 'same question' rule should be respected, and the deal not be put to the Commons for a third time. The amendment wasn't voted upon, but used by Bryant to make a point.

Four days later, on 18 March, Speaker Bercow made a statement on this question to MPs. He noted that there were rumours of a third meaningful vote, and that if this was on a substantially different question to before it would be in order, but that the government 'cannot legitimately...resubmit to the House the same proposition or substantially the same proposition as that of last week, which was rejected by 149 votes'.[30]

This was one of Bercow's more controversial rulings during the period. It was welcomed immediately by Brexiteers, but strongly criticized by the government. In fact, while there was clear precedent on the 'same question' rule, what made this situation unusual was that it was being used to block proposals from ministers. In normal times of majority government, ministers would not need repeated attempts to gain Commons approval for their policy, and the rule primarily offers protection against time-wasting on nongovernment business (such as motions to introduce 10-minute rule bills—see Erskine May 2019: 20:12). So Bercow's unusually combative approach was in part a product of circumstances. But he subsequently went noticeably beyond precedent, by suggesting that the government could not circumvent the rule by seeking MPs' agreement to a 'notwithstanding' motion to set it aside.[31] This denied rights not just to the government but to MPs themselves, and was both unprecedented and difficult to defend.[32] In response to Bercow's first ruling, ministers suggested that they too could push the boundaries of convention. Appearing on BBC News, Solicitor General Robert Buckland pointed out that the government could if necessary sidestep the rule by proroguing parliament and starting a new parliamentary session (Elgot 2019b).

Backbenchers Take Control

So by late March, the government had been defeated twice on its Brexit deal, and the House of Commons had made clear that it rejected the idea of a no-deal exit. An extension to Article 50 had been agreed by MPs, and secured with the EU, but the clock was ticking down, and very soon the UK faced the unpalatable prospect of requesting a second extension and preparing for European elections. Despite Theresa May's protestations that the Commons had rejected all of the options except delay, the government had still not facilitated the kind of indicative votes process that had been proposed for months, and was supported by several Cabinet ministers. The deal had not met with MPs' approval, but the government had yet to test the alternatives.

The First Disapplication of Standing Order no. 14

Under Section 13 of the EU (Withdrawal) Act, the second meaningful vote defeat now needed to be followed by a government 'next steps' motion, which would again be amendable. This debate took place shortly after the extension had been granted, on 25 March. The usual variety of amendments were tabled, but the key decision was on a proposal from Oliver Letwin, alongside a long cross-party list of signatories drawn from the 'grandees' and key figures from other groupings described in Chapter 6 (House of Commons 2019b).[33] This sought to set aside Standing Order no. 14 on 27 March, in order to debate a series of motions on the Brexit options—in effect, to facilitate indicative votes.

Leading for the government, David Lidington again indicated that ministers planned to provide a similar process, suggesting that it would occur later that same week. But no firm details were provided, and MPs were no longer willing to back down in response to vague reassurances, given the government's previous reluctance to act. Crucially, time was rapidly running out. Lidington was among those in the debate who argued that setting aside Standing Order no. 14 would be constitutionally problematic, claiming that it 'would upset the balance between legislature and Executive in a way that would set an unwelcome precedent'.[34] The most outspoken proponents of this argument were hardline Brexiteers, including Bill Cash, who denounced the proposal as a 'constitutional revolution', and suggested—somewhat oddly in the context of minority government—that Standing Order no. 14 must be respected, because it upheld the rights of 'the majority of Members of Parliament, who form the Government'.[35]

In response to Cash, Speaker Bercow advised that 'the House is the owner of the Standing Orders', and therefore perfectly entitled to set them aside by majority vote.[36] Oliver Letwin argued that the principle of default government control was a relatively recent one in Westminster parliamentary history, and suggested that there was 'no revolutionary intent behind the amendment'.[37] Letwin emphasized that he had sought consistently to bring members together in support of the Prime Minister's deal, and had voted for it twice himself, but that he feared May might now be forced into exiting without a deal. Other Conservatives supporting him were sharply critical of members on their own side. Nicholas Soames pointed out that he had voted for the deal while Boris Johnson, Jacob Rees-Mogg, Steve Baker, and others had not, suggesting that it was 'ironic that those who apparently wish most fervently to leave are those who have most consistently voted against the withdrawal agreement and thus inhibited any real progress'.[38] Those members were absent from the debate, but would likely have argued that the deal that May had presented was not an authentic Brexit. Speaking for the Labour frontbench, Keir Starmer supported Letwin's initiative, and the principle of 'exploring whether there is a majority for a different approach', suggesting that this was 'actually what we should have done two years ago'.[39] Starmer echoed the Vote Leave mantra in supporting Letwin's tactic, suggesting that 'Parliament must take back control'.[40] Expressing regret that this was necessary, Dominic Grieve suggested that due to 'their intransigence over many months', 'the Government have only themselves to blame'.[41]

The Letwin amendment passed relatively easily, by 329 votes to 302, with 30 Conservative MPs voting in support—three of them resigning from the government to do so.[42] This moment of drama appealed to the media, which widely reported MPs 'seizing' control. The *Daily Telegraph* suggested that 'Parliament leaves May powerless with plot to seize agenda' (Rayner 2019), and similar wording appeared in the *Times* (Elliott and Wright 2019) and *Guardian* (Stewart and Elgot 2019). The *Daily Express* adopted the more dramatic framing of a betrayal by 'Remainer' MPs, claiming '[t]hey've now stolen what's left of Brexit' (Hall 2019b).

The Indicative Votes of 27 March

Following several false starts, the Commons was therefore now finally set to stage indicative votes.

The Process

As is well known, the indicative votes did not succeed in breaking the Brexit deadlock. Proponents ended up frustrated when none of the options tabled found majority support. Some critics have suggested that there were ways in which the votes could have been more carefully designed and managed, to provide a more constructive result. Others always considered failure to be inevitable. Chief Whip Julian Smith (2020) was among those warning that the process was 'doomed from the start'. Such objections had clearly contributed to the government's reluctance to instigate such a procedure itself.

The most obvious problem, as seen with the recent precedents (discussed earlier in the chapter), was that members might not vote sincerely when presented with different options—instead seeking to game the system. This could potentially have been addressed through the design of the voting process. From the earliest stage of discussion in the context of Brexit, key proponents of indicative votes had argued that that these should use a preferential voting system, whereby MPs would rank the options on offer, rather than voting yes or no to each individual proposition. Such a procedure is used, for example, by MPs for the election of Speaker and select committee chairs. A key advocate of this approach was former Labour frontbencher and member of the Commons Procedure Committee Helen Goodman, who worked on detailed proposals with Conservative grandee Ken Clarke. For example, the pair had tabled an amendment to this effect to the government's motion of 14 February (House of Commons 2019a). Goodman (2019) had argued convincingly that yes/no votes were unsuited to the task, and many MPs assumed that a preferential system would be adopted. But Letwin was among those who believed that a more conventional parliamentary decision-making mechanism was needed. While an exhaustive ballot (where failed options are eliminated, and votes are redistributed among remaining options until a winning proposal emerges) might guarantee a majority of sorts, this could appear manufactured. An interviewee close to the process therefore suggested that 'the only thing that would actually have an effect on the price of eggs was if you could get a parliamentary majority in favour of something: a straight, simple parliamentary majority'. Despite 'endless discussion' about voting systems, the group of 'grandees' who devised the process to be followed on 27 March ultimately based this on yes/no voting.

The point about the importance of a 'real' majority was linked to the more fundamental difficulty with indicative votes mentioned earlier in the chapter: that while parliament might in principle approve a solution, in practice the government's cooperation would be required to implement it. A key insider recalled the dilemma of 'what happens if something gets a majority that in government we fundamentally disagree with, or…the Conservative Party refuses to vote for?' Hence a Labour frontbencher commented, 'I always thought it was a long shot because, in a sense, there was no enforcement on the other side'. In principle the Prime Minister could perhaps have committed to implementing the result but, even had she tried, her party might well not have let her do so.

The Options

Debate on 27 March began with agreement of the process, whereby the Speaker would select a suitable range of motions from those submitted by members, to be debated and voted upon simultaneously on paper.[43] Sixteen proposals were submitted, and Bercow (2020b: 386) recalled that 'I was able quite easily to whittle down the motions chosen to eight, on the grounds of how many colleagues ha[d] signed them and breadth of support they enjoyed'. The eight selected motions are summarized in Table 8.2, and covered a range of options from no deal, through softer forms of Brexit, to a further referendum or revoking Article 50.[44] These broadly reflected the various conflicting options that had been touted at earlier stages.

It fell to the proposers of the motions, and others working with them, to convince MPs of their merits. Given the complexity of the options, figure-heads and informal whipping would be important in communicating to MPs which they should support. The hard Brexit options came from

Table 8.2 Options in the indicative votes of 27 March 2019

Proposition	Lead sponsor (party)	Voting result	Margin of loss	Con/Lab supporters	Con/Lab opponents
Leave on 12 April without a deal	John Baron (Con)	160–400	240	157 Con 3 Lab	94 Con 237 Lab
If no deal, transition period and trade agreement ('Malthouse compromise')	Marcus Fysh (Con)	139–422	283	126 Con 3 Lab	122 Con 233 Lab
EEA/EFTA	George Eustice (Con)	64–337	273	59 Con 4 Lab	200 Con 124 Lab
Customs union	Ken Clarke (Con)	265–271	6	34 Con 226 Lab	235 Con 12 Lab
Norway plus arrangement ('Common Market 2.0')	Nick Boles (Con)	189–283	94	37 Con 143 Lab	225 Con 42 Lab
Labour frontbench plan	Jeremy Corbyn (Lab)	237–307	70	1 Con 232 Lab	276 Con 4 Lab
Confirmatory referendum on any deal ('Kyle–Wilson' plan)	Margaret Beckett (Lab)	268–295	27	8 Con 198 Lab	254 Con 27 Lab
Revoke Article 50 to prevent no deal	Joanna Cherry (SNP)	184–293	109	10 Con 111 Lab	259 Con 22 Lab

Conservative-only groups of supporters, advocating a no-deal exit or the Malthouse compromise. Another group led by George Eustice proposed an EEA arrangement, while opposing any customs union, and urging the government to find an alternative solution for the Northern Ireland border. One option was purely sponsored by the Labour frontbench, restating its preference for a permanent customs union, close alignment with the Single Market, and continued alignment on matters such as employment rights. Other proposals came from the increasingly well-organized cross-party groups introduced in Chapter 6, sponsored by key figures within them. Ken Clarke's proposal of a permanent customs union was co-sponsored by Oliver Letwin, and Labour's Hilary Benn, Yvette Cooper, and Helen Goodman. The motion from Nick Boles for a 'Norway plus' arrangement was co-sponsored by Labour's Stephen Kinnock and Lucy Powell. Margaret Beckett's motion presented the compromise frequently touted by Labour's Peter Kyle and Phil Wilson, who co-sponsored it, indicating in-principle support for a deal, on the condition that it would be put to a referendum. Other signatories included Conservative Justine Greening and representatives of the SNP and Greens. Finally, Joanna Cherry of the SNP proposed what she called 'a revocation backstop', requiring the government to revoke Article 50 if two days before exit day there was still no agreed deal and parliament had not approved a no-deal exit. This route was now known to be possible, following a December 2018 ruling by the European Court of Justice in the *Wightman* case that Article 50 could be unilaterally revoked by the UK government.[45] Cherry had been a litigant in the case, and her proposal was co-sponsored by Dominic Grieve, Labour's Ben Bradshaw, Sarah Wollaston of TIG, and others from the Liberal Democrats and Plaid Cymru.[46]

A further process question concerned whether it was appropriate for all of these options to run simultaneously, as they related to different dimensions. Notably, a referendum was not a substitute for the various forms of Brexit, but a mechanism through which the public might be consulted on the desirability of them. Though MPs could vote for more than one option, the risk was that including the referendum on the same ballot as the forms of Brexit presented them as alternatives, increasing the likelihood that MPs' votes would be split—most obviously between a soft Brexit and a referendum—and both would lose. As was pointed out at the time, it could hence have been more rational to vote on these two dimensions separately (Guardian 2019b, Russell 2019). That is, MPs might logically have been invited to vote in principle on whether there should be a referendum before expressing a preference for the form of Brexit which the public should be asked to consider, or vice versa. But such a process, while ostensibly rational, could have led to gaming—for example through anti-Brexit MPs voting for what they considered the least attractive Brexit option to put to the public. Some advocates of a referendum were also concerned that if their proposition failed first, this would encourage supporters to move to support for a soft Brexit, rather than continuing to fight another day. The cross-party grandees who worked up the indicative votes plan discussed this conundrum, but concluded that the only way of accommodating different views was to present the referendum on an equal footing with the various Brexit options.

The Debate and the Results

In debate, the sponsor of each motion set out their case, with Labour's proposal presented by Keir Starmer. He called the occasion 'a historic day for this Parliament and for the power of MPs', and indicated that Labour members would be encouraged to vote not only for the frontbench motion but also for the proposals from Boles, Clarke, and Beckett.[47] Various interviewees described this Labour whipping as quite 'limited' or 'soft'. In contrast, Brexit Secretary Steve Barclay argued that the government's position remained to back the deal, and confirmed that MPs would have another chance to vote on it at a sitting on Friday 29 March. Barclay offered little comfort to the proposers of any of the motions, each of which he rejected, and had no warm words about the need for compromise or the benefit that might arise from such a process. The whips' guidance on the government side was not made public, though members of the Cabinet had been told to abstain. By now clearly the whips' priority was to get Conservatives to vote for the deal two days later. The proposers of each motion were also running their own informal backbench whipping operations.

Among other contributors to the debate, there was much talk of the need for compromise. Ken Clarke suggested that:

> the House is moving into a mood where it is going to be possible to end the catastrophic shambles of the last six months. We are beginning to talk about actually being able to take decisions founded on some sort of cross-party consensus and some search for a majority...It seems to me that it is up to the House to respond to that properly and deal with this procedure, with a willingness to compromise with one another and move towards some eventual binding recommendation to the Government.[48]

Nick Boles reiterated that 'I, too, want to make the case for compromise, not as something cowardly but as something courageous'.[49] Yvette Cooper suggested that '[i]t is in all of our interests to build consensus, come together and do what we should have done two years ago' in seeking a Brexit compromise.[50] Behind the scenes, proponents of different outcomes had been working earnestly together to try and encourage individual MPs to support any option that they could live with, in order (in the absence of preferential voting) to maximize the chances that there would be a majority for something.

In the event, there was no majority for any option, though Clarke's proposal on a customs union came very close, falling just six votes short. The hard Brexit options were all heavily defeated. Unsurprisingly, Labour's official proposal failed, attracting just one Conservative vote, from Clarke. The proposal for a second referendum did somewhat better, and the Norway proposal somewhat worse, with the referendum motion securing more votes in favour than any other option, but also more opposition than either of the soft Brexit proposals. After the vote, there were widespread recriminations about splits among opponents of hard Brexit. In particular, the SNP and most Liberal Democrats had abstained on the soft Brexit solutions in favour of the revoke and referendum options, while Caroline Lucas (Green) and members of TIG went further, actively opposing the Labour, Boles, and Clarke proposals. Had these members behaved differently, there would have been a clear majority for Clarke's motion. Several interviewees spoke bitterly about these splits.

But what was really more striking was the behaviour of Conservative MPs. One bloc of 32 Brexiteers, including David Davis and John Redwood, voted in favour of the no deal motion, and against everything else. An additional bloc of 98 voted for no deal and for the Malthouse compromise, and against everything else. This appeared to be the ERG line, attracting group officers Jacob Rees-Mogg, Steve Baker, and Mark Francois, alongside others including Boris Johnson, Priti Patel, Dominic Raab, and Rishi Sunak. A further grouping of 26 Conservatives, all of whom had supported May's deal, voted against every single option on offer. They appeared to be loyalists, holding out for the vote due two days later. This action clearly suppressed the number of votes available for any form of compromise, as did the enforced abstention by the Cabinet. Overall, very few Conservatives voted for the soft Brexit options proposed by their co-partisans Boles and Clarke—only 36 and 33 respectively. The latent support for such a compromise seemed likely to be far higher, but was discouraged by the whips given the impending vote on 29 March.

Alongside this, there were fears among loyalists about a majority forming around such solutions. A key government interviewee noted a real threat that, 'if the customs union vote had got through, what would have happened then in my view was that the ERG and others...would have triggered a confidence vote in Theresa May'. Added to this were pressures from local Conservative associations. One interviewee reported that Conservatives were being advised that a vote for Clarke's motion would lead to local no-confidence votes, which would strip them of their right to stand again as a candidate for the party. Dominic Grieve, who abstained on soft Brexit, and voted for the motions on a referendum and revoking Article 50, was rejected in such a local vote three days later (Rawlinson 2019).

The Brexit-supporting media's reaction to the inconclusive outcome was damning. The *Daily Express* referred to the 'shambolic series of votes' (Hall 2019e). The *Daily Mail* (2019d) again urged Conservatives to back May's deal, but this time shifted its anger away from the Brexiteers who had blocked most proposals, instead accusing the MPs who had supported the soft Brexit options of 'pitting themselves against the people' and seeking to 'dilute or kill off Brexit'.

The Third Attempt and the Second Extension

The Failed Third Vote on the Deal: 29 March

The conditions set by the EU on the timing of the extension made the government keen to give MPs one last chance to support the Brexit deal by 29 March. Despite the previous defeats, the stakes at this point were far higher: a failure to approve the deal would drive ministers towards seeking a further Article 50 extension, likely requiring participation in the European elections. Beyond that, the prospects were unknown—potentially including the collapse of Brexit and/or a further referendum. There were hence increased hopes that recalcitrant Brexiteers, confronted by these risks, would fall into line.

The Speaker's position to the 'same question' rule (discussed above) clearly presented obstacles. The government's chosen solution was to split the Withdrawal Agreement from the Political Declaration, and to limit the vote to the first of these alone. This would not fit the criteria of Section 13 of the EU (Withdrawal) Act, so would not formally be a 'meaningful vote' in that sense; but it would satisfy the EU's conditions for unlocking an extension to 22 May. For the government it had the potential advantage of limiting the vote to an ostensibly less contested question: many of the arguments about the form that Brexit should take concerned the future relationship, rather than the Withdrawal Agreement itself. But both Barwell (2021) and

Smith (2020) have claimed that Bercow's announcement destabilized attempts to get the DUP on board for this third vote. Meanwhile, even without the Political Declaration, a vote for the Withdrawal Agreement was a vote for Brexit, and for the backstop, hence retaining the capacity to attract opposition from both Brexit-sceptics and hardline Brexiteers.

More than at previous rounds, there were concerted attempts by ministers to bring round different groups of voters to support the deal. Particular effort was put into changing the positions of the ERG and DUP, but also into convincing Labour MPs from Leave-voting constituencies to support the government. Numerous behind-the-scenes meetings were held to try and persuade all of these groups, including with the Prime Minister herself.

By this point, Theresa May's position in her own party was extremely fragile. Following the votes on no deal, and on the Article 50 extension, both of which had only been carried thanks to opposition support, 1922 Committee chair Graham Brady was allegedly 'bombarded' by messages from Conservative MPs saying that she must go (Swinford, Hope, and Maidment 2019). But May was formally protected against a no-confidence vote by the committee's rules. The *Sunday Times* claimed that 11 Cabinet ministers favoured her removal (Shipman 2019a). Barwell (2021: 345) reports that on 19 March Boris Johnson had visited the Prime Minister, and said that his price for supporting her deal would be that 'someone else would be taking over the party leadership'. That weekend she invited him and other ERG members, including Iain Duncan Smith and Jacob Rees-Mogg, to Chequers to discuss what would be needed to get them on board; they confirmed that she needed to set a date for her departure (Swinford 2019b). May subsequently addressed the 1922 Committee on 27 March, and acknowledged the desire for 'new leadership' for the next stage of the Brexit negotiations. That same day, Johnson and Rees-Mogg publicly indicated that they were now prepared to support the deal (Elliott, Coates, and Wright 2019). This was the day of the indicative votes, and clearly influenced how Conservative MPs voted.

Intense negotiation had also gone on with the DUP. Its core concern remained post-Brexit divergence between arrangements in Northern Ireland and the British mainland. In terms of the future relationship, this required bringing Great Britain as far as possible into alignment with EU standards, in order to match the arrangements already proposed for Northern Ireland. Raoul Ruparel (2020), then closely involved in discussions in Number 10, recalled that by this point '[w]e'd offered them full alignment for the entire UK as long as the backstop lasted plus an NI say, via the UK, over any new laws involving the backstop, plus unfettered access to the UK, plus an economic package'. There was a high degree of optimism that this would bring the DUP on board. But these promises, of course, pushed in the reverse direction to that wanted by the ERG. Julian Smith (2020) has commented that, having previously been 'solid bedfellows', increasingly 'the position of the ERG and the DUP was diverging'—and it 'became more apparent... that Brexit was more important than the union' for the ERG.

The third group involved in keen discussions were Labour MPs from Leave-supporting constituencies, some of whom were tempted to vote for the government's deal in order to ensure that Brexit was delivered. Various of these members had been in discussion with Number 10 for some time. Thus far, only four such MPs (three on each occasion) had been persuaded to vote for the deal, but a significant further number feared the consequences of a cancellation of Brexit or a referendum.[51] Conservative whips hoped that MPs such as these might also be persuaded to support the government on a Brexit that promised a relatively close future relationship—which was officially Labour's position. But this not only flatly contradicted what the ERG wanted, it also presented difficulties to these Labour members. They were under significant pressure from their own whips not to support the government, and faced possible deselection as future party candidates if they did so.

To encourage Labour members to switch sides, Number 10 had promised to bring forward a Withdrawal Agreement Bill immediately if the deal was approved, privately suggesting that it could help to tie the government's hands over the negotiating objectives for the next stage. As a step in this direction, on 29 March a group of Labour members, headed by Lisa Nandy and Gareth Snell, proposed an amendment to the government's motion to require parliamentary approval for the negotiating mandate. Julian Smith was advised that various Labour members would vote for the government's motion if this amendment passed (Pogrund and Maguire 2020). The government signalled a willingness to endorse it, but the Speaker did not select it for decision.

Even if it had been approved, such a motion would not have been binding. Indeed, there was also no guarantee that the government's promised bill would pass, or that it wouldn't be subsequently overturned. Crucially, May's offer to go had imperilled all of these offers of future action, because any concessions could be reneged upon if she was replaced by a hard Brexiteer. A key Labour interviewee explained that:

> There were a lot of people who didn't vote for Theresa May's deal because the presumption was 'it will be overturned by Boris Johnson, we don't have trust, it's a blind deal'. In theory it's got the provisions that could lead you to a sort of sensible, manufacturing customs deal... In theory it's got the sort of Northern Ireland

provisions and so on in it, but the danger is you could vote for it, and then it'd be overturned three days later by Boris Johnson becoming Prime Minister and doing something mad.

All in all, despite the government's efforts to woo these different groups, there were substantial obstacles: particularly that the promises needed to bring one group on board were liable to drive another away. As an interviewee closely involved in the process said, 'when you're trying to build a complex coalition of people and views, every move you make risks another group, and that was the bind we were in; whichever way you moved, somebody else on the other side fell off the edge'. An additional problem was that no group wanted to jump first, and switch sides to support the government if the deal was going to be defeated. Labour members, particularly, would face retribution from their whips, but zero reward, if this happened. Meanwhile, Conservative MPs who had previously opposed the deal from a more pro-European position were also making calculations. Dominic Grieve (2020) has recalled:

> I thought to myself, 'Should I vote for this, because the situation is getting so bad, just to show solidarity against the ERG?' But we did the arithmetic, and the arithmetic was that whatever we did, she was going to lose. And so I stuck to my guns.

A similar comment could have been made by representatives of any of these four target groups.

In the debate on 29 March itself Theresa May made the usual call for unity, telling MPs that 'if you want to deliver Brexit, this is the moment'.[52] Other heartfelt pleas included some from committed Brexiteers. Iain Duncan Smith suggested that if the motion was defeated 'we will rue this day', as it would lead to 'a damaging and destructive extension that means we never leave the European Union'.[53] Meanwhile, Charles Walker, vice-chair of the 1922 Committee, lamented the lack of compromise, commenting that '[i]t seems to me that the losers do not know how to lose and the winners do not know how to win'.[54] Hardliners such as Bill Cash, however, still spoke out against the deal, while Sammy Wilson of the DUP dismissed it as 'a con trick that breaks up the United Kingdom'.[55]

The result of the vote was another defeat, albeit again by a reduced margin of 344 to 286. A hard core of 34 Conservative MPs—28 of them Brexiteers, dubbed 'the Spartans' (Goodman, P. 2019)—voted against the deal, as did the DUP. In the end, just five Labour members supported it.[56] Very unusually, the ERG had split, after some agonized internal discussions (Francois 2021). Among the Brexiteers switching from opposition to support were, as previously signalled, Boris Johnson and ERG chair Jacob Rees-Mogg (neither of whom contributed to the debate), plus Iain Duncan Smith and Dominic Raab. Other ERG officers Steve Baker and Mark Francois, and group members such as Suella Braverman and Priti Patel, maintained their opposition. Had these 28 'Spartans' and the 10 DUP MPs voted for rather than against the deal, it would have passed on this third occasion, even without the support of the handful of anti-Brexit Conservatives such as Grieve.

Given subsequent events, there has been significant interest in why Boris Johnson chose to shift his vote at this point—having previously spoken so passionately against the deal. Perhaps like others he was influenced by the fear of losing Brexit altogether. But his calculations were no doubt also bound up with positioning for the future. Theresa May had given in to pressure regarding her departure, opening up possibilities to change direction in the subsequent stages. In addition, one ERG interviewee recalled, in the light of Theresa May's promises to go, that 'I thought that it was very important that he should vote in favour of it, if he wanted to become leader of the party...I thought that if he had voted against the deal that last time, he would have found it very difficult to get sufficient votes from MPs to get to the final ballot.'

The Brexit-supporting media responded angrily, with the Spartans taking their share of the blame. The *Daily Mail* proclaimed '[t]he Brexit betrayal', noting, 'Corbyn conspires with hard Brexiteers to block deal' (Groves and Stevens 2019), while the *Sun* (2019c) declared itself 'Brexsick of the lot of you', arguing, 'Shame on them all. Shame on Labour. Shame on the Tory Remainers, the hard-core Brexiteers and the DUP'.

Table 8.3 Conservative MPs' votes on May's deal versus Remain/Leave support in 2016

	Backed Remain in 2016		Backed Leave in 2016		2016 position unknown	
	Aye	No	Aye	No	Aye	No
First vote, 15 January	144	26	49	90	2	2
Second vote, 12 March	155	12	76	62	3	1
Third vote, 29 March	161	6	111	28	4	0

Notes: Some MPs changed their Brexit stance post referendum (as discussed in Chapter 7). The total number of Conservative MPs decreased over this period as the result of defections. Voting based on data from the parliamentary website; MPs' Brexit stances drawn from Cygan, Lynch. and Whitaker (2019, 2021).

The Second Round of Indicative Votes: 1 April

The third vote on May's deal having failed, the House of Commons returned to the indicative votes process, again at backbenchers' instigation. This second day suspending Standing Order no. 14 had been secured through a vote at the beginning of business on 27 March, before the initial indicative votes took place (Cowie and Samra 2019). This linked process of setting aside time (sometimes referred to as the 'daisy chain') secured time on 1 April. On that day it also continued further, with an in-principle agreement to suspend Standing Order no. 14 on 3 April—which was used for the 'Cooper–Letwin' bill (as discussed below). Hence Standing Order no. 14 was suspended for three days in total over this period, allowing members of the House of Commons collectively, rather than the government, to decide how time was used.

The repetition of the indicative votes process had the potential to whittle down the Brexit options in the light of the results of the first round votes. Taking place after the third defeat on the deal, it also created a potential opportunity to bring more Conservatives over to alternative options. Again, there was lively debate about the appropriate voting system, and whether a preferential ballot, whereby options would be eliminated one by one until something secured a majority, should now be used. Several external commentators suggested that an approach of this kind was necessary to generate a conclusive result (Renwick 2019, Sullivan 2019). The cross-party group of 'grandees' discussed these issues carefully, including whether the question of holding a referendum should be treated separately from that of the preferred form of Brexit; but the decision ultimately, in the words of one of those present, was to 'keep it simple'. MPs would again just be asked to vote yes or no to a range of propositions.

The other way of concentrating support would be to limit the range of options to be voted upon. On this occasion, the Speaker selected just four motions (see Table 8.4)—which led to some criticism at the start of the debate. In particular, John Baron objected that Bercow had failed to select motions in support of dropping the backstop, and in favour of a no-deal exit. The Speaker responded that the second of these had been overwhelmingly rejected the week before, while the first was clearly unattainable in negotiations with the EU. The remaining options repeated the four cross-party motions presented on the previous occasion—on a permanent customs union, 'Norway plus', further referendum, and revocation—and were sponsored by the same groups of proponents.[57]

Table 8.4 Options in the indicative votes of 1 April 2019

Proposition	Lead sponsor (party)	Voting result	Margin of loss	Con/Lab supporters	Con/Lab opponents
Customs union	Ken Clarke (Con)	273–276	3	37 Con 230 Lab	236 Con 10 Lab
Norway plus arrangement ('Common Market 2.0')	Nick Boles (Con)	261–282	21	33 Con 185 Lab	228 Con 25 Lab
Confirmatory referendum on any deal ('Kyle–Wilson' plan)	Peter Kyle (Lab)	280–292	12	15 Con 203 Lab	253 Con 24 Lab
Revoke Article 50 to prevent no deal	Joanna Cherry (SNP)	191–292	101	10 Con 121 Lab	260 Con 18 Lab

Aspects of the debate were a rerun of that the week before. Steve Barclay for the government criticized all of the options on offer, and various of their sponsors. Keir Starmer encouraged members to support as many options as they felt able to, and indicated that Labour would whip in support of the two soft Brexit options and the referendum motion. Ken Clarke urged MPs to show greater pragmatism than previously, specifically encouraging the Liberal Democrats and SNP to support his motion. Peter Kyle suggested that the appropriate compromise was to allow the government's deal to be put to the voters.

Notwithstanding these entreaties, the changed circumstances, and the greater opportunities to build support since the first votes, the results were remarkably similar—with no option reaching a majority. The customs union proposal again came closest, being rejected by just 276 votes to 273. However, only 37 Conservative MPs supported it (up four on the previous occasion), while the SNP retained its position of abstention, and most Liberal Democrats and members of TIG voted against. The Boles proposal was also more narrowly rejected than previously, largely thanks to winning support from the SNP; but its number of Conservative supporters actually declined, from 37 to 33. The referendum motion won 12 more votes than previously, but still faced defeat, and attracted just 15 Conservatives. Joanna Cherry's revoke motion was rejected by a very similar margin to before. Members of the Cabinet again abstained, while an extraordinary 213 out of 312 Conservative MPs—including but not limited to the hardline Brexiteers—opposed all of the options. At the end of the debate Nick Boles announced dramatically that 'I have given everything to an attempt to find a compromise…I have failed chiefly because my party refuses to compromise. I regret therefore to announce I can no longer sit for this party', before departing both the chamber and the Conservative Party.[58]

Hence, despite the best efforts of backbenchers and the intense levels of cross-party working, the Commons had failed to find support for any alternative Brexit option in the absence of support for the deal. Tabloid fury with MPs was summed up by the *Daily Express* front page, which proclaimed '[w]e voted for Brexit, all you say is no' (Hall 2019d).

The Cooper–Letwin Bill and the Extension to 31 October

Failure to agree the deal forced attention onto the need for a further Article 50 extension, to avoid the otherwise default position of a no-deal exit on 12 April. The cross-party coalition of MPs opposed to no deal used the next day on which the 'daisy chain' had suspended Standing Order no. 14, 3 April, to force action. Given the uncertainties over whether the government would implement a decision taken by the House of Commons by motion (particularly given the Prime Minister's own perilous position), the cross-party coalition pursued this via legislation. The day set aside was used to rush through a private member's bill headed by Yvette Cooper, with support from Oliver Letwin and others. This would statutorily require the government to seek House of Commons approval for an extension to Article 50, and to put this request to the EU if the motion was approved.[59]

These were controversial actions at various levels. In addition to the continued 'seizure' of the Commons agenda by MPs, the proposal to pass a bill with such rapidity through both chambers raised inevitable questions about the necessary time for debate and reflection. More fundamentally, some figures questioned whether it was constitutionally proper for a private member's bill to be used to force action on a government, and whether the government could potentially block such a bill. These questions had first arisen earlier in the year, in the context of the first Cooper bill. Stephen Laws (2019), a previous head of the Parliamentary Counsel Office (responsible for drafting government legislation), wrote a piece for the centre-right think tank Policy Exchange suggesting that ministers could respond to a bill passed against their wishes by advising the monarch to withhold royal assent. To become law, any bill needs both the approval of parliament and royal assent, but the latter was generally considered a formality, and no bill had been denied it for over 300 years. This intervention thus generated a strong counterreaction from other experts. For example, a blog post by the legal adviser to the House of Lords Constitution Committee described it as 'highly problematic', arguing that such actions would breach the principle of parliamentary sovereignty, under which 'Parliament—not the *Government*, but *Parliament*—has the right to make or unmake any law' (Elliott, M. 2019b, italics in original). These same arguments re-emerged in the context of the Cooper–Letwin Bill, in a joint-authored *Sunday Times* article suggesting that ministers could block the bill either by proroguing parliament, which would cause all legislation to fall, or by advising against giving royal assent (Ekins and Laws 2019). A further piece by a senior legal academic in the *Telegraph* also proposed prorogation (Finnis 2019a). Again, other specialists hit back (Elliott, M. 2019a, Poole 2019). As various of these authors noted, such controversies arose due to the very unusual circumstances in which the government was unable to command a majority in the House of Commons. In more 'normal' times ministers would simply use their majority to block unwelcome measures (Evans 2020). In the absence of this ability, fundamental disputes arose about where the border between governmental and parliamentary power should lie.

The bill itself proceeded quickly, albeit amidst extremely heated debates. A Business of the House motion from Oliver Letwin, to set its timetable, was approved by a mere 312 votes to 311. Less than 90 minutes later the bill's second reading was agreed by 315 votes to 310, and subsequently its third reading by 313 votes to 312.[60] The following day it reached the Lords, where there is normally no formal programming of legislation or use of the 'guillotine' to put time limits on debates. To speed the bill, these conventions needed to be set aside. From the Labour frontbench, Baroness (Dianne) Hayter of Kentish Town proposed a motion to suspend the relevant standing orders. This provoked significant controversy, with numerous amendments from Brexit-supporting peers and attempts to 'filibuster' (delay) proceedings. Supporters of the bill blocked these by proposing repeated 'closure' motions to move the debate on, with six such motions approved within seven hours. In contrast, just seven had previously been approved since 1900 (Lee and Berry 2020). Once the bill's supporters had made their determination clear, the government conceded agreement to the programme motion. The bill completed its Lords stages on 8 April with limited further disruption, and received royal assent the following day.

Even before the Cooper–Letwin Bill had completed its passage, Theresa May had written to Donald Tusk requesting an Article 50 extension until 30 June. On 11 April the EU offered a substantially longer extension, to 31 October. May (2019a) had in fact indicated her intention to seek an extension on the day of the bill's introduction. But interviewees claimed that the breakdown of trust, and the Prime Minister's weak position, necessitated the bill. One Conservative ringleader commented that 'however much assurance we got that the government was going to do something, if we didn't make it ironclad in legislation, the next day, the ERG would be in and the decision would be reversed'. But the bill fed further negative media headlines about parliament, and was characterized by the *Sun* as 'a controversial power grab drawn up by Remainer rebels' (Clark and Newton Dunn 2019).

While the coalition against no deal succeeded in passing the Cooper–Letwin Bill, and arguably in forcing the second extension, it failed to retain control of the Commons agenda. On 3 April, MPs had been invited to support a further suspension of Standing Order no. 14 for 8 April. This resulted in a tied vote, by 310–310, requiring the Speaker to cast a deciding vote. In line with precedent, and demonstrating that he wasn't always the Remainers' friend, he voted against the proposal. This meant the daisy chain was broken, and the initiative passed back to the government.

The Failed Talks with Labour and the Downfall of May

By this point, the options available to the government following the failure of the first meaningful vote had mostly been exhausted. The deal had been repeatedly defeated, but MPs had also emphatically rejected a no-deal exit. Backbenchers' takeover of the agenda, and the staging of indicative votes, had failed to find a way through the impasse—particularly thanks to Conservative MPs' reluctance to support compromise options. At this eleventh hour, an enfeebled Theresa May, already forced to state that she would shortly be stepping down, and facing growing pressure from her parliamentary party to go immediately, finally opened formal talks with Labour. Like all previous strategies, these failed. Meanwhile, the results for the Conservatives in the local and much-resented European elections were catastrophic. Ultimately May had no option but to admit defeat, and to tender her resignation.

The Cross-party Talks

On 2 April, the day after the inconclusive second indicative votes, the Prime Minister announced an offer to open formal talks with the opposition in order to seek joint agreement on a Brexit plan (May 2019a). She noted that this decision followed 'seven hours of Cabinet meetings'—where interviewees reported that key Brexiteer ministers were prepared to countenance a softer form of Brexit, but that there was no clear agreement. Despite the Labour leader's previous reservations, he accepted this offer.

The talks, which formally included Theresa May, David Lidington, Steve Barclay, and Julian Smith on the government side, and Jeremy Corbyn, Keir Starmer, Shadow Business Secretary Rebecca Long Bailey, and Chief Whip Nick Brown for the opposition, clearly always had limited chance of success. The *Financial Times* (2019b) commented that such talks 'should have happened at the start of the withdrawal process—or when the government lost its majority in 2017—not as a final, desperate step', while other commentators noted that May's imminent departure meant that any agreement could easily be reneged upon by her successor (Freedland 2019). In any case, the divisions on the Labour side, as well as within the government, were deeper than ever. While some Labour members remained prepared to accept a form of soft Brexit, increasing numbers were now wedded to a referendum, which the government (and indeed some others within Labour) were very reluctant to concede.

The cross-party talks were not well received on the Conservative side, and ERG members told journalists that they 'fear[ed] for Brexit' (Syal and Stewart 2019). But Barwell (2021: 370) recalled one Cabinet minister objecting that 'we should remind those colleagues who were criticising us for talking to Labour that we were only doing it because some Conservatives had spent the last few months voting with them' against May's Brexit deal.

Significant time and effort were put into the talks, which explored detailed aspects of a possible future relationship with the EU (Barwell 2021, Pogrund and Maguire 2020). At times, optimistic signals were issued by both sides. But levels of distrust—within the parties, as well as between them—were unmanageably high, and pressures were worsened both by the impending elections and May's promised departure. To guard against the risks of the latter, it was reported that Labour was seeking a 'Boris lock', to provide legal certainty that what was agreed could not subsequently be overturned by a future Conservative leader (Elgot 2019a).

Reports differed over what was the biggest stumbling block, but a very significant problem was the question of a referendum. Labour negotiators claimed that their MPs could be persuaded to support a deal subject to a public vote—essentially the Kyle–Wilson plan; but offering a referendum was anathema to May and others in her team. A Labour interviewee close to the negotiations recalled talking to a centrist Conservative minister, 'and him saying he couldn't understand why Theresa May wasn't prepared to offer that'. The obvious answer was that other members of the Cabinet wouldn't accept it. Conservative negotiators got as far as promising to facilitate a House of Commons vote on a referendum, but could not offer to whip their members in favour. However, the indicative votes had already demonstrated that without this a majority in favour was unlikely. In any case, as discussed earlier in the chapter, an agreement in principle to stage a referendum would have had to be followed by legislation on its detailed implementation—where any agreement could quickly have fallen apart.

On 17 May, six days before the European elections, Jeremy Corbyn (2019a) wrote to the Prime Minister officially ending the cross-party talks, citing an inability to 'bridge important policy gaps' and the 'increasing weakness and instability' of the government. This, he claimed, had created 'growing concern in both the Shadow Cabinet and Parliamentary Labour Party about the government's ability to deliver on any compromise agreement'.

The Withdrawal Agreement Bill

Theresa May's very final Brexit move was an attempt to sidestep the talks by returning the question to parliament, in the shape of a Withdrawal Agreement Bill. This was the same tactic explored a few weeks earlier, when seeking to bring MPs on board for the third vote on the deal. On 14 May the government announced that, whatever the outcome of the talks, MPs would be invited to vote on the bill implementing the Brexit agreement in early June.

A week later, the Prime Minister made a last-ditch attempt to secure agreement, in a speech badged 'seeking common ground in parliament', in which she set out 10 proposals designed to maximize parliamentary support behind a Brexit plan (May 2019c). These encompassed many of the key points previously discussed in the talks. They included continuing to seek alternative arrangements to the backstop, ensuring that Great Britain would retain the same standards as Northern Ireland, guaranteeing workers' rights and environmental protections, and making the negotiating objectives for the next stage subject to parliamentary approval. Crucially, May also pledged that MPs would be offered a vote on whether there should be a referendum on the deal—but made no promises about whipping arrangements. These same pledges were set out in a statement to MPs the following day, on 22 May.

Despite the Prime Minister's attempted optimistic tone, there was little sign that this offer would attract any new support. Unsurprisingly, given his abandonment of the talks, Jeremy Corbyn dismissed the proposals as 'a repackaged version of her three times rejected deal'.[61] Brexiteers were equally damning, and one media outlet published a list of Conservative MPs believed to oppose the package, including 42—such as David Davis, Boris Johnson, and Jacob Rees-Mogg—who had voted for the deal on the third occasion.

The final blow to the plan came on the evening of 22 May, when Andrea Leadsom announced that she was resigning as Leader of the House of

Commons, citing her belief that a referendum would be 'dangerously divisive', and her objection to offering this as a concession (PoliticsHome 2019). She had hence concluded that 'I cannot fulfil my duty as Leader of the House tomorrow, to announce a Bill with new elements that I fundamentally oppose'. The following day her place at the dispatch box was taken by government whip Mark Spencer, who did not announce the bill.

The Local and European Elections

Even before the European elections took place, the Conservatives suffered major setbacks at the English local council elections in early May. The party lost 44 councils and 1,330 councillors, with the main overall beneficiaries being the Liberal Democrats and Greens (BBC News 2019l). This further fed dismay and dissatisfaction with Theresa May's leadership in the party. On 8 May, Conservative backbencher Andrea Jenkyns used the very public forum of Prime Minister's Questions to ask, 'Is it not time to step aside and let someone new lead our party, our country and the negotiations?'[62]

But the bigger electoral challenge was still to come. Following the third defeat on the deal, and the request for the Article 50 extension, the government had reluctantly conceded that the European Parliament elections must go ahead. Legislation to facilitate this was passed on 8 April. Consequently, TIG registered as a political party, under the name 'Change UK—The Independent Group', in order to contest the elections. But they were not the only newcomers. In February, former UKIP leader Nigel Farage had registered a new Brexit Party, which officially launched in April, claiming 'betrayal' by the Conservatives, and urging a 'clean' Brexit (Dennison 2020). The Conservatives, meanwhile, struggled to put together a platform and did not publish a manifesto. The party's main pitch was to seek support for May's deal, with literature claiming (in words which were to reach significantly greater prominence later) to be the 'only party which can get Brexit done' (Conservative Party 2019b). Labour stood on a platform of rejecting no deal and supporting a second referendum. Few Conservative activists could be motivated to campaign, and it was rumoured that some of the party's MPs planned to vote for the Brexit Party.

The election results were terrible for the Conservatives. The party came fifth, losing 15 of its 19 seats, while the Brexit Party topped the poll on 31.6 per cent of the vote and won 29 seats (BBC News 2019g). The unequivocally pro-European Liberal Democrats came second on 20.3 per cent and 16 seats. Labour was third, while Change UK won less than 4 per cent of the vote and no MEPs at all. Within two weeks the party had split, and founding MPs Heidi Allen, Luciana Berger, Angela Smith, Chuka Umunna, and Sarah Wollaston went on to join the Liberal Democrats.

Theresa May Agrees to Go

For weeks, the pressure from within her own party for Theresa May to step down had been enormous. She had relied on opposition votes to rule out no deal, and to support an Article 50 extension, entered unwelcome talks with Labour, and led the party into disastrous elections that it had never wanted to hold. The Prime Minister had been determined to stay on long enough to see a Brexit deal approved, but had ultimately failed to find a majority, principally due to opposition from her own Brexiteers. With the repeated pledges to depart the EU by 29 March broken, and a media narrative of parliamentary chaos, MPs were increasingly demanding her departure.

The no-confidence vote in her leadership staged by the party in December had formally protected her from further challenges for a year, under the rules of the 1922 Committee. But pressure had mounted for amending the rules. On 13 April, two former 1922 Committee chairs pointed out in the *Telegraph* that such a rule change was within the power of MPs (Spicer and Hamilton 2019). This possibility was reportedly discussed by the 1922's executive on 24 April and only narrowly rejected. After the meeting, 1922 chair Graham Brady told journalists that members had instead asked Theresa May 'to offer clarity about the timetable and schedule for her departure' (ITV News 2019). At this point the cross-party talks were still underway.

Ultimately on 22 May, the day of the Prime Minister's speech setting out proposals for the Withdrawal Agreement Bill (and of Andrea Leadsom's resignation), the 1922 executive reportedly voted again on a rule change to facilitate a no-confidence vote. However, before the votes were counted, the Prime Minister was offered an opportunity to tender her resignation (Stewart 2019b). She reluctantly complied in a statement outside Number 10 two days later. Theresa May (2019e) stated that 'I negotiated the terms of our exit and a relationship with our closest neighbours that protects jobs, our security and our union. I have done everything I can to convince MPs to back that deal. Sadly I have not been able to do so.' She therefore announced that she would be formally resigning as leader of the Conservative Party on 7 June, at which point a leadership election would be triggered.

Jeremy Corbyn's (2019c) response came in a tweet, which suggested that 'Theresa May is right to resign.... Whoever becomes the new Tory leader must let the people decide our country's future, through an immediate general election.'

Conclusion

The early months of 2019 were particularly tumultuous ones in parliament. Having reviewed the options available after the failure of the first meaningful vote, Theresa May essentially chose not to change direction, and her deal was defeated on three occasions in total. There were also multiple votes on alternative Brexit options, instigated by backbench parliamentarians. Yet in the end the only thing that MPs could agree on was delay. They voted emphatically against a no-deal exit on several occasions, and narrowly supported extensions to the Article 50 period. But neither the deal nor an alternative Brexit formulation (or indeed a referendum) found parliamentary support.

This was a hugely controversial period, in which parliament increasingly came under criticism by the media, and by the Prime Minister herself. Various questions, therefore, deserve consideration—and some of these are easier to answer than others.

One of the most straightforward questions is who was responsible for the defeat of Theresa May's Brexit deal. Numerically, it fell thanks to an 'unholy alliance' of opposition parties, and predominantly hardline Brexiteers. The behaviour of Labour and the other non-government parties was unsurprising. As King (1976) highlighted, UK governments rarely expect the cooperation of the opposition, but crucially rely on the votes of their own backbenchers. On the government side, a handful of former Remain-supporting Conservatives opposed the deal, but the main blocking contingent was the ERG, alongside the smaller DUP. Speaking after the event, ERG supporter and 'Spartan' Mark Francois proudly recalled that, 'if it hadn't been for us, the Withdrawal Agreement would have passed' (BBC 2020). Since they were the group that had most vigorously called for Brexit, such behaviour was counter-intuitive, and went relatively unnoticed by observers outside parliament.

Previous chapters have highlighted Theresa May's rhetoric that 'no deal is better than a bad deal', which had partly been intended as a threat to the EU, and also to bring former Remainers into line. But it inadvertently galvanized hardline Brexiteers, encouraging them to believe that a complete break with the EU was possible, and even desirable. As discussed in previous chapters, the Leave campaign had no blueprint for Brexit, and when it became clearer that frictionless trade and stability in Northern Ireland depended on continued close alignment, they increasingly embraced an exit 'on WTO terms'—viewing anything less as not being an authentic Brexit. Many interviewees spoke bitterly about these developments. A Conservative supporter of the deal described the government's original hope that 'the threat of the cliff edge' (i.e. a no-deal exit) would bring parliament round. But 'the cliff edge gave the no deal proponents the prospect of us being able to leave without a deal. That was the trouble.' Consequently, Cabinet member Amber Rudd (2021) argued that 'the whole idea that Parliament was trying to stop Brexit was one that I found quite frustrating, because it clearly wasn't true. What was stopping Brexit was the ERG failing to vote for the Withdrawal Agreement, and Labour not engaging with it at all.' Increasingly, a Brexit dividing line developed between those who were prepared to compromise and those who were not. Most former Conservative Remain supporters reluctantly accepted the referendum result, and fell in behind May's deal, while the original proponents of leaving the EU rejected it as falling short of a real Brexit. As a senior backbench organizer said in interview, 'the mistake that I made early on in this process is I had thought that "look if we took time over things, consensus would grow". And actually, the longer it went on the greater the polarisation.'

There were many things that the Prime Minister could have handled better, but once the formal negotiations had begun she fought hard to find a workable compromise. In return she was punished (indeed, arguably was bullied) by Brexiteers in her party who championed an idealized model of exit which almost certainly didn't exist. This ended in Theresa May's downfall, and replacement with one of her most outspoken critics. Looking back, one of May's biggest errors appears to have been her continued determination to hold her party together. She embraced the Brady amendment, and re-entered doomed talks with the EU, rather than confronting her MPs with hard realities. When repeatedly subject to defeat at the hands of rebel Brexiteers, she never singled them out for criticism, or punishment—preferring to heap blame on an undifferentiated 'parliament'. Had she done so, this might not only have better preserved the reputation of the institution but could potentially have got the public and the media on her side, and isolated her internal opponents. But the risk was a party split, or at least far more public infighting, which May did not want to bear.

In the absence of support for the government from large numbers of its own backbenchers, other parliamentarians eventually sought to take matters into their own hands and to seek an alternative majority. Two questions arise here: of whether this was in any way constitutionally improper, and whether it ever could have worked.

The situation was unprecedented in modern British politics: a minority government, which was not even able to keep its own troops together, but which was mandated to act upon a national referendum result. The rules of the House of Commons were certainly not designed to accommodate such a scenario. Standing Order no. 14 (and various other rules and conventions) gave the government almost total power to set the agenda, and to determine what MPs should be able to debate and decide. This was already mildly controversial before Brexit (Select Committee on the Reform of the House of Commons 2009), but became far more so in the context of minority government (Russell and Gover 2021). Formally, the Commons retains complete control of its own standing orders and can change them by majority vote. There was hence nothing procedurally incorrect in the setting aside of Standing Order no. 14, or indeed in the passage of a private member's bill without government support—but these were undoubtedly very unusual. The ingrained nature of the previous working arrangements, which had been stable under successive majority governments, allowed some Brexit supporters to question the propriety of setting them aside. This opened up further controversies about parliamentary sovereignty, beyond those discussed in previous chapters, in terms of whether—when the two were in conflict—it was really parliament that should have control, or the government. While different groups articulated divergent views couched in constitutional principle, their motivations were often instrumental ones—based heavily on their preferences over Brexit.[63]

There were also specific questions in this period about the decisions of the House of Commons Speaker. John Bercow, notwithstanding his previous support for backbench Brexiteers, was frequently accused of siding with the opponents of Brexit. The Speaker clearly faced more difficult procedural questions than many of his predecessors, in particular regarding handling minority government. Bercow (2020a) himself has said that 'my feeling about it was that it wasn't for me to facilitate Brexit and it wasn't for me to stop Brexit. It certainly wasn't my responsibility to protect the Government from the absence of a majority.' This is essentially correct. Nonetheless, in making procedural decisions the Speaker normally follows the advice of the neutral parliamentary clerks, and at times Bercow chose not to do so. It was on these occasions—the 'forthwith' ruling in January 2019, and particularly his later handling of the 'same question' rule—that he was on weakest ground. But the first time that Bercow had rejected the clerks' advice was in 2013, in favour of the hardline Brexiteers (see Chapter 2), and some of them have defended his neutrality (Francois 2021: 278). His grandstanding may sometimes have increased tensions, but it seems unlikely that his decisions (at either stage) fundamentally altered the direction of Brexit.

A further question is whether, having gained control of the order paper, the cross-party groupings of MPs ever could have succeeded in garnering a majority for a different direction on Brexit. These groups worked hard, over a long period, to build support for different options and to facilitate indicative votes, which ultimately proved inconclusive (though several proposals did come closer to a majority than did May's deal). This suggested that there was no ready majority in the House of Commons for anything. But it also demonstrated the enormous difficulty of organizing parliamentary decisions in the absence of cohesive parties. The party whips are well practised at canvassing members on their views, and putting decisions to the vote once a majority exists. Crucially, they guide members on positions to take on complex policy questions with which they often have little familiarity (Cowley 2005). On Brexit, members undoubtedly often didn't fully understand the options in front of them. So, one Conservative interviewee suggested that 'right up until the indicative votes themselves, a very large number of my colleagues had actually no idea at all what the Single Market or the Customs Union was'. This left MPs seeking signals on how to vote from organized and credible figures, which suited the highly disciplined ERG. In contrast, the proponents of other Brexit options outside the government were fragmented, and their communications less well established. There was no agreement even among proponents of 'soft' Brexit about what form that should take, while others rejected this route in favour of a further referendum. But crucially, a weakness of the backbench organizers was that—unlike whips—they couldn't promise that the government would deliver on what MPs voted for. Indeed, had the Commons found a majority for a soft Brexit or a referendum, and the Prime Minister embraced this, her parliamentary party might have forced her out.

This leads to a final question, of whether with greater leadership from government some other kind of agreement would have been possible. Certainly, government-sponsored indicative votes at an earlier stage (distinctly anathema to May's closed style) would have had greater authority. Various interviewees believed that, if Theresa May had put her weight behind a softer form of Brexit, or given in to pressure for a confirmatory referendum on her deal, a majority involving a substantial number of Labour MPs could have been built. A Labour interviewee suggested that there were 'various customs union Brexits, Single Market Brexits, EFTA and EEA Brexits. And if the government had ever put those forward as a proposition, she would have had a majority for them', also suggesting that 'we kept being told that there were a significant number of extra Tories who would be prepared to vote for a second referendum, if it was the only option left'. Certainly, behaviour by the Conservative whips around the indicative votes helped to turn Conservative MPs away from such options, and more would undoubtedly have voted for them if instructed by the whips to do so. But Conservative whips were—in part—seeking to protect the Prime Minister. Even key figures in her government would not have tolerated such moves. The bigger problem here was not therefore parliamentary procedure, the skills of the Prime Minister, or the role of the opposition, but the lack of cohesiveness on the government side—upon which a functioning House of Commons usually depends.

With Theresa May having tried and failed to persuade her party to compromise, and having been hounded out by her own hardliners, the stage was now set for them to take over.

Notes

1. Two of these exceptions are long-standing, while backbench business dates to the changes implemented in 2010 following the recommendations of the 'Wright Committee'.
2. House of Commons Hansard, 15 January 2019, column 1126.
3. Ibid., 17 December 2018, column 541.
4. Ibid., 7 January 2019, column 44.
5. All of these were entitled European Union (Withdrawal) Bill, starting with European Union (Withdrawal) (No. 2) Bill—the first such bill having been the government's. Two of them (as discussed later in this and the next chapter) went on to become law.
6. House of Commons Hansard, 29 January 2019, column 783.
7. Ibid., column 724.
8. Ibid., column 778.
9. Ibid., column 721.
10. Ibid., column 670.
11. The European Union (Withdrawal) (No. 4) Bill.
12. House of Commons Hansard, 26 February 2019, column 165.
13. Ibid., 11 March 2019, column 130.
14. Ibid., 12 March 2019, column 210.
15. Ibid., 12 March 2019, column 225.
16. Ibid., 12 March 2019, column 264.
17. Ibid., 12 March 2019, column 262.
18. Of the former Remainers who had previously voted against, three (Heidi Allen, Anna Soubry, and Sarah Wollaston) had now left the party, and one (Douglas Ross) abstained. The other 11 voted in favour of the government. As before (see Chapter 7), several of the previous 26 still opposing the government (e.g. Mark Harper, Shailesh Vara) did so from a pro-Brexit position.

19. House of Commons Hansard, 13 March 2019, column 383.

20. Conservatives were divided, with 149 voting for the amendment, 66 against, and 94 not voting. Cabinet members Jeremy Hunt and Sajid Javid voted in favour, while Greg Clark, David Gauke, David Lidington, Amber Rudd, and Rory Stewart voted against.

21. House of Commons Hansard, 14 March 2019, column 562.

22. The first of these, oddly, was the Brexit secretary Steve Barclay, who had formally moved the motion. Others were Liam Fox, Chris Grayling, Andrea Leadsom, Penny Mordaunt, Liz Truss, and Gavin Williamson.

23. As discussed in Chapter 6, the ERG had pressed the government to put exit day on the face of the bill, but this had failed due to opposition from moderate Conservatives. The government was now boxed into the very corner that the moderates had feared, but their intervention meant that ministers retained legislative flexibility.

24. House of Commons Hansard, 20 March 2019, column 1037.

25. Ibid., column 1038.

26. Peter Bone, ibid., column 1040.

27. The two had been contemporaries at Oxford University as undergraduates, among other things.

28. House of Commons Hansard, 20 March 2019, column 1123.

29. Johnson continued, 'The reason we are not leaving on Friday [29 March] is not the fault of MPs. We are not leaving this Friday because the government has chickened out'— suggesting that, in the absence of support for her deal, the Prime Minister should have embraced a no-deal exit (which, of course, the Commons had rejected). The article ran with the headline 'Theresa May is a chicken who's bottled Brexit'.

30. House of Commons Hansard, 18 March 2019, column 776.

31. Subsequent statement: House of Commons Hansard, 27 March 2019, column 370. This approach was rumoured at the time of Bercow's first statement.

32. Any government 'notwithstanding' motion to push the deal against MPs' wishes could have been defeated if MPs didn't want to vote again. So rather than acting for MPs, Bercow could have allowed them to act for themselves.

33. Conservative signatories included Nick Boles, Dominic Grieve, Nicholas Soames, and Caroline Spelman. Labour signatories included Hilary Benn, Yvette Cooper, Stephen Doughty, Stephen Kinnock, Peter Kyle, Alison McGovern, and Phil Wilson, alongside representatives of the SNP, Liberal Democrats, and TIG.

34. House of Commons Hansard, 25 March 2019, column 68.

35. Ibid., columns 144; 68.

36. Ibid., column 69.

37. Ibid., column 81.

38. Ibid., column 92.

39. Ibid., column 74.

40. Ibid., column 80.

41. Ibid., column 97.

42. Steve Brine, Alistair Burt, and Richard Harrington.

43. This procedural innovation did differ from the previous processes (e.g. on Lords reform), meaning that MPs could not base their decisions on the outcome of preceding rounds of voting.

44. The motions in full can be found in House of Commons Hansard, 27 March 2019, columns 370–2.

45. Case C-621/18 *Wightman and others v Secretary of State for Exiting the European Union* [2019] 1 CMLR 29. For discussion see Garner (2018).

46. House of Commons Hansard, 27 March 2019, column 385.

47. Ibid., column 381.

48. Ibid., column 382.

49. Ibid., column 378.

50. Ibid., column 401.

51. On the first occasion, the deal had been supported by Ian Austin, Kevin Barron, and John Mann. The second time it was supported by Barron, Mann, and Caroline Flint. The 18 Labour members who broke the whip to vote against a referendum on 14 March, and the (largely overlapping) 19 who voted against this in the indicative votes, were among the possible additional allies. They included, for example, Rosie Cooper, Stephanie Peacock, Ruth Smeeth, Gareth Snell, Melanie Onn, and long-time Eurosceptic Kate Hoey.

52. House of Commons Hansard, 29 March 2019, column 769.

53. Ibid., column 721.

54. Ibid., column 731.

55. Ibid., column 734.

56. Kevin Barron, Rosie Cooper, Jim Fitzpatrick, Caroline Flint, and John Mann.

57. Margaret Beckett was a supporter of the proposal headed by Peter Kyle on this occasion, rather than the other way around.

58. House of Commons Hansard, 1 April 2019, column 880.

59. The European Union (Withdrawal) (No. 5) Bill. Other signatories included Oliver Letwin, Caroline Spelman, Jack Dromey, Alison McGovern, and Dominic Grieve.

60. The motion was supported by 14 Conservative rebels, while eight Labour MPs voted against. The respective numbers at the second reading were 15 and seven, and at the third reading 14 and nine.

61. House of Commons Hansard, 22 May 2019, column 374.

62. Ibid., 8 May 2019, column 553.

63. As explored further in Chapter 11, these attitudes were complex, and not just based on 'parliament good, government bad', or vice versa. Hardline Brexiteers opposed both the government's position and parliamentary interference—whenever these were targeted at avoiding a no-deal Brexit.

9

Shut Down Parliament! Boris Johnson and the Prorogation Crisis

Following Theresa May's final announcement of her departure, it fell to the Conservative Party to choose a new leader, who would almost certainly become the new Prime Minister. By this point, the government's position in parliament was more fragile than ever, and there was no obvious way forward on Brexit. May's deal and various alternatives had been defeated, thanks to opposition from hardline Brexiteers, and most other Conservatives had not been prepared to support alternatives. The only solution found had been to extend the Article 50 period, which was now due to end on 31 October. A no-deal exit was still the legal default, but had been repeatedly and roundly rejected by the House of Commons. The parliamentary mood was bleak, with many feeling exhausted and unable to see a way forward.

Various candidates presented themselves as potential successors to Theresa May, but the front runner was always the charismatic former Foreign Secretary and London Mayor Boris Johnson. He had been a leading light in the Vote Leave campaign, and had quit May's Cabinet over Brexit, thereafter being highly critical of both her leadership and her deal. The contest to succeed her saw fierce arguments about how to secure Brexit, and suggestions (initially from former Brexit Secretary Dominic Raab) that parliament could be prorogued—i.e. effectively shut down—in order if necessary to facilitate a no-deal exit. This proposal was rejected by most leadership candidates, and Johnson declared himself 'not attracted' to it. But having won the leadership, and after a torrid summer of speculation, including about his possible removal and replacement by an alternative cross-party government, in late August he announced his intention to prorogue. This led to a second Supreme Court ruling against the government over Brexit, and fed an increasingly negative rhetoric about the role of the courts and parliament versus 'the people'.

This chapter begins with a discussion of populism and democratic backsliding. Growing populist rhetoric pitting a Brexit-supporting public against out-of-touch 'elites' had been seen since the referendum, and reached a high point during this period. The chapter then discusses the Conservative leadership contest, parliament's own initial attempts to guard against prorogation, and the uncertainties over the summer. After this, it describes the announcement of the prorogation, and parliament's response—which included the 'Benn–Burt Act' to demand a third Article 50 extension. This is followed by a summary of the *Miller/Cherry* case in the Supreme Court, and the increasingly vitriolic responses of the Johnson government to both the court judgment and the Benn–Burt Act. This chain of events pushed the flexibility of the UK constitution to its limits.

Populism and Democratic Backsliding

Recent years have seen growing international concerns about two interconnected phenomena: populism and 'democratic backsliding'. Numerous academic and more popular accounts have warned of the threats that these hold for the stability of democracy. While some of the cases most frequently noted concern countries—such as Hungary, Poland, and Turkey—where democracy is relatively young and might already have been considered fragile, disquiet has subsequently spread to more mature and previously robust democracies, such as the US.

Significant academic debate has focused on both the definition, and the causes, of populism. The most widely accepted treatment considers it a 'thin' or 'thin-centred' ideology, which presents society as divided into two competing groups: a 'pure people' and a 'corrupt elite' (Mudde 2004: 30:79, Mudde and Rovira Kaltwasser 2013a). It is 'thin' (or arguably more of a rhetorical form than an ideology), because it does not in itself require position-taking on many of the key questions central to other ideologies—such as market regulation or the role of the welfare state. Populist positions can thus be adopted by politicians of either the left or the right. Left-wing populist leaders typically cited include Venezuela's Hugo Chavez and others in Latin America (Panizza and Miorelli 2009), while in the UK some have explored Jeremy Corbyn's populist tendencies (Watts and Bale 2019). But greater attention has tended to fall on right-wing populism, and particularly the 'populist radical right' (Mudde 2017). While on the left populism may largely focus on criticism of economic elites, on the right the notion of 'the people' is often nativist, and 'elites' are seen as including those who serve explicitly to protect various kinds of minorities.

This connects to a key point noted in the literature, that by their nature 'populists are always *antipluralist*' (Müller 2016: 3, italics in original). In populist logic, 'the people' are a unified force, with a single 'will'. This is, of course, a gross oversimplification: in modern, complex societies the people will in practice almost invariably be diverse, both in terms of their identities and their opinions (Weale 2018). But populism elides the majority or dominant view with that of the people as a whole. Those who disagree can then be dismissed as 'enemies of the people'. Hence a populist leader claiming to speak directly for 'the people' may dispute the typical constitutional checks and balances that exist to constrain their power. Bodies such as legislatures, opposition parties, courts, regulators, and independent media may be branded as 'enemies' or 'out-of-touch elites'. This results in an inherently uneasy relationship between populism and democracy (Urbinati 2019a). As Urbinati (2019b: 121) has put it,

In a textbook manner, the trajectory of the populist leader starts with the attack against the political establishment... he has to go on humiliating the other state elites and institutions that obstruct his government, and attacking the checks and balances and independent institutions that limit his power.

European scholars frequently note the links between the populist right (in particular) and anti-EU sentiments (Flood and Soborski 2017, Vasilopoulou 2018). The supranational basis of European Union institutions means that they can readily be presented as 'out-of-touch elites', which constrain national politicians and interfere unduly with the domestic sovereignty of 'the people'. Indeed, even mainstream UK political leaders have tended historically to adopt anti-EU populist rhetoric of this kind (Daddow 2013, 2015). Extreme examples of such rhetoric were regularly articulated by Boris Johnson in the 1990s when he served as the *Daily Telegraph*'s Brussels correspondent (Oborne 2021, Rankin and Waterson 2019). Meanwhile, a favoured democratic device of populist leaders is the referendum, as Mudde (2004: 559) suggests, 'mainly as an instrument to overcome the power of "the elite"'. Thus British Euroscepticism in general, and the Brexit referendum in particular, have often been cited internationally as examples of populism at work (Müller 2021, Norris and Inglehart 2019).

Populism's antipluralist tendencies, and the tensions that it creates with the typical checks and balances intrinsic to constitutional democracy, strongly link it to the second worrying contemporary phenomenon of 'democratic backsliding'. Backsliding is defined as a rolling back of the institutions of democracy, not through a sudden collapse or coup, but due to a gradual erosion instigated by elected leaders. This may not, at least initially, be deliberately intended to undermine democracy or usher in authoritarianism, but can end up having that effect. Various international studies of backsliding point to underlying causes and characteristics that are familiar from the post-Brexit UK. Scholars emphasize how it is facilitated by political polarization (itself often a result of populist rhetoric), which leads opposing political movements to become so concerned about the threat presented by their rivals that they are prepared to weaken or eliminate key democratic institutions in order to lock them out of power (Haggard and Kaufman 2021, McCoy and Somer 2019). In line with this, Naím (2022) has suggested that '3 Ps' underlie backsliding: populism, polarization, and post truth. Applebaum (2020) has reviewed past developments in Hungary and Poland, noting how a division opened up on the political right between those who prioritized defending political pluralism and the rule of law, and those who were willing to sacrifice those ideals in order to remain in power. This facilitated the dismantling of democratic norms and institutions. Hence, as such authors emphasize, responses from members in the governing party—including in the legislature—can be key to frustrating leaders with authoritarian tendencies.

Regarding what those tendencies are, Levitsky and Ziblatt (2018: 23–4) have presented a checklist of behaviours, which include accusing political rivals of being 'subversive, or opposed to the existing constitutional order', claiming baselessly that such opponents are working in collusion with foreign powers, and suppressing basic aspects of the constitution. Their case studies illustrate how such moves may initially be deployed by leaders in order to achieve policy objectives or cling onto power, but may ultimately lead to a slow and inadvertent death of democracy.

Some of these patterns certainly became visible during the Brexit process, particularly in the final stages.[1] What is surprising, and troubling, is that they won support from leading figures in the traditionally mainstream Conservative Party. Chapter 2 noted how the UK's 'first-past-the-post' electoral system encourages political parties to be 'broad churches'; in line with that, Conservative ideology has long encompassed different strands (Green 2004, Heppell and Hill 2005). But, at least historically, the party had been a staunch defender of the traditional institutions of the UK's constitution and the rule of law (Norton 2005, 2012). Later stages of the Brexit process brought this into question.

The Conservative Leadership Election and the Threat of Prorogation

The timetable for the Conservative leadership contest had been signalled by Theresa May a fortnight before it began, when she announced that she would formally resign as party leader on 7 June 2019. The rules of the contest required candidates to be nominated by Conservative MPs, who would then narrow them down to a final two through successive rounds of voting, with the final choice being put to a ballot of the wider party.

The Candidates

Initially, 13 candidates expressed their interest in standing as leader. Each was required to have the support of eight MPs to enter the first ballot, and three hopefuls (James Cleverly, Sam Gyimah, and Kit Malthouse) dropped out at this stage. As shown in Table 9.1, this left 10 to go forward to the first MP ballot.

Six of these candidates (Matt Hancock, Jeremy Hunt, Michael Gove, Andrea Leadsom, Sajid Javid, and Rory Stewart) had been members of Theresa May's Cabinet at the time of the meaningful votes, so were bound by collective responsibility to vote consistently for her Brexit deal. Former Foreign Secretary Boris Johnson, and former Brexit Secretary Dominic Raab, as discussed in Chapter 7, had both resigned from the Cabinet over Brexit. Both had voted against the deal on the first two occasions, but switched to support it third time round. Esther McVey, who had resigned as a junior minister over Brexit, and Mark Harper, a former Chief Whip to David Cameron, had done the same. Of all of the candidates on offer, Rory Stewart was seen as most sympathetic to a soft Brexit. He had joined May's Cabinet

Table 9.1 MPs' voting in the leadership election of 2019

	First ballot (13 June)	Second ballot (18 June)	Third ballot (19 June)	Fourth ballot (20 June)	Fifth ballot (20 June)
Boris Johnson	114	126	143	157	160
Jeremy Hunt	43	46	54	59	77
Michael Gove	37	41	51	61	75
Sajid Javid	23	33	38	34	
Rory Stewart	19	37	27		
Dominic Raab	27	30			
Matt Hancock	20				
Andrea Leadsom	11				
Mark Harper	10				
Esther McVey	9				

Source: Figures taken from Johnston (2019).

only a month beforehand, having previously been a junior minister, and was instrumental behind the scenes in organizing for Ken Clarke's customs union proposal during the indicative votes.

The first ballot took place on 13 June, and required candidates to have the support of at least 16 MPs to progress to the second stage. Three candidates failed this test, and a fourth, Secretary of State for Health Matt Hancock, chose to withdraw. In subsequent rounds, Dominic Raab, followed by Rory Stewart, then Sajid Javid, then Michael Gove, were each eliminated. This left Boris Johnson and Foreign Secretary Jeremy Hunt on 20 June to go forward to the member ballot. Johnson led at every stage, albeit having begun on only 36 per cent of MPs' votes. Several candidates, including Leadsom, Hancock, Raab, and Javid, pledged support to Johnson as they dropped out. Michael Gove, the final candidate eliminated by MPs, expressed no view between Johnson and Hunt. Rory Stewart came out for Hunt and strongly against Johnson.

The result of the member ballot was announced on 23 July; Boris Johnson had secured 92,153 votes (66 per cent) to Jeremy Hunt's 46,656.

Debates during the Contest about Brexit and Prorogation

Despite the fast-moving early stages of the leadership contest, there was plenty of room for public debate about the candidates' policy positions, and a significant focus inevitably fell on Brexit. A key question, given the context, was their attitudes to potentially exiting without a deal. Johnson and Raab had supported this position in the indicative votes (as had Harper and McVey), while the candidates in the Cabinet had followed the collective line of abstention. Hunt and Gove expressed reluctance to embrace this position, while Stewart vociferously rejected it. But the dominant question remained how the Brexit deadlock could be broken.

At an early stage, on 5 June, Dominic Raab suggested at a hustings meeting for Conservative MPs that he might be prepared to prorogue parliament in order to ensure that Brexit happened by 31 October (Schofield 2019). Here he was acting on advice from Theresa May's former Director of Legislative Affairs Nikki da Costa (2021). Prorogation had been mooted occasionally in the preceding months, including as a means of starting a new parliamentary session to circumvent the 'same question' rule, and more controversially as a potential means for killing off an unwelcome private member's bill (see Chapter 8). A prorogation imposes a complete shutdown on parliamentary proceedings in both chambers, causing all uncompleted legislation to fall, and preventing all meetings, debates, and publications. But despite the profound effect on parliament, parliamentary approval for prorogation is not required. Instead it relies on a prerogative power, exercised through direct ministerial advice to the monarch. Hence suggestions that it could be used to block a bill had raised concerns that MPs' expressed support for a policy could be overridden by government (Elliott, M. 2019b). The suggestion of proroguing to facilitate a no-deal Brexit, which the Commons had repeatedly and roundly voted against, took these concerns to a new level. Given the government's perilous position in the Commons, a prorogation could even potentially be attempted in order to deny MPs the opportunity to launch a no-confidence vote. This would not only frustrate MPs' policy priorities but potentially undermine the constitutional fundamental of government accountability to parliament.

Raab's suggestion provoked strong opposition from most of his opponents. Rory Stewart immediately condemned the proposal, arguing that 'It would be unconstitutional. It would be undemocratic. And it wouldn't work.' His Cabinet colleague Amber Rudd described the idea as 'outrageous' (both quoted in Schofield 2019). The following day, Matt Hancock (2019) published a letter to MPs, arguing that '[t]o suspend Parliament explicitly to pursue a course of action against its wishes is not a serious policy of a Prime Minister in the 21st century', and that such a policy 'would mean the end of the Conservative Party as a serious party of government'. Andrea Leadsom, until a fortnight earlier Leader of the House of Commons, firmly rejected the idea, commenting that 'we live in a parliamentary democracy, I think bringing the Queen in and actually trying to do something that shuts down our parliamentary democracy would be entirely wrong' (BBC 2019). Michael Gove likewise commented that 'proroguing parliament in order to get no deal through, I think would be wrong', while Sajid Javid responded by suggesting that 'you don't deliver on democracy by trashing democracy' (Murphy 2019).

Other key figures weighed in equally strongly. House of Commons Speaker John Bercow insisted in the chamber on the day after Raab's initial comments that 'Parliament will not be evacuated from the centre stage of the decision-making process on this important matter', while Leadsom's successor, Mel Stride, commented that 'Her Majesty should be kept out of the politics of our Parliament'.[2] On 14 June former Conservative Prime Minister John Major made excoriating comments in a speech, suggesting that a prorogation of this kind would be 'fundamentally unconstitutional', and that 'com[ing] from the people who in the Brexit debate talked about parliamentary sovereignty being at stake, it is not just fundamentally distasteful, it is hypocrisy on a gold-plated standard' (Mairs 2019).

While Raab was knocked out of the contest early, and condemnations of his proposal came from far and wide in the Conservative Party, Boris Johnson was markedly less vocal. The *Times* reported that Johnson had privately told senior members of the ERG that he would leave open the option of proroguing parliament to force through a no-deal Brexit (Elliott, F. 2019). This seems to have been the same meeting of 5 June where Mark Francois (2021) reports that Johnson won the official backing of the group's leadership—by guaranteeing to take the UK out of the EU by 31 October, with or without a deal. Later, during the member ballot, he was asked whether he would rule out such action, and responded somewhat elliptically that 'I don't envisage the circumstances in which it will be necessary to prorogue parliament, nor am I attracted to that expedient' (Elliott and Courea 2019). In contrast, his opponent Jeremy Hunt (2019) told Sky News that 'we voted to leave the EU because we wanted to restore parliamentary democracy; you cannot in that situation force through a no-deal Brexit by closing down parliament', stating clearly that he would '100% not' attempt this manoeuvre.

Particularly given Johnson's equivocation, his rival Rory Stewart took a strong stance against prorogation, suggesting that if it were tried, parliament should find other ways to meet. Drawing on a tactic that had successfully been used to persuade Tony Blair to recall the House of Commons to discuss Iraq in 2002, he claimed on 13 June that 'I, and every other member of parliament will sit across the road in Methodist Central Hall and we will hold our own session of parliament, and we will bring [Johnson] down', should he attempt this (Heffer 2019).[3] In early July Stewart expanded on this idea, suggesting that former Speaker Betty Boothroyd might be approached to preside (Wintour 2019).

Stewart also made other procedural suggestions during the leadership contest which attracted public attention. In particular, he proposed that the Brexit deadlock should be resolved through creating a citizens' assembly, perhaps chaired by the Archbishop of Canterbury, to bring ordinary voters in to resolve the dilemmas. Although Stewart drew on recent UK and French experience in making this proposal, Raab colourfully dismissed it during a TV debate as the 'Venezuelan option' (Bartlett and Bloom 2019). Generally, Stewart captured wide public interest through his frank interventions about the difficulties of resolving Brexit, and through a lively social media campaign. But many of his supporters were undoubtedly Brexit-sceptics who were not Conservative voters, and it was always unlikely that party members would choose him over Johnson. That opportunity never arose, after he was knocked out by MPs in the third round of the contest.

The Departure of May and Arrival of Johnson

Boris Johnson's victory was announced on 23 July, and he became Prime Minister the following day. A week beforehand, Theresa May (2019d) had given her last major speech in the role, where she declared herself 'worried about the state of politics'. While May had been bombastic at times about the role of parliament, and occasionally reached for populist rhetoric in frustration, she had also often implored MPs to recognize the need for compromise. Her speech, at Chatham House, focused on this theme, suggesting that:

> Today an inability to combine principles with pragmatism and make a comprom-
> ise when required seems to have driven our whole political discourse down the
> wrong path. It has led to what is in effect a form of 'absolutism' – one which
> believes that if you simply assert your view loud enough and long enough you will
> get your way in the end.

While these words could have applied to Jeremy Corbyn, or people who advocated a second Brexit referendum, they seemed particularly well suited to Johnson and the ERG, whom May had repeatedly avoided singling out for criticism. More directly, she remarked that '[s]ome argue I should have taken the United Kingdom out of the European Union with no deal on 29th March…but most people across our country had a preference for getting it done with a deal'. Commenting specifically on populism, she noted that populist movements internationally 'promote a polarised politics which views the world through the prism of "us" and "them"—a prism of winners and losers, which views compromise and cooperation…as signs of weakness not strength'. Such movements 'have embraced the politics of division; identifying the enemies to blame for our problems and offering apparently easy answers'. This did all seem a portent of things to come, but it is unfortunate that May did not recognize—and tackle—such dangers earlier.

Johnson's first speech as Prime Minister was made on the steps of Downing Street on 24 July. It was typically upbeat, criticizing the 'pessimists at home and abroad' who suggested that, three years after the referendum, 'we are incapable of honouring a basic democratic mandate'. He claimed that 'we are going to restore trust in our democracy and we are going to fulfil the repeated promises of parliament to the people and come out of the EU on October 31, no ifs no buts' (Johnson 2019a). In a statement to the House of Commons the following day, he repeated the pledges to 'restore trust in our democracy' and an 'absolute commitment to the 31 October date for our exit'. With a distinctly populist twist, Johnson suggested that '[i]t is this party now, this Government who are clearly on the side of democracy in this country... we are the party of the people'.[4] While touching clearly on Brexit, much of both speeches focused on various domestic matters, such as policing, social care, economic prosperity, and achieving net zero carbon emissions.

One of Johnson's first tasks was to construct his Cabinet. In this he was aided by the departure of several of Theresa May's most senior ministers. Cabinet members David Lidington, Philip Hammond, David Gauke, and Rory Stewart had all handed in their resignations to May in advance of his arrival; Chris Grayling gave his resignation to the new Prime Minister. Jeremy Hunt resigned rather than accept a demotion, and Johnson sacked various others who had supported his rival's leadership bid. In their place, he rewarded Brexit hardliners and other leadership rivals who had proffered him their support. Sajid Javid became Chancellor of the Exchequer, Dominic Raab became Foreign Secretary, Priti Patel was made Home Secretary, Michael Gove replaced David Lidington at the Cabinet Office, Andrea Leadsom returned as Secretary of State for Business, Energy and Industrial Strategy, and Jacob Rees-Mogg replaced Mel Stride as Leader of the House of Commons. Of the five new Cabinet members who were not ministers during the votes on May's deal, two—Patel and Theresa Villiers—were Spartans, and two others—Raab and Grant Shapps—had like Johnson voted against it twice.[5] Rees-Mogg, who was not a full member of Cabinet, had done the same.

Perhaps Johnson's most eye-catching appointment was not to his Cabinet, but his choice of Dominic Cummings, former Campaign Director of Vote Leave, as his Chief Adviser. Several other members of that team also gained backroom roles in Number 10, and Nikki da Costa (who had previously resigned over May's deal) also returned to her position as Director of Legislative Affairs. Just a few months earlier, in March 2019, Cummings had been found in contempt of parliament by the House of Commons Privileges Committee (2019), for refusing to give evidence to a select committee on Vote Leave's activities during the referendum campaign. This conclusion had been endorsed by a resolution of the House of Commons in April.[6] However, it was no formal bar to him being appointed to a senior post in government.

Attempts at Parliamentary Fightback

Talk of prorogation, and the prospect of a new Prime Minister intent on taking the UK out of the EU by 31 October, if necessary without a deal, raised significant concerns among MPs. As prorogation does not need parliamentary approval, it wasn't immediately obvious what they could do to guard against it. But there were three notable parliamentary initiatives during the leadership contest, which achieved varying levels of success.

The 12 June Opposition Day on Agenda Control

A week after Dominic Raab's original comments, on 12 June, Labour was granted an opposition day. Its motion proposed to take control of the Commons agenda on a subsequent day (25 June) to debate 'matters relating to the United Kingdom's withdrawal from the European Union'.[7] This was the first attempt to use an opposition day in such a way. Previous proposals to wrest agenda control from the government had depended on amendable 'next steps' motions under Section 13 of the EU (Withdrawal) Act—not least because, in recent months, so few opposition days had been granted.

This initiative faced two significant obstacles. First, it is always difficult to persuade government backbenchers to support opposition frontbench proposals. In an attempt to avoid this problem, the motion had been signed not only by Labour, and by the parliamentary leaders of most other opposition parties, but additionally by leading Conservative backbench organizer Oliver Letwin.[8] Keir Starmer claimed in debate that Rory Stewart had also come close to signing, but his Cabinet position clearly proscribed this. The second obstacle was the proponents' lack of clarity about precisely how they planned to use the allotted time. They stated an intention to bring forward a bill, but not what it would do.

Starmer framed the motion's purpose as being 'that if the next Prime Minister were foolish enough to pursue no deal without gaining the consent of this House, or to prorogue Parliament to force through no deal, Parliament would have the means to prevent that'; but he failed to articulate, when questioned, exactly how.[9] This was strongly criticized by Brexit Secretary Steve Barclay, and led ERG supporter Bill Cash to dub Starmer's proposal 'a phantom motion for a phantom Bill', with hints that it could even be used to revoke Article 50.[10] Notwithstanding pleas from Oliver Letwin and Dominic Grieve that this could prove MPs' last opportunity to prevent total government control of the Commons agenda up to 31 October, the motion was defeated by 309 votes to 298. A total of 10 Conservatives rebelled to support it, but eight Labour members voted against.[11] Grieve issued a noteworthy warning in his contribution to the debate that:

> if we get to a point where a Prime Minister is intent on taking us out of the EU with
> no deal, the only way of stopping that Prime Minister will be to bring down their

Government. I have to say here and now that I will not hesitate to do that, if that is attempted, even if it means resigning the Whip and leaving the [Conservative] party.[12]

Passions were running high, but the opposition day seemingly occurred too soon for enough concerned Conservatives to be prepared to break with precedent to support it.

The Northern Ireland (Executive Formation) Bill

The next opportunity came in the shape of a government bill which allowed for extension of the time available to form a Northern Ireland executive. The province was still without a political executive, and the provisions allowing its civil service to function in the absence of ministers were otherwise set to expire in August. The cross-party alliance against no deal used the bill to attach amendments aimed at preventing a lengthy prorogation of parliament. The bill was introduced in the very last throes of Theresa May's government, receiving its Commons second reading during the Conservative Party membership ballot, on 8 July. There was a notable reticence on the part of insiders interviewed to discuss the details, but clearly some senior ministers sought to facilitate this opportunity for the rebels. As one recalled in interview, 'we had come to fear that the successor government might effectively seek to mount a constitutional coup, and shut parliament down'. Another senior interviewee, asked why ministers didn't simply legislate against prorogation, commented that 'we were functioning as a caretaker government in effect at that point', and that this 'would have poisoned the leadership election'. It would likely also have met with resistance from some Cabinet members.

The bill's 'long title', which helps determine the amendments that will be considered 'in scope', was to 'Extend the period for forming an Executive under section 1(1) of the Northern Ireland (Executive Formation and Exercise of Functions) Act 2018 and to impose a duty on the Secretary of State to report on progress towards the formation of an Executive in Northern Ireland'. One interviewee suggested that the words on reporting had been deliberately framed to facilitate the changes that followed. These began at committee stage in the Commons, with a group of amendments headed by Dominic Grieve, co-sponsored by various Conservative and ex-Conservative MPs, as well as opposition members.[13] Their basic purpose was to insert requirements for regular ministerial reporting to parliament over the autumn, and one key amendment (not selected for debate) explicitly stated that parliament should be recalled for this purpose if it had been prorogued. One of Grieve's amendments was narrowly approved, by 294 votes to 293, and another narrowly defeated.

In the Lords, there were attempts to toughen up the provisions, led by Crossbench lawyer Lord (David) Anderson of Ipswich, with support from Conservative Viscount Hailsham and others. The minister suggested that the amendments were inappropriate, as they were not really about Northern Ireland at all. His Conservative backbench Brexiteer colleague Lord (Nicholas) True (who became a minister some months later) argued vehemently that the amendments were politically motivated, and were based on an unjustified allegation:

> Mr Johnson does not wish to prorogue Parliament. He has not said so, and he does not need to...It is simply rubbish to say that there might be an attempt to stop Parliament legislating on Brexit. Parliament has already legislated, and talk about a so-called unlawful shutdown of Parliament or hyperbole about a ban on Parliament sitting reflects nothing Mr Johnson has ever said. It is so much chaff thrown up by the ditchers among the more extreme referendum deniers.[14]

Unconvinced by these arguments, peers solidly approved Anderson's proposals by 272 votes to 168 (with 13 Conservatives in favour). When the bill returned to the Commons on 18 July, Hilary Benn moved an amendment to shore up the requirements, inserting Grieve's original demand that parliament should if necessary be recalled from a prorogation if it was not meeting at the reporting times set out in the bill. This proposal was comfortably passed, by 315 votes to 274, with 17 Conservative MPs voting in favour. A further 30 Conservatives were absent from the vote, notably including Secretary of State for Northern Ireland Karen Bradley, and her Cabinet colleagues Greg Clark, David Gauke, Philip Hammond, Jeremy Hunt, and Rory Stewart, alongside several junior ministers. A senior Labour interviewee reported that the MP whipping for the cross-party group had been told in advance that precisely this would happen. The carefully premeditated outcome reflected the increased anxiety on the Conservative benches about prorogation by this point. No action was taken against the Cabinet absentees, all of them by now set to quit the government one week later. Had they not been guaranteed leniency for abstention, Theresa May's Chief of Staff Gavin Barwell (2021) recalled that they had threatened instead to vote for Benn's proposal.

The changes to the bill meant that ministers would be required to report to parliament on the Northern Ireland situation, therefore effectively requiring parliament to be sitting, on or before 4 September, and fortnightly from 9 October onwards. But in what later became clear was a serious tactical error, the rebels had left a gap for what would normally be a recess period in late September and early October during the party conferences. Conservative interviewees suggested that this gap had been included at the insistence of Jeremy Corbyn.

A Potential Vote of No Confidence in Boris Johnson

As seen in Dominic Grieve's comments on 12 June, and those of Rory Stewart during the leadership contest, another potential means to resist a Boris Johnson government was a parliamentary no-confidence vote. As the numbers in the Commons were already on a knife-edge, a Prime Minister acting in conflict with the wishes of MPs could potentially be brought down, so long as parliament was sitting. In July, when the contest was still underway, the *New Statesman* published names of several Conservative MPs—including Chancellor of the Exchequer Philip Hammond—who had publicly stated that they were prepared to contemplate voting no confidence in Johnson (Walsh 2019).[15] Assuming that such members were joined by the opposition parties, this would be adequate to bring the government down.

Before the contest ended, Alan Duncan, who had served as a junior minister under Johnson when he was Foreign Secretary, devised a plan for an debate on his suitability as Prime Minister, to take place on the day that the result was announced.[16] Duncan (2021) has described his behind-the-scenes conversations with senior clerks, who advised him that his proposal for an emergency debate under Standing Order no. 24 was completely in order, and the discretion lay with John Bercow as Speaker to decide if it went forward. But on the day in question Bercow turned down the request. This left Duncan (2021: 504) perplexed and angry, believing that the Speaker had scuppered his initiative 'on a whim'.

It is not wholly clear why Duncan's initiative failed. The new Prime Minister was due to be in office for just one day before the House of Commons was set to break for its long summer recess (see below). It undoubtedly seemed appropriate for MPs to debate whether they supported him remaining in post over the summer—particularly given the prorogation threat. However, Duncan was not firmly allied with any of the rebel groups, so his scheme lacked coordinated backing, and there were other routes that could more plausibly have been taken to test confidence.

A more conventional such test could have been triggered by Labour, and a formal motion of no confidence from the opposition would normally, by convention, be given time for debate—but this route was not tested. Labour may have correctly surmised that, until the new leader chosen by party members had done anything actually wrong, Conservative MPs would be unlikely to vote to unseat him. This was particularly the case with Corbyn at the helm, as the most likely person to replace a Prime Minister who had lost MPs' confidence would normally be the leader of the opposition.[17] Speaking about the Duncan initiative, a senior Labour interviewee said 'the trouble is, it never would have worked. Because throughout all of this, people would vote for a number of things, but they weren't voting to have the remotest possibility that Jeremy Corbyn might be asked to form a government'. This presumably prevented a formal Labour move against Johnson, and seems likely to have been a factor influencing Bercow's decision.

A Summer of Uncertainty

As already seen, Boris Johnson became Conservative Party leader on 23 July 2019, and—without any attempt by MPs to withdraw Commons confidence—assumed office as Prime Minister the following day. On 25 July, the House of Commons was set to rise for its long summer recess. This clearly left virtually no time for Johnson and his new government to be scrutinized, including on his Brexit plans. The start date for the recess had been agreed a month earlier, notwithstanding the known leadership timetable. Recess dates are proposed by the government, but officially approved by the House of Commons on a motion which is taken 'forthwith'—i.e. with no opportunity for amendment or debate. Liaison Committee chair Sarah Wollaston (a former Conservative, now independent) had sought on 24 June to organize opposition to the government motion. But given the procedural obstacles, plus MPs' exhaustion and desire for a summer break, just 25 members voted against the motion, while 223 supported it (Labour chose to abstain). Consequently, following his upbeat statement on 25 July, Johnson was free to formulate his Brexit plans over the summer entirely relieved of parliamentary oversight. This did appear an important opportunity missed.

Over the summer, as discussed in the next chapter, Johnson's rhetoric continued to be that the 31 October exit date was immoveable, come what may. Both the Prime Minister and his newly appointed Brexit negotiator, David Frost, made clear that the UK was preparing if necessary for a no-deal exit.

Although Johnson reopened negotiations with the EU on the backstop (see Chapter 10), Brussels sources suggested that a 'no deal now appear[ed] to be the UK government's central scenario' (Tominey 2019b). This, combined with the tone of the Prime Minister's rhetoric, alarmed the anti-no deal parliamentarians—who, in response, continued to develop various cross-party initiatives designed to prevent such an outcome.

One option that received both public and private attention was the possibility of a citizens' assembly to recommend the way ahead on Brexit. Rory Stewart had proposed this during the Conservative leadership campaign, but it had also been under discussion for some time among other senior MPs opposed to a no-deal exit, led by Yvette Cooper and Caroline Spelman. In August the *Times* reported that the Archbishop of Canterbury, Justin Welby, was talking to them about possibly chairing such an assembly (Courea 2019). He later issued a public statement indicating his in-principle willingness to do so, provided that the new body was carefully organized, had cross-party support, and was not 'a Trojan horse intended to delay or prevent Brexit in any particular form' (Welby 2019). As mentioned in Chapter 5, the only previous attempt to host such a public deliberative exercise on Brexit—by researchers, rather than government or parliament—had come down in favour of a soft Brexit (Renwick et al. 2017, 2018). Proponents of such an exercise in 2019 clearly hoped that citizens would continue to be more open to compromise than MPs had been, and would reject the hardline ERG position that was now taking hold. ERG members, meanwhile, firmly rejected the proposal. Steve Baker suggested that 'There can be no excuse for undermining our essential institutions. Parliament is the people's assembly' (quoted in Courea and Devlin 2019). Without formal backing from government or parliament it proved impossible to get such an initiative off the ground.

The cross-party grouping of 'grandees' continued to meet and communicate regularly over the summer. It was now joined by new senior figures who had until recently served in government, such as Philip Hammond, David Gauke, and Rory Stewart. During the recess it vacated its usual meeting place of Hilary Benn's parliamentary office, and began meeting at offices in Holborn, causing members to dub it 'the Kingsway group'.

A significant proposal, which attracted a good deal of media speculation, was the idea of staging a no-confidence vote in Johnson's government when parliament returned from summer recess, to replace it with an alternative cross-party government. Under the terms of the Fixed-term Parliaments Act, a formal no-confidence vote would trigger a 14-day period in which a new government could be formed, failing which a general election would be held.

The levels of concern about Johnson were such that the numbers could have been there for a no-confidence vote (and indeed these numbers worsened over the summer, after the Conservatives lost the Brecon and Radnorshire by-election in August). The central problem remained who would lead an alternative government. Here, Jeremy Corbyn's leadership of Labour was undoubtedly a major obstacle. This was publicly highlighted, in particular, by Jo Swinson, who had become leader of the Liberal Democrats in July. In mid-August, Corbyn (2019b) publicly proposed that he should lead a temporary government after a no-confidence vote, to pursue a further Article 50 extension, followed by a general election in which Labour would support a second Brexit referendum. Swinson was particularly vocal in stating that this wouldn't work, attracting criticism from some of his supporters. However, she was only voicing an evident truth—that Conservative rebels would not be prepared to back a Corbyn-led government (indeed, even some Labour MPs were firmly opposed). This reality is clear from public statements by key Conservative figures. David Gauke (2020) has noted that the 'Jeremy Corbyn factor essentially ruled out any possibility' of an alternative government, while Dominic Grieve (2020) likewise remarked on 'the extent to which Corbyn was massively destructive' in this regard. The names of various more unifying figures from either side—such as Labour's Hilary Benn, Margaret Beckett, or Harriet Harman, or Conservatives Ken Clarke or David Lidington— were therefore mooted publicly instead. But a senior Labour interviewee recalled that 'Jeremy would never agree to anyone else heading it', and without his blessing Corbynite MPs would not have voted for such a plan. Consequently, the idea of a cross-party government (sometimes dubbed a 'government of national unity') also foundered.

In practice, the cross-party grandees spent more of their time fleshing out plans for a further backbench bill to be proposed in the autumn, facilitating another extension to the Article 50 process beyond 31 October. Even without the risk of prorogation, there were severe challenges to such an enterprise; as Letwin and Grieve had emphasized on the opposition day in June, there was no obvious procedural 'hook' for backbenchers to take control of the agenda before the scheduled exit date. Knowing backbenchers' intentions, the government would be very unlikely to grant opposition time and, without a Section 13-style government motion that could be amended, it might prove impossible to force a vote on the suspension of Standing Order no. 14. In these circumstances, a procedural route that came increasingly to be discussed (including in the media) was use of an emergency debate under Standing Order no. 24. This was again a procedurally 'innovative' approach, as such debates usually take place on a neutral motion. However, there had been some partial exceptions, some of them noted in Erskine May, which could (and in due course, would) be used by Speaker Bercow to justify allowing such a debate (Lee and Berry 2020).

As recess wore on, some MPs grew increasingly restive, and publicly demanded a parliamentary recall. However recall is another power which lies solely in the government's hands—a limitation which has frequently been controversial (Russell and Gover 2021). On 17 August, over 100 MPs sent a public letter to Boris Johnson asking that parliament should be recalled, on the basis that the risk of a no-deal Brexit amounted to a 'national emergency'. The letter, headed by former Labour member Luciana Berger (2019), argued that 'This is no time for Parliament to be in recess. Waiting until 3 September when your Brexit deadline will be only a matter of weeks away is unacceptable'. But Number 10 quickly rejected these calls (Zeffman 2019). In a similar way, cross-party support also emerged for cancelling the usual autumn recess period allowed for the party conferences (Mason and Elgot 2019). Unlike recall (or prorogation), recess dates do require approval by MPs, via the mechanism that Wollaston had unsuccessfully sought to use in June. The conference recess had not yet been approved, and MPs were due to vote on this in the autumn.

The Prorogation Announcement and Parliament's Response

A Prorogation is Announced

Before parliament's prearranged meeting date of 3 September, and notwithstanding the earlier protestations from some of his supporters, Johnson's government announced on 28 August that the Queen had been advised to grant a five-week prorogation. He wrote to inform MPs that same day (Johnson 2019b). His stated reasoning was that the parliamentary session had been very long, and it was time for a new Queen's Speech to set out his government's programme. But what was proposed was the longest prorogation since 1930. Since then, the average prorogation period—to mark the break between one parliamentary session and the next, sometimes with a general election in between—had been 4–5 calendar days (Purvis 2019). But Johnson proposed that parliament would rise in early September, and not return until mid-October. During a prorogation, MPs would have no opportunity to question the government, pass legislation, or mount a no-confidence vote. Subsequently, Nikki da Costa quite openly admitted that the prorogation was a tactic to block parliamentary resistance to a no-deal Brexit (UK in a Changing Europe 2022).[18]

Most Cabinet ministers seemingly had no warning that the prorogation was coming. Amber Rudd (2021), kept on by Johnson as Secretary of State for Work and Pensions, has reported that there was no consultation, and the Cabinet was told of the decision only after it had been made. The only minister to resign in immediate response to the announcement was Lord (George) Young of Cookham, who issued a statement suggesting that it 'risks undermining the fundamental role of parliament at a critical time in our history, and reinforces the view that the government may not have the confidence of the House [of Commons] for its Brexit policy' (quoted in Stewart 2019a). Young was a junior minister, but had held various senior government roles under Margaret Thatcher and John Major, and had been David Cameron's Chief Whip and Leader of the House of Commons. Conspicuously, none of the leadership candidates who had been so critical of Raab's prorogation proposal a few months earlier—Hancock, Gove, Javid, or Leadsom—spoke out in protest. But the Prime Minister's brother Jo Johnson (2019) (brought back into government only in July) did resign a few days later, citing 'unresolvable tension' experienced 'between family loyalty and the national interest'. Ruth Davidson also resigned as Scottish Conservative leader on the day after the prorogation was announced.

Reactions from some outside government to the news were fierce. John Bercow issued a statement denouncing the proposal as a 'constitutional outrage' and 'an offence against the democratic process and the rights of parliamentarians as the people's elected representatives' (quoted in Bercow 2020b: 13). Dominic Grieve suggested that it was 'tantamount to a coup, really, against parliament', and that Johnson was 'behaving like a revolutionary rather than a Conservative Prime Minister' (Sky News Politics 2019). Many (though not all) ERG supporters took the opposing view.[19] Peter Bone went so far as to suggest that 'this is actually restoring parliamentary democracy' (BBC Newsnight 2019), while Jacob Rees-Mogg (who had flown to Balmoral for the required meeting with the Queen) did the media round to defend the government's proposal. He dismissed a 'candyfloss of outrage... from people who never wanted to leave the European Union' (quoted in BBC News 2019m), repeatedly claiming that the prorogation was perfectly normal—as it added only a few days onto the standard autumn break for the party conferences. What was not publicly conceded (and seems very likely to have been omitted from the private advice to the Queen) was that MPs had the discretion to vote against a conference recess, and looked likely to do so.[20] In contrast, they had no automatic ability to overturn a prorogation.

The Emergency Debate and Purging of Conservative Moderates

This all led to exceedingly tense scenes when the Commons reconvened on 3 September. The prorogation timing had not sought to interfere with this meeting, which was effectively now required due to the rebel amendments to the Northern Ireland (Executive Formation) Act. Notably, the proposed prorogation almost exactly filled the window which had been left by those amendments. The rebels had failed to block the prorogation, but at least had ensured that it was preceded by some sitting days, and also prevented it from, as some proponents had initially contemplated, extending beyond the Brexit deadline.

In line with the rumours over the summer, but with added urgency given the events of the preceding days, Oliver Letwin made an application to the Speaker for an emergency Standing Order no. 24 debate to discuss EU withdrawal—which was granted for that day. Before the debate began, Conservative rebel and former minister Phillip Lee crossed the floor of the House of Commons during a statement by the Prime Minister, to join the Liberal Democrat benches. Officially, this erased the fragile Conservative–DUP majority.

Letwin's motion for the emergency debate did as had been planned by the cross-party alliance: proposing to suspend Standing Order no. 14 for 4 September, to allow expedited passage of a bill requiring the Prime Minister to request a further Article 50 extension. This was an unprecedented use of a Standing Order no. 24 debate, but the government's own actions, in seeking a prorogation of a length unparalleled in modern times, drew attention away from the Speaker's break with convention, and offered it some justification. While the debate focused in part on the merits of the proposal to proceed with the cross-party bill, much of it also focused on the connected matter of the attempted prorogation. Central to both questions was the appropriate role of parliament.

Leader of the House Jacob Rees-Mogg spoke for the government. He repeatedly insisted that the prorogation was nothing out of the ordinary, stating for example that 'Prorogation is a routine start for a new Session, and we are losing a similar number of days to the number we would lose in a normal Prorogation', and that '[t]he Prorogation is the normal Prorogation to have a new Session; it is not to stop debate on matters related to the European Union.'[21] Its unusual length was purely because 'we are taking four or five days of parliamentary time and simply going over the normal recess' held annually for the party conferences.[22] But these protestations were transparently untrue. Conservative backbencher Antoinette Sandbach roundly rebuffed them, contending:

> It is claimed that this Prorogation is a normal Prorogation, but it is not. This Parliament would have expected the Leader of the House to table a recess motion, which would have asked us to agree to the party conference recess. That motion has never been put to us. As Members of Parliament, we have never been asked to agree to the recess, and it is highly likely that we would not have done so given the scale of the crisis that faces our country.[23]

Dominic Grieve lamented that 'a section of my party has become hijacked by a narrow sector of those who voted to leave, and who are simply using the will of the people as an instrument of potential tyranny against any of those who disagree with them'.[24] This perceived tension between different conceptions of democracy was echoed by senior Brexiteer Bernard Jenkin, who suggested that '[t]he bitterness of tonight's exchanges reflects the breakdown of our shared understanding about which mandate is legitimate: the representative or the direct'.[25] While not defending the prorogation, he argued that it would be incorrect to proceed with the proposed cross-party bill.

At the end of the debate, the government was comfortably defeated on Letwin's motion, by 328 votes to 301. A total of 21 Conservatives supported it. Boris Johnson's response was to immediately strip them all of the Conservative whip. This was a complete departure from normal practice and, of course, a markedly different response to that from Theresa May— who had tolerated multiple rebellions, including from Johnson himself. On just the third parliamentary day of his premiership, Johnson had expelled not only Dominic Grieve and three others who had opposed May's deal, but 17 Conservatives, including Oliver Letwin, who had voted for it on all three occasions. Among them were four recently departed members of her Cabinet: former Chancellor of the Exchequer Philip Hammond, Justice Secretary David Gauke, Secretary of State for Communities and Local Government Greg Clark, and Johnson's own leadership rival Rory Stewart. Other targets included 'Father' of the House of Commons Ken Clarke, who had served as a Conservative MP for 49 years and held multiple Cabinet roles under three previous prime ministers, and Winston Churchill's grandson, Nicholas Soames.[26] In response to this extraordinary action Amber Rudd, who condemned it as an 'assault on decency and democracy', resigned from the Cabinet and surrendered the Conservative whip (Helm et al. 2019).

The Benn–Burt Act

Proceedings on the bill began the following day.[27] Its lead sponsor was Hilary Benn, though he was clearly acting as a figurehead for the senior cross-party group. Alistair Burt, another former minister from May's government who had just been stripped of the whip, was second sponsor.

The bill had all of its stages in the House of Commons on the day of its introduction. At second reading, Benn emphasized its cross-party nature, and the need to prevent a no-deal exit. He was supported from the Labour frontbench by Keir Starmer, who was strongly critical of the prorogation, suggesting that the government's claim that it was normal, and simply intended to facilitate a new Queen's Speech, was an 'obvious untruth', and that its true purpose was 'to silence this House and frustrate attempts to prevent no deal'.[28] Philip Hammond, who was listed as a sponsor of the bill and now spoke from the backbenches as a former Conservative MP, claimed that numerous EU sources indicated that no real negotiations were going on, and that time was anyway running out for approval of a new deal before exit day. The bill's opponents argued that it 'hands the decision back to the European Union', by requiring the Prime Minister to request an Article 50 extension that he did not want, which would only be granted at EU discretion.[29] Bill Cash therefore dubbed it a 'Subservience Bill'.[30] During the debate it emerged that the Conservative Party was tweeting about the debate using the hashtag #SurrenderBill. This moniker was to appear repeatedly in subsequent weeks.

Second reading was approved by 329 votes to 300, with a single Conservative rebel: Caroline Spelman. She was, in effect, the only one of the rebel leaders who retained the party whip, having voted against Letwin's motion the previous day. The subsequent Commons stages of the bill were fairly uneventful, and it passed swiftly to the Lords. There was then a near repetition of proceedings over the Cooper–Letwin Bill earlier in the year. The Labour frontbench proposed a timetable motion, to limit the options for delay, which led to lengthy debates and multiple attempts by Brexit-supporting peers to 'filibuster' the motion. This resulted in 17 divisions, six of them on 'closure' motions from the bill's supporters to speed up the debate.[31] The clear impression was that the government had hoped to block the bill via the Lords, notwithstanding the elected chamber's support.[32] But ministers eventually relented and agreed a timetable motion. The bill passed the Lords unamended on 6 September, and attained royal assent three days later.

What was now the EU (Withdrawal) (No. 2) Act 2019 required that, if parliament had not approved either a deal or no-deal exit by 19 October, the

Prime Minister must request a further extension to the Article 50 period to 31 January 2020. As the bill left the Commons, the *Daily Express* ran with the headline 'Parliament surrenders to the EU'. On 5 September, Boris Johnson claimed that he would rather be 'dead in a ditch' than agree a further Article 50 extension (BBC News 2019n). Speculation hence quickly began as to whether he would comply with the Act's provisions, and what might happen if he didn't.

Johnson's Attempts to Get a General Election

While MPs were trying to bind the Prime Minister into extending the Brexit timetable, he was hoping to go over their heads to the voters, by triggering a general election. In the summer, almost immediately after Johnson took over the premiership, reports began circulating—almost certainly based on briefings from Number 10—that he wanted a showdown with parliament over Brexit, and would seek to generate a 'people versus politicians' election (e.g. Mason and Elgot 2019).

Johnson's first attempt came on 4 September, the day that the Benn–Burt Bill was introduced. Following proceedings on the bill, he moved a formal motion under the Fixed-term Parliaments Act that there should be an early general election, which he suggested should take place on 15 October. Notwithstanding the earlier reports, he insisted that 'I do not want an election, the public do not want an election and the country does not want an election, but this House has left no option other than letting the public decide who they want as Prime Minister'—inviting a choice between himself and Jeremy Corbyn.[33] Corbyn insisted in response that 'We want an election because we look forward to turfing this Government out', but argued—quite reasonably—that dissolving parliament in the face of a potential no-deal Brexit would be reckless.[34] He pressed Johnson to focus instead on securing his promised new Brexit deal, suggesting that the Prime Minister's attempts to prorogue parliament, and to use the Lords to block the Benn–Burt Bill, indicated 'anti-democratic instincts'.[35] Labour abstained on the motion, which was supported by 298 votes to 56; but motions of this kind required a two-thirds majority of all members of the House of Commons. Hence Johnson's proposal was blocked.

The Prime Minister made a second attempt on 9 September, the final parliamentary sitting day before the prorogation took effect. Referring scornfully to the 'Surrender Act', he claimed that parliament in general, and the opposition in particular, had for three years 'schemed to overturn the verdict of the British people, delivered in a referendum which, in a crowning irony, almost all of them voted to hold'.[36] These were, of course, strange words from a man who had contributed to the three-year delay by denouncing and voting against the previous Conservative Prime Minister's Brexit deal. Jeremy Corbyn insisted that Labour would not support a general election until the Prime Minister had complied with the Benn–Burt Act and secured an Article 50 extension. Labour abstained, and the motion again failed, by 293 votes to 46.

The Final Sitting Day

This final day of sitting included various other dramas. Speaker Bercow announced that he would step down on 31 October after 10 years in the role, to allow a successor to be chosen before a potential general election. He also granted two emergency debates. The first was proposed by Dominic Grieve on a humble address to require publication of internal government corres-pondence about the prorogation, which was approved by 311 votes to 302. The second was at the request of Jeremy Corbyn, to question whether the Prime Minister intended to comply with the terms of the Benn–Burt Act. The general tone from Conservative Brexiteers was that of course he would, as this was the law, but that the Act was inappropriate. Foreign Secretary Dominic Raab, responding for the government, claimed that 'Across the country, millions of voters are concluding that Parliament is refusing to allow Brexit to happen, because some MPs just do not like it and because some politicians think the voters got it wrong in 2016'.[37] By now a very deliberate Brexiteer narrative was establishing itself, that the blame for delay over Brexit lay with parliament, and by implication with Remainers—rather than with MPs such as Raab and Johnson, who had repeatedly voted down Theresa May's deal.

The final business was the formal prorogation ceremony, which takes place in the House of Lords. At the end of business in the Commons there were unhappy scenes, with MPs shouting and booing, and holding up signs read-ing 'silenced'. In the Lords, the Labour and Liberal Democrat leaders refused to play their normal role in the prorogation ceremony, but it simply took place nonetheless. In the words of one closely involved interviewee, the opponents had taken legal advice, which concluded that 'you don't have to have a ceremony to have a prorogation'. Despite the earlier threats, nothing came of Rory Stewart's 'alternative parliament'. Presumably preferring not to rock the boat, even his closest former allies on the Conservative side declined to participate.

The Miller/Cherry Cases

The Johnson government's attempted prorogation led to the second major case over Brexit in the Supreme Court, which again was in part initiated by Gina Miller. Again, the government's position was rebuffed by the court. The result was a determination that, legally, the prorogation was null and void and had hence never officially taken place.

Background to the Cases

The idea of legal action first emerged due to the concerns during the Conservative leadership contest. Two separate complainants pursued matters through two separate routes. Gina Miller began correspondence with the government before the contest was over, and remained in regular contact throughout the summer. She claims that the 'final letter from the government's legal department arrived on 27 August at 5 p.m., promising I need not go to court because Prime Minister Johnson would not be proroguing Parliament' (Miller 2019a: 203–4). In fact, the prorogation was announced the very next day. Separately, in late July, a cross-party group of 75 parliamentarians led by the SNP's Joanna Cherry had lodged a challenge in the Scottish courts, which was subsequently joined by the Scottish government. This case sought to take pre-emptive action, based on the hypothetical notion that parliament might be prorogued, and gained legal permission to proceed in early August.

When the prorogation was announced, both complainants were therefore ready. But the early trajectory of the cases was quite different. In Scotland, the initial ruling by the Outer House of the Court of Session was that the question of prorogation was 'non-justiciable': that is, that it was not a matter for the courts (instead being a matter of politics). However, on 11 September a higher Scottish ruling from the Inner House concluded the reverse. The judges agreed unanimously that prorogation was indeed justiciable, and that the Prime Minister had exercised his power improperly.[38]

In contrast, Gina Miller lodged proceedings in the High Court of England and Wales on the day that the prorogation was announced, 28 August. Two days later, former Conservative Prime Minister John Major announced that he would join the case (Elgot 2019c). But it was dismissed by the court, and on 11 September, the same day as the Cherry ruling, a detailed judgment was published stating that prorogation was not justiciable.[39] It was the combination of these two cases, and their contemporaneous but conflicting judgments, which ended up being fast-tracked to appeal in the Supreme Court. Hearings took place on 17–19 September, and the judgment was handed down on 24 September. Unsurprisingly, given the mixed results in the courts so far, legal experts had conflicting opinions about the litigants' chances of success (e.g. Tierney 2019, Young 2019). The Supreme Court proceedings attracted widespread attention, with as many as 30 million views of its live video feed over the four days (Hussain 2019).

The Key Arguments in the Supreme Court

In line with proceedings at the earlier stage, the arguments in the case rested on two questions: first, whether the matter of prorogation was justiciable at all; and second, if it was, whether the requested five-week prorogation was lawful. Both of these questions fundamentally concerned the relationship between parliament, government, and the courts.

With respect to justiciability, the government argued that the matter of prorogation, under the prerogative, was 'intrinsically one of high policy and politics, not law'.[40] It was therefore not something in which the courts should get involved. Parliament had not chosen to limit the power of prorogation (aside from in a few specific circumstances), and its rightful exercise by the executive remained largely a matter of convention.[41] Furthermore, the government argued, the 'commission' which sits in the House of Lords for the prorogation ceremony is a 'proceeding in parliament'. As such, it is a process in which the courts cannot rightfully interfere, according to Article 9 of the Bill of Rights 1689. This is the provision underlying the principle of parliamentary privilege, which states that 'the freedom of speech and debates or proceedings in Parliament ought not to be impeached or questioned in any court' (quoted in Joint Committee on Parliamentary Privilege 1999: 1).

The government's opponents made contrasting arguments on justiciability. They pointed out that it was legally well established that prerogative powers are subject to limits and are not beyond judicial review. Further, by suspending parliament, particularly for such a long time and at a crucial moment, the government was seeking to prevent it conducting its functions as a sovereign legal body.[42] Parliamentary sovereignty is a fundamental principle of the UK constitution; another fundamental principle is that the government must be accountable to parliament.[43] If prorogation was not justiciable, they argued, there would be nothing to prevent the Prime Minister from advising the monarch to prorogue for a year or more. It was therefore essential that the courts should be able to step in if this power was misused. They dismissed the argument about Article 9 as 'unsustainable nonsense'.[44] Essentially, their challenge was against the government's instruction to prorogue, not against the prorogation itself.

With respect to legality, the arguments were rather different, relating to the specific nature of this prorogation request. The government claimed, as it had done politically, that there was nothing inherently unusual about it—that the proposed five-week shutdown included 'a period in which both Houses would customarily have been in recess on account of the party conferences'.[45] Parliament had been able to sit in September before the prorogation, and would be able to sit again in October in the run-up to the Article 50 deadline. Indeed, it had clearly not been prevented from legislating, given that it had passed the Benn–Burt Act. The government further argued that in the time available parliament 'could have legislated, but did not legislate, to ensure that Parliament continued to sit during the prorogation if that had been Parliament's wish'.[46] The cross-party grandees had in fact considered this as a potential response to the prorogation announcement, but rejected it on two grounds. First, that the time available was extremely limited, and if it was not used to pass the Benn–Burt Act, the sole opportunity to extend the Article 50 period before a no-deal crash-out might have been lost. Second, there were concerns that an attempt to legislate on prorogation might have resulted in ministers seeking to block the proposition by withholding so-called Queen's consent (now King's consent), on the basis that it interfered with the prerogative powers.[47] This was a very hazy area, and there was no guarantee that the government could use such a blocking power (Evans 2020), but it risked opening a fresh constitutional controversy with uncertain consequences, at a point when time was very short. Suffice to say, the suggestion that parliament could readily have prevented the prorogation if it wished was distinctly questionable. As was the suggestion in court from the government's lawyer, James Eadie, that the various bills that would inevitably fall as a result of prorogation could be quickly and easily resurrected by parliamentarians if they wished. Both arguments seemed distinctly detached from the day-to-day parliamentary realities of government agenda control.

The arguments on legality from the government's challengers rested on some of the points already raised by parliamentarians, as discussed earlier in the chapter. Particularly that this was an unprecedentedly long proposed prorogation in modern times, and that it would prevent parliament from scrutinizing government and potentially taking action during a crucial period. The point was also made that the adjournment for the conference recess would, unlike prorogation, have been a decision of parliament itself. Significant attention focused on internal correspondence between the Prime

Minister and members of his team regarding whether a parliamentary shutdown was desirable and appropriate. In response to a memorandum from Nikki da Costa, which recommended the move, Johnson had scribbled that 'the whole September session [of parliament] is a rigmarole introduced by girly swot [David] Cameron', and that he saw nothing shocking about a lengthy prorogation given the usual conference recess (Walker 2019). A minute from the Cabinet meeting of 28 August, also released to the court, noted that 'Parliament would not normally be prorogued for a longer period than one to two weeks. It should be explained why in this case the period was significantly longer' (Bowcott and Carrell 2019).

Fundamentally, those challenging the government maintained that parliament had been shut down deliberately in order to allow ministers to avoid scrutiny and accountability at a crucial moment—as Nikki da Costa subsequently admitted (UK in a Changing Europe 2022). In his summing up, Lord (David) Pannick, acting for the second time as lead advocate for Gina Miller, reiterated that a central principle of the constitution is that 'the executive is answerable to parliament'. Therefore:

> The executive – the junior partner – cannot claim a legally unfettered power to close down the senior partner, for as long as the executive likes, for whatever reason it likes, and however substantial the damage to the ability of parliament to perform its scrutiny functions.   (**Supreme Court 2019**)

The Judgment and the Reaction

Unusually, 11 Supreme Court justices had sat in this case and, uniquely, the 11 delivered a unanimous ruling. This strongly rejected the government's position, and accepted many of the arguments from Miller and Cherry's teams. An oral summary of the judgment was broadcast live from the Supreme Court by its President, Baroness (Brenda) Hale of Richmond (who was quickly dubbed by supporters a 'girly swot'). In her statement, Hale (2019) indicated that 'there is no doubt that the courts have jurisdiction to decide upon the existence and limits of a prerogative power', and that therefore the case was justiciable. In terms of legality, she indicated that the court had been guided by the need to respect two principles: of parliamentary sovereignty, and parliamentary accountability. In deciding what the limits on prorogation should be, she presented reasons very similar to those of Lord Pannick:

that a decision to prorogue (or advise the monarch to prorogue) will be unlawful if the prorogation has the effect of frustrating or preventing, without reasonable justification, the ability of Parliament to carry out its constitutional functions as a legislature and as the body responsible for the supervision of the executive.

Hale emphasized that the proposed length of the prorogation made it far from 'normal' and that '[p]roroguing Parliament is quite different from Parliament going into recess', criticizing the da Costa memo for omitting to point out this distinction. She also noted that 'it is quite clear that the pro- rogation is not a proceeding in Parliament. It takes place in the House of Lords chamber in the presence of members of both Houses, but it is not their decision. It is something which has been imposed upon them from outside.'

The court concluded that the timing of the proposed prorogation in the context of Brexit meant that the 'effect upon the fundamentals of our democ- racy was extreme'. Hence, in summary, 'the decision to advise Her Majesty to prorogue Parliament was unlawful' and the court judged it 'void and of no effect', concluding that 'Parliament has not been prorogued'. These arguments were set out more fully in the formal judgment document published simultaneously.[48]

Reactions were predictably mixed. Many legal commentators were sur- prised by the judgment's strength and unanimity, but some pleasantly so. Its significance was undoubted, but opinion ranged between seeing it as a defence of the constitution, a logical development, or a maverick rewriting. Some suggested that there had been an unwelcome incursion by the court into the executive–legislative relationship, which had hitherto been governed by convention (Finnis 2019b, McHarg 2020). But others argued that the court had—while further developing the scope of judicial review—defended the long-standing principle of parliamentary sovereignty 'in circumstances where the legislature [was] unable to ensure its powers are not usurped by the executive' (Barber 2019, Young 2021: 360). Lord (Jonathan) Sumption, a former Supreme Court justice who was seen as a critic of judicial power, having recently delivered the BBC Reith Lectures on the dangers of overreach by the courts (Sumption 2020c), congratulated his former colleagues for 'reinstat[ing] parliament at the heart of the decision making process…in circumstances where the government has tried to kick away the conventions' (quoted in Rozenberg 2020: 187–8).

Others were more outspoken. Jacob Rees-Mogg was reported as having gone so far as to suggest to Cabinet colleagues that the judgment represented a 'constitutional coup' (Demianyk 2019). The newspapers, unsurprisingly, were divided to the point of polarization—though the detractors stopped short of the much-criticized 'enemies of the people' rhetoric that had followed the first *Miller* case (Anderson and Hazell 2019). The *Guardian* (2019a) and *Independent* (2019) both argued that the Prime Minister's misjudgement, and his consequent legal humiliation, now demanded his resignation, while the *Financial Times* (2019a) described the ruling as a 'devastating indictment of [his] abuse of power'. The *Sun* (2019e), meanwhile, splashed that 'Political judges must face scrutiny after doing the bidding of braying Remainers', accusing the justices of 'constitutional vandalism'.

This same polarization could also be found in the polls. As reported by Curtice (2020), in early September, before the case, 59 per cent of former Leave voters had supported the prorogation of parliament (and 16 per cent opposed), while 58 per cent of former Remain voters opposed the prorogation (versus 19 per cent who supported it). Mirroring this pattern, 76 per cent of former Remain voters now expressed support for the Supreme Court's decision (and just 9 per cent were opposed), while 62 per cent of Leave voters disagreed with the decision (and just 18 per cent supported it). It was clear that by this point, on core constitutional questions about the role of both parliament and the courts, public opinion was firmly divided along Brexit lines.

The Political Aftermath

Particularly given the need to stay out of parliamentary proceedings, the Supreme Court had not specified what should happen next, returning that question to parliament. John Bercow was quick to respond, indicating that the Commons would sit the following day—25 September.

The first business that day was an urgent question from Joanna Cherry, which asked Attorney General Geoffrey Cox to 'make a statement about his legal opinion on the advice given to her Majesty the Queen to prorogue parliament'.[49] Cox walked a difficult line, insisting that he accepted the outcome of the Supreme Court case, while also making it clear that he disagreed with it. He denied that the government's defeat in such a major case was cause for his own resignation. But increasingly needled by parliamentarians, he blurted out the first of several overtly populist lines emerging from the government on that day, with his widely reported remarks that 'This Parliament is a dead Parliament. It should no longer sit. It has no moral right to sit on these green benches'.[50] Like Theresa May's anti-parliamentary comments earlier in the year, Cox's words attracted widespread criticism, inside parliament and beyond. Lord Sumption (2020b) later suggested that they had been 'outrageous', and 'surely one of the most extraordinary statements ever made in public by a Law Officer of the Crown'.

Later in the day came a statement from the Prime Minister. Johnson was unrepentant, blaming the opposition parties for frustrating the referendum result, and accusing them of damaging democracy. As ever, with no reference to his own role in Theresa May's difficulties, he criticized parliament for 'three years of dither and delay', arguing that only he and the Conservatives were on the side of 'the people'.[51]

The Prime Minister came under significant pressure on the question of whether he would now commit to complying with the Benn–Burt Act, and to seeking an extension to the Article 50 period if its conditions were met. During the course of the debate, Johnson referred to this measure 14 times as the 'Surrender Act', often in direct response to MPs who were specifically requesting that he restrain his language. He also referred to the 'Humiliation Act' and the 'Capitulation Act'. At one point Johnson was challenged by Labour MP Paula Sherriff, a friend and constituency neighbour of Jo Cox, the MP murdered during the referendum campaign, who commented:

> Many of us in this place are subject to death threats and abuse every single day. Let me tell the Prime Minister that they often quote his words – surrender Act, betrayal, traitor – and I, for one, am sick of it. We must moderate our language, and that has to come from the Prime Minister first, so I should be interested in hearing his opinion.[52]

Johnson's response to Sherriff was that 'I have to say that I have never heard so much humbug in all my life'.[53] To add insult to injury, he then commented on her murdered colleague, who had been an ardent Remain campaigner, suggesting that 'the best way to honour the memory of Jo Cox…would be, I think, to get Brexit done'.[54] John Bercow (2020b: 7–8) described the atmosphere in this debate as 'one of raw, intense, undiluted anger on both sides of the House of Commons', suggesting that he 'had never known a mood so toxic'. A subsequent analysis by the *Financial Times* found that the debate sparked floods of abusive tweets towards MPs (Blood, Elliott, and Burn-Murdoch 2019).

The following day, 26 September, the House of Commons was asked to vote on a motion from the government to adjourn until 3 October for a conference recess. As previously widely predicted, this proposal was defeated by 306 votes to 289. By now, such figures more or less illustrated the outcome of a straight party vote: Conservative and DUP MPs, and five independents, voted for the motion, with all other parties, and 16 independents, against. Its consequence was that parliament sat through the Conservative Party conference the following week (Labour's event having by now been held). Johnson (2019c) used his leader's speech at the event in Manchester to launch a further attack on parliament, commenting that 'If parliament were a laptop, then the screen would be showing the pizza wheel of doom. If parliament were a school, Ofsted would be shutting it down.' This was another remarkably unrepentant statement from a Prime Minister who had just lost a case in the UK's highest court for attempting to do exactly that.

Johnson's frequent hints, both inside and outside parliament, that he might not comply with the Benn–Burt Act led to significant concerns among government lawyers. Former Head of the Government Legal Department Jonathan Jones (2021) has indicated that he and others, likely including Geoffrey Cox, would have resigned if the Prime Minister had failed to comply.[55] In the end (as discussed in the next chapter) the Prime Minister did go along with the Act, but not before Downing Street had deployed another established device from the backsliding toolbox, in suggesting that it had resulted from collusion with 'foreign powers' by figures including Dominic Grieve, Philip Hammond, Oliver Letwin, and Hilary Benn. A banner headline in the *Mail on Sunday* on 29 September, echoed in several other papers, quoted briefing from 'a senior No 10 source' that 'extensive investigations' had begun into this matter (Owen 2019). Subsequent inquiries to Number 10 officials found these claims to be completely baseless, indicating that they had been briefed by those on the political side (Oborne 2021). Beyond even this, there were widespread reports in early October that Johnson might refuse to resign if subjected to a parliamentary no-confidence vote, and 'dare the Queen to sack him'—citing briefings from 'senior aides' and 'Cabinet ministers' (Shipman and Wheeler 2019).[56] Far from being deterred by the outcome of the Supreme Court case, the Prime Minister and his advisers seemed set on stretching constitutional conventions to their limits.

The long 2017–19 parliamentary session finally ended on 8 October, with a relatively standard prorogation which lasted until 14 October, at which point there was a Queen's Speech. It was by now perfectly obvious that Johnson wanted to hold a general election, and he had no desire (and quite possibly no ability) to keep battling on for another parliamentary year. This caused some experts to criticize the Prime Minister for 'heaping more embarrassment on the Queen' by requiring her to set out a political programme that there was no genuine intention to enact (Hazell 2019). The speech itself restated the intention to depart the EU by 31 October, and 'to work towards a new partnership with the European Union, based on free trade and friendly cooperation'.[57] Despite the controversies of the preceding weeks, MPs narrowly approved the speech, with some former Conservatives voting for it, and a handful abstaining.

Conclusion

Theresa May's premiership was tumultuous, and marked by significant Brexit-related conflict with MPs. It saw parliament's role brought into question, including sometimes by the Prime Minister herself, and development of a populist rhetoric of parliamentary and judicial 'elites' thwarting the 'will of the people'. But Boris Johnson's premiership took this to a completely new level.

The troubles during May's years as leader, essentially caused by a divided Conservative Party, but amplified by the loss of the government's narrow majority in 2017, fed a mood that parliament, and parliamentary scrutiny and accountability, were a problem. This created the environment that allowed Dominic Raab to float what would otherwise have been an outlandish idea—that parliament should be shut down (prorogued) in order to give the government unimpeded freedom to act. While Raab's proposal was widely condemned, and he exited the leadership contest relatively early, he had laid the ground for the subsequent actions of Boris Johnson. By this point, notwithstanding that ERG members had used numerous parliamentary mechanisms, first to force the referendum on a reluctant leadership, and subsequently to thwart Theresa May's attempts to agree a Brexit deal, the closure of parliament was a proposal that attracted many Brexiteers. This fitted a typical populist narrative: that the leader spoke for 'the people', against an out-of-touch parliamentary elite who sought to block their will. That the leader—be it Raab or Johnson (or indeed other now senior ministers, such as Jacob Rees-Mogg and Priti Patel)—had been part of the parliamentary blocking majority remained conveniently unspoken.

The divisions in the Conservative Party had been rife throughout the period covered by this book, and particularly since the referendum. More than ever, during these final stages, such tensions became very public and very bitter. Rory Stewart served to an extent as the voice of parliament during the leadership contest, articulating more firmly than Theresa May had done the complexity of agreeing Brexit in a minority government situation, and the need for compromise. He spoke out particularly vocally against the prorogation idea, though he was joined by others including Jeremy Hunt, and, from outside parliament, John Major. Other members of May's Cabinet, many of whom were soon to resign or be sacked on the changeover to Johnson, offered tacit support to backbench initiatives to try and keep parliament sitting, but did not feel able openly to block the prorogation. Ultimately, Johnson's extraordinary stripping of the whip from 21 largely loyal Conservatives literally broke the party apart—something that Theresa May had steadfastly avoided, to her own great cost. She understandably considered it a self-defeating act to expel parliamentary party members when the majority was already non-existent or wafer thin. But she assumed that proceeding with MPs' consent was necessary, and almost certainly would never have considered the option of shutting parliament down.

Johnson, in contrast, seemed to reject the fundamental constraints inherent in parliamentary democracy. He arrived in office on a very fragile mandate—the votes of barely half his parliamentary party, and hence just a quarter of the House of Commons, followed by those of 92,153 Conservative Party activists. It was fairly clear that he did not have the full confidence of the House of Commons—particularly to pursue a no-deal Brexit. Yet the timing of the summer recess left this untested. Johnson claimed a mandate from the people based on the referendum, in order to trump parliamentary resistance, notwithstanding that when May had sought to respect the self-same mandate, she had been blocked by Johnson and his supporters. But her determinedly non-specific rhetoric about the problem of 'parliament' provided cover, enabling him to arrive with a simple populist message that he was the man to sort out the intractable problems that he had in fact helped to ferment.

This deepened the muddled argument over sovereignty. The executive sought to act on the expression of the people against parliament, despite the referendum having identified no detailed vision for Brexit, and that executive having no independent democratic mandate of its own. But Johnson went further than May, seemingly sensing a personal mandate that had no relation to parliament. His rhetoric extended to threats to flout what he consistently dubbed the 'Surrender Act', and even to refuse to step aside if subjected to a parliamentary no-confidence vote. It enabled him to break with convention by applying brutal parliamentary discipline to internal party dissenters that had not been applied to himself, with the lasting effect of cowing his internal Conservative parliamentary opponents. In all of these actions, Johnson profited from a mood of increasing public frustration with parliament and other constitutional constraints. A poll by the Hansard Society (2019) published in April had found a majority of respondents ready to support 'a strong leader willing to break the rules'. In a far cry from traditional Conservatism, Johnson's populist approach carefully sought to exploit this.

Labour in this period was relatively united in condemning Johnson's actions and working with Conservative (and ex-Conservative) rebels to prevent a no-deal Brexit. But the party's leader was a huge obstacle to resolving the situation. Had the opposition leader been a more moderate figure, or a more pragmatic one willing to stand aside for someone behind whom anti-no deal MPs could unite, Johnson might well have been toppled in a vote of no confidence—if not in July, then in September or October. As a senior ERG interviewee put it:

> If you go through the next few months, up until the election, I think it's amazing we got Brexit. I think we were so close to it all going, from my point of view, catastrophically wrong. I think – you're no doubt speaking to David Lidington and all sorts of people like that – they were so close to forming an alternative government, and actually it's Jeremy Corbyn who saves the situation in two ways. One is that he wasn't acceptable to the other side, they could not have him as leader. And the other was that he wouldn't make way for anybody else. But if he had made way…there was Philip Hammond, there was David Lidington…you had a whole host of people who could have commanded a majority in the House of Commons.

As well as potentially easing the way towards a no-deal Brexit, the prorogation, of course, narrowed the window that was available for a potential no-confidence vote. This was one consideration in the extraordinary Supreme Court case that saw Boris Johnson's actions ruled unlawful. That ruling was highly significant in articulating some of the core principles of the UK constitution, emphasizing the well-established centrality of parliamentary sovereignty and the more novel legal principle of the government's accountability to parliament (Young 2021). But while the Supreme Court rightly sought to protect parliament's role at the core of the constitution, this risked further fuelling anti-elite populist sentiments among Brexit supporters—which resisted checks and balances on executive power. Amidst mounting public frustrations about the Brexit deadlock, an unrepentant Johnson was able to redouble his efforts to stage a divisive anti-parliament election campaign, on a promise to 'get Brexit done'—as the next chapter describes.

Notes

1. See, for example, the description of judges as 'enemies of the people' (Chapter 4), the description of Theresa May's parliamentary opponents as 'saboteurs' (Chapter 5), her 'on your side' speech (Chapter 8), and several of the events described later in this chapter.

2. House of Commons Hansard, 6 June 2019, columns 281, 276.

3. The organizer of this previous event (which never actually took place, but forced Blair's hand politically) was Labour MP Graham Allen (see House of Commons Hansard, 2 April 2009, columns 1094–9).

4. House of Commons Hansard, 25 July 2019, columns 1458–9, 1464.

5. The sixth, Nicky Morgan, had voted for the deal on all three occasions.

6. House of Commons Hansard, 2 April 2019, columns 941–62.

7. Ibid., 12 June 2019, column 690.

8. Letwin's words, that 'I have taken the uncomfortable step of signing a motion that has at the head of it the name of the Leader of the Opposition, whose party I do not follow and with whose policies I generally profoundly and radically disagree', communicated well how unusual this move was (ibid., 12 June 2019, column 715).

9. Ibid., 12 June 2019, column 691.

10. Ibid., 12 June 2019, column 716.

11. Conservative rebels were Guto Bebb, Ken Clarke, Jonathan Djanogly, Justine Greening, Dominic Grieve, Sam Gyimah, Phillip Lee, Oliver Letwin, Antoinette Sandbach, and Caroline Spelman. Labour rebels were Kevin Barron, Ronnie Campbell, Jim Fitzpatrick, Caroline Flint, Stephen Hepburn, Kate Hoey, John Mann, and Graham Stringer.

12. House of Commons Hansard, 12 June 2019, column 720–1.

13. Among them Heidi Allen, Nick Boles, Justine Greening, Sam Gyimah, Phillip Lee, Anna Soubry, Ed Vaizey, and Sarah Wollaston, plus key Labour figures such as Hilary Benn, Stephen Doughty, and Alison McGovern.

14. House of Lords Hansard, 17 July 2019, column 249.

15. Others included Roger Gale, Margot James, Phillip Lee, and Antoinette Sandbach.

16. Duncan was among the ministers who voted for Hilary Benn's amendment to the Northern Ireland (Executive Formation) Bill, and who resigned from the government once the outcome of the leadership contest was known.

17. Constitutional experts were divided at the time on whether the opportunity to form a government would automatically be extended to the leader of the opposition, or whether protracted negotiations would follow, with possible parliamentary votes, to establish who could command the Commons' confidence.

18. She suggested that 'the point was to change the dynamic', in order that a no-deal Brexit could viably be threatened in the talks with the EU. So, 'it's essentially about controlling time. How do you create an interval in which the PM can go and negotiate without the EU saying, well, we don't need to do business with you, because you can't deliver?' There was no doubt in her remarks that this was driven by Brexit, and overruling MPs' objections to no deal. See also da Costa (2021).

19. Clearly some who were less comfortable with the decision stayed publicly silent. A senior ERG member recalled in interview that 'I remember when I heard the news…and my heart sank. I really thought this was very, very bad. Really very bad, I really didn't like it.'

20. Notably, this was omitted from the da Costa memo, later cited in the court case and criticized in the Supreme Court ruling. It also seems very likely that the public protestations by Jacob Rees-Mogg and other members of the government—which steadfastly ignored this point—were consistent with the information offered to the Palace.

21. House of Commons Hansard, 3 September 2019, columns 99, 95.

22. Ibid., column 94.

23. Ibid., column 122.

24. Ibid., column 116.

25. Ibid., column 120.

26. The others were Guto Bebb, Richard Benyon, Steve Brine, Alistair Burt, Justine Greening, Sam Gyimah, Stephen Hammond, Richard Harrington, Margot James, Anne Milton, Caroline Nokes, Antoinette Sandbach, and Ed Vaizey.

27. Formally the European Union (Withdrawal) (No. 6) Bill.

28. House of Commons Hansard, 4 September 2019, column 230.

29. Bernard Jenkin, ibid., column 222.

30. Ibid., column 237.

31. As noted in Chapter 8, such motions are very unusual in the Lords. Six had taken place on the Cooper-Letwin Bill, contrasting with a mere seven in the preceding 119 years.

32. Notably, former Conservative Leader of the House Lord (Tom) Strathclyde, who had so vehemently spoken out against attempts by the Lords to block the Wharton bill on a referendum on the basis that this had been approved by the House of Commons (see Chapter 2), voted for the blocking amendments.

33. House of Commons Hansard, 4 September 2019, column 292.

34. Ibid., column 292.

35. Ibid., column 293.

36. House of Commons Hansard, 9 September 201, column 616.

37. Ibid., column 580.

38. Opinion of Lord Carloway, the Lord President, *R (Joanna Cherry QC and others) v The Advocate General* [2019] CSIH 49 P680/19.

39. *R (Miller) v The Prime Minister* [2019] EWHC 2381 (QB).

40. 'Case for the Prime Minister and Advocate General for Scotland', *R (Miller) v The Prime Minister, and R (Cherry and others) v Advocate General for Scotland,* UKSC 2019/0192 and 2019/0193, at [126(1)], https://www.supremecourt.uk/docs/written-case-for-the-prime-minister-and-advocate-general-for-scotland.pdf.

41. Notably, the Reserve Forces Act 1996 and the Civil Contingencies Act 2004 specifically provide that a meeting of parliament must be facilitated in certain cases of emergency, even if it stands prorogued.

42. 'Written case for the appellant, Mrs Gina Miller', *R (Miller) v The Prime Minister*, UKSC 2019/0192, https://www.supremecourt.uk/docs/written-case-for-mrs-gina-miller.pdf.

43. 'Case for the respondents', *R (Cherry) v Advocate General for Scotland* UKSC 2019/0193, https://www.supremecourt.uk/docs/written-case-for-joanna-cherry-qc-mp.pdf.

44. Ibid. at [1.3].

45. 'Case for the Prime Minister and Advocate General for Scotland', *R (Miller) v The Prime Minister, and R (Cherry and others) v Advocate General for Scotland,* UKSC 2019/0192 and 2019/0193, at [33].

46. Ibid., at [9].

47. Queen's (or King's) consent represents the monarch's permission for parliament to debate legislation, and is required for bills relating to topics covered by the royal prerogative or which affect the monarch's personal interests. Consent is sought by the government and signified on the monarch's behalf at third reading. Those claiming that this might be used to block the bill suggested that the government could simply refuse to seek consent. Their opponents argued that parliament could, in response, vote to set aside the requirement.

Queen's/King's consent is an arcane and little-discussed area, but had previously received some recent examination from the Political and Constitutional Reform Committee (2014).

48. *R (Miller) v The Prime Minister* [2019] UKSC 41.
49. House of Commons Hansard, 25 September 2019, column 652.
50. Ibid., column 660.
51. Ibid., columns 774, 776.
52. Ibid., columns 793–4.
53. Ibid., column 794.
54. Ibid., column 802.
55. Jones later did resign his post, in protest at the Internal Market Bill (discussed in Chapter 11).
56. At this time, anonymous briefings from a 'Downing Street source' became somewhat ubiquitous. The source was often assumed to be Dominic Cummings, but this may not always have been the case (Rutter 2019).
57. House of Lords Hansard, 14 October 2019, column 2.

10

The 2019 General Election and the Brexit Mandate

The Supreme Court's judgment in the *Miller/Cherry* case had guaranteed parliament's right to sit, but it still remained for the government, and MPs, to resolve the Brexit deadlock. Prime Minister Boris Johnson strongly desired a general election; many MPs, on the other hand, were still focused on ruling out a no-deal exit—which they suspected he would happily have embraced.

Johnson had reopened negotiations with the EU shortly after becoming Prime Minister, and surprised many by agreeing a new Brexit deal in mid-October. This was accepted in principle, though with significant reluctance, by the hardline ERG and some other former Conservative rebels. But the Commons attached conditions to its approval—first to safeguard against reversion to a no-deal exit, and then to ensure adequate time for parliamentary scrutiny. Recognizing that such scrutiny could see support for the deal unravel, Johnson abandoned any attempts at parliamentary approval and instead intensified efforts to secure a general election. As seen in the previous chapter, MPs had already twice denied this to him. But opposition parties ultimately switched to support it once Johnson had relented over the Benn–Burt Act, and secured a further Article 50 extension. A general election was hence held on 12 December, whose campaign was marked by consistent populist and anti-parliamentary rhetoric from Johnson's Conservatives, alongside a simple but appealing pledge to 'get Brexit done'. These tactics secured an 80-strong Commons majority for the party. The new parliament then quickly went on to pass Johnson's deal.

This chapter begins with a discussion of the Fixed-term Parliaments Act, which governed the process for calling general elections during this period, and would later be widely but inaccurately blamed for having generated the Brexit deadlock. Following this, it briefly describes the Prime Minister's new Brexit deal and reactions to it, including from the House of Commons. The chapter then maps the process of securing a general election, the campaign, and the result. Finally, it describes the eventual passage of Johnson's European Union (Withdrawal Agreement) Bill, which paved the way for the UK to leave the European Union on 31 January 2020.

The Fixed-term Parliaments Act

As seen in the previous chapter, Boris Johnson's initial attempts to trigger an early general election in 2019 were prevented by other political parties under the terms of the Fixed-term Parliaments Act 2011 (FTPA)—a measure introduced by the Conservative/Liberal Democrat coalition government.

Prior to the FTPA, the timing of general elections lay essentially in the hands of the Prime Minister, within a maximum five-year window set down by the 1911 Parliament Act. The ability to call an early election rested on a prerogative power. The Prime Minister could request a dissolution of parliament by the monarch, who in anything other than exceptional circumstances would comply. Parliaments relatively rarely ran to their full five years, with elections frequently called at around the four year point, and occasional very early elections (as in 1951, 1966, and October 1974). This arrangement had attracted criticism, for handing undue discretion to the Prime Minister (which could be used to their party's electoral advantage) and creating uncertainty for the civil service and other public authorities. Proposals to move to a system of fixed terms were therefore made in a series of private members' bills, and appeared in both the Labour and Liberal Democrat general election manifestos in 2010 (Hazell 2010). Change was seen as part of the general move to bring prerogative powers under greater control by parliament, as discussed in Chapter 6.

Although the Conservative Party had not proposed this, legislation to introduce fixed-term parliaments became part of the coalition agreement with the Liberal Democrats in 2010, and offered stability to the smaller partner. The resultant Act removed the dissolution power from the Prime Minister and gave it instead to parliament. It set the standard length of a parliamentary term at five years, but also allowed an early general election to be called, provided that two-thirds of MPs voted for it. As indicated in the previous chapter, it also set out a statutory route for votes of no confidence in the government. If MPs passed a specifically worded no-confidence motion, this triggered a 14-day countdown during which a potentially new government could form and demonstrate that it had the confidence of the House of Commons. Should no such government be established, a general election would be held. At the subsequent 2015 general election, the Conservative manifesto celebrated the FTPA as an achievement for parliament, referring to it as 'an unprecedented transfer of Executive power' (Conservative Party 2015: 49).

These changes brought the UK into line with many other comparable democracies, where dissolution requires either parliamentary approval or approval by an elected head of state (Schleiter and Morgan-Jones 2009). In very few of those countries are terms completely rigidly fixed, and it is common to have clauses allowing early general elections if approved by parliament. The use of this mechanism in the UK was demonstrated in 2017 (see Chapter 5), when Theresa May proposed a motion under the FTPA to secure the Commons' support for her snap election. However, the FTPA did prevent a weak Prime Minister from calling an election against the wishes of the House of Commons. This became a source of major frustration for Boris Johnson.

The circumstances of Brexit, however, also demonstrated some of the constitutional arguments in favour of requiring parliamentary approval for dissolution. Many MPs feared that Johnson wanted to time an election to either force parliamentarians to accept a Brexit deal that they opposed or to facilitate a no-deal Brexit—possibly even during the period when parliament was dissolved. Such a danger existed because the FTPA had left discretion to the Prime Minister to set the precise date of an early election, after the principle had been approved by the House of Commons. This was one reason why MPs repeatedly rebuffed Johnson's motions under the Act.

Both at the time, and subsequently, various sources have claimed that the FTPA played a key role in the Brexit deadlock during Theresa May's premiership, by preventing her from using a confidence vote to force her deal through the House of Commons (e.g. Bogdanor 2020, Craig, R. 2020). Such a tactic had been used by John Major in the debates over Maastricht, as described in Chapter 2. But this interpretation rested on two assumptions, neither of which was wholly correct (Russell 2021b). First, that the FTPA provided the only route for the government to make its survival dependent on securing MPs' support for its policy. In fact, in principle, nothing had prevented May from announcing that she would resign should her deal be defeated—as the Public Administration and Constitutional Affairs Committee (2018a) pointed out. Second, such claims relied on an assumption that rebellious Conservative MPs would have been cowed by such a threat, in sufficient numbers to prevent May's deal being defeated. But the size of the defeats was so overwhelming that this is very unlikely; and unless Labour had changed position, approval for the deal would have required the so-called 'Spartans' to come round. But in interview a senior ERG member argued that some hardliners (including this interviewee) would have voted against the deal regardless, and if necessary run in any ensuing election as independent candidates. Anyway, May's authority in her party was by now so low that, had she attempted such a manoeuvre, she would likely have been immediately ousted as leader. This could have left the Conservatives needing to pick a new leader in the midst of an election campaign—which seems to be an argument in favour of the parliamentary control provided by the FTPA.

Once Johnson had taken over, this control was undoubtedly more of a constraint. Ultimately it caused him to exploit one of the FTPA's known weaknesses. The UK's principle of parliamentary sovereignty meant that the required two-thirds majority to secure an early general election could be overridden by subsequent legislation. Hence a bill authorizing an election would require only a simple majority (albeit in both chambers) to pass. It was to this route that Johnson eventually turned to secure the general election that took place in December 2019, as described below. Subsequently, the FTPA was replaced by the Dissolution and Calling of Parliament Act 2022, which returned the largely unconstrained power to call general elections to the Prime Minister.

Johnson's Brexit Deal

The Terms of the Deal

Boris Johnson had reopened negotiations with the EU soon after becoming Prime Minister, with his new EU adviser David Frost leading talks for the UK. Throughout the summer, both sides briefed about their hardline stances; BBC News (2019a) reported on 25 July that the EU would not reopen the question of the backstop, while Frost emphasized the government's willingness to embrace a no-deal exit (Boffey and Mason 2019), and the UK began to withdraw its officials in Brussels from all non-Brexit EU business (Miller 2019b). The Prime Minister was particularly keen to emphasize that the only alternative to a new deal was to leave without a deal, as witnessed in his many statements on the Benn–Burt Act (see Chapter 9).

The week before the Act's deadline of 19 October, Johnson met with Irish Prime Minister Leo Varadkar. Varadkar, who had been coordinating closely with EU negotiators, now proposed the outline of a revised deal which aimed to break the negotiating deadlock. To a degree of surprise, the leaders briefed after the meeting that an agreement was in sight, and the meeting was followed by formal negotiations in Brussels. The terms of a new deal were then announced by Johnson and European Commission President Jean-Claude Juncker on 17 October. May's plan had included some Northern Ireland-only regulatory alignment with the EU, but had sought to minimize the post-Brexit differences between the province and Great Britain by including a UK-wide customs union with the EU, and associated alignment with its 'level playing field' provisions. Johnson's deal removed these all-UK elements from the Northern Ireland Protocol—instead, both its customs arrangements and provisions on regulatory alignment would apply to Northern Ireland only. The province would stay legally part of the same customs territory as Great Britain—allowing the UK to apply common external tariffs—but, unlike Great Britain, it would continue to apply the EU's customs code. The plan avoided the need for customs checks at the border between Northern Ireland and the Republic but, unlike May's backstop, would require them for goods moving between it and Great Britain. The Protocol also ceased to be a 'backstop' (i.e. coming into force only in the absence of another agreement), becoming instead the preferred, avowedly permanent, solution (Menon and Wager 2021).

In effect, Johnson had signed up to the Northern Ireland-only arrangement that the EU had originally wanted, and that May (as discussed in Chapter 6) had refused to accept in order to prevent a border down the Irish Sea. The deal included a new 'consent mechanism' which provided a regular opportunity for the Northern Ireland Assembly to vote in the future to dis-apply most of the Protocol's trade provisions.[1] But it was difficult to see how a hard border on the island of Ireland could be avoided, should it choose to do so (Hayward 2020).

David Gauke (2020) later speculated, very plausibly, that the Benn–Burt Act had forced Johnson's hand—by making it clear to him that parliament would not back a no-deal Brexit. This left the Prime Minister with a choice between accepting further delay, or accepting a deal that he knew to be problematic. But Johnson proclaimed his agreement a great success, calling it 'a real Brexit' and 'an excellent deal that achieves our priorities' (Johnson 2019h, Sun 2019b). He also claimed that the agreement protected the Belfast/Good Friday Agreement and kept the Union together—conveniently ignoring the highly contentious nature of the border down the Irish Sea.[2]

The DUP (2019) was predictably appalled by the revised Northern Ireland Protocol, and declared shortly before the deal was announced that it 'could not support' Johnson's approach. The fact that he had spoken at the party's conference the previous year, and declared that 'no British Conservative government could or should sign up' to just the sort of deal he had now negotiated, only worsened the offence (Steerpike 2018). Johnson's willingness to go back on this statement—which he had repeated as recently as the previous month (BBC News 2019c)—may not have come as a total surprise. Raoul Ruparel (2020), the former adviser to both David Davis and Theresa May, recalled a meeting with the DUP during the 2019 leadership contest in which the party was fully aware that Johnson might try to sell them out. Its representatives had, however, apparently sounded fairly unconcerned, relying on their position as power brokers in a hung parliament to guard against any such deal. A general election could change all that.

The ERG, which had vocally espoused both unionism and Brexit, now had to decide its priorities. Johnson's deal delivered, as the group had wanted, looser regulatory alignment for the British mainland than May's had. One member of the group summed this up as Johnson having 'played a blinder' in the negotiations, and succeeding where May had failed (Francois 2021: 378). But in truth, she had explicitly rejected this option, given the concerns of the unionist community in Northern Ireland, and potential risks to the Union itself. ERG members' level of sincerely felt unionism had always been distinctly questionable (Kenny and Sheldon 2021, O'Toole 2020). Nonetheless, one senior member interviewed described the new Protocol as 'a nightmare', recalling that 'we had to be lashed to the mast' to support the deal. Francois (2021: 347) claims that ERG officers made it 'absolutely crystal clear' that the plan was unacceptable. But some compromise was needed, because they were now concerned that rejecting Johnson's deal would risk sacrificing Brexit altogether. Plus, some also feared for their own personal positions. The same interviewee who described the Protocol as a 'nightmare' suggested that some ERG members thought that if they didn't vote for the deal, 'they'd already chucked a lot of Europhiles out of the party...and it was quite obvious that they'd do the same to us if we didn't cooperate'.

By this point the government and the ERG were thus metaphorically holding a gun to each other's heads, with either able to destroy the other. It seems clear that the government also recognized the flaws in its deal, but feared that Brexit might be lost. David Frost (2022) later admitted:

> We faced a choice—take this deal and try to get it through Parliament, and sort out the detail in 2020 while we were negotiating the trade agreement...or walk away, fail to deliver Brexit on 31 October, and almost certainly see the Government collapse. At that point we would have seen, at best, a second referendum, quite possibly Brexit taken off the agenda for good.

Given the group's concerns, Francois (2021: 381) recounts that the ERG therefore agreed to vote for the deal 'on the strict understanding...that the [Protocol] was unsustainable in the longer-term and would one day have to be re-negotiated, or ideally replaced'.

Like the ERG, the more centrist former Conservatives were conflicted about their response to the deal. As noted in Chapter 6, Conservative moderates had always been split between those whose primary goal was to avoid a no-deal exit and those seeking a soft Brexit or Remain outcome. Most such members had supported Theresa May's deal, but Johnson's harder Brexit presented all of them with a fresh dilemma. Amber Rudd (2021), for example, accepted it on the basis that it was preferable to a no-deal exit, later reflecting that Johnson had 'sort of gaslit us all to that stage'. Like for the ERG, electoral considerations were also at play for those previously stripped of the whip by Johnson. As Dominic Grieve (2020) later noted, with an election clearly on the horizon any rebels who wanted to stand for the Conservative Party again were running out of time to reconcile with the government.

'Super Saturday' and the Letwin Amendment

The deal was reached just two days before the Benn–Burt Act's deadline for the Commons to agree a deal, or agree to a no-deal exit, or else for the government to seek an Article 50 extension. The government therefore quickly brought forward a motion providing for the Commons to sit on the day of the deadline itself—Saturday, 19 October—in order to approve the deal. Dubbed 'super Saturday' by many media outlets, it was to be the first Saturday sitting since 1982, and only the fourth in the post-war era.[3]

In the lead-up to the vote, concern revived among Brexit-sceptic MPs about the risk of a no-deal exit. This anxiety stemmed from a loophole in the Benn–Burt Act. It had specified that the government must seek an extension should the deal not pass a Commons vote, but was silent on the need for implementing legislation—which was necessary if a deal was to be ratified. Particularly given the concerns above, it was hence possible that Johnson's deal might pass the Saturday vote, satisfying the terms of the Act and allowing the government to avoid an extension, but subsequently that the implementing legislation might be voted down—resulting in a no-deal exit. The fear was that the ERG might deliberately engineer this.[4] Oliver Letwin (2020) discussed these worries with the Prime Minister, and concluded that Johnson's primary goal was simply to leave the EU on 31 October, without any further extension, and that he was less concerned about whether the implementing legislation was actually approved. It might pass, or there might be a no-deal exit: 'either way he would have left; either way he would have been a hero'.

Letwin therefore took matters into his own hands. First, he tabled an amendment to the business motion for the Saturday sitting, extending the debate from the government's proposed 90 minutes to around five hours to allow time for backbench amendments to be debated. This proposal was approved with the support of one Conservative rebel (Caroline Spelman) and various former Conservatives including Nick Boles, Ken Clarke, David Gauke, and Dominic Grieve. Letwin then tabled a second amendment for debate at the Saturday sitting itself. This would withhold the Commons' support until the implementing legislation had been passed—allowing MPs to endorse Johnson's deal in principle, but ensuring that the legal requirement to seek an extension remained in place.

Immediately before the debate on the government motion the Prime Minister made a statement, formally announcing his deal to the Commons. Though he took the opportunity to promote it once more as a 'real Brexit' and an opportunity to 'heal this country', the DUP's Nigel Dodds complained that it '[drove] a coach and horses through the Belfast agreement'.[5] In the debate on the motion itself, Letwin and his supporters argued that his amendment was a necessary 'insurance policy'.[6] Mark Francois claimed that this was unnecessary, because the ERG had agreed to vote for both the deal and the implementing legislation. But trust was far too low for Letwin's supporters to take such claims at face value, and his amendment passed by 322 votes to 306. It was supported by the DUP, as well as opposition parties and most of the 21 formerly Conservative MPs who had been stripped of the whip. The media widely claimed (likely based on briefings from Number 10) that the government had in retaliation 'pulled' the vote on the deal itself, but this was incorrect. The Commons had amended the government's motion, and ministers therefore had no power to ask the Commons to vote on it in its unamended form (James and Russell 2019). MPs had refused to approve the deal until the legislation had passed, but had indicated a conditional willingness to do so.

Johnson responded by announcing that the implementing legislation would be introduced the following week. But he also signalled his willingness to defy the Benn–Burt Act, claiming, 'I will not negotiate a delay with the EU; neither does the law compel me to'.[7] But perhaps under pressure from the risk of senior resignations (described in the previous chapter), Johnson (2019d, 2019e) did ultimately write to European Council President Donald Tusk that same evening. He did so by sending a pointedly unsigned copy of the extension request compelled by the Act, along with a side letter claiming that an extension was unnecessary because he hoped and expected to pass the implementing legislation by 31 October. The government also initially proposed to bring back the deal for a further in-principle vote on Monday.[8] When the Speaker announced, entirely predictably, that this violated the 'same question' rule as previously discussed during Theresa May's tenure (see Chapter 8), a Number 10 spokesperson claimed that Bercow had 'yet again denied us the chance to deliver on the will of the people' (Lister 2019). As seen in the previous chapter, such populist rhetoric was becoming an increasing mainstay of the Downing Street operation.

The Withdrawal Agreement Bill

The Speaker's decision had no impact on the implementing legislation, and the European Union (Withdrawal Agreement) Bill (or 'WAB') was duly introduced and had its second reading on Tuesday, 22 October. The bill established the domestic systems and ministerial powers necessary to allow the implementation of the Withdrawal Agreement. It also laid out parliament's role in the future relationship negotiations, and here the government appeared to include some pre-emptive concessions, to avoid the kind of battles which had previously been fought to secure the meaningful vote (see Chapter 7). Thus the bill required the government to win a parliamentary vote on its 'statement of objectives' before commencing the next set of negotiations, to report regularly on its progress, and to lay the eventual treaty before the Commons for approval. It also gave the Commons the right to veto any proposed extensions of the transition period—but no automatic right to propose one, or to require the government to accept one if proposed by the EU.

Ostensibly still set on meeting the original exit day of 31 October, which he had promised so many times to do, Johnson proposed an expedited passage for the bill.[9] But by the time of its second reading, just seven sitting days remained before that date. The government's proposed programme motion (setting the timetable for the bill) allowed only three days for its remaining Commons stages. This was an extremely truncated timetable for a bill of this scale and complexity; the EU (Withdrawal) Act 2018 had, by contrast, had ten Commons sitting days. Crucially, the proposed timetable would leave little opportunity for amendments and for Conservative MPs to look too closely at the deal.

Opening the second reading debate, Johnson argued that his deal would restore democracy and sovereignty to the UK, and uphold the Belfast/Good Friday Agreement. The DUP Brexit spokesperson Sammy Wilson disagreed, arguing that it left Northern Ireland 'a semi-detached part of the United Kingdom'.[10] Responding for Labour, Jeremy Corbyn likewise criticized the bill's potential impact on Northern Ireland, as well as on workers' and citizens' rights. The ERG gave the deal a lukewarm reception, with long-standing Eurosceptics Bill Cash and John Redwood both citing concerns about

Northern Ireland, and Redwood declaring 'a spirit of disappointment'.[11] ERG members indicated in-principle support for the deal, but the voicing of their concerns, along with the objections of the DUP, did not bode well for a committee stage.

The topic of the bill's timetable was raised frequently in the second reading debate. Jeremy Corbyn called it 'an abuse of Parliament', while Dominic Grieve accused Johnson of 'playing bully-boy tactics with this House'.[12] Ken Clarke drew a contrast with the more than 100 hours spent on the Maastricht debates. But other MPs (such as Oliver Letwin) were either resigned to the timetable or dismissive. Iain Duncan Smith, for example, claimed that the Commons had already 'debated and thrashed to death' Brexit—notwithstanding the new and surprising elements of Johnson's deal.[13]

The bill passed its second reading by 329 votes to 299. All Conservative MPs, including the 28 'Spartans', voted for it. Most of those recently stripped of the whip also did so, although Dominic Grieve, Guto Bebb, and Justine Greening joined Labour and the other opposition parties in the 'no' lobby—as did the DUP. Meanwhile, from the Labour benches 19 MPs rebelled to vote in favour of the bill—14 of whom, including Jon Cruddas, Lisa Nandy, Melanie Onn, and Gareth Snell, had voted against May's deal on all three occasions.[14] Without these rebel Labour votes, the second reading would not have passed.

The programme motion, however, was defeated by 322 votes to 308. Six former Conservatives who had voted for the bill voted against it, while only five Labour rebels voted in favour.[15] This was not a direct rejection of the bill, but an invitation to the government to return with a new offer for the legislative timetable. However, ministers flatly refused to do so.

In fact, it seems unlikely that Johnson ever really wanted his WAB considered further. Had it reached committee stage, it is certain that MPs would have sought to amend it. Nandy, for example, had argued in debate that a vote for the bill at second reading would provide an opportunity for subsequent changes to the detail. For the Labour rebels, this would likely have meant amendments to require a guarantee of greater environmental and employment protections at the next negotiating stage—diametrically opposed to the deregulatory direction in which Johnson sought to go. The proponents of a second referendum had also been hoping for an opportunity to press their claim, though it was far from certain that a referendum amendment would have passed. One Labour frontbencher suggested in interview that the second referendum group was now within three votes of a majority—though most other interviewees considered this too optimistic, and had believed at the time that any such attempt was doomed to fail. More ominous for Johnson was how the ERG might have reacted given the opportunity to amend the bill—particularly in the light of the DUP's outspoken concerns. Had an alternative programme motion been offered, it almost certainly would have passed—Labour reportedly requested eight days for the remaining Commons stages (Waugh 2019), which was consistent with the timetables for previous Brexit legislation. But the more attractive option for Johnson was clearly a general election, where he could present himself as vanquishing a Remainer parliament.

The defeat on the programme motion was presented by Johnson's supporters as an attempt to block Brexit. An anonymous Downing Street source briefed that 'this parliament is broken' and that an election was necessary (Stewart and Boffey 2019). Though misleading, this rhetoric was lapped up by the Brexit-supporting media, with the *Daily Express* accusing Remainers of 'fresh parliamentary skulduggery' (Hall 2019a) and the *Daily Telegraph* (2019) arguing that 'this parliament has forfeited its right to remain in existence'. This laid the ground perfectly for Johnson.

Getting Parliament's Approval for an Election

With the WAB's second reading underway, anonymous Number 10 sources had briefed journalists that, should the programme motion fall, the government would take the unprecedented step of seeking 'essentially to go on strike' and refusing to put further business before parliament (Kuenssberg 2019). Johnson's Cabinet reportedly was split over this strategy, with some ministers, including the now Secretary of State for Northern Ireland Julian Smith, urging the Prime Minister to concentrate on getting his deal through parliament, while others—and Johnson's chief adviser Dominic Cummings—pressed instead for a December election (BBC News 2019e). The Prime Minister's own preference was clear. Following a Cabinet meeting on 24 October, Johnson wrote to Corbyn to announce that a Commons vote on a 12 December general election would be held the following week, on a motion under the FTPA (BBC News 2019b). Though his letter also offered extended hours and weekend sittings to allow parliament to consider the WAB in the meantime, this still allowed only nine sitting days for the bill to complete its stages in both chambers—far less than Labour had asked for. Meanwhile, Treasury sources briefed that the planned 6 November budget would be cancelled (BBC News 2019d).

Up to this point, the opposition parties had been unanimous in their desire to avoid an early election, with party leaders meeting weekly to agree their strategies (Cowley 2021). But as the vote, scheduled for 28 October, approached, this unity crumbled. Labour's official line was that the party would support an election only if a no-deal exit was ruled out, noting that the UK was still awaiting the EU's decision on Johnson's extension request (BBC News 2019f). But behind the scenes the Shadow Cabinet was divided, with some Corbynites increasingly in favour of an election, while other members remained firmly opposed (Pogrund and Maguire 2020). Meanwhile, the SNP and Liberal Democrats grew increasingly attracted to an early election, for different reasons. For the Liberal Democrats, the party's strong performance in the European elections and the Brecon and Radnorshire by-election, plus subsequent encouraging polling, suggested that it might win as many as 100 seats (Liberal Democrats 2020, Sloman 2020). Senior interviewees from the party suggested, in the belief that a Commons vote on a further referendum would fail, that an election was effectively 'the last roll of the dice' to block Brexit. For the SNP, the upcoming trial of former party leader Alex Salmond for sexual assault threatened a slew of negative publicity which could damage the party's prospects if an election occurred later. The day before Johnson's vote took place, these two parties hence effectively conceded, by signalling support for a December election, on the condition that an Article 50 extension had been granted to the end of January. Though their votes combined with those of the Conservatives would still fall short of the two-thirds majority required for a motion under the FTPA, they were enough to create a majority in favour of an early general election bill.

On the morning of 28 October, the EU granted the UK's extension request, offering to move 'exit day' to 31 January 2020. When the debate began that evening, Corbyn argued that, as the UK government was yet to formally accept the proposal, Labour could still not support an early election. However, this argument was running out of road: Johnson's (2019d) letter accepting the extension appeared in the media while the debate was underway. Labour and the SNP abstained on his FTPA motion, denying the government the required two-thirds supermajority. But immediately following the vote, Johnson announced that the government would introduce an Early Parliamentary General Election Bill the following day.

The next morning, the Shadow Cabinet met, having been backed into a corner. The pivot by the other key opposition parties left Labour with a choice between voting for an election or having one forced upon it. Shadow Chancellor John McDonnell (2021) would later comment that, 'as soon as the SNP decided they wanted the general election, we were stuffed, basically'. The Shadow Cabinet agreed to vote for Johnson's bill.

Introducing its second reading, Johnson once more attacked parliament, arguing that MPs had 'voted to delay Brexit yet again' and claiming somewhat implausibly that 'the government have tried to be reasonable'.[16] These arguments were rebutted by Ken Clarke, who pointed out not only that Johnson could easily have brought forward another programme motion for the WAB but also that he had himself delayed Brexit by—unlike the now-exiled Clarke—voting against May's Brexit deal. Nonetheless, the bill passed the Commons unamended.[17] At third reading, only 20 MPs from Labour and the minor parties, including Peter Kyle and Anna Soubry, voted against the bill—though 104 other Labour MPs were absent from the vote. It passed to the Lords the next day and—unsurprisingly given its topic and over-whelming Commons support—passed quickly and easily.

With an election now confirmed, some MPs faced a hard choice about whether or not to run again. Those with the most obvious dilemma were the former Conservative rebels. Of the 21 who had lost the whip in early September, 10 had it restored as the election bill passed through parliament, though only four of them ultimately decided to stand again.[18] But the rest of that group—as well as those who had defected from the party—confronted the difficult prospect of running either as independent candidates or for minor parties. Dominic Grieve, David Gauke, and Anne Milton stood as independents, while Anna Soubry became Change UK's only previously Conservative candidate.[19] Former Conservatives Phillip Lee, Sam Gyimah, Antoinette Sandbach, and Sarah Wollaston all ran for the Liberal Democrats—as did former Labour (and Change UK) members Luciana Berger and Chuka Umunna. But various other backbench figures, including Nick Boles, Ken Clarke, Oliver Letwin, and Caroline Spelman, chose to step down. They were joined by former ministers Philip Hammond, Jo Johnson, David Lidington, Nicky Morgan, Amber Rudd, and Rory Stewart. Several of the women, in particular, cited the vicious abuse that they had received over Brexit as a key factor in their decision (Spelman 2019, Swinford, Wright, and Zeffman 2019).

The Campaign and the Result

Reports that Johnson would frame any general election as a populist 'people vs parliament' contest had been circulating since August (Devlin 2019), and turned out to be well founded. Launching the election outside Downing Street on 6 November, the Prime Minister repeated his implausible earlier claim (see Chapter 9) that he had not wanted a general election—instead blaming MPs for 'just refusing time and again to deliver Brexit and honour the mandate of the people'. This was followed by the demonstrably false claim that parliament had 'blocked' his Queen's Speech—when in fact MPs had voted to approve it on 24 October (BBC News 2019h). The Conservative manifesto, likewise, borrowed the classic populist trope of betrayal to claim that the country had been 'paralysed by a broken parliament' and criticized 'the way so many MPs have devoted themselves to thwarting the democratic decision of the British people in the 2016 referendum' (Conservative Party 2019a: 2, 47–8). This was a flat reversal of the previous claim by Johnson (2019g) that Theresa May had been 'wrong in every sense to blame MPs for blocking Brexit' (see Chapter 8). Looking to the future, the manifesto proposed a comprehensive constitutional review, including examination of the relationship between 'Government, Parliament and the courts' (Conservative Party 2019a: 48)—which critics feared was code for a planned enhancement of executive power.

Johnson's core campaign message was the simple promise (also borrowed from May) to 'get Brexit done', repeated relentlessly in his public appearances, and often supplemented by references to his 'oven-ready deal' (Ford et al. 2021). The manifesto—titled 'Get Brexit Done: Unleash Britain's Potential'—offered little detail about what the next steps might entail, promising only to keep the UK out of the Single Market and 'any form of customs union' (Conservative Party 2019a: 5). This promise was perhaps technically true of Johnson's new Brexit deal, but ignored the fact that Northern Ireland would continue to apply the EU's customs rules. The manifesto further promised that there would be no extension to the transition period; experts pointed out that this allowed little time for the formidably complex future relationship negotiations (UK in a Changing Europe 2019). But the core Conservative messaging sidestepped these details in favour of repeating the straightforward pledge to end the convulsions of the Brexit process— offering, as one commentator put it, to 'make the pain go away' (O'Toole 2020: xv). This was of course a pain that, at various levels, Johnson himself had been central to inflicting.

The Labour campaign notably did not point this out. The party's Brexit policy was nuanced, and less easily communicated in a campaign setting than Johnson's. Labour's manifesto promised to renegotiate the Brexit deal within three months, aiming for a new agreement based on a comprehensive customs union and close Single Market alignment. It then promised to put this deal to a referendum, with Remain as the alternative option, within a further six months. This left Labour failing to endorse either a Leave or a Remain stance—worsened by Corbyn's insistence that he would stay neutral in the promised referendum. In addition, Corbyn's own public approval rating, according to one poll, was the worst of any opposition leader since 1977 (Goes 2020). The Liberal Democrats (2019) had now moved to a radical position of pledging to revoke Article 50 without a further referendum. The DUP reiterated opposition to any deal that would result in a border down the Irish Sea (Democratic Unionist Party 2019).

Parties on both sides of the Brexit divide sought tactical advantages through forming alliances. In the Brecon and Radnorshire by-election, an alliance with Plaid Cymru and the Green Party had successfully delivered a Liberal Democrat victory, but the combined Conservative and Brexit Party vote exceeded that of the winning party—providing important lessons for both sides. Unite to Remain, which brought together Plaid Cymru, the Liberal Democrats, and Greens, identified 60 seats in which it would run a single candidate. But Labour's absence from the alliance significantly limited its potential impact. On the Leave side, the key development was the Brexit Party's decision not to stand in seats that the Conservative Party had won in 2017. Nigel Farage had hinted at the possibility of an alliance long before the election was called, suggesting in April 2019 that he might not stand candidates against the 28 Conservative 'Spartans'. His announcement in November confirmed what he called a 'unilateral' Leave alliance (quoted in BBC News 2019i). Consequently, Conservative and Brexit Party candidates were left competing in seats held by other parties. But the threat of a split in the pro-Leave vote in 317 constituencies was removed, while Farage had signalled to Leave voters that Johnson and his deal had Brexit Party support.

The Conservative campaign attracted criticism not only for its anti-parliamentary rhetoric but for other aspects of its conduct. Johnson's team largely kept him away from potentially tricky interviews, including with the famously tough questioner Andrew Neil (Power, Bale, and Webb 2020)—perhaps fearing, as Dominic Cummings (2021b) later put it, that the Prime Minister would be exposed as 'a gaffe machine clueless about policy'. Johnson participated in two head-to-head leaders' debates against Corbyn, but refused to participate in a third, planned by Channel 4. The campaign operation was also accused of seeking to mislead voters through a string of incidents. These included the renaming of the Conservative Press Office's Twitter account to 'factcheckUK' during the first leaders' debate, and various campaign videos which used edited or doctored footage (Whale 2019). Nonetheless, by 10 December, two days before the election, YouGov predicted a 28-seat Conservative majority (Fitzpatrick et al. 2019).

The actual scale of Johnson's victory far exceeded this. The Conservatives won an 80-seat majority, with a net gain of 48 seats and a total of 365, on a vote share of 43.6 per cent (Uberoi et al. 2020). Johnson was aided by a collapse in Labour support. The party dropped from 40 per cent of the UK vote in 2017 to 32.1 per cent, and from 262 seats to 202—with 54 of those that it had held in the 2017–19 parliament passing into Conservative hands. The Brexit Party's decision to stand candidates in Labour-held seats saved the party from even worse disaster, splitting the Leave-supporting vote in a way that allowed Labour to retain 25 seats that it would otherwise have lost (Curtice, Fisher, and English 2021). Without the presence of Farage's party, Johnson's majority might have been closer to 130. Meanwhile, only a small handful of Conservative MPs owed their re-election to the Brexit Party's decision not to run against them.[20] The Liberal Democrat share of the vote increased from 7.4 per cent to 11.5 per cent; but far from winning the 100 seats that it had hoped for, the party dropped from 12 to 11, and its leader Jo Swinson personally lost to the SNP. A post-mortem identified the radical revoke policy as a key strategic mistake (Liberal Democrats 2020). The SNP's electoral calculation, by contrast, paid off, with the party making a net gain of 13 seats. The DUP made a net loss of two, dropping from 10 to eight.

The Conservative result was undoubtedly impressive. However, the 2019 election cemented trends which had been apparent for some time (Curtice, Fisher, and English 2021, Ford and Sobolewska 2020). Theresa May had increased the Conservative vote share significantly more in 2017 than her successor did in 2019, by 5.5 percentage points compared to his 1.3. Johnson's success was the product of these longer-term changes, combined with his own ability to consolidate the Leave vote efficiently in certain constituencies, partly through his attractiveness to former UKIP and Brexit Party supporters (Evans, de Geus, and Green 2021). The proportion of Leave supporters voting Conservative rose by 9 per cent between 2017 and 2019, to 74 per cent. Meanwhile Labour's support among this group dropped from 24 per cent to just 14 per cent. In polling conducted shortly after the election, voters who had switched from Labour to Conservative cited Labour's Brexit policy as one of the most important reasons for their decision (Ashcroft 2020). At the same time, the party failed to consolidate the Remain vote; Remain voters swung away from both main parties, with 49 per cent backing Labour and 19 per cent the Conservatives, compared to 55 per cent and 25 per cent respectively in 2017 (Uberoi et al. 2020). Johnson was undoubtedly also helped by Jeremy Corbyn's deep unpopularity, with 75 per cent of the voters who switched from Labour to Conservative citing his leadership as a factor (Ashcroft 2020).

Perhaps most striking was the Conservatives' gain of a swathe of Northern and Midlands seats in what was dubbed the 'Red Wall': Labour-held seats with a significant Leave vote, and a substantial and growing Conservative vote in previous general elections (Kanagasooriam and Simon 2021). Conservative strategists had identified 42 such seats in the run-up to the election, of which the party won 30. These included Don Valley, Labour-held since 1922, and Bolsover, held by Labour's Dennis Skinner since 1970. Many Labour MPs who had been prominent in the Brexit battles of the previous years were among the losers in these Red Wall seats—including some who had supported Johnson's Brexit deal, such as Caroline Flint in Don Valley, Melanie Onn in Great Grimsby, and Gareth Snell in Stoke-on-Trent Central, as well as others such as Phil Wilson in Sedgefield. The former Conservative rebels, meanwhile, were wiped out. Without exception, Grieve, Gauke, Soubry, Wollaston, and their peers who had stood as independents or for other parties lost their seats to Conservative candidates, as did Labour defectors Luciana Berger and Chuka Umunna.[21]

Getting Brexit 'Done'

Boris Johnson's commanding new majority—strengthened by the pre-election purge of his Conservative opponents—made approval of his deal all but certain after the election. On the following morning, the Brexit-supporting press celebrated, with the *Daily Express* proclaiming 'Victory for Boris...and for Brexit!' (Hall 2019c), while the *Daily Mail* urged its readers to 'Rejoice' (Groves 2019). But not all of the media shared this jubilation; the *Independent*'s front page carried instead the bleak conclusion that 'Populism wins' (Grice 2019).

The Prime Minister's speech outside Downing Street on the morning following the election seemed designed to allay this concern (Johnson 2019f). While promising to deliver a 'parliament that works for the people', he abandoned his divisive campaign rhetoric, urging listeners to 'find closure and let the healing begin' and promising to focus on domestic priorities. The Queen's Speech, delivered on 19 December, shared this emphasis, saying of Brexit only that the government would secure a 31 January exit and then turn to the future relationship negotiations, seeking a free trade agreement.

Nonetheless, there was no doubt that Brexit topped the government's agenda. A new Withdrawal Agreement Bill was introduced to parliament on the same day as the Queen's Speech. The following day—the last before the Christmas recess—it had its second reading. With the new Conservative majority promising it an easy passage, the government had taken the opportunity to make important revisions to the bill, significantly reducing parliament's oversight of the future relationship negotiations (Cowie 2019). The provisions for a parliamentary vote on the negotiating mandate for the future relationship, and the text of any resulting treaty, were removed. The parliamentary vote on any transition period extension was replaced by a clause which expressly forbade ministers from agreeing any such extension.

This new WAB passed quickly and easily through parliament. Opening the second reading debate, Johnson claimed that its purpose was to 'reject any further delay', promising that 'Brexit will be done—it will be over...we will be able to move forward'.[22] This optimistic statement ignored, most obviously, the continuing need to negotiate a future relationship deal. It also dodged the continued difficult challenges around the Northern Ireland Protocol. During the election campaign, doubts emerged about the extent to which Johnson fully understood the implications of his deal—at one point he claimed that there would be 'no barriers of any kind' to trade between Northern Ireland and Great Britain, and that anyone asked to complete customs paperwork should simply 'throw that form in the bin' (Daly and Baynes 2019). Nonetheless, at this stage Conservative MPs loudly backed the Prime Minister. ERG supporters Bill Cash and Suella Braverman hailed the bill's passage respectively as 'a watershed moment in our history' and an opportunity to '[rebuild] trust with the British people'.[23]

Jeremy Corbyn had resigned as Labour Party leader as the election night disaster unfolded, but remained as caretaker until his successor could be identified (Keir Starmer was subsequently elected to the position in April 2020). He declared that Labour opposed the government's deal, and would vote against the bill, and was joined by Liberal Democrat and SNP frontbenchers in voicing anxieties about its consequences for the economy, rights, and standards. The DUP's new Westminster Leader Jeffrey Donaldson (Nigel Dodds having just lost his seat) expressed 'grave concerns about the potential impact on Northern Ireland, where economic prosperity goes hand in hand with political stability'.[24] The DUP joined the other opposition parties in voting against the bill at second reading. But with the Conservative Party united, it passed by 358 votes to 234—a far cry from the gridlock of the previous parliament.[25] Immediately afterwards the Commons passed the government's programme motion, endorsing the same truncated scrutiny timetable that the previous parliament had rejected. Opposition attempts to amend the bill during its remaining Commons stages—including to restore aspects of parliamentary scrutiny, or to protect citizens' and workers' rights—were easily rebuffed. The unamended bill duly passed its third reading vote by 330–231. Although there were five government defeats in the Lords, partly addressing concerns raised by the chamber's select committees (Constitution

Committee 2020, Delegated Powers and Regulatory Reform Committee 2020, European Union Committee 2020), these were easily overturned when the bill returned to the Commons. And while all three devolved legislatures refused their consent to the bill, this had no formal force. It passed unamended, gaining Royal assent on 23 January. Eight days later, on 31 January, the UK finally left the EU—hailed by the triumphant *Daily Mail* (2020) as 'A New Dawn for Britain'.

Conclusion

By the end of the 2017–19 parliament, the Brexit battle was at an impasse. Arriving in office without a parliamentary majority, and with no clear alternative plan beyond exiting without a deal, Boris Johnson was highly restricted. What he craved most was a resounding general election victory, through which he could break free of these parliamentary constraints. Meanwhile, his opponents remained unable to unite around any alternative except yet another extension to Article 50. A key Labour MP, heavily involved in the anti-no-deal effort, recalled in interview that 'there came a point where I just thought I can't see the way through this at all'. As the battle dragged on, both MPs and the public grew increasingly polarized in their views, making compromise ever more difficult. Many MPs interviewed spoke about the acrimonious atmosphere of these final months in the Commons, as well as the abuse that they were receiving from the public. A senior Conservative Brexiteer recalled a mood of 'real misery that felt like there was simply no end to it' and 'a certain amount of desperation to see almost anything that would...let us move on and start again'. Another interviewee suggested that many MPs 'didn't much care about the outcome, they just wanted it to stop'.

Johnson did secure an alternative Brexit deal, but essentially only under the pressure of the constraints still upon him—that MPs would block a no-deal exit, leaving nowhere else to turn except to options previously rejected by Theresa May. This allowed looser alignment with the EU, but presented very serious problems with respect to Northern Ireland.

In terms of 'what-ifs', a significant question is what might have happened had Johnson's Withdrawal Agreement Bill been given proper time for parliamentary scrutiny at this stage. It was not accurate to claim, as Johnson did (and some media outlets reported), that MPs had blocked his deal—they had, rather, demanded proper time to consider it. Closer scrutiny of the bill would have exposed the continuing splits within the Conservative Party, providing space for the concerns of the DUP, and Theresa May's supporters, to be aired. Given that even the ERG was far from enamoured with the deal, its fragile majority at second reading could very well have unravelled. Johnson's own team recognized that the government was at risk of collapse; the longer that he spent arguing over the detail of his deal, the weaker his premiership and his future election prospects were likely to become. Some both inside and outside parliament believed that a majority might finally have formed at committee stage in favour of a further referendum, conceivably leading in the end to reversal of the 2016 result. Judging by interviewees' accounts, this seems unlikely to have been achieved through amendments to the bill itself. But the collapse of Johnson's proposals might finally have raised doubts about whether there was any form of Brexit at all around which agreement could be reached.

While Theresa May had endured hour upon hour of parliamentary cross-questioning on her negotiations and her Brexit deal, Johnson had tolerated only one sitting day before seeking a prorogation, a further two sitting days before first proposing a general election, and a total of just 28 sitting days before parliament dissolved for that election. He claimed implausibly to have never wanted an election, but it appeared always to have been his central strategy, allowing him to fulfil his prime ministerial ambitions, while bouncing his reluctant party into finally accepting a Brexit deal. Amidst the parliamentary mood of desperation, the opposition parties eventually conceded to this demand.

Johnson's divisive election campaign extended and amplified the kind of populist rhetoric that he had used consistently since becoming leader. By casting parliament as the villain of the story, and the blocker of Brexit, he depicted himself instead as the hero who could 'get Brexit done'. This was an essentially dishonest narrative, which deliberately obscured the central role that he and his allies had played in voting down Theresa May's deal. She herself had propagated a similar narrative at earlier stages, and the Brexit-supporting media were only too happy to disseminate it. Meanwhile, Corbyn's Labour was too conflicted, and insufficiently well led, to challenge it effectively. A different and more capable Labour leader might have secured a different election result. But Johnson's message proved popular, and delivered him the majority that he craved—while his pre-election purge of the parliamentary party at least temporarily reunited his backbenches.

The speedy passage of Johnson's second Withdrawal Agreement Bill after the election demonstrated the difference made by a comfortable governing majority. Although ERG supporters remained unenthusiastic about his deal, they could no longer plausibly challenge the Prime Minister, and accepted something that they would almost certainly have rejected, had it been put to them by Theresa May. The DUP disliked his deal far more than May's, which had been carefully constructed to avoid the hated border down the Irish Sea. But Johnson broke his promise to the party, while the general election saw its influence at Westminster drain away. The way things ended led many MPs to question whether they had made mistakes at earlier stages. One former centrist Conservative commented in interview that 'looking back you know, with the benefit of hindsight, you think "oh goodness, maybe I should have just voted for her deal and helped to get it through and at least then it might have been a less harmful Brexit". That's something…I will always be asking myself.' Likewise, a senior Labour interviewee said, 'people have asked me "Shouldn't you have backed Theresa May's deal because you've ended up with Boris Johnson's nightmare?", and I find that quite a hard question to answer, frankly'. DUP members almost certainly felt the same.

To claim that Brexit was now 'done' was, of course, an overstatement; the future relationship had yet to be negotiated, and disputes over Johnson's hastily negotiated Northern Ireland Protocol would soon emerge. Three and a half years after the referendum, the UK had finally left the European Union—but the long-term ramifications of the tortuous and hotly contested Brexit process for British politics, and for the UK's democratic institutions, remained to be seen.

Notes

1. The clause required a vote four years after the end of the transition period. The vote would be repeated after eight years if the Protocol was approved with cross-community consent, or after four years if approved by a simple majority. In the case of a vote to dis-apply the Protocol's trade provisions, the UK and EU would be required to identify a new solution consistent with the Belfast/Good Friday Agreement.
2. For example, House of Commons Hansard, 19 October 2019, column 571.
3. The others were: in 1982, to debate the invasion of the Falkland Islands; in 1956, over the Suez Crisis; and in 1949, to finish business before the summer recess (UK Parliament 2019).
4. For example, Oliver Letwin, House of Commons Hansard, 17 October, column 495.
5. House of Commons Hansard, 19 October 2019, columns 571, 573, 580–1.
6. Ibid., column 621.
7. Ibid., column 653.
8. Announced by Jacob Rees-Mogg, ibid., column 658.
9. No further vote on the deal would be required should the legislation pass, because it contained a clause repealing the meaningful vote provisions of the EU (Withdrawal) Act. It also disapplied the provisions of the Constitutional Reform and Governance Act (described in Chapter 6).
10. House of Commons Hansard, 22 October 2019, column 878.

11. Ibid., column 880.

12. Ibid., columns 845, 876.

13. Ibid., columns 914, 853.

14. The other Labour rebels were Kevin Barron, Rosie Cooper, Jim Fitzpatrick, Caroline Flint, and John Mann (all of whom had voted for May's deal), plus Sarah Champion, Gloria De Piero, Mike Hill, Dan Jarvis, Emma Lewell-Buck, Grahame Morris, Stephanie Peacock, Jo Platt, Ruth Smeeth, and Laura Smith (all of whom hadn't).

15. The former Conservatives were Ken Clarke, Philip Hammond, Richard Harrington, Anne Milton, Antoinette Sandbach, and Rory Stewart.

16. House of Commons Hansard, 29 October 2019, column 233.

17. Labour amendments to expand the franchise to 16- and 17-year-olds and EU citizens were not selected for debate.

18. Steve Brine, Greg Clark, Stephen Hammond, and Caroline Nokes. The six MPs who had the whip restored but did not stand for re-election were Richard Benyon, Alistair Burt, Richard Harrington, Margot James, Nicholas Soames, and Ed Vaizey.

19. Former Labour MPs Mike Gapes and Chris Leslie also stood for the party, which ran under the full name Independent Group for Change.

20. They included Iain Duncan Smith, in Chingford, and Dominic Raab, in Esher.

21. Mike Gapes and Chris Leslie both lost to Labour.

22. House of Commons Hansard, 20 December 2019, column 147.

23. Ibid., columns 177, 166.

24. Ibid., column 165.

25. Six Labour rebels also voted with the government: Sarah Champion, Rosie Cooper, Jon Cruddas, Emma Lewell-Buck, Grahame Morris, and Toby Perkins.

11

Conclusion: Brexit, Parliament, and the Constitution

As recounted in the previous chapter, the UK formally left the European Union on 31 January 2020. This followed years of uncertainty and bitter arguments over Brexit. But it was, in a way, just a staging post. The next steps, towards negotiating the future relationship with the EU, still lay ahead, as did the remainder of Boris Johnson's premiership.

This closing chapter primarily draws together conclusions from the analysis earlier in the book, which ended on exit day. But it first very briefly summarizes subsequent developments, including the next stages of the Brexit process and the political style of the Johnson regime—which was toppled in summer 2022, resulting in his eventual replacement by Rishi Sunak. This period was fundamentally affected by the Covid-19 pandemic, which drew attention away from both Brexit and the government's manifesto pledges of constitutional reform. Following on from the Brexit period, the pandemic response further unsettled the relationship between government and parliament, preventing any desired return to 'politics as usual'.

The remainder of the chapter then looks back on the developments described in the book, returning to the questions originally laid out in Chapter 1. This begins with a summary of what happened, drawing out some key moments and themes described in earlier chapters. That is followed by a review of some of the key 'what-ifs', asking whether the bitter and damaging arguments over Brexit and the role of parliament could have been avoided, and whether Brexit itself might have turned out differently. Leading directly on, the chapter then reflects on what the Brexit battle tells us about key aspects of UK politics. This starts with a discussion of parliament's role in the constitution. Next it considers whether the Brexit period suggests a need for institutional changes, particularly surrounding parliament itself. Finally, the chapter considers the significant cultural changes wrought by Brexit in UK politics, and their worrying resonances with democratic pressures around the world.

Afterword: Brexit and the Covid-19 Pandemic

The emergence of the global Covid-19 pandemic in early 2020 abruptly shifted attention away from Brexit, with the UK's first confirmed Covid cases announced on the very same day that it left the EU (BBC News 2020). By late March the whole country had entered lockdown, with most businesses and schools closed, and residents forbidden from leaving their homes except to carry out certain narrowly prescribed activities. With both the death toll and economic damage mounting, the pandemic rapidly became the predominant focus of UK politics.

Parliament itself was significantly affected—both through the need to develop a policy response, and due to the impact of the lockdown on its own mode of working. On both fronts, the government's attitude echoed previous behaviour over Brexit, with the House of Commons often sidelined (Russell et al. 2021). The emergency Coronavirus Act, containing key powers used by the government to respond to the pandemic, was understandably rushed through the Commons very quickly. But there followed many months when delegated legislation, subject to minimal parliamentary scrutiny, was used to implement successive lockdown restrictions. Parliamentary criticism over this followed the previous widespread concerns about the scale of such legislation relating to Brexit (Constitution Committee 2021, Public Administration and Constitutional Affairs Committee 2020).

The Commons' own sitting arrangements were very significantly affected by Covid, given the emphasis on limiting social contact to prevent the spread of infection. Downing Street sources initially suggested that parliament could shut down completely for several months (Craig, J. 2020)—which thankfully did not come to pass. But, in line with standard government control over the Commons agenda (as discussed in Chapter 8), it was ministers who largely set the parameters for procedural change, while backbenchers got little say. This resulted in a series of lurches between physical, virtual, and 'hybrid' proceedings, often failing to respect the fundamental principle of equal participation for all MPs (Gover and James 2021), which significantly worsened the challenges of maintaining scrutiny.

Meanwhile, Brexit was still not 'done', and parliament exercised minimal oversight of the future relationship negotiations. Notwithstanding the previous delays, and the new demands of the pandemic, the Johnson government refused to consider extending the transition period beyond 31 December 2020. A deal—the Trade and Cooperation Agreement (TCA)—was struck only on 24 December. This permitted Great Britain in principle to diverge from EU level playing field provisions, in line with the long-time objectives of Eurosceptics. But it made clear that too much divergence could have consequences, most obviously through imposition of tariffs on its exports to the EU (Fella et al. 2020). Hence the inevitable tension between the desire for new regulatory freedoms post Brexit and the reality of free trade in an interconnected world remained (Grey 2021).

Parliament was recalled from its Christmas recess for a single day on 30 December 2020 to pass the implementing legislation.[1] The scrutiny that this permitted was significantly more cursory even than that for Johnson's Withdrawal Agreement (covered in Chapter 10). Critics suggested that ministers could have facilitated fuller oversight by seeking only provisional approval of the agreement before the deadline, followed by substantive agreement later (King 2021)—which was the process followed by the EU.[2] But ministers preferred to force the bill through Westminster at speed. Former Brexit Secretary David Davis was among those who complained that '[o]ne day, frankly, is not enough for us to deal with a 1,200 page treaty'.[3] For the Labour opposition, the bill presented significant dilemmas. Internal unhappiness with the deal, and with Brexit in general, placed pressures on new party leader Keir Starmer to whip Labour MPs to vote against it, or at least to abstain (Scott 2020). But Starmer faced twin dangers: that rebels on the Conservative side could potentially have forced a new form of 'no-deal' outcome, and that the party would appear—even after the event—to be anti-Brexit. Ultimately, Labour whipped in favour of the bill, and there were no rebels on the government side.[4]

Soon after the general election victory, Johnson and members of his team had begun to criticize the 'oven-ready' deal that they had so enthusiastically promoted to the electorate. As indicated in Chapter 10, key figures openly suggested that he had signed up to—and sold—the legal agreement only on the basis that he did not expect to be bound by its conditions (Frost 2022; see also Cummings 2021a). This was consistent with the private assurances that Johnson had apparently given to ERG hardliners in 2019 that the Northern Ireland Protocol would be renegotiated. Having initially voted for the deal, that group came to voice its disapproval increasingly publicly (ERG 2021). Meanwhile, the DUP had been implacably opposed to Johnson's deal from the outset, which created significant instability in Northern Ireland.

The Johnson government hence controversially sought to circumvent the Protocol that it had negotiated. First, in late 2020, it proposed powers in the Internal Market Bill—a Brexit-related bill designed to limit intra-UK regulatory divergence—allowing ministers to make regulations in breach of the Protocol (Hogarth 2020). The Northern Ireland Secretary openly admitted that this plan would breach international law, unconvincingly assuring MPs that it would do so only 'in a specific and limited way'.[5] The proposal was dropped following objections from former prime ministers John Major, Tony Blair, Gordon Brown, and Theresa May, pro-Brexit former Conservative leader Michael Howard, various senior backbenchers, the EU, and the House of Lords (Elgot and Stewart 2020, Elgot, Syal, and Boffey 2020). But in spring 2022 elections to the Northern Ireland Assembly were followed by the DUP's refusal to allow an Executive to be formed unless the Protocol was changed. Johnson's government responded with a bill which sought unilaterally to disapply parts of it—which experts again argued would breach international law (Cormacain 2022, Elliott 2022). Sunak inherited this stand-off, while Steve Baker, now a Northern Ireland minister, ominously warned that the ERG would 'implode' his government if it reversed Johnson's policy (Leebody 2022).

A further development in early 2022 was Johnson's Retained EU Law (Revocation and Reform) Bill (dubbed the 'Brexit Freedoms Bill'). This would repeal en masse the large volume of EU law transferred onto the UK statute book by the EU (Withdrawal) Act 2018 (see Chapter 6), allowing ministers to decide what to retain or amend with only minimal parliamentary oversight. It promised the Eurosceptics' desired post-Brexit regulatory divergence, but risked undermining environmental and employment protections, and generating major uncertainty for business, while further sidelining parliament (Fox 2022). Again, the ERG was determined that Sunak should stick to the plans.

The Johnson government's approach, including to the Covid pandemic and the continued implementation of Brexit, demonstrated a consistent tendency to empower the executive, at the expense of parliament, the courts, and regulators, alongside a continued willingness to break constitutional norms. Meanwhile, the Constitution, Democracy and Rights Commission promised by the Conservative Party's 2019 general election manifesto did not emerge, though a series of piecemeal reviews were held (Schleiter and Fleming 2022). Some changes were made to arrangements for judicial review, and the government moved towards replacing the Human Rights Act with a new Bill of Rights. These proposals were based on claims of judicial overreach, and a stated desire to protect parliamentary sovereignty (Braverman 2020)—as examined below. In spring 2022, the Fixed-term Parliaments Act was replaced by a new Dissolution and Calling of Parliament Act, which restored the Prime Minister's de facto personal power to call general elections.

Johnson himself was ultimately ousted in summer 2022. This followed a string of complaints about his apparently casual willingness to breach constitutional norms and standards of propriety (David-Barrett 2022).

Two holders of the post of Prime Minister's Independent Adviser on Ministers' Interests (responsible for overseeing adherence to the Ministerial Code) resigned over Johnson's behaviour. He became the first Prime Minister to appoint a peer in defiance of propriety recommendations from the House of Lords Appointments Commission, and later the first to be referred for inquiry by the House of Commons Privileges Committee for misleading parliament. This followed months of headlines about social gatherings in Number 10 which breached the very lockdown restrictions that the government had imposed on the public. Johnson had repeatedly denied any wrongdoing in the Commons chamber, but (along with Sunak, then his Chancellor of the Exchequer, and multiple Downing Street staff) went on to be fined by the Metropolitan Police. Conservative MPs' support gradually leached away from Johnson, over these incidents and various others. Although he survived a no-confidence vote by his parliamentary party in June 2022, he was forced to resign the next month following an unprecedented raft of ministerial resignations, including Sunak's. Two leadership contests ensued (see below), initially selecting Liz Truss, whose brief and chaotic premiership was followed by Sunak taking over in October.

Brexit and Parliament: the Story in Brief

This book has focused on the disputed role of parliament in the Brexit process, exploring how this most central UK democratic institution became embroiled in such controversy, and what the Brexit period demonstrates about the wider state of politics. The rest of this closing chapter returns to the questions set out at the start of the book, the first and most basic of which is what actually happened in these troubled years. This is a long and complex story. As noted in Chapter 1, different narratives developed around it, often fed by competing players, which were frequently partial and sometimes downright misleading. The book has sought to provide an objective account, based on the public record and interviews with insiders. What follows is only a very brief summary, drawing out some important themes from earlier chapters.

The need to restore sovereignty to parliament was a long-time argument of Eurosceptics. While the institution's own role in Brexit rose to prominence after the referendum, it also served (as discussed in Chapter 2) as a key forum for helping to bring this vote about. Backbench MPs—assisted on occasion by Speaker John Bercow's unconventional interpretation of the rules—generated significant pressure for a referendum.[6] Notably, not all of them favoured exiting the EU. Some, in a similar way to Prime Minister David Cameron, saw the referendum as a way to make an awkward question go away. Based on polling, there was little expectation of a Leave victory, and this prospect was not taken particularly seriously. Parliament held no major debate on the merits of Brexit to air the arguments; the Leave campaign set out no detailed prospectus to voters; and the civil service was forbidden from preparing. Consequently, the dilemmas and trade-offs that dominated subsequent debates were barely mentioned before the referendum. As an ERG interviewee acknowledged, 'it was only [after the referendum] that different types of Brexit started coming to the fore. Soft Brexit and hard Brexit had never been canvassed before the referendum; the expressions were coined afterwards'. This lack of definition greatly stoked the bitterness of the following years.

The unexpected Leave result triggered the Prime Minister's resignation, and Conservative MPs elected Theresa May in his place (Chapter 3). She was, in the words of one interviewee, 'blood and bone a party woman', with her deep commitment to public service if anything surpassed by her commitment to the Conservative Party. But that party was severely divided over Brexit. Labour, too, was now internally split, with some party heartlands having voted strongly for Remain and others for Leave. Labour leader Jeremy Corbyn was already unpopular in his parliamentary party, and it tried but failed to remove him after his lacklustre performance in the referendum campaign. This left both party leaders significantly compromised.

The uncertain question of how to implement Brexit now passed over to parliament. Many feared that a Remainer-dominated House of Commons would seek to undermine the referendum result, and May's instinct was to rely as far as possible on pursuing Brexit using prerogative powers. But the enormity of the question understandably led parliamentarians to seek oversight of the next steps (Chapter 4). This provoked an institutional conflict between government and parliament. The courts were also drawn in, via Gina Miller's first legal case arguing for parliament's role in the triggering of Article 50. This resulted in defeat for the government and the infamous *Daily Mail* headline labelling the judges 'enemies of the people' (Slack 2016). Rather than cooling down the conflict, May's government sought to exploit it, in order to appear the people's defender.[7]

Shortly afterwards, the Prime Minister justified her calling of a snap election in 2017 (Chapter 5) by arguing—on shaky empirical grounds—that parliament was standing in the way of Brexit. But the election weakened her position, resulting in a minority government, dependent on a confidence-and-supply agreement with the Northern Ireland DUP. The closeness of the result raised hopes among former Remainers that Brexit might be blocked, which further fuelled polarization and discouraged the spirit of compromise required to navigate the subsequent stages.

May's early positioning (her initial 'red lines') incorporated the demands of her party's hardliners—including that the UK should leave the Single Market and Customs Union. But when formal negotiations with the EU began (Chapter 6), her team came to recognize the trade-offs, particularly concerning the protection of the Belfast/Good Friday Agreement. Avoidance of a hard border on the island of Ireland would require continued close alignment with the EU, which was unacceptable to hardline Brexiteers, while a 'border down the Irish Sea' between Great Britain and Northern Ireland was unacceptable to unionists, and in particular the DUP.

These difficulties, and May's rhetoric that 'no deal is better than a bad deal', raised concerns about failure to reach an agreement with the EU, and a possible no-deal Brexit. That would imply a hard border for Northern Ireland, and likely severe economic consequences. Partly to avoid it, a small number of moderate Conservative rebel MPs backed demands for a 'meaningful vote' in parliament on the final Brexit plan (Chapter 7). The extent of Conservative splits became very apparent when David Davis and Boris Johnson resigned from May's Cabinet over her 'Chequers' proposals in July 2018, and further ministers departed in November over her final Brexit deal. The primary sticking point was the 'backstop'—a compromise arrangement to avoid the border problem, demanding significant future all-UK alignment with EU rules (plus some special arrangements for Northern Ireland). When MPs voted on this deal in January 2019 it was overwhelmingly defeated, by 432 votes to 202. More than a third of the parliamentary Conservative Party—118 MPs—opposed it, 90 of whom were former Leave supporters. Most former Conservative Remain supporters, in contrast, voted for the deal.

There followed months of parliamentary wrangling, during which May's deal was defeated twice more (Chapter 8). Crucially, hardline Conservative Brexiteers (dubbed the 'Spartans') repeatedly refused to accept it. May expressed strong frustrations with parliament, but never explicitly criticized her backbench opponents. Boris Johnson (2019g)—who had voted against the deal on the first two occasions—responded by arguing that it was 'wrong in every sense to blame MPs for blocking Brexit'.

At this point, Conservative backbench moderates took further action to avoid a no-deal Brexit, including through backing temporary suspension of ministers' control of the Commons agenda to facilitate 'indicative' votes on alternative Brexit options. But with near-universal Conservative opposition to every option, they were all defeated. Meanwhile, other parties continued to reject the deal. All that MPs could agree on was instructing Theresa May to negotiate extensions to the Article 50 period. The polarization and failure to compromise which characterized this period was painfully summed up by senior Conservative Brexiteer Charles Walker, who commented that 'the losers do not know how to lose and the winners do not know how to win'.[8]

It was in these circumstances that Boris Johnson—who had adopted a mantle as the authentic voice of Brexit, denouncing May and voting against her deal—was elected in her place (Chapter 9). Parliament entered its 2019 summer recess immediately afterwards, without any formal test of confidence in Johnson. Before its return, he requested a five-week prorogation, potentially to help facilitate a no-deal Brexit. This led to the second government defeat in the Supreme Court on a Brexit-related matter. Before the court case, Johnson had stripped the whip from 21 Conservative MPs (17 of whom had consistently voted for May's deal), for facilitating what he dubbed the 'Surrender Act'—a non-government bill requiring pursuit of a further Article 50 extension unless parliament voted for a Brexit plan.

This parliamentary blocking of a no-deal Brexit drove Johnson to agree an alternative deal with the EU, which was put to the House of Commons in October (Chapter 10). It was essentially a package previously rejected by Theresa May, which included close EU alignment for Northern Ireland only, thus requiring a 'border down the Irish Sea'. Rather than subjecting the deal to parliamentary scrutiny, Johnson demanded a new general election, which was eventually conceded by MPs. He fought this on a slogan to 'get Brexit done', and a manifesto which—in direct contradiction to his own earlier comments—accused MPs of 'refus[ing] to deliver Brexit', and of 'thwarting the democratic decision of the British people' (Conservative Party 2019a: 2, 47–8). The Conservatives won an 80-seat majority, and the UK's exit from the EU followed on 31 January 2020.

This story clearly contains many contradictions. In particular, Johnson's rhetoric that parliament had failed to 'get Brexit done' was fundamentally inaccurate. He himself had voted with the hardliners against May's deal on the basis that it wasn't an authentic Brexit. They dismissed it instead as 'BRINO'—Brexit in name only. But this group never had a detailed plan of its own. A 'pure' Brexit, eschewing all EU regulatory alignment, would have required a hard border on the island of Ireland, and presented major obstacles to an ambitious trade deal with the EU. May's negotiated compromise sought to avoid these risks, while delivering on the Leave result. Johnson only 'got Brexit done' by returning to a version of the deal that May had rejected, due to the problems that it threatened for Northern Ireland. This central disagreement about what Brexit should mean was facilitated by the original lack of clarity in the referendum. But it took place between May's government and Johnson's supporters—not between the institution of government and the institution of parliament. The Conservative MPs who blocked May's deal, including Johnson himself, believed that they were defending Brexit, rather than undermining it. This made it wholly misleading to blame *parliament* for 'thwarting' Brexit, when those involved had in fact used parliament to pursue an argument with May's *government*. Yet this was the story that Johnson's manifesto told, profiting from a growing anti-parliamentary rhetoric that had developed under her premiership.

Summing up, a saga that began with demands to enhance the sovereignty of parliament gradually developed into one where parliament was vilified. The central arguments over Brexit were always—and indeed remain—those inside the Conservative Party. However, it suited most of these internal protagonists for parliament to get the blame.

How Might Things Have Turned Out Differently?

This leads to the second question identified in Chapter 1, of whether the problems arising after the referendum could have been avoided, and what else might have turned out differently. These are actually two interconnected questions, explored below in turn. First, whether the Brexit process could have been handled better, with less acrimony and negative fallout for UK politics—and specifically for the reputation of parliament. Second, whether there might have been a different outcome regarding Brexit itself. As the book has charted, the post-referendum period saw leaders, MPs, and other key players face difficult decisions, and there were many knife-edge parliamentary votes—suggesting various paths not taken. This section hence draws together conclusions on some particularly central 'what-ifs', while many others were explored in earlier chapters.

How Could Brexit Have Been Handled Better?

As already identified, the referendum itself could clearly have been handled better. The means for doing so are discussed in greater detail below. The central problem was the lack of serious focus on the desired model of Brexit, but also on the process for achieving it. Greater clarity about the meaning of Brexit might not have resulted in a different referendum outcome, but it could have avoided many of the bitter conflicts which subsequently occurred both inside and outside parliament. Even a clearer indication of parliament's necessary role in the event of a Leave vote could have eased things somewhat.

The fallout from the referendum was left for government and parliament to deal with, under the leadership of Theresa May. She was undoubtedly dealt a difficult hand, but there are significant questions about how she might have managed things better.

One potentially important missed opportunity was that of appealing to the public immediately after the referendum. Having voted for Brexit, they were essentially shut out of the subsequent stages. Voters were clearly polarized after the referendum result; but had May presented herself as a unifier, and sought public, industry, and other views on the way forward, this might have helped to go some way to healing the divide. Crucially, it might have helped shield May from her party hardliners, and boxed Labour into accepting some kind of compromise.[9] Parliament is always mindful of the public mood; but there was no serious effort by government to explore that mood on the form of Brexit. The only such exercise held, independent of government, suggested a willingness to compromise around a soft Brexit deal (Renwick et al. 2017, 2018).

In contrast, May's instinctive approach was closed, and politically tribal. With a narrow Commons majority, she focused on shoring up support on her own side. Combined with the lack of civil service preparedness for the complexity ahead, that led to adoption of her hastily drawn red lines, and her rhetoric that no deal was 'better than a bad deal'. This echoed the position of Brexit hardliners, initially helping her to secure their support. But it had the dual effect of heightening their expectations and alarming more moderate Conservatives.

Meanwhile, as indicated above, the establishment of a dividing line with parliament began early. May was instinctively reluctant to be open with MPs, which fuelled parliamentary suspicions. The government's response to the first Miller case, including its rejection of the short, simple bill to avert it preferred by David Davis (as discussed in Chapter 4), stoked up serious problems. May herself used the case to feed a narrative that parliament was anti-Brexit, while her Lord Chancellor, Liz Truss, failed to defend the courts against media attacks. This negativity towards key institutions continued in May's dubious public arguments for the 2017 general election (Chapter 5), and later her 'I am on your side' speech of 2019 (Chapter 8). From an early stage, she steered public frustration towards parliamentary Remainers, when one of her biggest challenges to finding agreement was actually hardliners on her own side. Her failed attempt to achieve a larger majority via the 2017 election might have given her greater freedom to face down these internal opponents, but the result left her more dependent on them than ever.

Until the very end of her premiership, May's deep-rooted party tribalism saw her flinch from building alliances with those beyond her party, and also from criticizing those on her own side. As a Conservative interviewee noted, she struggled to comprehend that her backbenchers would treat her with the kind of disloyalty that they did. But even once they had rejected her deal, she continued to lash out at her traditional political opponents, rather than chastising the ERG rebels. This may have been her worst mistake (and is one from which Rishi Sunak may seek to learn). At key stages, when Brexit-supporting newspapers were themselves directing anger at the hardliners, May missed opportunities to argue publicly for this group to come onside, instead continuing to criticize a generalized 'parliament'. This tainted parliament's reputation, while allowing her internal opponents to dodge blame, and ultimately to launch even fiercer criticisms of key institutions. After Johnson had taken over, May and her supporters largely remained silent about these contradictions. Even senior figures who had spoken out strongly against the prospect of a parliamentary prorogation chose to stay in Cabinet when it took place. Come the 2019 general election, Labour was too compromised on Brexit to highlight the dishonesty of Johnson's position.

The Conservative Party is often said to have a remarkable self-preservation instinct, supported by pragmatism and an ability to bend to the political weather (Heppell 2014, Jackson 2021). The efforts by May and her supporters to hold the party together at all costs were consistent with such traditions, but ultimately served both her and the institutions of UK politics very badly. Brexit hardliners who had previously lauded parliament, and used it to achieve their goals, were complicit in this behaviour.

Might Brexit Itself Have Turned Out Differently?

When the referendum took place, most parliamentarians did not support leaving the EU. The result of the public vote was then very narrow. Even afterwards, Brexit hardliners remained a minority even on the Conservative benches; but ultimately they proved very influential. The balance of parliamentary opinion, plus the various knife-edge votes, often made a different outcome appear more likely. Hence it is reasonable to ask, as other authors have, 'why was there a hard Brexit?' (Quinn, Allen and Bartle 2022) and 'who killed soft Brexit?' (Rutter and Menon 2020). Related questions include whether a further Brexit referendum was ever a realistic prospect, and indeed whether—given the finely balanced parliamentary numbers—the whole Brexit project might have fallen apart.

The positions of Theresa May and the Labour opposition are central to such questions. As Quinn, Allen, and Bartle (2022: 19) explore, the ingrained traditions of UK politics placed obstacles in the way of seeking a cross-party deal on a soft Brexit, and ultimately 'Labour unintentionally helped to deliver a hard Brexit'—through joining a blocking majority against the government whose Conservative members were mostly hardline Brexiteers. This may appear an unlikely alliance between ideological polar opposites, but such alliances are commonplace in the context of backbench rebellions at Westminster. Pre-referendum examples were seen in Chapter 2 with respect to Maastricht, and the purdah provisions in the EU Referendum Bill of 2015.

For the ERG, in the words of one interviewee from the group, the 'constant fear' and 'biggest anxiety' was that Labour would choose to support May's deal. Earlier chapters have explored the difficulties in forming this kind of centrist parliamentary alliance. Jeremy Corbyn was a particularly unattractive potential ally for May; and Labour's own problems with doing a deal were very great. Nearly all of the party's MPs had opposed Brexit at the referendum, and this remained the position of most party activists. Many Labour constituencies had tilted strongly to Remain, while many others tilted to Leave (a factor also existing on the Conservative side). There were real risks of party splits in this environment. While the governing party by necessity had to take a position, it was rational for the opposition to maintain ambiguity, and a typical stance of not helping the government out. As a Labour frontbencher put it in interview,

> I've asked myself the question, so many times that maybe if we had reached out to May and we could have landed some sort of softer Brexit, wouldn't that have been the more responsible thing to do? And I guess that I reconcile myself to what we did...on the basis that it would not only have destroyed the Labour Party, but also the hardliners within the Tory party were waiting for the opportunity to get rid of May anyway. And any deal that she struck would not have out-survived her. It would have probably destroyed the Labour Party pointlessly.

Theresa May's natural tribalism meant that she did not try to instigate such cooperation herself at the early stages. Had she done so, her own divided party might well have been the one to split. As already touched upon, her efforts to hold the Conservatives together proved to be of dubious merit given what happened later—including the purge of some of her own supporters under Johnson, and the direction in which he subsequently took the party.

May was under maximum pressure to change tactics and build cross-party alliances after the defeat of her deal, as explored in Chapter 8. Instead, following the first defeat, she continued to prioritize party unity by supporting the doomed Brady amendment. Options at this point included facilitating indicative votes in government time, backing a permanent customs union deal, or offering a referendum—which most Labour MPs now supported. But, as the interviewee above indicates, the fragility of her own position was by now a major problem. In the indicative votes themselves, the fragmentation among opponents of a no-deal Brexit was much lamented at the time; but the larger obstacle to agreement was near-universal rejection of soft Brexit or a referendum by Conservative MPs. A stronger Prime Minister might have instructed her troops (many of whom were not following the complexities closely) to support such compromise. But by this point May probably lacked the capacity. Organized resistance from Johnson and the ERG held the ingredients for her downfall, while MPs feared retribution from local Conservative associations if they supported the softer options.

When Johnson took over, he faced even more perilous numbers in the House of Commons than Theresa May. Had the Labour leader been a more palatable figure, Johnson might have been brought down in favour of a cross-party alliance (Chapter 9). Without that pressure, he eventually reached an uneasy agreement with the ERG to back his alternative Brexit deal (Chapter 10), taking care to avoid close parliamentary inspection of its detail. Had his Withdrawal Agreement Bill reached its committee stage in autumn 2019, support for it might have fallen apart completely. Meanwhile, the space for his more moderate opponents to extract compromise appeared limited. Despite Labour's official support for a further referendum, insufficient MPs seemed willing to back even the principle of this, let alone the detail of a bill to bring it about. Rather than holding out, exhausted MPs responded to the gridlock by supporting Johnson's demand for a general election, after which his little-scrutinized deal was hurried through.

To external observers, the failure to compromise may seem puzzling, and even frustrating. But a key additional factor is that the 'compromise' position of a soft Brexit was viewed by opponents at both ends of the spectrum—Remainers and hard Brexiteers—as the 'worst of all worlds' (Rutter and Menon 2020). It meant being out of the EU, but governed by its rules without having influence over their formation. Hence, although many considered it preferable to a potentially damaging hard Brexit, few felt enthusiastic about embracing it. Meanwhile, there were significant complexities in staging a further referendum (Sargeant, Renwick, and Russell 2018), and concerns—including from Labour MPs in Leave-supporting areas—that this would stir up further bitterness and polarization.

A final 'what-if' (discussed in more detail in Chapter 7) relates to parliament's intervention to require the 'meaningful vote'. Some moderate Conservatives worked with opposition parties to achieve this, in part to prevent a no-deal 'crash-out' at the end of the Article 50 period. But the votes that it facilitated against May's deal largely benefited the ERG. This led some to view the intervention as a mistake. Had May's government retained greater freedom to agree a deal without parliament's in-principle approval, as she initially wanted, implementing legislation would still have been needed—which did leave the door open to blocking by the ERG. But if defeat of the legislation had meant a no-deal Brexit, this would have radically changed calculations on the Labour side, likely forcing the opposition to at least abstain, or to whip in favour (as Starmer ultimately did on Johnson's future relationship legislation in December 2020). There were certainly strong principled arguments against parliament being 'bounced' into a Brexit deal on a take-it-or-leave-it basis. But, tactically, this might indeed have been to May's advantage, and resulted in the passage of her deal.

Throughout this period, the most important thing that could have altered dynamics in parliament was a change in the public mood. The obstacles created by steps such as the meaningful vote helped parliamentarians retain potential to change direction later. Interviewees repeatedly insisted that parliament was never going to overturn Brexit, which was clearly true while the policy maintained public support. Nonetheless, many parliamentarians might have welcomed a public backlash, had it occurred. Instead, throughout this period, the polls remained remarkably stable, with support for both Remain and Leave consistently hovering around 40–50 per cent, and 10–15 per cent of voters undecided (YouGov 2022a). Hence, for all of the controversy about parliament's divisions and struggles to reach agreement, in the words of one interviewee, 'I think it was really, looking back on it, just that parliament reflected what was happening [outside]...what was happening in families across the country'.

The Role of Parliament

Chapter 1 opened by quoting some fierce criticisms of the role of parliament and parliamentarians during the Brexit saga, and others appear throughout the book. The accounts above have already begun to reflect on the extent to which these were justified. This section continues that theme, while turning more squarely to the third question set out in the opening chapter, of what the Brexit process demonstrated about the constitutional role of parliament.

The Functions of Parliament

Chapter 1 briefly reviewed parliament's core functions, which have been seen played out throughout the book. First, the House of Commons is a *representative* institution, bringing together MPs from different parties and constituencies throughout the UK. As illustrated by the quotation at the end of the preceding section, parliament intrinsically brings together diverse voices, making it natural that it was divided over Brexit. Parliament also serves as a *deliberative* forum for the nation, where these diverse voices can be heard. It is crucially a very open environment, whose *oversight* function forces ministers to explain themselves on the public record—which can be uncomfortable for governments whose policies are controversial or have not fully been thought through. By demanding transparency, and providing democratic accountability, parliament served as the forum in which many of the contradictions and difficult trade-offs involved in Brexit were flushed out. In all of these respects, parliament fulfilled its functions entirely appropriately; though this exposed conflicts, given the lack of clarity about interpretation of the referendum outcome.

The role of parliament in *policymaking* has always been more contested. In comparative legislative studies, Westminster is classically seen as 'reactive' rather than 'active' in this regard (Mezey 1979, Norton 2013). That is, it primarily responds to policy that is formulated by the government. In fact, close study shows that parliament shapes government's thinking more than is often assumed, including through putting new policies onto the agenda (Russell and Gover 2017)—as was clearly illustrated by backbenchers' successful demand for the Brexit referendum (Chapter 2). Nonetheless, it is government that has the resources and internal coordination, particularly through the civil service, to develop major policies. Behind this generally lies a fairly cohesive governing party (or parties), whose whips shepherd proposals through parliament. But Brexit threw these standard dynamics into disarray.

The preceding sections have already highlighted how the key clashes between government and parliament over Brexit were those inside the Conservative Party. This is in line with the central conclusion by King (1976), nearly 50 years ago, that it is simplistic to talk of 'executive-legislative relations', because parliament is not a unitary actor—it is made up of various groups with different views. King emphasized that the most important relationship is generally that between the government and its own backbenchers; ministers will struggle to maintain a majority if they lack support on their own side. And when it came to Brexit, government backbenchers were deeply divided. This was clearly exacerbated by the unusual context of minority government; but, more importantly, it was worsened by very similar divisions existing inside the government itself. Theresa May's Cabinet, described to us by one of its former members as divided into 'armed camps' over Brexit, was extremely poorly equipped to deliver such a controversial policy. Historically, governments have often dropped major policies on which their own parties cannot agree. Yet in the context of the referendum, this was politically impossible. To make things worse, Brexit could not be shaped by the UK alone, but depended on international negotiations.

This created a uniquely difficult environment for parliamentary decision-making. But the Article 50 clock was ticking, so when May's deal failed to find support from her own backbenchers, parliamentarians increasingly took matters into their own hands (as discussed in Chapter 8)—seeking effectively to approximate the usual role of government. It is not unusual for ad hoc groupings of parliamentarians to form across party lines to influence policy. But even experienced 'grandees' such as Oliver Letwin, Ken Clarke, Hilary Benn, and Yvette Cooper lacked the capacity for policymaking on this scale. They also lacked the government's access to the Commons agenda, its whipping apparatus to secure MPs' support for complex policy proposals that many did not fully understand, and crucially, the ability to deliver on those policies if agreed. Unsurprisingly, their attempt to succeed where the government itself had failed proved fruitless. Some may conclude that parliament sought to overreach itself; but the primary failure was one of government, not parliament.

The Sovereignty of Parliament

Right from the start, the arguments over parliament's role recounted in the book often centred on the core concept of parliamentary sovereignty—the traditional notion that parliament is the UK's ultimate constitutional authority. The best-known account of this dates to Dicey (1962 [1885]: 39–40), who emphasized that parliament has 'the right to make or unmake any law whatsoever', and that 'no person or body...[has] a right to override or set aside' the law made by parliament. Reasons to think that this principle had subsequently eroded were summarized in Chapter 1. EU membership was one of these, and Eurosceptics often argued in terms of needing to restore the sovereignty of parliament.

The 2016 referendum could be seen as challenging one version of parliamentary sovereignty, by handing the Brexit decision directly to the people. The fact that referendums were consistently called for on European matters (see Chapter 2) indicated a degree of long-standing distrust in parliament to make the right decisions. Parliament itself seemed to accept this, by backing the referendum and then leaving the question of Brexit wholly to the public to decide, without even debating the principle beforehand. This suggested a drift towards support for a principle of popular, rather than parliamentary, sovereignty.

After the result, the government claimed a mandate for Brexit on the basis of the referendum—effectively seeking to translate this popular sovereignty into an argument for executive sovereignty, further boosted by the traditional use of the prerogative in foreign affairs. Such claims were at their strongest around the time of the first Miller case, where the policy question was a straightforward one of whether to trigger Article 50 or not, which mirrored the dichotomous choice presented to voters in the referendum itself. But the court's intervention was on a procedural point, serving to defend parliament's control over statute law—the most fundamental aspect of its sovereignty. Theoretically, parliamentarians could have used this procedural lever to overturn the referendum result, but politically that was never likely to happen. Unfortunately the government did little to reassure the public on this point.

At subsequent stages, ministers' grounds to argue that they were acting on a mandate from the people were distinctly weaker. In the absence of a detailed prospectus for Brexit, ministers faced important political decisions on which the people themselves had not spoken. It was essential that the choices made in implementing Brexit had clear democratic authority, requiring reversion to more conventional accountability through parliament.

While Eurosceptics had traditionally been keen to uphold the principle of parliamentary sovereignty, after the referendum many Brexit supporters inclined to defend the executive-sovereignty-as-popular-sovereignty line, for fear that parliamentarians would undermine the referendum result. In contrast, their opponents were more vocal in claiming that parliament should use its powers to decide the way forward. For example, in arguing for a meaningful vote, Heidi Allen (2017) claimed that '[t]his is what the Parliamentary sovereignty so desired by many Leavers looks like'; subsequently, when arguing for indicative votes, Hilary Benn (2018) borrowed from the Vote Leave slogan to suggest that this was 'the moment for Parliament to take back control'. But hardline Brexiteers opposed the two mechanisms that Allen and Benn were espousing. Such apparent contradictions illustrated how different participants were attaching different meanings to the concept of parliamentary sovereignty. Semantic differences of this kind had previously been pointed out by scholars. Most obviously, the rhetoric of traditional Eurosceptics tended not to distinguish between 'external' and 'internal' sovereignty—that is, essentially *national* sovereignty on the world stage versus the question of which constitutional body should be sovereign *domestically* (Gordon 2016: 335). So, for example, when Nigel Farage (2016) complained that 'Our Parliament is no longer sovereign and the majority of our laws are made for us by the EU', this was largely a defence of national sovereignty wrapped up in the language of parliament. The elision of internal and external sovereignty—and use of 'parliament' as a kind of shorthand for 'nation'—explains how some Eurosceptic champions of a referendum saw themselves as defending parliament.

Later, when those wishing to block a no-deal Brexit deliberately echoed the Brexiteer narrative, parliament's perceived adversary was not the EU but a recalcitrant government. This invoked a constitutional essential—of parliament's authority within the domestic sphere, as the institution to which the government is answerable, and on whose confidence it depends. But it raised the contested question of parliament's role in policymaking, as discussed above. One Brexit-supporting historian protested, at the height of the clashes between parliament and Theresa May's government, that '[w]hatever Remainers now say Parliament is not sovereign. It never has been…Parliament does not govern. Its job is to make laws' (Tombs 2019). While apparently contradicting Farage, this comment clearly referred to a different meaning of 'parliamentary sovereignty'—not only through a different interpretation of 'sovereignty' (see preceding paragraph), but also potentially of 'parliament' itself. Howarth (2021), building on Birch (1964), has referred to these latter conflicts as reflecting alternative 'Whitehall' and 'Westminster' readings of the ultimate authority in the UK constitution. Both represent versions of 'internal' domestic sovereignty. But a Whitehall reading rests on assumptions that parliament is really a creature of government, whereas a Westminster perspective places emphasis on the government's accountability to parliament. The former makes parliamentary sovereignty largely synonymous with executive sovereignty, while the latter supports parliamentary sovereignty in a far more literal sense.

Once Boris Johnson had assumed the premiership, the executive-sovereignty-as-popular-sovereignty justification was reasserted, through his repeated claims to be defending the referendum mandate. But Johnson's previous rejections of May's deal made clear that his interpretation of this mandate was different to hers. His own personal mandate extended no further than the votes of around a quarter of MPs and fewer than 100,000 Conservative Party members; yet he felt secure enough in his reading of the 'will of the people' to propose a lengthy parliamentary prorogation in order to pursue it, against the will of MPs. The irony of this action, given the traditional Eurosceptic rhetoric, was not lost on the commentators. The *Daily Mail* (2019a) lamented, on the day of the prorogation announcement, that it was 'not glorying in this sobering, significant step. Leave campaigners always insisted quitting the EU meant regaining Parliamentary sovereignty—not circumventing it. But in truth, what choice has [Johnson] got?' A casual reader might well have assumed that an exasperated Johnson was seeking, finally, to achieve the policy objective pursued by Theresa May; but his objective was actually opposed to hers.

As explored in Chapter 9, the Supreme Court subsequently reinstated parliament, recognizing its democratic authority over the government. The court was criticized for this by many Brexiteers, on the basis that its activism had undermined parliamentary sovereignty (e.g. see Braverman 2020). The courts (and particularly EU courts) had long attracted suspicion from some defenders of parliament's sovereignty, and had been seen as contributing to its erosion (e.g. Ekins and Gee 2017, Sumption 2016). But even some of those who had previously criticized judicial power welcomed the Supreme Court decision as upholding the proper constitutional role of parliament (Sumption 2020a). Politicians who attacked the court for undermining parliamentary sovereignty seemed to be espousing a hardline defence of the Whitehall version of the term—which was disingenuous when they themselves had recently used parliament's power to defeat the May government's Brexit policy.

Suella Braverman became Johnson's Attorney General in 2020, and in that guise used claims of parliamentary sovereignty as a justification for legislating against the Northern Ireland Protocol, in breach of international treaty obligations (HM Government 2020). This returned the argument full circle, deploying claims about internal (domestic) sovereignty to assert external (international) sovereignty. But as constitutional law professor Mark Elliott (2020) suggested, 'Treaty obligations are binding upon the UK, and to suggest that they are not "because Parliament is sovereign" is as embarrassing as it is dangerous'.[10] At the time of writing, these arguments about the Protocol were yet to reach their conclusion.

As this discussion has demonstrated, the 'sovereignty of parliament' has been used in very different ways by different protagonists during the Brexit debates, to support competing ends. It has variously been invoked against international actors, the people, the government, the courts, and also (as touched on below) the UK's devolved bodies. This lack of clarity significantly muddied the waters, obscuring public understanding over both Brexit and the constitution. It indicates a need to discuss and clarify what parliamentary sovereignty is intended to mean.

The Power of Parliament

These different arguments all touch upon the appropriate power of parliament, to make decisions and hold the government to account. The previous chapters showed that the government's relative numerical weakness in the House of Commons during 2016–19 resulted in significant shows of parliamentary assertiveness, but that there was also a clear counterreaction, in terms of executive retrenchment. The Brexit process itself, and subsequent developments, have tended to see parliament's role eroded.

Prior to Brexit, the dominant narrative had become one of growing (or previously unrecognized) parliamentary power (Cowley 2006, Norton 2015, Russell and Cowley 2016, 2018, Russell and Gover 2017). Changes such as the increasingly well-resourced select committees, latterly with their elected chairs, the decline in party voting cohesion, and the increased assertiveness of the post-1999 House of Lords all added up to an environment that had become more testing for government. Likewise, parliamentary oversight over the executive's prerogative powers had gradually been enhanced, both by convention and by statute (Hazell and Foot 2022).

In contrast, the Brexit period was marked by a notable reluctance from ministers to face parliamentary accountability. This was to a degree understandable, given the undoubted potential for defeat. The referendum, and the ensuing international negotiation, saw the government seeking to rely as far as possible on prerogative powers. The complexity of Brexit implementation (as discussed in Chapter 6) caused an unprecedented turn to delegated legislation, allowing ministers to put changes in place with only the most limited of oversight by parliament. But, as indicated earlier in the chapter, such trends did not end with minority government—they continued under the 2019 Johnson regime. Reliance on delegated legislation intensified further during the Covid crisis, raising concerns about 'government by diktat' (Secondary Legislation Scrutiny Committee 2021) and 'the urgent need to rebalance power between parliament and the executive' (Delegated Powers and Regulatory Reform Committee 2021). The government showed increased tendencies to rush primary legislation through both chambers of parliament, and proposed fast-track procedures to allow post-Brexit amendment of retained EU law. Johnson's ministers were criticized for a growing failure to engage with select committee scrutiny (Jenkin 2022a, 2022b). His tactics for managing the Conservative parliamentary party were also unusually heavy-handed (as further discussed below).

The 2017–19 parliament was unique, given the governing party's deep divisions over a controversial policy question, overlaid by the unusual circumstances of minority government. But in multiple ways, a Brexit campaign that had begun by championing a strengthening of the power of parliament ended, in a reversal of prior trends, with a greater entrenchment of executive power. While at the height of the crisis some specialists had begun to ask whether parliament had become too powerful (Norton 2019), more recent analyses have instead tended to lament the increasing sidelining of the institution (Barnard 2022, Judge 2021, White 2022).

What Changes Are Needed in Our Institutions?

Leading on from this discussion, an obvious question raised by the parliamentary battle over Brexit is whether it exposed flaws in the UK's constitutional arrangements. This is the fourth question posed in Chapter 1. As emphasized at the start of the book, parliament is central to the functioning of UK democracy—and, more fundamentally, such bodies are central to all democracies. It is therefore essential that the UK parliament is supported and can work effectively. This section first reviews three key constitutional interactions involving parliament, before very briefly reflecting on the wider constitution.

Referendums and Parliament

As already emphasized, the single most obvious constitutional flaw in the Brexit process arose at the very outset, in terms of arrangements for the referendum. The integration of the little-used mechanism of a national referendum with the traditional centrality of parliament was not well thought through.

These problems have subsequently been closely explored by bodies such as the Constitution Unit's Independent Commission on Referendums (2018) and parliamentary committees. The Commons Public Administration and

Constitutional Affairs Committee (2017: 12) strongly criticized the practice of holding a 'bluff-call' referendum, facilitated by the government solely to try and shut down a difficult political issue, rather than sincerely to enable change. The failure by David Cameron's government to prepare for a Leave vote, or to facilitate a serious public discussion about what this would mean, created the conditions for the very difficult parliamentary clashes that followed.

Two key components were clearly missing from the 2016 referendum: adequate information, and space for deliberation. On the first, it is essential that such votes should take place on a clear and detailed prospectus for change. The Independent Commission on Referendums concluded that, where this is difficult because the change will require negotiations, a pre-planned follow-up referendum may be needed.[11] On the second point, the decoupling of the Brexit referendum from the parliamentary process set up damaging tensions between the two. Fuller parliamentary debates on the Brexit options before the referendum would have helped to tease out the trade-offs and clarify what the public was voting for. In turn, greater public engagement in debates after the referendum could have better enabled parliamentarians to navigate the process.[12]

Looking back at Brexit, even senior supporters of change recognized some of these problems. One such interviewee commented that the 2019 indicative votes were 'almost like parliament bothering to have the debate that it probably should have had before the referendum was legislated for, but doing it after the people had voted'. The bluff-call criticism came from the committee chaired by long-time Eurosceptic Bernard Jenkin, while Vote Leave chair Gisela Stuart (alongside key Brexit critic Dominic Grieve) was a member of the Independent Commission on Referendums—whose most central recommendation was that this practice should never be repeated.

Parties and Parliament

Political parties are central actors in all modern parliaments, helping to aggregate opinion and provide electoral accountability to voters. As discussed in Chapter 2, cohesion within parliamentary parties is the norm. Recent changes at Westminster, summarized above, have encouraged greater backbench independence and more cross-party working, helping to boost scrutiny and accountability. But the Brexit process took internal party divisions to new levels. Again, the root of this was the referendum. Originally called thanks to a divided Conservative Party, it cut across the party structures upon which parliament usually depends, with splits emerging among both government and opposition. The growth of internal factions, and the fragmented organization for example around the indicative votes, demonstrated how parliament can struggle when parties cease to operate as reliable, cohesive blocs. It offered a painful proof by counterexample of how the traditional pattern of party organization can be beneficial.

Nonetheless, the subsequent actions by Boris Johnson to control his MPs, and to crush his internal party critics, went far beyond the norms of preceding decades. His removal of the whip from the 21 previously mostly loyal Conservatives in September 2019 (Chapter 9) was wildly disproportionate when compared to the treatment of Conservative Eurosceptic rebels over many years (latterly including Johnson himself), and of rebels such as Jeremy Corbyn within the Labour Party (Cowley 2005). This was not entirely a one-off by Johnson; his heavy-handed approach continued subsequently.[13] Such actions can have a significant 'chilling effect', leaving MPs fearful of retribution if they dare to express independent views, thereby undermining scrutiny and weakening parliament against the executive. They can also breed backbench resentment, which subsequently played a part in Johnson's fall. This demonstrates that cohesion is a matter of balance. It requires both a tolerance for some independent voting in parliament, and acceptance that collective decision-making and accountability through parties has important merits.

A further party organizational feature that contributed substantially to the difficulties over Brexit shares some similarities with the dynamic of referendums. This is the means by which parties now elect their leaders.

During the period covered by the book, problems were particularly evident in the case of Labour. Its post-2010 process for leadership elections largely removed the decision from the hands of MPs and gave it to grassroots party supporters (Dorey and Denham 2016, Quinn 2016). This allowed members to impose a leader on MPs who lacked parliamentary party support, while preventing MPs from unseating him even after an overwhelming vote of no confidence in his leadership (Chapter 3). Like the referendum, this mechanism took a key decision out of parliament but left parliamentarians to deal with the outcome. Far more directly than the referendum, it cut across the basic logic of parliamentary democracy. If a leader lacks even the confidence of their own parliamentary party, then attaining the confidence of the House of Commons is likely to be impossible. Corbyn's leadership proved a problem at various stages, but this conflict became particularly clear in the summer of 2019. Boris Johnson very probably lacked MPs' confidence, but Corbyn—considered undesirable even by a majority in his own parliamentary party—was not a viable replacement.

Prior to the 1980s, leaders of both main parties were selected exclusively by MPs. Thereafter both systems opened up gradually. The parallel Conservative Party system maintains a greater role for MPs, allowing them to unseat leaders, and also to select the final two candidates to go forward to a membership ballot.[14] But this too can leave MPs with a leader who does not have their majority support. In the initial leadership contest to replace Boris Johnson, in summer 2022, Liz Truss went into the membership ballot with the votes of only 113 Conservative MPs out of 359 (31 per cent). Rishi Sunak had led at every round of the MPs' ballot, and had MPs chosen between the final two, it is quite likely that he would have been elected at that point. Truss's premiership swiftly fell apart, and after just seven weeks Sunak was overwhelmingly nominated by MPs to replace her, in a contest that avoided a further membership ballot.

The cases of Corbyn and Truss show how the disempowering of MPs by the use of membership ballots effectively weakens parliament, and can prevent the system from functioning appropriately. Though the issue is complex and disputed, the arguments for returning this power to parliamentary parties have increasingly been recognized (Finkelstein 2022, Russell 2020, 2022, Saunders 2019)—including by William Hague (2022), the Conservative leader who originally introduced the reforms within that party.

Government and Parliament

The central relationship in the UK system is that between government and parliament. The Brexit process opened up many controversies about where the balance of power should lie between the two, and which is most suited to taking what kind of decisions.

Core to these was the question of prerogative powers, exercised by the executive without the need for parliamentary approval. As indicated above, the period prior to Brexit had seen a gradual parliamentary encroachment in these areas. This included, for example, greater input into decisions on military action, and parliamentary approval for early general elections via the Fixed-term Parliaments Act 2011 (FTPA) (Hazell and Foot 2022). During the Brexit period, disputes over the use of prerogative powers led to the two Miller cases in the Supreme Court (Chapters 4 and 9), through which the court upheld the power of parliament. In the latter case, the Johnson government had sought a lengthy prorogation, seemingly to maintain freedom to push through a policy (a no-deal Brexit) that the Commons had explicitly rejected. As discussed in Chapter 9, Johnson sought to evade other constraints as far as possible; and in 2022 the Dissolution and Calling of Parliament Act returned power to the Prime Minister to call elections without parliamentary approval—a highly unusual revival of prerogative power. Soon afterwards, fears arose that Johnson would seek to use this power to avoid being toppled by his own

MPs—which he was forced to publicly deny (Liaison Committee 2022), but which journalistic accounts suggest was under active consideration in the hours before his premiership collapsed (Payne 2022).

Throughout the Brexit period there was significant controversy about the balance of prerogative power and parliamentary control in foreign affairs. This still continues, with important questions about parliamentary oversight of treaties and other international agreements, where the UK had previously been able to rely on scrutiny at the EU level. Despite some changes (Hayter 2022), structures for oversight at Westminster are widely seen as inadequate (Natzler and Sayers-Carter 2022, Smith, Bjorge, and Lang 2020). There are delicate matters of balance here, but the time is ripe for a fresh review of the use of prerogative powers, and strong arguments for greater control by parliament in all of the aforementioned areas.

Likewise, the Brexit period saw severe tensions over the government's control of the House of Commons agenda (Chapter 8). Long beforehand, the Select Committee on the Reform of the House of Commons (2009)—commonly known as the 'Wright Committee'—had proposed change in this area. It recommended that the Commons weekly agenda should be drawn up by a cross-party House Business Committee, rather than by the government, and, most importantly, that it should be put to MPs for decision and possible amendment. But these proposals were never put into effect. Although minority government was not considered by the Wright Committee, its arrival in 2017 made the pattern of agenda control particularly problematic. Government control allowed, for example, the cancellation of the December 2018 vote on Theresa May's Brexit deal, and saw many months during which ministers withheld opposition days. Ultimately, this contributed to non-government MPs' controversial 'seizing' of the agenda in 2019. Disputes subsequently re-emerged under majority government in 2020–21, over the handling of the Covid pandemic. The procedural controversies in both of these periods could have been avoided, to a significant extent, by implementation of the Wright Committee's plan for the Commons to vote on its own weekly agenda. Likewise, giving MPs meaningful control over when the Commons goes into recess, and when it is recalled, could have eased tensions in both cases (Russell and Gover 2021). Such changes would be in line with the basic principle that the government is accountable to parliament.

There is also an urgent need to reverse the trend towards government undermining standards of parliamentary scrutiny. As with respect to the prerogative, and political party cohesion, there is a balance to be struck. The Brexit period demonstrated some of the risks of parliament overreaching itself in policymaking, and the benefits of stable government as the prime 'maker' of policy. But proper examination of proposals in parliament is essential to democratic accountability. It is also necessary for good-quality decision-making, allowing policies to be tested in a public arena and potential flaws to be identified in advance (Benton and Russell 2013, White 2015). Post Brexit, particular emphasis has been placed on the need to rein in over-use of delegated legislation, and to improve processes for its parliamentary examination (Hansard Society 2021). But under the Johnson government primary legislation was also too often rushed. Meanwhile, the repatriation of numerous complex policy responsibilities from the EU demands strength-ened infrastructure in both government and parliament.

The Wider Constitution

The areas discussed above all relate directly to parliament. But there are other aspects of the constitution about which Brexit has raised significant concerns. Just two are considered here.[15]

First, as the House of Lords European Union Committee (2017: 12) commented early on in the Brexit process, the 'European Union ha[d] been, in effect, part of the glue holding the United Kingdom together since [devolution occurred in] 1997'. Subsequently, Brexit has put serious strains on the UK's territorial constitution, and the Union itself. The fact that majorities in both Scotland and Northern Ireland voted Remain in 2016 fuelled pre-existing separatist pressures (McEwen and Murphy 2022). The SNP quickly began pressing for a further referendum on Scottish independence, and Sinn Féin likewise raised the prospect of a 'border poll' on Irish unification. Both of these open up complex constitutional, as well as political, questions (Hepburn, Keating, and McEwen 2021, Working Group on Unification Referendums on the Island of Ireland 2021). In Northern Ireland, Brexit has reopened sectarian wounds which had previously been healing (Murphy and Evershed 2022), with very difficult arguments left to resolve about the Protocol as a result of Johnson's Brexit deal. In addition, tensions have arisen due to passage of Brexit legislation through Westminster despite objections from the devolved legislatures (McEwen 2021), and over the distribution of policy competences post Brexit. These leave difficult questions to be resolved, including regarding the appropriateness of parliamentary sovereignty from a territorial point of view (Keating 2021, 2022).

Such problems, and various others visible during the Brexit process, have fed wider questions about whether the UK should finally adopt a codified constitution—in the shape of a single document—as now applies in most other states. Brexit has been identified as a 'constitutional moment', or 'crisis', of the kind often associated with the writing of such documents (Bogdanor 2019,

King 2019). Some saw the Johnson period as signalling a collapse in the UK's so-called 'good chaps' culture—a term popularized by Peter Hennessy in the 1980s for the importance of unwritten rules, conventions, and norms—implying the need to move to a more formal document (Blick and Hennessy 2019, Clark 2022).

But it is difficult to see this as an easy answer to the UK's constitutional malaise. In fact, since the 'good chaps' epithet was coined, substantially more of the UK's constitutional arrangements have already been written down in statute (Melton, Stuart, and Helen 2015). These documents remain scattered, but the key difference to most other states is that they are not 'entrenched' by any special process for amendment. This retains the principle of parliamentary sovereignty, while change could result in more power transferring to the judges.

Even if the end point of a new written constitution were considered desirable, it is currently quite hard to envisage the realistic political steps towards agreement. The post-Brexit moment of wide-ranging constitutional contention and uncertainty—encompassing the roles of parliament, government, courts, territorial arrangements, and even monarchy—would be a difficult one in which to fix arrangements rigidly. Indeed, to do so could prove unwise.

In truth, all constitutions ultimately depend on norms of good behaviour. Most systems recently associated with 'democratic backsliding' (such as Hungary, Poland, and the US) have entrenched written constitutions—which indicates how these documents alone are an imperfect protection against political actors going 'rogue'. Leaders who reject previously accepted constraints, particularly if they enjoy strong electoral support, can readily undermine norms, and even dismantle written checks. This suggests that the democratic problems of our age are more cultural than institutional, which is the focus of the closing section.

What Has Happened to Our Politics?

At least as important as thinking about institutional flaws—indeed almost certainly more so—is considering the final question set out in Chapter 1, regarding the culture of UK politics, and the effects upon it of the Brexit process. Here the conclusions are troubling, and the need for solutions is clearly urgent.

Although the concepts are contested, there are some clear connections between aspects of Euroscepticism and populism (Gifford 2014, Vasilopoulou 2018). While Euroscepticism may be rooted in legitimate support for national sovereignty, and traditionally for (in the UK case) UK institutions, some advocates have emphasized the role of distant and out-of-touch

European 'elites' in disadvantaging a downtrodden British people (MacMillan 2017, Tournier-Sol 2014). The contrast between out-of-touch elites and a pure, unified people is the central defining feature of populism (Mudde 2004, Mudde and Rovira Kaltwasser 2013b), as described in Chapter 9. This plays to deep human instincts of tribalism, and activates identities of 'us' and 'them' (Obradović, Power, and Sheehy-Skeffington 2020). The demand for referendums to advance the Eurosceptic cause has also sometimes had a populist edge: seeking to take decisions out of the hands of 'out-of-touch' domestic political elites, and hand them directly to the people.

It would hence be wrong to see the Brexit referendum as the root cause of a rise in populism in UK politics; it can more sensibly be considered an early symptom. But the referendum itself certainly accelerated such trends. Referendums by their very nature hold significant risks of polarization: simplifying complex questions into a binary choice. To reach and mobilize a broad base of supporters, campaign messages may adopt a populist tone. This characteristic is not confined to Brexit, or to the political right; for example, proponents of change in the 2011 referendum on the UK voting system presented an (essentially ill-founded) argument that it would make politicians work harder, and root out corrupt MPs (Seawright 2013). Likewise, the campaign by Dominic Cummings for a No vote in the 2004 referendum on North-East devolution deployed a white elephant mascot and was characterized as 'anti-politician and anti-tax' (Tickell, John, and Musson 2005: 493). The Brexit referendum was clearly far more high-profile and passionately fought than either of these, and crucially it created polarized identities which long outlasted the campaign. Researchers have found that Leave and Remain identities were more firmly held than political party identities, even years after the result (Ford and Sobolewska 2020, Hobolt, Leeper, and Tilley 2020). Following the referendum, holders of one of these identities were less likely to think that holders of the other were honest, intelligent, or open-minded, or to welcome the idea of such people either taking up public office or marrying into their families. This polarization, once established, could potentially be exploited by politicians.

Such problems were seen played out through the Brexit debates, with 'parliament' (alongside the courts) falling victim, due to its frequent implicit or explicit association with 'Remainers'. Such narratives often obscured the true story, as discussed above. More worryingly, this media and political rhetoric, which developed into a broader public discourse, served to turn opinion against traditional institutions of British democracy. Such divisions reached their height around the prorogation crisis, when (as discussed in Chapter 9) public attitudes to the courts and parliament were highly polarized along Brexit lines (Curtice 2020). In this period the Twitter hashtag '#PeopleVersusParliament' gained currency, including among some advocating violence against parliamentarians.

Boris Johnson's rise to the premiership was a product of this toxic political mood, and he subsequently sought to profit from it. Johnson gained the leadership having actively undermined Theresa May's efforts to agree a Brexit compromise. Aided by Cummings, he presented himself as able to succeed where others had failed, on a mission to 'get Brexit done' even if this meant flouting conventions, shutting down democratic institutions, and potentially even breaking the law. By this point in the process there was widespread public tolerance for such behaviour, as witnessed in the Hansard Society's (2019) poll showing majority support for 'a strong leader willing to break the rules'. Johnson was subsequently rewarded with a comfortable Commons majority in December 2019.

The UK is far from alone in having been tempted by such 'strong' leaders to cut through the mundane frustrations of politics. As Bernard Crick (1962) classically articulated many years ago, politics is a necessarily imperfect process, entailing messy compromise and negotiation to reach workable solutions whereby most people do not ultimately get quite what they want.[16] Disillusionment with the imperfections of politics has been well documented for decades (Hay 2007, Mounk 2018, Runciman 2018, Russell 2005, Stoker 2006). In the UK, such disillusionment has sometimes been directed specifically at parliament, most notably after the 2009 MPs' expenses crisis (van Heerde-Hudson 2014). But there is now a growing concern about the state of democracy worldwide, and about actions by authoritarian leaders—themselves often democratically elected—to pursue democratic backsliding (as also discussed in Chapter 9). This results in a gradual breakdown of norms and dismantling of democratic checks and balances, consistent with the fundamentally anti-pluralist, and anti-political, nature of populism (Müller 2016, Urbinati 2019b). Political polarization, which enables leaders to demonize their opponents and take radical action to lock them out of power, can further facilitate backsliding (Haggard and Kaufman 2021, Naím 2022). It may also be assisted by, and encourage, campaigns of political disinformation, so that electorates are no longer sure what is true or who (if anyone) they can trust (McChesney 2014, Moore 2019). Such trends have been well documented in numerous countries, while others are struggling to keep them at bay.

The role played by traditional centre-right political parties in these developments has drawn recent attention. Applebaum (2020) carefully describes how mainstream parties in Hungary, Poland, and the US gradually bifurcated between those politicians with a solid commitment to democratic constitutional principles and those willing to see checks and balances eroded in order to remain in power. In all three cases the latter groups won. Bale and

Rovira Kaltwasser (2021) have explored the response of centre-right parties in various European democracies to the challenge posed by the populist radical right. Here the UK is unusual, in how a long-established centre-right party moved to adopt policies and electoral strategies previously championed by fringe right parties. This was partially a response to UKIP; but Trump's US showed how similar shifts can occur even without such direct electoral challengers. In the UK and US two of the world's longest-established centre-right parties, previously stern defenders of moderation and institutional checks on executive power, have moved towards more radical positions and threats to dismantle such checks. This broad international pattern provides essential context for the 2019 Conservative manifesto promise to rebalance 'the relationship between Government, Parliament and the courts' (Conservative Party 2019a: 48).

Boris Johnson's style was inseparable from the politics of Brexit. His charismatic presence in the Vote Leave campaign was undoubtedly a key factor in its popularity (Clarke, Goodwin, and Whiteley 2017, Curtice 2017b). Post referendum, a prevailing populist mistrust of elites—at times encouraged by Theresa May—coupled with an aversion to the messy compromise essential to politics, benefited those who rejected the deal that she had negotiated, including Johnson. All of this created an opportunity for a politician willing to offer a bolder approach, which he then did. Johnson had not originally been a hardline Eurosceptic, having long been considered relatively non-ideological, and having presented himself as a traditional 'one nation' centrist Conservative (Bower 2020). But by the end of his premiership, he was renowned as a serial constitutional rule-breaker, and cited as one of the new international breed of authoritarian 'strongman' leaders (Rachman 2022). His polarizing rhetoric by then extended to claiming that the 'deep state' would seek to overturn Brexit (Schofield 2022), while his allies continued to lambast 'Remainer' civil servants (Harris 2022). This persistent appeal to polarized identities sought to sustain a shaky pro-Brexit electoral coalition, long after the act of Brexit itself.

The Brexit period, marked by a divided public, the uncompromising campaign style of Dominic Cummings, a Labour leader drawn from the fringe left of his own party, and finally the premiership of Boris Johnson, established a degree of political polarization unknown in the preceding decades. This eroded the very spirit of compromise on which politics depends, sparking attempts to undermine traditional institutions and reject many of the norms of propriety upon which the system had long depended. Post Brexit, and post Johnson, rebuilding these norms and standards, and a political culture in the Crickean sense, is a critical priority. UK polling showed some positive signs in 2021, including a strong public preference for honesty and integrity in politics, and for constitutional checks and balances (Renwick et al. 2022). This suggests that politicians seeking to restore such values may be rewarded, and may help to explain why Prime Minister Rishi Sunak (2022) entered Downing Street on a promise to restore 'integrity, professionalism and accountability' and to rebuild trust. But restoration of constitutional norms is not an easy task, or a challenge in which the UK is alone. It is part of an international struggle, to defend democracy and its institutions.

Notes

1. The recall began with last-minute changes to the Commons' standing orders to allow participation by the many MPs who had been excluded from legislative debate for months due to pandemic rules.
2. The European Council agreed on 29 December 2020 to apply the TCA provisionally pending its full ratification by the European Parliament, which followed on 28 April 2021.
3. House of Commons Hansard, 30 December 2020, column 556.
4. Just one Labour member voted against its second reading, while 36 did not vote—including two junior shadow ministers who resigned in order to abstain (Rodgers 2020).
5. Brandon Lewis, House of Commons Hansard, 8 September 2020, column 509.
6. Bercow's role was often publicly controversial, but is not discussed in this chapter. For a very brief assessment see the conclusion to Chapter 8.
7. Indeed, the author of the controversial article, James Slack, was appointed to a senior communications role at Number 10 soon afterwards by Theresa May, and continued to serve under Boris Johnson.
8. House of Commons Hansard, 29 March 2019, column 731.
9. Although the proposals were never really developed, this bears some similarity to the ideas put forward by Yvette Cooper, Stephen Kinnock, Seema Malhotra, and others after the referendum, as described in Chapter 4.
10. See also Elliott (2022).
11. This is a different proposition from claiming that a further referendum on Brexit was the right course. The key point is that the process for acting upon the (first) referendum should be set out clearly and unambiguously in advance.
12. There are also various means by which better public deliberation could be built into the referendum process itself, as explored by the Independent Commission on Referendums (2018).
13. A key example was Johnson's stripping of the whip from Julian Lewis, who stood against his preferred candidate for chair of the largely non-political Intelligence and Security Committee (Sabbagh 2020), but there were various other cases.
14. As recounted in earlier chapters, May was elected without a member ballot in 2016, after the second-placed candidate dropped out (Chapter 3); she survived one no-confidence vote (Chapter 7) and resigned when threatened with another (Chapter 8).

15. There are additional areas, including the role of the monarchy (particularly with respect to ministers' exercise of prerogative powers), and the courts. In the interest of brevity, these are omitted. Various other authors' reflections on the role of the courts can be found via references cited in the sections on the two Miller cases (Chapters 4 and 9), and in the earlier section of this chapter on the sovereignty of parliament.
16. Notably, this description fairly accurately matches the culture of the EU.

Glossary of Parliamentary Terms

Italics denote a term which has its own glossary entry.

10-minute rule bill A form of *private member's bill* initially proposed in the House of Commons via a 10-minute speech. Often the bill itself is never actually introduced.

Act of parliament A law made by parliament, known during its passage through parliament as a *bill*. Bills become Acts once they have completed their passage and gained *royal assent*. Acts may also be referred to as *primary legislation*.

Amendment A text proposing a specific change to the wording of a *bill* or *motion*.

Backbench business Commons business proposed by *backbenchers*. A minimum quantity of time for this in each session is guaranteed by *Standing Order* no. 14(4), though the government determines on which days it will take place. Proposals for debate are chosen by the Backbench Business Committee.

Backbencher An MP who is not a minister, shadow minister, *whip*, or frontbench spokesperson for their party. Parliamentary Private Secretaries (PPSs), who assist ministers without themselves holding ministerial office, have a more ambiguous role between *frontbencher* and backbencher.

Bill A proposed Act of parliament, also known as *primary legislation*. Bills go through several stages in both the House of Commons and House of Lords, including *first reading*, *second reading*, *committee stage*, *report stage*, and *third reading*. They may also undergo *ping-pong* between the two chambers, before the final wording is agreed and the bill receives *royal assent*.

Business motion A *motion* proposing to change the content or timing of business in either chamber of parliament.

Clause *Bills* are generally made up of multiple clauses (and sometimes additional 'schedules'). Once a bill becomes an *Act of parliament*, the clauses become known as sections.

Committee stage The second substantive stage of a *bill*'s consideration in each chamber, following *second reading* and preceding *report stage*. The bill is considered in detail, and can be amended.

Confidence motion A *motion* proposed in the House of Commons, asking MPs to express their confidence in the government. Alternatively, a motion of no confidence may be tabled, asking MPs to reject the government. A failed confidence motion or successful motion of no confidence is expected to lead to formation of a new government, or else a general election.

Delegated legislation Law which is usually created by ministers using powers given (or 'delegated') to them by an *Act of parliament*. Delegated legislation is subject to less parliamentary scrutiny than *primary legislation*. Also commonly known as secondary legislation.

Division A formal vote in the House of Commons or House of Lords, in which parliamentarians pass through the division lobbies to record their votes.

Early day motion (EDM) A text submitted by an MP for publication by the House of Commons, expressing an opinion on a topic; other MPs may add their names to show support. Early day motions are rarely debated, but allow MPs to demonstrate the strength of feeling in the House of Commons on a particular matter.

Emergency debate A debate granted at short notice by the Speaker of the House of Commons at the request of an MP, on 'a specific and important matter that should have urgent consideration'. Such debates are granted under *Standing Order* no. 24, and are normally on *motions* in 'neutral terms', though this became controversial in September 2019 (see Chapter 9).

Erskine May The definitive written guide to parliamentary procedure and conventions used by those inside and outside parliament. It details how key rules are interpreted, often illustrated by examples of past precedents.

First reading A *bill*'s introduction into the House of Commons or House of Lords. No debate takes place at this stage.

Free vote A vote in which parliamentarians in a given party are not whipped to follow a party line.

Frontbencher A minister, shadow minister, *whip*, or party spokesperson.

Humble address A type of *motion* addressed to the monarch. Humble addresses can be used to call for the release of information; unlike many other types of motion, they are considered binding if agreed.

Implementing legislation *Legislation* to implement an international agreement in domestic law.

Legislation A term used to describe draft laws which are currently passing through parliament, or laws which have been passed. This can take the form of either *primary legislation* or *delegated legislation*.

Money resolution A House of Commons *resolution*, proposed by the government and required for *bills* that, if enacted, would authorize new public spending. A decision on the money resolution usually follows *second reading*; if the government declines to put forward a money resolution, or the Commons votes it down, the bill cannot progress.

Motion A text put forward for debate and/or decision, in either chamber. Motions are binding when they relate to parliament's own activity, or in a small handful of other cases including *confidence motions*. Other motions are non-binding for example, a Commons motion expressing disagreement with government policy may put political pressure on the government, but would not bar it from pursuing the policy.

Neutral terms Used to describe Commons *motions* that do not indicate a particular position on topic at hand. Such motions may be used to facilitate debate without any expectation that the chamber will take a decision. They are generally considered to be unamendable, which became controversial over the Brexit 'meaningful vote' (see Chapter 7).

Opposition day A day on which Commons time is allocated to a non-government party, for it to facilitate debate on topics of its choice. The minimum number of opposition days per *session* is set at 20 in *Standing Order* no. 14(2). Additional days may be granted at the government's discretion, but are not guaranteed, even in longer sessions. The government determines which specific days will be treated as opposition days.

Parliamentary questions Questions asked of government ministers, in either the House of Commons or House of Lords. They may be either oral or written. Oral questions occur on most days, with the most famous (but not necessarily most important) being weekly Prime Minister's Questions in the House of Commons.

Ping-pong The colloquial term for the process by which the final wording of a *bill* is agreed following its passage through both chambers, if the bill was subject to *amendments* in the chamber which considered it second. In this case, it must return to the chamber where it began, for those changes to be considered, and can then shuttle back and forth between the chambers until both approve it in identical form.

Primary legislation An *Act of parliament* or, prior to its completing passage through parliament, a *bill*. Contrasted with *delegated legislation/secondary legislation*.

Private member's bill A *bill* introduced by a *backbench* MP or peer, rather than by the government. Only limited time is available for debating private members' bills and—unless supported by the government—they rarely become law.

Prorogation The end of a parliamentary *session*. While parliament is prorogued, no parliamentary business can take place, and any *legislation* which has not passed before the prorogation

ceremony falls (unless prior agreement has been reached that it should be 'carried over' to the next session). The timing of prorogation lies in the hands of the government, though the Miller/Cherry Supreme Court case of 2019 (see Chapter 9) confirmed that there are some limits on the government's discretion.

Queen's Speech The speech read out by the monarch, as part of the State Opening of parliament which begins a new parliamentary *session*. The Queen's Speech (now the King's Speech, following the accession of King Charles) is written by the government, and sets out its legislative priorities for the session. It is followed by a debate over several days on its content, known as the 'Debate on the Address'.

Reasoned amendment In the House of Commons, an *amendment* tabled to the motion proposing *second reading* or *third reading* of a *bill*, indicating why the bill should be rejected. In the House of Lords, reasoned amendments have slightly wider uses.

Report stage Typically, the third substantive stage of a *bill's* consideration in the House of Commons or House of Lords. The bill—as amended at *committee stage*—is reviewed, and further *amendments* can be made. Report stage may be omitted under certain circumstances.

Resolution A word used to describe a decision of the House of Commons or House of Lords, or alternatively to describe some types of *motion* (see, for example, *money resolution*).

Royal assent The monarch's formal approval of a *bill* which has completed its passage through both the House of Commons and House of Lords. At this point, the bill becomes an *Act of parliament*.

Royal prerogative Powers formally retained by the monarch and used by ministers on their behalf. Parliamentary approval of their use is not required.

Secondary legislation See *delegated legislation*.

Second reading The first substantive stage of a *bill*'s consideration in each chamber of parliament, following its introduction in the (largely ceremonial) *first reading*. At this stage, the general principles underlying the bill are debated.

Select committee A small group of MPs or peers, established to carry out oversight or scrutiny of a particular policy area. Select committees set their own agendas, initiating inquiries, taking evidence from ministers, officials, and external experts, and publishing reports on their findings. The best-known select committees are those in the House of Commons which 'shadow' each government department—covering, for example, health, education, or foreign affairs.

Session A parliamentary 'year', several of which normally take place between one general election and the next. The timing of sessions is in the hands of the government, and they may be longer or shorter than a calendar year. Each session begins with the State Opening of parliament (see *Queen's Speech*) and is brought to an end by a *prorogation*.

Standing orders The rules governing parliamentary business. The House of Commons and House of Lords each have their own standing orders.

Statement An address to parliament, typically (although not always) made by government ministers in order to explain government policy or respond to urgent events. Statements may be either oral or written; oral statements are often followed by questions to the minister.

Statute Laws set out in *primary legislation*. The collection of all such law is often referred to as the 'statute book'.

Statutory instrument The most common form of *delegated legislation*.

Third reading Typically, the fourth substantive scrutiny stage which a *bill* undergoes in the House of Commons and House of Lords. The chamber considers the bill, as amended at *committee stage and report stage*, and votes to pass or discard it. In the Lords only, the bill may be further amended at this stage.

Urgent question A type of oral *parliamentary question* addressed by an MP to the government. MPs must apply to the Speaker for permission to ask such a question, justifying its urgency. If permission is granted, a government minister must provide an answer in the House of Commons the same day, which is normally followed by numerous follow-up questions and answers. The equivalent mechanism in the House of Lords is a 'Private Notice Question'.

Whip A party management role, existing in both the House of Commons and House of Lords. Whips are appointed by their parties to communicate between *frontbenchers* and *backbenchers*. One of their roles is to encourage backbenchers to vote as recommended by the party line (itself often referred to as 'the whip').

Bibliography

Allen, H. (2017), 'We're No Mutineers—But Parliament Must Have a Binding Vote on the Final Brexit Deal', *Daily Telegraph*, 13 December.

Anderson, S., and Hazell, R. (2019), 'Miller 2/Cherry and the Media—Finding a Consensus?', *Constitution Unit blog*, 14 October.

Applebaum, A. (2020), *Twilight of Democracy: The Failure of Politics and the Parting of Friends* (London: Allen Lane).

Ashcroft, M. A. (2017), *The Lost Majority: The 2017 Election, the Conservative Party, the Voters and the Future* (London: Biteback).

Ashcroft, M. A. (2020), *Diagnosis of Defeat: Labour's Turn to Smell the Coffee* (London: Lord Ashcroft Polls).

Asthana, A., and Elgot, J. (2017), 'Theresa May Buys Time with Apology to Tory MPs Over Election "Mess"', *Guardian*, 12 June.

Baczynska, G. (2019), 'EU's Tusk Says Brexit "Backstop" Not Renegotiable', *Reuters*, 29 January.

Baker, D., Gamble, A., and Ludlam, S. (1994), 'The Parliamentary Siege of Maastricht 1993: Conservative Divisions and British Ratification', *Parliamentary Affairs*, 47(1), 37–60.

Baker, S., and Wilson, S. (2018), 'We Will Vote Against a Deal That Prioritises the EU Over the UK', *Sunday Telegraph*, 11 November.

Bale, T. (2006), 'Between a Soft and a Hard Place? The Conservative Party, Valence Politics and the Need for a New "Eurorealism"', *Parliamentary Affairs*, 59(3), 385–400.

Bale, T. (2016), *The Conservative Party: From Thatcher to Cameron* (Cambridge: Polity Press).

Bale, T. (2018), 'Who Leads and Who Follows? The Symbiotic Relationship Between UKIP and the Conservatives—and Populism and Euroscepticism', *Politics*, 38(3), 263–77.

Bale, T., Cygan, A., and Russell, M., eds (2020), *Parliament and Brexit* (London: UK in a Changing Europe).

Bale, T., and Rovira Kaltwasser, C., eds (2021), *Riding the Populist Wave: Europe's Mainstream Right in Crisis* (Cambridge: Cambridge University Press).

Bale, T., and Webb, P. (2018), '"We Didn't See it Coming": The Conservatives', *Parliamentary Affairs*, 71(Supplement 1), 46–58.

Bale, T., Webb, P., and Poletti, M. (2019), *Footsoldiers: Political Party Membership in the 21st Century* (Abingdon: Routledge).

Ball, S. (2003), 'The Conservatives in Opposition, 1906–79: A Comparative Analysis', in M. Garnett and P. Lynch, eds, *The Conservatives in Crisis* (Manchester: Manchester University Press).

Banks, A. (2016), *The Bad Boys of Brexit: Tales of Mischief, Mayhem and Guerrilla Warfare in the EU Referendum Campaign* (London: Biteback).

Barber, N. (2011), 'The Afterlife of Parliamentary Sovereignty', *International Journal of Constitutional Law*, 9(1), 144–54.

Barber, N. (2019), 'Prorogation, Prerogative, and the Supreme Court', *Harvard Law Review blog*, 3 October.

Barber, N. (2021), *The United Kingdom Constitution: An Introduction* (Oxford: Oxford University Press).

Barber, N., Hickman, T., and King, J. (2016), 'Pulling the Article 50 "Trigger": Parliament's Indispensable Role', *UK Constitutional Law Association blog*, 27 June.

Barber, N., Hickman, T., and King, J. (2018), 'Reflections on Miller', in D. Clarry, ed., *The UK Supreme Court Yearbook, Volume 8: 2016–17 Legal Year* (Barlaston: Appellate Press).

Barnard, C. (2022), 'Taking Back Control: Rule by Law(s) and the Executive in the Post-Brexit World', *Oxford Review of Economic Policy*, 38(1), 11–26.

Barnard, C., and Menon, A., eds (2018), *What Would 'Trading on WTO Terms' Mean for the UK?* (London: UK in a Changing Europe).

Barnier, M. (2018), 'Statement by Michel Barnier at the Press Conference Following His Meeting with Dominic Raab, UK Secretary of State for Exiting the EU', *European Commission website*, 26 July.

Bartlett, N., and Bloom, D. (2019), 'Furious Tory Hopefuls Round on "Dictator" Dominic Raab's Brexit Plan', *Daily Mirror*, 16 June.

Barwell, G. (2020), *Brexit Witness Archive interview*, 1 and 25 September (London: UK in a Changing Europe).

Barwell, G. (2021), *Chief of Staff: Notes from Downing Street* (London: Atlantic Books).

Bate, A., Baker, C., Uberoi, E., Audickas, L., Dempsey, N., Hawkins, O., Cracknell, R., McInnes, R., Rutherford, T., and Apostolova, V. (2019), *General Election 2017: Results and Analysis*, CBP-7979 (London: House of Commons Library).

BBC (2019), 'Today', *BBC Radio 4*, 10 June.

BBC (2020), 'Episode 22: The Spartans', *Brexit: A Love Story*, 31 August, https://www.bbc.co.uk/sounds/play/p08q3nf8.

BBC News (2016a), 'Boris Johnson: Brexit Would Not Affect Irish Border', *BBC News*, 29 February.

BBC News (2016b), 'Corbyn: I'm "Seven out of 10" on EU', *BBC News*, 11 June.

BBC News (2016c), 'Reality Check: Has Corbyn Changed His Mind on Article 50?', *BBC News*, 22 July.

BBC News (2017), 'Arlene Foster: Brexit Deal Paper Was a "Big Shock" for DUP', *BBC News*, 5 December.

BBC News (2018), 'Brexit: "People's Vote" Campaign Group Launched', *BBC News*, 15 April.

BBC News (2019a), 'Boris Johnson's Brexit Policy "Unacceptable" – EU Negotiator', *BBC News*, 25 July.

BBC News (2019b), 'Boris Johnson's Letter to Jeremy Corbyn Calling for a General Election', *BBC News*, 24 October.

BBC News (2019c), 'Brexit: Boris Johnson Has Ruled Out NI-Only Backstop', *BBC News*, 11 September.

BBC News (2019d), 'Brexit: Boris Johnson to Try for 12 December Election', *BBC News*, 24 October.

BBC News (2019e), 'Brexit: EU Extension Decision Expected on Friday', *BBC News*, 24 October.

BBC News (2019f), 'Corbyn: We Will Support Election if No-Deal Is "Off the Table"', *BBC News*, 24 October.

BBC News (2019g), 'European Election 2019: UK Results in Maps and Charts', *BBC News*, 27 May.

BBC News (2019h), 'General Election 2019: Boris Johnson's interview with Andrew Marr fact-checked', *BBC News*, 1 December.

BBC News (2019i), 'General election 2019: Brexit Party Will Not Stand in Tory Seats', *BBC News*, 11 November.

BBC News (2019j), 'Independent Group: Three MPs Quit Tory Party to Join', *BBC News*, 20 February.

BBC News (2019k), 'Labour Prepared to Back New Brexit Referendum', *BBC News*, 25 February.

BBC News (2019l), 'Local Elections: Results in Maps and Charts', *BBC News*, 3 May.

BBC News (2019m), 'Parliament Suspension Sparks Furious Backlash', *BBC News*, 29 August.

BBC News (2019n), 'PM: I'd Rather Be Dead in Ditch Than Delay Brexit', *BBC News*, 5 September.

BBC News (2020), 'Coronavirus: Two Cases Confirmed in UK', *BBC News*, 31 January.

BBC Newsnight (2019), Tweet of 28 August (@BBCNewsnight), https://twitter.com/BBCNewsnight/status/1166832299649855488.

Benn, H. (2018), 'Indicative of the Times', *The House magazine*, 20 December.

Benn, H. (2021), *Brexit Witness Archive interview* (London: UK in a Changing Europe).

Benton, M., and Russell, M. (2013), 'Assessing the Impact of Parliamentary Oversight Committees: The Select Committees in the British House of Commons', *Parliamentary Affairs*, 66(4), 772–97.

Berberi, C. (2017), 'Northern Ireland: Is Brexit a Threat to the Peace Process and the Soft Irish Border?', *Revue Française de Civilisation Britannique*, 22(2).

Bercow, J. (2020a), *Brexit Witness Archive interview*, 21 July (London: UK in a Changing Europe).

Bercow, J. (2020b), *Unspeakable: The Autobiography* (London: Weidenfeld & Nicolson).

Berger, L. (2019), Tweet of 17 August (@lucianaberger), https://twitter.com/lucianaberger/status/1162823999048601602.

Berry, J. M. (2003), 'Validity and Reliability Issues in Elite Interviewing', *PS: Political Science & Politics*, 35(4), 679–82.

Birch, A. H. (1964), *Representative and Responsible Government: An Essay on the British Constitution* (London: George Allen & Unwin).

Blair, T. (2018), 'The In-Betweener Solution is the Worst of All Worlds: Parliament Should Reject it', *Tony Blair Institute for Global Change blog*, 15 July.

Blick, A., and Hennessy, P. (2019), *Good Chaps No More? Safeguarding the Constitution in Stressful Times* (London: Constitution Society).

Blondel, J. (1997), 'Political Opposition in the Contemporary World', *Government and Opposition*, 32(4), 462–86.

Blood, D., Elliott, O., and Burn-Murdoch, J. (2019), '"Toxic" Tweets Aimed At MPs Soar After Johnson Outburst', *Financial Times*, 27 October.

Boffey, D., and Mason, R. (2019), 'Boris Johnson Has No Intention of Renegotiating Brexit Deal, EU Told', *Guardian*, 5 August.

Bogdanor, V., ed. (1985), *Representatives of the People? Parliamentarians and Constituents in Western Democracies* (Aldershot: Gower).

Bogdanor, V. (1999), *Devolution in the United Kingdom* (Oxford: Oxford University Press).

Bogdanor, V. (2009), *The New British Constitution* (Oxford: Hart).

Bogdanor, V. (2012), 'Imprisoned by a Doctrine: The Modern Defence of Parliamentary Sovereignty', *Oxford Journal of Legal Studies*, 32(1), 179–95.

Bogdanor, V. (2019), *Beyond Brexit: Towards a British Constitution* (London: Bloomsbury).

Bogdanor, V. (2020), *Written Evidence to the House of Lords Constitution Committee's 'Fixed-term Parliaments Act 2011' Inquiry*, FTP0001 (London: House of Lords).

Boles, N. (2018), 'Only the "Norway Plus" Plan Can Save Brexit', *Financial Times*, 27 November.

Bowcott, O., and Carrell, S. (2019), 'Government Forced to Reveal Confidential Memos on Prorogation', *Guardian*, 5 September.

Bowcott, O., Mason, R., and Asthana, A. (2017), 'Supreme Court Rules Parliament Must Have Vote to Trigger Article 50', *Guardian*, 24 September.

Bower, T. (2020), *Boris Johnson: The Gambler* (London: W.H. Allen).

Bowler, S., Farrell, D. M., and Katz, R. S. (1999), 'Party Cohesion, Party Discipline, and Parliaments', in S. Bowler, D. M. Farrell, and R. S. Katz, eds, *Party Discipline and Parliamentary Government* (Columbus: Ohio State University Press).

Brady, G. (2018), 'Blue Letter Day', *The House magazine*, 18 December.

Braverman, S. (2020), 'People We Elect Must Take Back Control From People We Don't. Who Include the Judges', *ConservativeHome*, 27 January.

BrexitCentral (2019), 'The "Star Chamber" Has Reported on the Government's Latest Legal Advice; The Advice Does Not Meet the Tests the Government Set Itself', *BrexitCentral*, 12 March.

Burke, E. (2000 [1774]), 'Speech at the Conclusion of the Poll', in D. Bromwich, ed., *On Empire, Liberty and Reform: Speeches and Letters* (New Haven: Yale University Press).

Burt, A. (2018), Tweet of 17 November (@AlistairBurtUK), https://twitter.com/AlistairBurtUK/status/1063746585442623488.

Butterworth, B. (2018), 'Full Text of Boris Johnson's "Alternative Leader's Speech" at Conservative Party Conference Fringe', *i*, 2 October.

Cameron, D. (2006), 'Leader's Speech, Bournemouth', *UKpol.co.uk*, 1 October.

Cameron, D. (2013), 'EU Speech at Bloomberg', *Gov.UK*, 23 January.

Cameron, D. (2015a), 'A New Settlement for the United Kingdom in a Reformed European Union', 10 November, https://assets.publishing.service.gov.uk/government/uploads/system/uploads/attachment_data/file/475679/Donald_Tusk_letter.pdf (London: HM Government).

Cameron, D. (2015b), 'Prime Minister's Speech on Europe', *Gov.UK*, 10 November.

Cameron, D. (2015c), Tweet of 4 May (@David_Cameron), https://twitter.com/david_cameron/status/595112367358406656.

Cameron, D. (2016), 'PM Statement Following Cabinet Meeting on EU Settlement', *Gov.UK*, 20 February.

Cameron, D. (2019a), *For the Record* (London: William Collins).

Cameron, S. (2019b), 'Unsung Officials', *The House magazine*, 4 March.

Campbell, A. (2021), *Brexit Witness Archive interview*, 5 March (London: UK in a Changing Europe).

Carey, J. M. (2007), 'Competing Principals, Political Institutions, and Party Unity in Legislative Voting', *American Journal of Political Science*, 51(1), 92–107.

Carter, N., Evans, M., Alderman, K., and Gorham, S. (1998), 'Europe, Goldsmith and the Referendum Party', *Parliamentary Affairs*, 51(3), 470–85.

Cherry, J. (2020), *Brexit Witness Archive interview*, 18 December (London: UK in a Changing Europe).

Clark, N., and Newton Dunn, T. (2019), 'No Commons Sense: MPs' Bid to Kill Off No Deal Brexit Backfires as Minister Claims it Has Actually Increased the Chance of it Happening', *Sun*, 3 April.

Clark, T. (2022), 'Peter Hennessy: Boris Johnson Has Killed Off the "Good Chaps" Theory of Government', *Prospect*, 21 January.

Clarke, H. D., Goodwin, M., and Whiteley, P. (2017), *Brexit: Why Britain Voted to Leave the European Union* (Cambridge: Cambridge University Press).

CNN (2017), 'Theresa May Attacks Jeremy Corbyn and "Coalition of Chaos"', *YouTube*, 3 May, https://www.youtube.com/watch?v=cn2iBVDLSMg.

Coakley, J., and Todd, J. (2020), *Negotiating a Settlement in Northern Ireland, 1969–2019* (Oxford: Oxford University Press).

Coates, S. (2018a), 'Brexit: Senior Tory Pleads for Delay to Brexit Vote', *Times*, 6 December.

Coates, S. (2018b), 'Brexiteers Sharpening Their Pens for Letters of No Confidence in May', *Times*, 15 November.

Cockburn, H. (2016), 'Brexit Campaigner Admits He Set Up Second EU Referendum Petition Signed by Three Million People', *Independent on Sunday*, 26 June.

Conservative Party (2010), *Invitation to Join the Government of Britain. The Conservative Manifesto 2010* (London: Conservative Party).

Conservative Party (2015), *Strong Leadership, a Clear Economic Plan, a Brighter, More Secure Future. The Conservative Party Manifesto 2015* (London: Conservative Party).

Conservative Party (2017), *Forward Together: Our Plan for a Stronger Britain and a Prosperous Future. The Conservative and Unionist Party Manifesto 2017* (London: Conservative Party).

Conservative Party (2019a), *Get Brexit Done: Unleash Britain's Potential. The Conservative and Unionist Party Manifesto 2019* (London: Conservative Party).

Conservative Party (2019b), *How to Show You Want a Brexit Deal Delivered as Soon as Possible* (London: Conservative Party).

Constitution Committee (2015), *European Union Referendum Bill (Fifth Report of Session 2015–16)*, HL Paper 40 (London: House of Lords).

Constitution Committee (2016), *The Invoking of Article 50 (Fourth Report of Session 2016–17)*, HL Paper 44 (London: House of Lords).

Constitution Committee (2017a), *European Union (Withdrawal) Bill: Interim Report (Third Report of Session 2017–19)*, HL Paper 19 (London: House of Lords).

Constitution Committee (2017b), *The 'Great Repeal Bill' and Delegated Powers (Ninth Report of Session 2016–17)*, HL Paper 123 (London: House of Lords).

Constitution Committee (2018), *European Union (Withdrawal) Bill (Ninth Report of Session 2017–19)*, HL Paper 69 (London: House of Lords).

Constitution Committee (2020), *European Union (Withdrawal Agreement) Bill (First Report of Session 2019–21)*, HL Paper 5 (London: House of Lords).

Constitution Committee (2021), *COVID-19 and the Use and Scrutiny of Emergency Powers (Third Report of Session 2021–22)*, HL Paper 15 (London: House of Lords).

Cooper, C., and Forster, K. (2016), 'EU Referendum: Nigel Farage Says it "Looks Like Remain Will Edge it" as Polls Close', *Independent*, 23 June.

Cooper, Y. (2017), 'After This Result, a Tory Cabal Cannot Be Allowed to Negotiate Brexit Alone', *Guardian*, 12 June.

Corbyn, J. (2017), 'Jeremy Corbyn Speech to Labour Party Conference', *Labour Party website*, 27 September.

Corbyn, J. (2018), 'Jeremy Corbyn Full Speech on Britain After Brexit', *Labour Party website*, 26 February.

Corbyn, J. (2019a), 'Cross-Party Brexit Talks Have "Gone as Far as They Can" – Corbyn's Letter', *LabourList*, 17 May.

Corbyn, J. (2019b), Tweet of 14 August (@jeremycorbyn), https://twitter.com/jeremycorbyn/status/1161751909788782594.

Corbyn, J. (2019c), Tweet of 24 May (@jeremycorbyn), https://twitter.com/jeremycorbyn/status/1131860524549967872.

Cormacain, R. (2022), *Northern Ireland Protocol Bill: A Rule of Law Analysis of its Compliance with International Law* (London: Bingham Centre for the Rule of Law).

Courea, E. (2019), 'Welby in Talks Over Citizens' Assembly to Avoid No-Deal Brexit', *Times*, 26 August.

Courea, E., and Devlin, K. (2019), 'Justin Welby's Brexit Citizens' Assembly Will Be a Broad Church', *Times*, 28 August.

Cowie, G. (2019), 'The New EU (Withdrawal Agreement) Bill: What's changed?', *House of Commons Library Insight*, 19 December.

Cowie, G., and Samra, S. (2019), 'Taking Control of the Order Paper', *House of Commons Library Insight*, 26 June.

Cowley, P., ed. (1998), *Conscience and Parliament* (London: Frank Cass).

Cowley, P. (2005), *The Rebels: How Blair Mislaid His Majority* (London: Politico's).

Cowley, P. (2006), 'Making Parliament Matter?', in P. Dunleavy, R. Heffernan, P. Cowley, and C. Hay, eds, *Developments in British Politics 8* (Basingstoke: Palgrave Macmillan).

Cowley, P. (2017), 'EU Referendum One Year on—MPs', *UK in a Changing Europe blog*, 26 June.

Cowley, P. (2019), 'Proportionally, This Brexit Rebellion Beats Even Iraq', *Times*, 16 January.

Cowley, P. (2021), 'The Calling of the Election', in R. Ford, T. Bale, W. Jennings, and P. Surridge, eds, *The British General Election of 2019* (Cham: Palgrave Macmillan).

Cowley, P., and Kavanagh, D. (2018), *The British General Election of 2017* (Cham: Palgrave Macmillan).

Cowley, P., and Stuart, M. (2010), 'Where Has All the Trouble Gone? British Intra-Party Parliamentary Divisions During the Lisbon Ratification', *British Politics*, 5(2), 133–48.

Cowley, P., and Stuart, M. (2012a), 'The Cambusters: The Conservative European Union Referendum Rebellion of October 2011', *Political Quarterly*, 83(2), 402–6.

Cowley, P., and Stuart, M. (2012b), 'A Coalition with Two Wobbly Wings: Backbench Dissent in the House of Commons', *Political Insight*, 3(1), 8–11.

Cox, G. (2019), 'Legal Opinion on Joint Instrument and Unilateral Declaration concerning the Withdrawal Agreement', 12 March, https://assets.publishing.service.gov.uk/government/uploads/system/uploads/attachment_data/file/785188/190312_-_Legal_Opinion_on_Joint_Instrument_and_Unilateral_Declaration_co.._2_.pdf (London: HM Government).

Craig, J. (2020), 'Coronavirus Could Shut Down Parliament for Months Under Emergency Plans', *Sky News*, 5 March.

Craig, P. (2017), 'Epilogue: Miller, the Legislature and the Executive', in S. Juss and M. Sunkin, eds, *Landmark Cases in Public Law* (Oxford: Hart).

Craig, P. (2018), 'The Withdrawal Bill, Status and Supremacy', *UK Constitutional Law Association blog*, 19 February.

Craig, R. (2020), *Written Evidence to the House of Commons Public Administration and Constitutional Affairs Committee's 'Fixed-term Parliaments Act 2011' Inquiry*, FTP10 (London: House of Commons).

Creasy, S. (2017), Tweet of 18 April (@stellacreasy), https://twitter.com/stellacreasy/status/854452349456265220.

Crewe, I., and King, A. (1995), *SDP: The Birth, Life, and Death of the Social Democratic Party* (Oxford: Oxford University Press).

Crick, B. (1962), *In Defence of Politics* (London: Weidenfeld & Nicolson).

Culbertson, A. (2018), 'Six Labour MPs Quit Frontbench Roles Over Key Brexit Vote', *Sky News*, 14 June.

Cummings, D. (2015), 'On the Referendum #6: Exit Plans and a Second Referendum', *Dominic Cummings's blog*, 23 June.

Cummings, D. (2021a), Tweet of 12 October (@Dominic2306), https://twitter.com/Dominic2306/status/1448018739623038982.

Cummings, D. (2021b), Tweet of 18 June (@Dominic2306), https://twitter.com/Dominic2306/status/1405827979029237762.

Curtice, J. (2013), 'Politicians, Voters and Democracy: The 2011 UK Referendum on the Alternative Vote', *Electoral Studies*, 32(2), 215–23.

Curtice, J. (2016a), 'How Leave Won the Battle but Remain May Still Win the War', *What UK Thinks EU blog*, 23 June.

Curtice, J. (2016b), 'Is David Cameron Now Leader of the Opposition?', *What UK Thinks EU blog*, 29 February.

Curtice, J. (2017a), 'General Election 2017: A New Two-Party Politics?', *Political Insight*, 8(2), 4–8.

Curtice, J. (2017b), 'Why Leave Won the UK's EU Referendum', *Journal of Common Market Studies*, 55(S1), 19–37.

Curtice, J. (2020), 'What Do the Public Think?', in T. Bale, A. Cygan. and M. Russell, eds, *Parliament and Brexit* (London: UK in a Changing Europe).

Curtice, J., Fisher, S., and English, P. (2021), 'The Geography of a Brexit Election: How Constituency Context and the Electoral System Shaped the Outcome', in R. Ford, T. Bale, W. Jennings, and P. Surridge, eds, *The British General Election of 2019* (Cham: Palgrave Macmillan).

Curtice, J., and Ormston, R., eds (2015), *British Social Attitudes 32* (London: NatCen).

Curtis, J. (2018), 'The Backstop Explained', *House of Commons Library Insight*, 12 December.

Cygan, A., Lynch, P., and Whitaker, R. (2019), *MPs' Positions on the UK's Referendum on European Union Membership 2016* (Colchester: UK Data Service).

Cygan, A., Lynch, P., and Whitaker, R. (2021), *2019 UK General Election Candidates' and Incumbents' Positions in the UK's Referendum on Membership of the European Union, 2019–2020* (Colchester: UK Data Service).

da Costa, N. (2021), 'The Nikki da Costa Edition', *Women With Balls Podcast (The Spectator)*, 22 October, https://www.spectator.co.uk/podcast/the-nikki-da-costa-edition.

Daddow, O. (2012), 'The UK Media and "Europe": From Permissive Consensus to Destructive Dissent', *International Affairs*, 88(6), 1219–36.

Daddow, O. (2013), 'Margaret Thatcher, Tony Blair and the Eurosceptic Tradition in Britain', *British Journal of Politics and International Relations*, 15(2), 210–27.

Daddow, O. (2015), 'Interpreting the Outsider Tradition in British European Policy Speeches from Thatcher to Cameron', *JCMS: Journal of Common Market Studies*, 53(1), 71–88.

Daily Express (2010), 'Get Britain Out of Europe', *Daily Express*, 25 November.

Daily Express (2017), 'Vote May or We Face Disaster: It's Time for Patriotic Realism Not Socialist Indulgence', *Daily Express*, 7 June.

Daily Express (2019a), 'Brussels Bullies Must Heed This Vote and Compromise', *Daily Express*, 16 January.

Daily Express (2019b), 'A Remainer Parliament Has Sought to Thwart the Will of the Majority', *Daily Express*, 13 March.

Daily Mail (2017), 'Crush the Saboteurs', *Daily Mail*, 19 April.

Daily Mail (2019a), 'Brexit Rebels Force PM to Fight Fire with Fire', *Daily Mail*, 29 August.

Daily Mail (2019b), 'Cease This Destructive Game of Vanity Politics', *Daily Mail*, 21 March.

Daily Mail (2019c), 'Daily Mail Comment', *Daily Mail*, 16 January.

Daily Mail (2019d), 'Don't Let Theresa's Sacrifice Be in Vain', *Daily Mail*, 28 March.

Daily Mail (2019e), 'These Tory Wreckers Will Not Be Forgiven', *Daily Mail*, 13 March.

Daily Mail (2020), 'A New Dawn for Britain', *Daily Mail*, 31 January.

Daily Telegraph (2016), 'EU Summit: David Cameron's Difficult Day is Exactly Why Europe Needs Reform', *Daily Telegraph*, 19 February.

Daily Telegraph (2017), 'The Tory Brexit Rebels Have Left Theresa May Exposed. Is That Really in the National Interest?', *Daily Telegraph*, 13 December.

Daily Telegraph (2019), 'Only an Election Can End This Saga', *Daily Telegraph*, 22 October.

Daly, P. and Baynes, M. (2019), 'Johnson Tells Northern Ireland Businesses to "Bin" Customs Forms', *Belfast Telegraph*, 8 November.

Daniels, P. (1998), 'From Hostility to "Constructive Engagement": The Europeanisation of the Labour Party', *West European Politics*, 21(1), 72–96.

D'Arcy, M. (2016), 'Brexit: How Rebel MPs Outfoxed Cameron to Get an EU Referendum', *BBC News*, 29 December.

Dathan, M., and Clark, N. (2017), 'Right Dog's Brexfast: Fresh Tory Civil War Erupts Over Brexit as Remainers Seek to Exploit Theresa May's Weakened Position to Push Pro-EU Agenda', *Sun*, 11 June.

David-Barrett, L. (2022), 'Is the UK Sliding Into State Capture?', *Constitution Society blog*, 5 May.

Davidson, D. (2020), *Brexit Witness Archive interview*, 14 September (London: UK in a Changing Europe).

Davis, D. (2018a), 'Labour Exit Bill Proposal Will Not Give Brits the Brexit They Deserve', *Sun*, 29 April.

Davis, D. (2018b), 'We Must Defeat Theresa May's Wretched Brexit Deal and Go Out Into the World with Hope and Imagination ', *Daily Telegraph*, 8 December.

Davis, D. (2021), *Brexit Witness Archive interview*, 8 July (London: UK in a Changing Europe).

Delegated Powers and Regulatory Reform Committee (2018), *European Union (Withdrawal) Bill (Twelfth Report of Session 2017–19)*, HL Paper 73 (London: House of Lords).

Delegated Powers and Regulatory Reform Committee (2020), *European Union (Withdrawal Agreement) Bill (First Report of Session 2019–21)*, HL Paper 3 (London: House of Lords).

Delegated Powers and Regulatory Reform Committee (2021), *Democracy Denied? The Urgent Need to Rebalance Power Between Parliament and the Executive (Twelfth Report of Session 2021–22)*, HL Paper 106 (London: House of Lords).

Demianyk, G. (2019), 'Jacob Rees-Mogg Calls Supreme Court Ruling a "Constitutional Coup"', *Huffington Post*, 24 September.

Democratic Unionist Party (2017), *Standing Strong for Northern Ireland. The DUP Manifesto for the 2017 Westminster Election* (Belfast: Democratic Unionist Party).

Democratic Unionist Party (2019), *Let's Get the UK Moving Again. Manifesto General Election 2019* (Belfast: Democratic Unionist Party).

Dempsey, N. (2017), 'Brexit: Votes by Constituency', *House of Commons Library Insight*, 6 February.

Denham, A., and O'Hara, K. (2007), 'The Three "Mantras": "Modernization" and the Conservative Party', *British Politics*, 2, 167–90.

Dennison, J. (2020), 'How Niche Parties React to Losing Their Niche: The Cases of the Brexit Party, the Green Party and Change UK ', *Parliamentary Affairs*, 73(Supplement 1), 125–41.

Denver, D. (2018), 'Results: How Britain Voted', *Parliamentary Affairs*, 71(Supplement 1), 8–28.

Devlin, K. (2019), 'Boris Johnson Lays Ground for "People Versus Politicians" General Election', *Times*, 5 August.

Diamond, P. (2016), 'Assessing the Performance of UK Opposition Leaders: Jeremy Corbyn's "Straight Talking, Honest Politics"', *Politics and Governance*, 4(2), 15–24.

Dicey, A. V. (1962 [1885]), *Introduction to the Study of the Law of the Constitution* (London: Macmillan).

Doherty, D. (2018), 'Brexit: The History of the Tories' Influential European Research Group', *BBC News*, 19 January.

Dominiczak, P., Hope, C., and McCann, K. (2016), 'The Judges Versus the People', *Daily Telegraph*, 4 November.

Dorey, P., and Denham, A. (2016), ' "The Longest Suicide Vote in History": The Labour Party Leadership Election of 2015', *British Politics*, 11(3), 259–82.

Döring, H. (2001), 'Parliamentary Agenda Control and Legislative Outcomes in Western Europe', *Legislative Studies Quarterly*, 26(1), 145–65.

Drewry, G. (2016), 'Euroscepticism and Parliamentary Sovereignty: The Lingering Shadows of Factortame and Thoburn', in A. Horne and A. Le Sueur, eds, *Parliament: Legislation and Accountability* (Oxford: Hart).

Dromey, J., and Spelman, C. (2018), Letter to Theresa May, 17 December, https://twitter.com/RupaHuq/status/1082200845964505088 (Twitter).

Duncan, A. (2021), *In the Thick of It: The Private Diaries of a Minister* (London: William Collins).

Dunleavy, P. (2005), 'Facing Up to Multi-Party Politics: How Partisan Dealignment and PR Voting Have Fundamentally Changed Britain's Party Systems', *Parliamentary Affairs*, 58(3), 503–32.

DUP (2019), Tweet of 17 October (@duponline), https://twitter.com/duponline/status/1184707245478678533.

Ekins, R., and Gee, G. (2017), 'Putting Judicial Power in its Place', *University of Queensland Law Journal*, 36(2), 375–98.

Ekins, R., and Laws, S. (2019), 'Stop This Power Grab by MPs Or Chaos Governs', *Sunday Times*, 31 March.

Electoral Commission (2013), *Referendum on the United Kingdom's Membership of the European Union: Advice of the Electoral Commission on the Referendum Question Included in the European Union (Referendum) Bill* (London: Electoral Commission).

Electoral Commission (2015), *Referendum on Membership of the European Union: Assessment of the Electoral Commission on the Proposed Referendum Question* (London: Electoral Commission).

Electoral Commission (2016), 'Results and Turnout at the EU Referendum', *Electoral Commission website*, 25 September.

Elgot, J. (2017), 'Osborne Says Theresa May is a "Dead Woman Walking"', *Observer*, 11 June.

Elgot, J. (2019a), 'Brexit Talks: Stumbling Blocks That Threaten a Labour and Tory Deal', *Guardian*, 9 April.

Elgot, J. (2019b), 'Brexit: John Bercow Rules Out Third Meaningful Vote on Same Deal', *Guardian*, 18 March.

Elgot, J. (2019c), 'John Major to Join Legal Fight to Stop Johnson Suspending Parliament', *Guardian*, 30 August.

Elgot, J., and Stewart, H. (2020), 'Brexit: Internal Market Bill Passes by 77 Votes Amid Tory Party Tension', *Guardian*, 14 September.

Elgot, J., Syal, R., and Boffey, D. (2020), 'Senior Tories Urge Ministers to Scrap "Illegal" Brexit Rule Plan', *Guardian*, 8 September.

Elliott, F. (2019), 'Boris Johnson "Won't Rule Out Suspending Parliament"', *Times*, 13 June.

Elliott, F., Coates, S., and Wright, O. (2019), 'Fearful Brexiteers Swing Behind May's Deal', *Times*, 27 March.

Elliott, F., and Courea, E. (2019), 'Accept No-Deal As an Option Or Lose Job, Boris Johnson Warns Cabinet', *Times*, 28 June.

Elliott, F., and Wright, O. (2019), 'MPs Seize Control of Brexit', *Times*, 26 March.

Elliott, F., Zeffman, H., and Webber, E. (2019), 'We're Not Enemies of the People: MPs Revolt After May's Onslaught Over Brexit Chaos', *Times*, 22 March.

Elliott, M. (2016), 'On Why, as a Matter of Law, Triggering Article 50 Does Not Require Parliament to Legislate', *Public Law for Everyone blog*, 30 June.

Elliott, M. (2017a), 'Does the Salisbury Convention Apply During a Hung Parliament?', *Public Law for Everyone blog*, 10 June.

Elliott, M. (2017b), 'The EU Withdrawal Bill: Initial Thoughts', *Public Law for Everyone blog*, 14 July.

Elliott, M. (2017c), 'The Supreme Court's Judgment in Miller: In Search of Constitutional Principle', *Cambridge Law Journal*, 76(2), 257–88.

Elliott, M. (2019a), 'Brexit, the Executive and Parliament: A Response to John Finnis', *Public Law for Everyone blog*, 2 April.

Elliott, M. (2019b), 'Can the Government Veto Legislation by Advising the Queen to Withhold Royal Assent?', *Public Law for Everyone blog*, 21 January.

Elliott, M. (2019c), 'Parliamentary Sovereignty in a Changing Constitutional Landscape', in J. Jowell, and C. O'Cinneide, eds, *The Changing Constitution* (Oxford: Oxford University Press).

Elliott, M. (2020), Tweet of 10 September (@ProfMarkElliott), https://twitter.com/ProfMarkElliott/status/1304076146154319872.

Elliott, M. (2022), 'The Northern Ireland Protocol Bill', *Public Law for Everyone blog*, 13 June.

Elliott, M., Williams, J., and Young, A. L. (2018), 'The Miller Tale: An Introduction', in M. Elliott, J. Williams, and A. L. Young, eds, *The UK Constitution After Miller: Brexit and Beyond* (Oxford: Hart).

Emmerson, C., Johnson, P., and Mitchell, I. (2016), *The EU Single Market: The Value of Membership Versus Access to the UK* (London: Institute for Fiscal Studies).

ERG (2018), *Your Right to Know: The Case Against Chequers and the Draft Withdrawal Agreement in Plain English* (London: European Research Group).

ERG (2021), *Re-Uniting the Kingdom: How and Why to Replace the Northern Ireland Protocol* (London: European Research Group).

Erskine May, T. (2019), 'Erskine May's Treatise on the Law, Privileges, Proceedings and Usage of Parliament (25th edn.)', *UK Parliament website*.

European Union Committee (2017), *Brexit: Devolution (Fourth Report of Session 2017–19)*, HL Paper 9 (London: House of Lords).

European Union Committee (2020), *Brexit: The Revised Withdrawal Agreement and Political Declaration (First Report of Session 2019–21)*, HL Paper 4 (London: House of Lords).

Evans, G., and Butt, S. (2007), 'Explaining Change in British Public Opinion on the European Union: Top Down or Bottom Up?', *Acta Politica*, 42(2), 173–90.

Evans, G., de Geus, R., and Green, J. (2021), 'Boris Johnson to the Rescue? How the Conservatives Won the Radical-Right Vote in the 2019 General Election', *Political Studies* [early view].

Evans, G., and Menon, A. (2017), *Brexit and British Politics* (Cambridge: Polity Press).

Evans, P. (2020), *Braking the Law: Is There, and Should There Be, an Executive Veto Over Legislation in the UK Constitution?* (London: Constitution Unit).

Evans-Pritchard, A. (2016), 'Brexit Vote is About the Supremacy of Parliament and Nothing Else: Why I Am Voting to Leave the EU', *Daily Telegraph*, 13 June.

Exiting the European Union Committee (2017a), *Oral Evidence: The Progress of the UK's Negotiations on EU Withdrawal*, 25 October, HC 372 (London: House of Commons).

Exiting the European Union Committee (2017b), *The Process for Exiting the European Union and the Government's Negotiating Objectives (First Report of Session 2016–17)*, HC 815 (London: House of Commons).

Exiting the European Union Committee (2018a), *The Future UK–EU Relationship (Fourth Report of Session 2017–19)*, HC 935 (London: House of Commons).

Exiting the European Union Committee (2018b), *The Progress of the UK's Negotiations on EU Withdrawal (March to May 2018) (Fifth Report of Session 2017–19)*, HC 1060 (London: House of Commons).

Exiting the European Union Committee (2018c), *The Progress of the UK's Negotiations on EU Withdrawal: December 2017 to March 2018 (Third Report of Session 2017–19)*, HC 884 (London: House of Commons).

Exiting the European Union Committee (2019), *Response to the Vote on the Withdrawal Agreement and Political Declaration: Options for Parliament (Eleventh Report of Session 2017–19)*, HC 1902 (London: House of Commons).

Farage, N. (2016), 'It Costs £55 Million a Day to be an EU Member—and For What?', *Daily Express*, 8 February.

Fella, S., Ferguson, D., Webb, D., Jozepa, I., Ares, E., and Kennedy, S. (2020), *The UK–EU Trade and Cooperation Agreement: Summary and Implementation*, CBP-9106 (London: House of Commons Library).

Fieldhouse, E., and Prosser, C. (2017), 'The Brexit Election? The 2017 General Election in Ten Charts', *British Election Study website*, 1 August.

Financial Times (2019a), 'Boris Johnson's Unlawful Conduct Has Been Called to Account', *Financial Times*, 24 September.

Financial Times (2019b), 'Theresa May Must Show Her Change of Heart is Serious', *Financial Times*, 3 April.

Finkelstein, D. (2022), 'Time to Cut Members out of Tory Leadership', *Times*, 19 July.

Finnis, J. (2019a), 'Only One Option Remains with Brexit—Prorogue Parliament and Allow Us Out of the EU With No-Deal', *Daily Telegraph*, 1 April.

Finnis, J. (2019b), *The Unconstitutionality of the Supreme Court's Prorogation Judgment* (London: Policy Exchange).

Fitzpatrick, S., Axe-Brown, A., Smith, M., Abraham, T., Curtis, C., and McDonnell, A. (2019), 'The Key Findings From Our Final MRP Poll', *YouGov website*, 10 December.

Fleming, T. G. (2021), 'Parliamentary Procedure Under Theresa May: Nothing Has Changed?', *Parliamentary Affairs*, 74(4), 943–63.

Fleming, T. G., and James, L. (2022), 'Parliamentary Influence on Brexit Legislation, 2017–2019', *Parliamentary Affairs* [early view].

Flinders, M. (2005), 'Majoritarian Democracy in Britain: New Labour and the Constitution', *West European Politics*, 28(1), 61–93.

Flinders, M., and Kelso, A. (2011), 'Mind the Gap: Political Analysis, Public Expectations and the Parliamentary Decline Thesis', *British Journal of Politics and International Relations*, 13(2), 249–68.

Flood, C., and Soborski, R. (2017), 'Euroscepticism as Ideology', in B. Leruth, N. Startin, and S. Usherwood, eds, *The Routledge Handbook of Euroscepticism* (Abingdon: Routledge).

Ford, R., Bale, T., Jennings, W., and Surridge, P. (2021), 'Get Brexit Done: The National Campaign', in R. Ford, T. Bale, W. Jennings, and P. Surridge, eds, *The British General Election of 2019* (Cham: Palgrave Macmillan).

Ford, R., and Goodwin, M. (2014), *Revolt on the Right: Explaining Support for the Radical Right in Britain* (Abingdon: Routledge).

Ford, R., and Sobolewska, M. (2020), *Brexitland: Identity, Diversity and the Reshaping of British Politics* (Cambridge: Cambridge University Press).

Fox, R. (2022), 'Five Problems with the Retained EU Law (Revocation and Reform) Bill', *Hansard Society blog*, 24 October.

Fox, R., and Baston, L. (2019), 'Indicative Votes: Options, Voting Methods and Voting Systems', *Hansard Society blog*, 26 March.

Fox, R., and Blackwell, J. (2014), *The Devil is in the Detail: Parliament and Delegated Legislation* (London: Hansard Society).

Francois, M. (2021), *Spartan Victory: The Inside Story of the Battle for Brexit* (Kindle Direct Publishing).

Freedland, J. (2019), 'Look Past the May-Corbyn Brexit Talks. There's Another Solution', *Guardian*, 3 April.

Frost, D. (2022), 'The Northern Ireland Protocol: How We Got Here, And What Should Happen Now? Keynote Speech by Rt Hon Lord Frost of Allenton CMG', *Policy Exchange website*, 27 April.

Full Fact (2018), 'Did 670,000 March for a People's Vote on Brexit?', *FullFact website*, 24 October.

Garner, O. (2018), 'Case C-621/18, Wightman v Secretary of State for Exiting the European Union: The European Court of Justice Confirms That Article 50 Notification Can Be Unilaterally Revoked', *European Law blog*, 11 December.

Gauke, D. (2020), *Brexit Witness Archive interview*, 26 June (London: UK in a Changing Europe).

Gay, O. (2005), 'MPs Go Back to Their Constituencies', *Political Quarterly*, 76(1), 57–66.

Geddes, A. (2013), *Britain and the European Union* (Basingstoke: Palgrave Macmillan).

George, S. (1998), *An Awkward Partner: Britain in the European Community* (Oxford: Oxford University Press).

George, S. (2007), 'Britain: Anatomy of a Eurosceptic State', *Journal of European Integration*, 22(1), 15–33.

Gifford, C. (2014), 'The People Against Europe: The Eurosceptic Challenge to the United Kingdom's Coalition Government', *JCMS: Journal of Common Market Studies*, 52(3), 512–28.

Gimson, A. (2016), *Boris: The Making of the Prime Minister* (London: Simon & Schuster).

Glencross, A. (2022), 'The Origins of "Cakeism": The British Think Tank Debate over Repatriating Sovereignty and its Impact on the UK's Brexit Strategy', *Journal of European Public Policy* [early view].

Glynn, J., and Menon, A. (2018), 'Brexit', in P. Cowley and D. Kavanagh, eds, *The British General Election of 2017* (Cham: Palgrave Macmillan).

Goes, E. (2020), 'Labour's 2019 Campaign: A Defeat of Epic Proportions', *Parliamentary Affairs*, 73(Supplement 1), 84–102.

Goodman, H. (2019), 'How to Break the Brexit Deadlock', *The House magazine*, 25 February.

Goodman, P. (2017), 'Why the Prime Minister Now Has No Alternative But to Broaden Her Cabinet. Today, She Should Bring Back Gove, Morgan and Grieve', *ConservativeHome*, 10 June.

Goodman, P. (2019), 'Enter—or Rather Exit—the Spartans', *ConservativeHome*, 18 March.

Goodwin, M., and Milazzo, C. (2015), *Britain, the European Union, and the Referendum: What Drives Euroscepticism?* (London: Chatham House).

Gordon, M. (2016), 'The UK's Sovereignty Situation: Brexit, Bewilderment and Beyond...', *King's Law Journal*, 27(3), 333–43.

Gordon, M. (2019), 'Parliamentary Sovereignty and the Political Constitution(s): From Griffith to Brexit', *King's Law Journal*, 30(1), 125–47.

Gove, M. (2016), 'The Facts of Life Say Leave: Why Britain and Europe Will Be Better Off After We Vote Leave', *Vote Leave website*, 19 April.

Gover, D., and James, L. (2021), 'The Hybrid House of Commons: The Problems of Government Control', *Constitution Unit blog*, 17 January.

Green, E. H. H. (2004), *Ideologies of Conservatism: Conservative Political Ideas in the Twentieth Century* (Oxford: Oxford University Press).

Grey, C. (2021), *Brexit Unfolded: How No One Got What They Wanted (and Why They Were Never Going to)* (London: Biteback).

Grice, A. (2019), 'Populism Wins', *Independent*, 13 December.

Grieve, D. (2020), *Brexit Witness Archive interview*, 9 and 20 November (London: UK in a Changing Europe).

Groves, J. (2017), 'Proud of Yourselves?', *Daily Mail*, 14 December.

Groves, J. (2019), 'Rejoice! Boris Set for Thumping Win', *Daily Mail*, 13 December.

Groves, J., and Doyle, J. (2017), 'Tory Rebels Threaten to Frustrate Brexit: Now Fifteen MPs Say They May Vote Against Bid to Enshrine Leaving Date in Law', *Daily Mail*, 15 November.

Groves, J., and Stevens, J. (2019), 'The Brexit Betrayal', *Daily Mail*, 29 March.

Guardian (2017), 'Crowdfunded High Court Challenge Against £1bn Tory–DUP Deal Fails', *Guardian*, 26 October.

Guardian (2019a), 'The Guardian View on Boris Johnson: Guilty But He Won't Go', *Guardian*, 24 September.

Guardian (2019b), 'The Guardian View on Parliament and Brexit: Take Back Control', *Guardian*, 25 March.

Gye, H., Clark, N., and Dathan, M. (2019), 'What a Brexs*itshow: Theresa May's Brexit Deal Crushed by MPs Again Meaning We're No Nearer to Quitting EU After 993 Days', *Sun*, 13 March.

Haggard, S., and Kaufman, R. (2021), *Backsliding: Democratic Regress in the Contemporary World* (Cambridge: Cambridge University Press).

Hague, W. (2017a), 'Brexit Will Defeat the Government Unless it Recognises That Everything Has Changed', *Daily Telegraph*, 13 June.

Hague, W. (2017b), 'The case for an early general election: Theresa May should be free to put her Brexit plans to the people', *Daily Telegraph*, 6 March.

Hague, W. (2022), 'Tory Members Must Not Pick Next Leader', *Times*, 31 October.

Hale, B. (2019), 'Supreme Court: Lady Hale's Statement on "Unlawful" Parliament Suspension', *BBC News*, 24 September.

Hall, M. (2016), 'Why MPs Won't Be Able to Block Brexit', *Daily Express*, 21 December.

Hall, M. (2017a), 'MPs Must Not Stop EU Exit', *Daily Express*, 25 January.

Hall, M. (2017b), 'PM's Brexit Minister Steve Baker Slaps Down Cameron as He Says May Will Not Soften Brexit', *Daily Express*, 15 June.

Hall, M. (2019a), 'Historic deal . . . But MPs Spoil it with Yet More Dithering', *Daily Express*, 23 October.

Hall, M. (2019b), 'They've Now Stolen What's Left of Brexit', *Daily Express*, 26 March.

Hall, M. (2019c), 'Victory for Boris . . . and for Brexit!', *Daily Express*, 13 December.

Hall, M. (2019d), 'We Voted for Brexit, All You Say is No', *Daily Express*, 2 April.

Hall, M. (2019e), 'What More Does She Have to Do?', *Daily Express*, 28 March.

Hammond, P. (2020), *Brexit Witness Archive interview*, 13 and 20 November (London: UK in a Changing Europe).

Hancock, M. (2019), Tweet of 6 June (@MattHancock), https://twitter.com/MattHancock/status/1136610833750994951.

Hanretty, C. (2016), 'Revised Estimates of Leave Vote Share in Westminster Constituencies', *Chris Hanretty's blog*, 18 August.

Hanretty, C. (2017), 'Areal Interpolation and the UK's Referendum on EU Membership', *Journal of Elections, Public Opinion and Parties*, 27(4), 466–83.

Hansard Society (2019), *Audit of Political Engagement 16: The 2019 Report* (London: Hansard Society).

Hansard Society (2021), *Delegated Legislation: The Problems With the Process* (London: Hansard Society).

Hardman, I. (2019), 'The Brady Amendment Gives Theresa May the Strength to Kick the Can Down the Road', *Spectator*, 29 January.

Harris, K. (2022), 'Furious Attorney General: EU-Loving Civil Servants Are Hell-Bent on Wrecking Brexit', *Daily Express*, 3 July.

Hay, C. (2007), *Why We Hate Politics* (Cambridge: Polity Press).

Hayter, D. (2022), Letter to Lord (Gerry) Grimstone of Boscobel, 19 May, https://committees.parliament.uk/publications/22312/documents/164995/default/ (London: House of Lords).

Hayward, K. (2020), 'Customs, Consent and Compromise: The Significance of the Brexit Protocol on Ireland/Northern Ireland', *Fortnight*, 479, 22–4.

Hazell, R. (2008), 'Conclusion: Where Will the Westminster Model End Up?', in R. Hazell, ed., *Constitutional Futures Revisited* (London: Palgrave Macmillan).

Hazell, R. (2010), *Fixed Term Parliaments* (London: Constitution Unit).

Hazell, R. (2019), 'Holding a Queen's Speech in October Risks Heaping More Embarrassment on the Queen', *Constitution Unit blog*, 3 October.

Hazell, R., and Foot, T. (2022), *Executive Power: The Prerogative, Past, Present and Future* (Oxford: Hart).

Hazell, R., Paun, A., Chalmers, M., Yong, B., and Haddon, C. (2009), *Making Minority Government Work: Hung Parliaments and the Challenges for Westminster and Whitehall* (London: Constitution Unit).

Heffer, G. (2019), ' "We Will Bring Him Down" – Tory Rival Rory Stewart's Threat to Boris Johnson', *Sky News*, 13 June.

Helm, T., Savage, M., Rawnsley, A., and Boffey, D. (2019), 'Amber Rudd Quits Cabinet and Attacks PM for "Political Vandalism"', *Guardian*, 8 September.

Helms, L. (2008), 'Studying Parliamentary Opposition in Old and New Democracies: Issues and Perspectives', *Journal of Legislative Studies*, 14(1–2), 6–19.

Hepburn, E., Keating, M., and McEwen, N., eds (2021), *Scotland's New Choice: Independence After Brexit* (Edinburgh: Centre on Constitutional Change).

Heppell, T. (2014), *The Tories: From Winston Churchill to David Cameron* (London: Bloomsbury).

Heppell, T. (2020), 'The Ideological Composition of the Parliamentary Conservative Party from Thatcher to May', in A. Mullen, S. Farrall, and D. Jeffery, eds, *Thatcherism in the 21st Century* (Cham: Palgrave Macmillan).

Heppell, T., and Hill, M. (2005), 'Ideological Typologies of Contemporary British Conservatism', *Political Studies Review*, 3(3), 335–55.

HM Government (2010), *The Coalition: Our Programme for Government* (London: Stationery Office).

HM Government (2016a), 'High Court Ruling on Article 50: Statement', *Gov.UK*, 3 November.

HM Government (2016b), *Why the Government Believes That Voting to Remain in the European Union is the Best Decision for the UK* (London: HM Government).

HM Government (2017), *The United Kingdom's Exit from and New Partnership with the European Union* (London: Stationery Office).

HM Government (2019), *Implications for Business and Trade of a No Deal Exit on 29 March 2019* (London: HM Government).

HM Government (2020), *HMG Legal Position: UKIM Bill and Northern Ireland Protocol* (London: HM Government).

Hobolt, S. B., Leeper, T. J., and Tilley, J. (2020), 'Divided by the Vote: Affective Polarization in the Wake of the Brexit Referendum', *British Journal of Political Science*, 51(4), 1476–93.

Hogarth, R. (2020), 'The Internal Market Bill Breaks International Law and Lays the Ground to Break More Law', *Institute for Government blog*, 9 September.

Hope, C. (2018), 'Jacob Rees-Mogg Submits Letter of No Confidence After Challenging Theresa May in Commons', *Daily Telegraph*, 15 November.

Horne, A. (2021), 'Scrutiny of Treaties by the House of Lords: An Insider's Reflections', *The Table*, 89, 56–65.

House of Commons (2018), *Order Paper, 5 December 2018* (London: House of Commons).

House of Commons (2019a), *Order Paper, 14 February 2019* (London: House of Commons).

House of Commons (2019b), *Order Paper, 25 March 2019* (London: House of Commons).

House of Commons (2021), *Standing Orders: Public Business 2021, 2 December*, HC 804 (London: House of Commons).

Howarth, D. (2021), 'Westminster Versus Whitehall: What the Brexit Debate Revealed About an Unresolved Conflict at the Heart of the British Constitution', in O. Doyle, A. McHarg, and J. Murkens, eds, *The Brexit Challenge for Ireland and the United Kingdom: Constitutions Under Pressure* (Cambridge: Cambridge University Press).

Hunt, J. (2019), 'Jeremy Hunt: I Will 100% Not Prorogue Parliament—Video', *Sky News*, 1 July, https://news.sky.com/video/hunt-i-will-100-not-prorogue-parliament-11752839.

Hunt, T. (2017), 'How Dare They?! Unelected Labour & Lib Dem Lords Plan "to Plunge Brexit into Chaos"', *Daily Express*, 22 June.

Hussain, A. (2019), 'Parliament Prorogation Case Racked Up 30 Million Views, Supreme Court Confirms', *Legal Cheek*, 15 October.

Independent (2019), 'Another Day, Another Disaster for Boris Johnson's Decaying Premiership', *Independent*, 24 September.

Independent Commission on Referendums (2018), *Report of the Independent Commission on Referendums* (London: Constitution Unit).

Institute for Government (2017), 'The Options for the UK's Trading Relationship with the EU', Institute for Government website.

International Trade Committee (2017), *UK Trade Options Beyond 2019 (First Report of Session 2016–17)*, HC 817 (London: House of Commons).

Islam, F. (2019), Tweet of 6 January (@faisalislam), https://twitter.com/faisalislam/status/1082045884593070081.

ITV News (2018a), '100,000 March Through London to Demand People's Vote Referendum on Terms of Brexit', *YouTube*, 23 June, https://www.youtube.com/watch?v=m9LSHXYMkIg.

ITV News (2018b), 'Nigel Dodds Says DUP Will "Be Voting Against Brexit Deal"', *ITV News*, 5 December.

ITV News (2019), Tweet of 24 April (@itvnews), https://twitter.com/itvnews/status/1121107570096259073.

Jackson, B. (2021), 'What We Have Learned About the Conservative Party', *Political Quarterly*, 92(1), 5–6.

James, L., and Russell, M. (2019), 'Parliament, Spin and the Accurate Reporting of Brexit', *Constitution Unit blog*, 24 October.

Jeffery, D., Heppell, T., Hayton, R., and Crines, A. (2018), 'The Conservative Party Leadership Election of 2016: An Analysis of the Voting Motivations of Conservative Parliamentarians', *Parliamentary Affairs*, 71(2), 263–82.

Jenkin, B. (2015), *Inquiry into the EU Referendum Bill: Purdah and Impartiality of the Civil Service*, 21 July, https://old.parliament.uk/documents/commons-committees/public-administration/Lidington.pdf (London: House of Commons).

Jenkin, B. (2017), 'May Must Remain for the Sake of Brexit: Tory MP Bernard Jenkin Says Those Who Voted Leave Cannot Be Betrayed', *Mail on Sunday*, 11 June.

Jenkin, B. (2022a), Letter to Mark Spencer: Facilitating Effective Scrutiny of Government, 20 May, https://committees.parliament.uk/publications/22343/documents/165191/default/ (London: House of Commons).

Jenkin, B. (2022b), Letter to Mark Spencer: Timeliness of Government Responses to Select Committee Reports, 30 March, https://committees.parliament.uk/publications/9564/documents/161990/default/ (London: House of Commons).

Jenkins, R. (1999), *Mr Balfour's Poodle: Peers vs People* (London: Papermac).

Johnson, B. (2016), 'Boris Johnson Exclusive: There Is Only One Way to Get the Change we Want—Vote to Leave the EU', *Daily Telegraph*, 16 March.

Johnson, B. (2017), 'My Vision for a Bold, Thriving Britain Enabled by Brexit', *Daily Telegraph*, 15 September.

Johnson, B. (2018a), 'Boris Johnson's Resignation Letter and May's Reply in Full', *BBC News*, 9 July.

Johnson, B. (2018b), 'My Brother is Right—Mrs May's Deal is the Biggest Statecraft Failure Since Suez', *Daily Telegraph*, 12 November.

Johnson, B. (2018c), 'We Must Take on Brussels with Steel and Unity When the PM's Deal Is Voted Down', *Sunday Telegraph*, 9 December.

Johnson, B. (2019a), 'Boris Johnson's First Speech as Prime Minister', *Gov.UK*, 24 July.

Johnson, B. (2019b), 'Boris Johnson's Letter to MPs in Full', *BBC News*, 28 August.

Johnson, B. (2019c), 'Boris Johnson's Speech to the 2019 Conservative Party Conference', *Politics Home website*, 2 October.

Johnson, B. (2019d), Letter to Donald Tusk, 28 October, https://assets.publishing.service.gov.uk/government/uploads/system/uploads/attachment_data/file/842622/20191028_HE_Mr_Donald_Tusk.pdf (London: HM Government).

Johnson, B. (2019e), Letter to Donald Tusk (Extension Request), 19 October, https://assets.publishing.service.gov.uk/government/uploads/system/uploads/attachment_data/file/840665/Letter_from_UK_to_EU_Council.pdf (London: HM Government).

Johnson, B. (2019f), 'PM statement in Downing Street', *Gov.UK*, 13 December.

Johnson, B. (2019g), 'Theresa May is a Chicken Who's Bottled Brexit. The Only Way Forward is to Come Out of the EU Now', *Sunday Telegraph*, 24 March.

Johnson, B. (2019h), Tweet of 17 October (@BorisJohnson), https://twitter.com/BorisJohnson/status/1184764798107602944.

Johnson, J. (2019), Tweet of 5 September (@JoJohnsonUK), https://twitter.com/jojohnsonuk/status/1169555292918571008.

Johnson, N. (1997), 'Opposition in the British Political System', *Government and Opposition*, 32(4), 487–510.

Johnson, S., and Hughes, L. (2017), 'Rethink Hard Brexit Plan—We Could Sink it, Scottish Tory leader Ruth Davidson Warns Theresa May', *Daily Telegraph*, 10 June.

Johnston, N. (2019), *Leadership Elections: Conservative Party*, CBP-1366 (London: House of Commons Library).

Johnston, P. (2017), 'To Get Brexit Through the Lords, Send in the Kamikaze Squad', *Daily Telegraph*, 3 January.

Joint Committee on Parliamentary Privilege (1999), *Parliamentary Privilege: Volume One—Report and Proceedings (First Report of Session 1998–99)* HL Paper 43-I, HC 214-I (London: House of Lords and House of Commons).

Jones, C., and Sturgeon, N. (2017), 'Joint Statement from First Ministers of Wales and Scotland in Reaction to the EU (Withdrawal) Bill', *Gov.Wales*, 13 July.

Jones, E., and Sands, A. (2020), *Ripe for Reform: UK Scrutiny of International Trade Agreements* (Oxford: Global Economic Governance Programme).

Jones, J. (2021), *Brexit Witness Archive interview*, 6 May (London: UK in a Changing Europe).

Judge, D. (2021), 'Walking the Dark Side: Evading Parliamentary Scrutiny', *Political Quarterly*, 92(2), 283–92.

Kaiser, A. (2008), 'Parliamentary Opposition in Westminster Democracies: Britain, Canada, Australia and New Zealand', *Journal of Legislative Studies*, 14(1–2), 20–45.

Kanagasooriam, J., and Simon, E. (2021), 'The Red Wall: The Definitive Description', *Political Insight*, 12(3), 8–11.

Keating, M. (2021), *State and Nation in the United Kingdom: The Fractured Union* (Oxford: Oxford University Press).

Keating, M. (2022), 'Taking Back Control? Brexit and the Territorial Constitution of the United Kingdom', *Journal of European Public Policy*, 29(4), 491–509.

Kenny, M., and Sheldon, J. (2021), 'When Planets Collide: The British Conservative Party and the Discordant Goals of Delivering Brexit and Preserving the Domestic Union, 2016–2019', *Political Studies*, 69(4), 965–84.

King, A. (1976), 'Modes of Executive–Legislative Relations: Great Britain, France and West Germany', *Legislative Studies Quarterly*, 1(1), 11–36.

King, J. (2019), 'The Democratic Case for a Written Constitution', *Current Legal Problems*, 71(1), 1–36.

King, J. (2021), 'Looking Back at the EU Future Relationship Act', *UCL Europe blog*, 11 January.

Kreppel, A. (2014), 'Typologies and Classifications', in S. Martin, T. Saalfeld, and K. Strøm, eds, *The Oxford Handbook of Legislative Studies* (Oxford: Oxford University Press).

Kuenssberg, L. (2017), 'Will Theresa May now have to change Brexit plans?', *BBC News*, 13 June.

Kuenssberg, L. (2018), 'Who Really Backed Down Over Brexit Vote?', *BBC News*, 20 June.

Kuenssberg, L. (2019), Tweet of 22 October (@bbclaurak), https://twitter.com/bbclaurak/status/1186622358603419650.

Labour List (2018), 'Labour's Brexit Composite Motion in Full', *Labour List*, 26 September.

Labour Party (2017), *For the Many Not the Few. The Labour Party Manifesto 2017* (London: Labour Party).

Laws, D. (2016), *Coalition: The Inside Story of the Conservative-Liberal Democrat Government* (London: Biteback).

Laws, S. (2019), *The Risks of the 'Grieve Amendment' to Remove Precedence for Government Business* (London: Policy Exchange).

Lee, C., and Berry, M. (2020), 'Taking Back Control? Initiatives in Non-Government Agenda Control in the UK Parliament in 2019', *The Table: The Journal of the Society of Clerks-at-the-Table in Commonwealth Parliaments*, 88, 55–91.

Leebody, C. (2022), 'Eurosceptics Will "Implode the Government" If Current Northern Ireland Protocol Policy Not Continued, Warns Minister Steve Baker', *Belfast Telegraph*, 23 October.

Letwin, O. (2020), *Brexit Witness Archive interview*, 11 December (London: UK in a Changing Europe).

Levitsky, S., and Ziblatt, D. (2018), *How Democracies Die* (New York: Penguin Random House).

Liaison Committee (2022), *Oral Evidence: The Work of the Prime Minister*, 6 July, HC 453 (London: House of Commons).

Liberal Democrats (2017), *Change Britain's Future. Liberal Democrat Manifesto 2017* (London: Liberal Democrats).

Liberal Democrats (2019), *Stop Brexit: Build a Brighter Future. Manifesto 2019* (London: Liberal Democrats).

Liberal Democrats (2020), *2019 Election Review Report* (London: Liberal Democrats).

Lijphart, A., ed. (1992), *Parliamentary Versus Presidential Government* (Oxford: Oxford University Press).

Lijphart, A. (1999), *Patterns of Democracy: Government Forms and Performance in Thirty-Six Countries* (New Haven: Yale University Press).

Lister, S. (2019), 'Bercow Accused of Shameless Brexit Bias for Blocking Major Vote on Boris Johnson's EU Deal', *Daily Express*, 22 October.

Loewenberg, G., and Patterson, S. C. (1979), *Comparing Legislatures* (Lanham, MD: University Press of America).

Lynch, P., and Whitaker, R. (2013), 'Where There is Discord, Can They Bring Harmony? Managing Intra-Party Dissent on European Integration in the Conservative Party', *British Journal of Politics and International Relations*, 15(3), 317–39.

Lynch, P., and Whitaker, R. (2019), 'Select Committees and Brexit: Parliamentary Influence in a Divisive Policy Area', *Parliamentary Affairs*, 72(4), 923–44.

McAllister, I., and Studlar, D. T. (2000), 'Conservative Euroscepticism and the Referendum Party in the 1997 British General Election', *Party Politics*, 6(3), 359–71.

McChesney, R. W. (2014), *Digital Disconnect: How Capitalism is Turning the Media Against Democracy* (New York: New Press).

McCoy, J., and Somer, M. (2019), 'Toward a Theory of Pernicious Polarization and How It Harms Democracies: Comparative Evidence and Possible Remedies', *Annals of the American Academy of Political and Social Science*, 681(1), 234–71.

McDonald, H., and Syal, R. (2017), 'DUP Leader Arlene Foster Vows to Bring Stability to UK with Conservatives', *Guardian*, 9 June.

McDonnell, J. (2021), *Brexit Witness Archive interview*, 19 February (London: UK in a Changing Europe).

McEwen, N. (2021), 'Negotiating Brexit: Power Dynamics in British Intergovernmental Relations', *Regional Studies*, 55(9), 1538–49.

McEwen, N., and Keating, M. (2017), 'Beyond the Referendum', in M. Keating, ed., *Debating Scotland: Issues of Independence and Union in the 2014 Referendum* (Oxford: Oxford University Press).

McEwen, N., and Murphy, M. C. (2022), 'Brexit and the Union: Territorial Voice, Exit and Re-Entry Strategies in Scotland and Northern Ireland After EU Exit', *International Political Science Review*, 43(3), 374–89.

McHarg, A. (2020), 'The Supreme Court's Prorogation Judgment: Guardian of the Constitution or Architect of the Constitution?', *Edinburgh Law Review*, 24(1), 88–95.

McKeown, L.-A. (2016), 'Tony Blair and John Major Warn a Brexit Could Threaten Peace Process During Visit to Derry', *Irish News*, 9 June.

McKinstry, L. (2017), 'Remoaners Must Now Accept That They Have Lost', *Daily Express*, 27 January.

McLachlan, C. (2014), *Foreign Relations Law* (Cambridge: Cambridge University Press).

McLean, I., Spirling, A., and Russell, M. (2003), 'None of the Above: The UK House of Commons Votes on Reforming the House of Lords', *Political Quarterly*, 74(3), 298–310.

MacMillan, C. (2017), 'Reversing the Myth? Dystopian Narratives of the EU in UKIP and Front National Discourse', *Journal of Contemporary European Studies*, 26(1), 117–32.

McNab, P. (2021), *Change: The Independent Group* (London: Grosvenor House).

McNeil, A. (2017), 'Miller and the Media: Supreme Court Judgement Generates More Measured Response', *Constitution Unit blog*, 9 February.

McTague, T. (2017), 'Battered and Bruised, Theresa May Limps Into Enemy Territory', *Politico*, 22 June.

Maddox, D. (2021), 'Hooray! MPs Say Yes to EU Exit', *Daily Express*, 8 November.

Maguire, K. (2016), 'Nigel Farage Wants Second Referendum if Remain Campaign Scrapes Narrow Win', *Mirror*, 16 May.

Maidment, J. (2018), 'Theresa May Under Pressure to Give MPs "Indicative Votes" on Brexit Options as Liam Fox Backs Plans', *Daily Telegraph*, 16 December.

Mairs, N. (2019), 'John Major: Plan to Shut Down Parliament to Force Through Brexit is "Gold-Plated Hypocrisy"', *PoliticsHome*, 14 June.

Major, J. (2000), *John Major: The Autobiography* (London: HarperCollins).

Malhotra, S., and Kinnock, S. (2016), 'Parliament Must Have a Role in Brexit Negotiations', *PoliticsHome*, 5 July.

Malnick, E., and Mikhailova, A. (2018), 'Brexit Deal Will Condemn Tories to Landslide Election Defeat, MPs Warn', *Sunday Telegraph*, 8 July.

Marshall, J., Lilly, A., Thimont Jack, M., and White, H. (2020), *Parliamentary Monitor 2020* (London: Institute for Government).

Martill, B., and Staiger, U. (2021), 'Negotiating Brexit: The Cultural Sources of British Hard Bargaining', *JCMS: Journal of Common Market Studies*, 59(2), 261–77.

Mason, R. (2017), 'Rebel MPs Form Cross-Party Group to Oppose Hard Brexit', *Guardian*, 10 July 2017.

Mason, R., and Elgot, J. (2017), 'Corbyn's Decision to Back Election Causes Serious Concerns Among His MPs', *Guardian*, 18 April.

Mason, R., and Elgot, J. (2019), 'New Rebel Bid to Halt No-Deal Brexit Amid Fury at PM's Enforcer', *Guardian*, 7 August.

May, T. (2016a), 'Conservative Conference: Theresa May's Speech in Full', *BBC News*, 5 October.

May, T. (2016b), 'Statement from the New Prime Minister Theresa May', *Gov.UK*, 13 July.

May, T. (2016c), 'Theresa May—Her Full Brexit Speech to Conservative Conference', *BBC News*, 2 October.

May, T. (2016d), 'Theresa May's Launch Statement: Full Text', *ConservativeHome*, 30 June.

May, T. (2017a), 'The Government's Negotiating Objectives for Exiting the EU: PM Speech', *Gov.UK*, 17 January.

May, T. (2017b), Letter to Donald Tusk, 29 March, https://assets.publishing.service.gov.uk/government/uploads/system/uploads/attachment_data/file/604079/Prime_Ministers_letter_to_European_Council_President_Donald_Tusk.pdf (London: HM Government).

May, T. (2017c), '"Nothing Has Changed!": May As She Announces Social Care U-Turn—Video', *Guardian*, 22 May, https://www.theguardian.com/society/video/2017/may/22/nothings-changed-may-claims-as-she-announces-social-care-u-turn-video.

May, T. (2017d), 'PM's Florence Speech: A New Era of Cooperation and Partnership Between the UK and the EU', *Gov.UK*, 22 September.

May, T. (2017e), 'PM Statement: General Election 2017', *Gov.UK*, 9 June.

May, T. (2017f), 'Theresa May's General Election Statement in Full', *BBC News*, 18 April.

May, T. (2017g), 'Theresa May – 2017 Speech in Bolton', *UKpol.co.uk*, 21 April.

May, T. (2018a), 'PM Speech on Our Future Economic Partnership with the European Union', *Gov.UK*, 2 March.

May, T. (2018b), 'PM's Statement on Brexit', *Gov.UK*, 14 November.

May, T. (2018c), 'Statement Made by the Prime Minister', *Gov.UK*, 15 November.

May, T. (2019a), '2019 Statement on Extending Article 50', *UKpol.co.uk*, 2 April.

May, T. (2019b), 'Full Text: May's Statement Calling on MPs to Back Her Deal', *Spectator*, 20 March.

May, T. (2019c), 'PM's Speech on New Brexit deal', *Gov.UK*, 21 May.

May, T. (2019d), 'PM Speech on the State of Politics', *Gov.UK*, 17 July.

May, T. (2019e), 'Prime Minister's Statement in Downing Street', *Gov.UK*, 24 May.

Mello, P. A. (2017), 'Curbing the Royal Prerogative to Use Military Force: The British House of Commons and the Conflicts in Libya and Syria', *West European Politics*, 40(1), 80–100.

Mellon, J., Evans, G., Fieldhouse, E., Green, J., and Prosser, C. (2018), 'Brexit or Corbyn? Campaign and Inter-Election Vote Switching in the 2017 UK General Election', *Parliamentary Affairs*, 71(4), 719–37.

Melton, J., Stuart, C., and Helen, D. (2015), *To Codify or Not to Codify? Lessons from Consolidating the United Kingdom's Constitutional Statutes* (London: Constitution Unit).

Mendez, M. (2017), 'Constitutional Review of Treaties: Lessons for Comparative Constitutional Design and Practice', *International Journal of Constitutional Law*, 15(1), 84–109.

Mendez, M. (2020), 'Neglecting the Treaty-Making Power in the UK: The Case for Change', *Law Quarterly Review*, 136(Oct), 630–57.

Menon, A. (2016), 'David Cameron's Renegotiation Has Failed to Win Tory MPs Around', *UK in a Changing Europe blog*, 24 February.

Menon, A. (2017), 'Brexit is Becoming a Masterpiece in Procrastination', *UK in a Changing Europe blog*, 11 December.

Menon, A., and Bevington, M. (2019), 'Where Did the Backstop Come From?', in A. Menon and K. Hayward, eds, *Brexit and the Backstop: Everything You Need to Know* (London: UK in a Changing Europe).

Menon, A., and Portes, J. (2018), 'If Only Theresa May Had Given This Speech 13 Months Ago At Lancaster House', *UK in a Changing Europe blog*, 5 March.

Menon, A., and Wager, A. (2021), 'The Long Goodbye: Brexit', in R. Ford, T. Bale, W. Jennings, and P. Surridge, eds, *The British General Election of 2019* (Cham: Palgrave Macmillan).

Mezey, M. L. (1979), *Comparative Legislatures* (Durham: Duke University Press).

Mile End Institute (2018), 'Survey of MPs Reveals Theresa May and Jeremy Corbyn Face Significant Political Challenges Over Brexit', *Mile End Institute blog*, 22 January.

Miller, G. (2019a), *Rise: Life Lessons in Speaking Out, Standing Tall and Leading the Way* (Edinburgh: Canongate).

Miller, V. (2019b), *A No-Deal Brexit: The Johnson Government*, CBP-8397 (London: House of Commons Library).

Millett, P. (2016), 'Article 50 and the EU Referendum Decision', *Times*, 4 July.

Montgomerie, T. (2012), '100 Tory MPs Call for Cameron to Prepare Legislation for EU Referendum', *ConservativeHome*, 28 June.

Moore, M. (2019), *Democracy Hacked: How Technology is Destabilising Global Politics* (London: Oneworld).

Moriarty, C. (2021), *Brexit Witness Archive interview*, 5 February (London: UK in a Changing Europe).

Morrison, J. (2016), 'Break-point for Britain? How UKIP's Image of "Hate" Set Race Discourse Reeling Back Decades', in N. Jackson, E. Thorsen, and D. Wring, eds, *EU Referendum Analysis 2016* (Poole: Bournemouth University).

Mounk, Y. (2018), *The People Versus Democracy: Why Our Freedom is in Danger and How to Save it* (Cambridge, MA: Harvard University Press).

Mudde, C. (2004), 'The Populist Zeitgeist', *Government and Opposition*, 39(4), 541–63.

Mudde, C. (2007), *The Populist Radical Right in Europe* (Cambridge: Cambridge University Press).

Mudde, C., ed. (2017), *The Populist Radical Right: A Reader* (Abingdon: Routledge).

Mudde, C., and Rovira Kaltwasser, C. (2013a), 'Populism', in M. Freeden and M. Stears, eds, *The Oxford Handbook of Political Ideologies* (Oxford: Oxford University Press).

Mudde, C., and Rovira Kaltwasser, C., eds (2013b), *Populism in Europe and the Americas: Threat or Corrective for Democracy* (Cambridge: Cambridge University Press).

Müller, J.-W. (2016), *What is Populism?* (London: Penguin).

Müller, J.-W. (2021), *Democracy Rules* (London: Allen Lane).

Murphy, M. C., and Evershed, J. (2020), 'Between the Devil and the DUP: The Democratic Unionist Party and the Politics of Brexit', *British Politics*, 15(4), 456–77.

Murphy, M. C., and Evershed, J. (2022), *A Troubled Constitutional Future: Northern Ireland After Brexit* (Newcastle: Agenda).

Murphy, S. (2019), 'Then and Now: What Senior Tories Say About Proroguing Parliament', *Guardian*, 29 August.

Naím, M. (2022), *The Revenge of Power* (New York: St. Martin's Press).

Nandy, L. (2019), Tweet of 20 March (@lisanandy), https://twitter.com/lisanandy/status/1108483900970594304.

Natzler, D., and Sayers-Carter, C. (2022), 'Parliamentary Scrutiny of International Agreements Should Not be Limited to Legally Binding Treaties', *Constitution Unit blog*, 12 July.

Negotiators of the European Union and the United Kingdom Government (2017), *Joint Report from the Negotiators of the European Union and the United Kingdom Government on Progress During Phase 1 of Negotiations Under Article 50 TEU on the United Kingdom's Orderly Withdrawal from the European Union* (London: HM Government).

Newson, N. (2017), *Salisbury Convention in a Hung Parliament*, LLN-2017–0030 (London: House of Lords Library).

Newton Dunn, T. (2016), 'See EU Later!', *Sun*, 24 June.

Newton Dunn, T. (2019), 'Power to the People', *Sun*, 21 March.

Norris, P., and Inglehart, R. (2019), *Cultural Backlash: Trump, Brexit, and Authoritarian Populism* (Cambridge: Cambridge University Press).

Northern Ireland Affairs Committee (2018), *The Land Border Between Northern Ireland and Ireland (Second Report of Session 2017–19)* HC 329 (London: House of Commons).

Norton, P. (2005), 'The Constitution', in K. Hickson, ed., *The Political Thought of the Conservative Party Since 1945* (Basingstoke: Palgrave Macmillan).

Norton, P. (2008), 'Making Sense of Opposition', *Journal of Legislative Studies*, 14(1–2), 236–50.

Norton, P. (2011), 'Divided Loyalties: The European Communities Act 1972', *Parliamentary History*, 30(1), 53–64.

Norton, P. (2012), 'Speaking for the People: A Conservative Narrative of Democracy', *Policy Studies*, 33(2), 121–32.

Norton, P. (2013), *Parliament in British Politics* (Basingstoke: Palgrave Macmillan).

Norton, P. (2015), 'Parliament: A New Assertiveness?', in J. Jowell, D. Oliver, and C. O'Cinneide, eds, *The Changing Constitution* (Oxford: Oxford University Press).

Norton, P. (2019), 'Is the House of Commons Too Powerful? The 2019 Bingham Lecture in Constitutional Studies, University of Oxford', *Parliamentary Affairs*, 72(4), 996–1013.

Oborne, P. (2021), *The Assault on Truth: Boris Johnson, Donald Trump and the Emergence of a New Moral Barbarism* (London: Simon & Schuster).

Obradović, S., Power, S. A., and Sheehy-Skeffington, J. (2020), 'Understanding the Psychological Appeal of Populism', *Current Opinion in Psychology*, 35, 125–31.

Oliver, C. (2016), *Unleashing Demons* (London: Hodder & Stoughton).

O'Toole, F. (2017), 'Fintan O'Toole: DUP's Crush on Britain Will End Badly', *Irish Times*, 17 June.

O'Toole, F. (2020), *Three Years in Hell: The Brexit Chronicles* (London: Head of Zeus).

Owen, G. (2019), 'No10 Probes Remain MPs' "Foreign Collusion", *Mail on Sunday*, 29 September.

Owen, G., and Carlin, B. (2017), 'Boris Bids to be PM: Johnson Team Circles Wounded Theresa May as She's Forced to Sacrifice Key Aides to Keep Her Job as Tory Leader', *Mail on Sunday*, 11 June.

Panizza, F., and Miorelli, R. (2009), 'Populism and Democracy in Latin America', *Ethics and International Affairs*, 23, 39–46.

Pannick, D. (2016), 'Why Giving Notice of Withdrawal From the EU Requires Act of Parliament', *Times*, 30 June.

Parker, G., Barker, A., and Beesley, A. (2017), 'How the Election Result Affects Brexit', *Financial Times*, 9 June.

Parsons, T. (2017), 'If Lords Hold Up Brexit... They'll Be Next Fur the Chop', *Sun*, 19 February.

Paun, A. (2017), 'The EU Withdrawal Bill Has Serious Implications for Devolution', *Institute for Government blog*, 26 September.

Payne, S. (2022), *The Fall of Boris Johnson: The Full Story* (London: Macmillan).

Peacock, T. N. (2018), *The British Tradition of Minority Government* (Manchester: Manchester University Press).

Penn, J. (2020), *Brexit Witness Archive interview*, 16 October and 17 November (London: UK in a Changing Europe).

Phillips, J. (2020), *Brexit Witness Archive interview*, 4 December (London: UK in a Changing Europe).

Pine, S. (2016), 'Corbyn: "Article 50 Has to Be Invoked Now"', *LabourList*, 24 June.

Pogrund, G., and Maguire, P. (2020), *Left Out: The Inside Story of Corbyn Under Labour* (London: Vintage).

Political and Constitutional Reform Committee (2014), *The Impact of Queen's and Prince's Consent on the Legislative Process (Eleventh Report of Session 2013-14)*, HC 784 (London: House of Commons).

PoliticsHome (2019), 'Andrea Leadsom's Resignation Letter and Theresa May's Reply', *PoliticsHome*, 23 May.

Poole, T. (2019), 'The Executive Power Project', *London Review of Books blog*, 2 April.

Pope, C. (2016), 'Corbyn Defiant After Being Trounced in MPs' Confidence Vote', *LabourList*, 28 June.

Power, S., Bale, T., and Webb, P. (2020), '"Mistake Overturned, So I Call it a Lesson Learned": The Conservatives', *Parliamentary Affairs*, 73(Supplement 1), 65–83.

Prasser, S. (2009), 'Opposition One Day, Government the Next: Can Oppositions Make Policy and Be Ready for Office?', *Australasian Parliamentary Review*, 25(1), 151–61.

Privileges Committee (2019), *Conduct of Mr Dominic Cummings (First Report of Session 2017-19)*, HC 1490 (London: House of Commons).

Procedure Committee (2013), *Committee of Selection and Membership of General Committees: Corrected Transcript of Oral Evidence*, 19 June, HC 216-I (London: House of Commons).

Procedure Committee (2018a), *Motions Under Section 13(1) of the European Union (Withdrawal) Act 2018 (Eighth Report of Session 2017-19)*, HC 1664 (London: House of Commons).

Procedure Committee (2018b), *Scrutiny of Delegated Legislation Under the European Union (Withdrawal) Act 2018 (Sixth Report of Session 2017-19)*, HC 1395 (London: House of Commons).

Public Administration and Constitutional Affairs Committee (2016), *Note from the Chair of PACAC to the Cabinet Office on Leaving the EU and the Machinery of Government*, 12 July, https://old.parliament.uk/documents/commons-committees/PACAC/Chair-PACAC-Cabinet-Office-Leaving-the-EU-and-the-Machinery-of-Government.pdf (London: House of Commons).

Public Administration and Constitutional Affairs Committee (2017), *Lessons Learned From the EU Referendum (Twelfth Report of Session 2016–17)*, HC 496 (London: House of Commons).

Public Administration and Constitutional Affairs Committee (2018a), *The Role of Parliament in the UK Constitution. Interim Report: The Status and Effect of Confidence Motions and the Fixed-term Parliaments Act 2011 (Fourteenth Report of Session 2017–19)*, HC 1813 (London: House of Commons).

Public Administration and Constitutional Affairs Committee (2018b), *Status of Resolutions of the House of Commons (Fifteenth Report of Session 2017–19)*, HC 1587 (London: House of Commons).

Public Administration and Constitutional Affairs Committee (2020), *Parliamentary Scrutiny of the Government's Handling of Covid-19 (Fourth Report of Session 2019–21)*, HC 377 (London: House of Commons).

Public Administration Select Committee (2004), *Taming the Prerogative: Strengthening Ministerial Accountability to Parliament (Fourth Report of Session 2003–04)*, HC 422 (London: House of Commons).

Punnett, R. M. (1973), *Front-Bench Opposition: The Role of the Leader of the Opposition, the Shadow Cabinet and Shadow Government in British Politics* (London: Heinemann).

Purvis, M. (2019), *Lengths of Prorogations since 1900*, LLN 2019–0111 (London: House of Lords).

Quinn, T. (2016), 'The British Labour Party's Leadership Election of 2015', *British Journal of Politics and International Relations*, 18(4), 759–78.

Quinn, T., Allen, N., and Bartle, J. (2022), 'Why Was There a Hard Brexit? The British Legislative Party System, Divided Majorities and the Incentives for Factionalism', *Political Studies* [early view].

Rachman, G. (2022), *The Age of the Strongman: How the Cult of the Leader Threatens Democracy Around the World* (London: Vintage).

Rankin, J., and Waterson, J. (2019), 'How Boris Johnson's Brussels-Bashing Stories Shaped British Politics', *Guardian*, 14 July.

Rawlings, R. (2017), *Brexit and the Territorial Constitution: Devolution, Reregulation and Inter-Governmental Relations* (London: Constitution Society).

Rawlinson, K. (2019), 'Dominic Grieve Loses Confidence Vote Held by Beaconsfield Tories', *Guardian*, 30 March.

Rayner, G. (2017), 'Leaving the EU Without a Deal on Brexit Would be "Perfectly OK", Boris Johnson Says, as Tory Rebellion Falters', *Daily Telegraph*, 12 March.

Rayner, G. (2019), 'MPs Vote to Take Control', *Daily Telegraph*, 26 March.

Rees-Mogg, J. (2018a), 'Leavers Will Have Concerns with Mrs May, But Now is Not the Time to Nitpick', *Daily Telegraph*, 2 March.

Rees-Mogg, J. (2018b), 'The Reins of Brexit Have Been Handed to Those Who Never Wanted to Leave', *Sunday Telegraph*, 8 July.

Reilly, J., and Newton Dunn, T. (2016), 'Who Do EU Think You Are?', *Sun*, 14 November.

Renwick, A. (2016), 'The Road to Brexit: 16 Things You Need to Know About the Process of Leaving the EU', *Constitution Unit blog*, 24 June.

Renwick, A. (2019), 'Could Innovative Voting Rules Break Parliament's Brexit Impasse?', *Constitution Unit blog*, 28 March.

Renwick, A., Allan, S., Jennings, W., McKee, R., Russell, M., and Smith, G. (2017), *A Considered Public Voice on Brexit: The Report of the Citizens' Assembly on Brexit* (London: Constitution Unit).

Renwick, A., Allan, S., Jennings, W., McKee, R., Russell, M., and Smith, G. (2018), 'What Kind of Brexit do Voters Want? Lessons From the Citizens' Assembly on Brexit', *Political Quarterly*, 89(4), 649–58.

Renwick, A., and Hazell, R. (2015), 'The EU Referendum Bill: Taking Stock', *Constitution Unit blog*, 3 October.

Renwick, A., Lauderdale, B., Russell, M., and Cleaver, J. (2022), *What Kind of Democracy Do People Want? Results of a Survey of the Population* (London: Constitution Unit).

Richards, D. (1996), 'Elite Interviewing: Approaches and Pitfalls', *Politics*, 16(3), 199–204.

Rigby, B. (2017), 'Theresa May's Future in Doubt as Election Gamble Backfires', *Sky News*, 9 June.

Rigby, B. (2018), Tweet of 10 October (@BethRigby), https://twitter.com/BethRigby/status/1050097720550219776.

Riley-Smith, B. (2017), 'The Caretaker PM Stays for Now, But No One Expects Her to Fight Another General Election', *Sunday Telegraph*, 18 June.

Roberts, D. (2017), 'Gina Miller to Launch Tactical Voting Initiative Against Hard Brexit', *Guardian*, 19 April.

Rodgers, S. (2020), 'Johnson's Brexit Bill Passes with Labour Backing—But 37 Rebels Defy Starmer', *Labour List*, 30 December.

Rogers, I. (2020), *Brexit Witness Archive interview*, 27 November (London: UK in a Changing Europe).

Rosenbaum, M. (2017), 'Local Voting Figures Shed New Light on EU Referendum', *BBC News*, 6 February.

Ross, T., and McTague, T. (2017), *Betting the House: The Inside Story of the 2017 Election* (London: Biteback).

Rothwell, J., and Bennett, A. (2018), 'Revealed: What Theresa May's Brexit Speech Means for Immigration, Free Trade and the Irish Border', *Daily Telegraph*, 2 March.

Rozenberg, J. (2020), *Enemies of the People? How Judges Shape Society* (Bristol: Bristol University Press).

Rudd, A. (2021), *Brexit Witness Archive interview*, 19 March (London: UK in a Changing Europe).

Runciman, D. (2018), *How Democracy Ends* (London: Profile Books).

Ruparel, R. (2020), *Brexit Witness Archive interview*, 11 August (London: UK in a Changing Europe).

Russell, M. (2005), *Must Politics Disappoint?* (London: Fabian Society).

Russell, M. (2011), ' "Never Allow a Crisis to go to Waste": The Wright Committee Reforms to Strengthen the House of Commons', *Parliamentary Affairs*, 64(4), 612–33.

Russell, M. (2013), *The Contemporary House of Lords: Westminster Bicameralism Revived* (Oxford: Oxford University Press).

Russell, M. (2019), 'How Did Parliament Get Into This Brexit Mess, and How Can it Get Out?', *Constitution Unit blog*, 24 March.

Russell, M. (2020), 'Why a Central Role for Party Members in Leadership Elections is Bad for Parliamentary Democracy', *Constitution Unit blog*, 6 February.

Russell, M. (2021a), 'Brexit and Parliament: The Anatomy of a Perfect Storm', *Parliamentary Affairs*, 74(2), 443–63.

Russell, M. (2021b), 'The Fixed-term Parliaments Act did not cause the Brexit impasse', *Constitution Unit blog*, 6 September.

Russell, M. (2022), 'Why Member Ballots for Party Leaders Threaten Parliamentary Democracy', *Prospect*, 23 October.

Russell, M., and Cowley, P. (2016), 'The Policy Power of the Westminster Parliament: The "Parliamentary State" and the Empirical Evidence', *Governance*, 29(1), 121–37.

Russell, M., and Cowley, P. (2018), 'Modes of UK Executive-Legislative Relations Revisited', *Political Quarterly*, 89(1), 18–28.

Russell, M., Fox, R., Cormacain, R., and Tomlinson, J. (2021), 'The Marginalisation of the House of Commons Under Covid Has Been Shocking: A Year on, Parliament's Role Must Urgently Be Restored', *Constitution Unit blog*, 21 April.

Russell, M., and Gover, D. (2017), *Legislation at Westminster: Parliamentary Actors and Influence in the Making of British Law* (Oxford: Oxford University Press).

Russell, M., and Gover, D. (2021), *Taking Back Control: Why the House of Commons Should Govern its Own Time* (London: Constitution Unit).

Russell, M., and Paun, A. (2007), *The House Rules?: International Lessons for Enhancing the Autonomy of the House of Commons* (London: Constitution Unit).

Rutter, J. (2019), 'Anonymous Number Ten Briefings Do the Public a Disservice. Journalists Should Stop Reporting Them', *UK in a Changing Europe blog*, 8 October.

Rutter, J., and Menon, A. (2020), 'Who Killed Soft Brexit?', *Prospect*, 9 November.

Rycroft, P. (2020), *Brexit Witness Archive interview*, 26 June (London: UK in a Changing Europe).

Sabbagh, D. (2019), 'Corbyn: No Talks with May Until No-Deal Brexit is Off Table', *Guardian*, 16 January.

Sabbagh, D. (2020), 'MP Who Beat Chris Grayling to Intelligence Chair Role Loses Tory Whip', *Guardian*, 15 July.

Samuelson, K. (2017), '7 Times Theresa May Said She Wouldn't Call for a General Election', *Time Magazine*, 18 April.

Sargeant, J., Renwick, A., and Russell, M. (2018), *The Mechanics of a Further Referendum on Brexit* (London: Constitution Unit).

Saunders, R. (2018), *Yes to Europe!: The 1975 Referendum and Seventies Britain* (Cambridge: Cambridge University Press).

Saunders, R. (2019), 'Why Party Members Should Never be Allowed to Elect Prime Ministers', *New Statesman*, 20 June.

Schleiter, P. and Fleming, T. G. (2022), 'Radical Departure or Opportunity Not Taken? The Johnson Government's Constitution, Democracy and Rights Commission', *British Politics* [early view].

Schleiter, P., and Morgan-Jones, E. (2009), 'Constitutional Power and Competing Risks: Monarchs, Presidents, Prime Ministers, and the Termination of East and West European Cabinets', *American Political Science Review*, 103(3), 496–512.

Schofield, K. (2019), 'Fresh Tory leadership Row as Dominic Raab Suggests He Could Shut Down Parliament to Secure Brexit', *PoliticsHome*, 6 June.

Schofield, K. (2022), 'Boris Johnson Says the "Deep State " Will Try to Take Britain Back Into EU', *Huffington Post*, 18 July.

Scott, J. (2020), 'Where Do the UK's Political Parties Stand on Brexit Vote?', *BBC News*, 29 December.

Sculthorpe, T., Tapsfield, J., and Ferguson, K. (2018), 'Rebels Blast May's "Unforgivable" Backtracking: Remainers Reject PM's "Sneaky" Offer Over "Meaningful Vote" on Final Brexit Deal and Threaten to Block It in New Commons Vote Next Week', *Daily Mail*, 14 June.

Seaward, P. (2019), 'Standing Order No. 14', *History of Parliament blog*, 28 March.

Seawright, D. (2013), ' "Yes, the Census": The 2011 UK Referendum Campaign on the Alternative Vote', *British Politics*, 8(4), 457–75.

Secondary Legislation Scrutiny Committee (2021), *Government by Diktat: A Call to Return Power to Parliament (Twentieth Report of Session 2021–22)*, HL Paper 105 (London: House of Lords).

Seldon, A., and Newell, R. (2019), *May at 10* (London: Biteback).

Select Committee on the Reform of the House of Commons (2009), *Rebuilding the House (First Report of Session 2008–09)*, HC 1117 (London: House of Commons).

Shipman, T. (2015), 'Boris Johnson Calls for "No" to Europe—Then "Yes"', *Sunday Times*, 28 June.

Shipman, T. (2016), 'The Owl Unseats the No 10 Pussycat', *Sunday Times*, 2 October.

Shipman, T. (2017a), *All Out War: The Full Story of How Brexit Sank Britain's Political Class* (London: William Collins).

Shipman, T. (2017b), *Fall Out: A Year of Political Mayhem* (London: William Collins).

Shipman, T. (2017c), 'Five Cabinet Ministers Urge Boris Johnson to Topple Theresa May', *Sunday Times*, 11 June.

Shipman, T. (2019a), 'Cabinet Coup to Ditch Theresa May for Emergency PM', *Sunday Times*, 24 March.

Shipman, T. (2019b), 'Theresa May in Brexit Meltdown', *Sunday Times*, 20 January.

Shipman, T., and Wheeler, C. (2018), 'Brexit: Theresa May "May Surrender Over Customs Union"', *Sunday Times*, 22 April.

Shipman, T., and Wheeler, C. (2019), '"Sack Me if You Dare," Boris Johnson Will Tell the Queen', *Sunday Times*, 6 October.

Sky News (2018a), 'Arlene Foster: Irish Sea Border Backstop Plan Unacceptable to DUP', *Sky News*, 9 November.

Sky News (2018b), 'David Davis Resignation Letter and Theresa May's Response', *Sky News*, 9 July.

Sky News Politics (2019), Tweet of 28 August (@SkyNewsPolitics), https://twitter.com/SkyNewsPolitics/status/1166657310569226240.

Slack, J. (2016), 'Enemies of the People', *Daily Mail*, 4 November.

Slack, J., Martin, D., and Groves, J. (2016), 'We're Out!', *Daily Mail*, 24 June.

Slack, J., and Stephens, J. (2016), 'Call That a Deal, Dave?', *Daily Mail*, 19 February.

Sloman, P. (2020), 'Squeezed Out? The Liberal Democrats and the 2019 General Election', *Political Quarterly*, 91(1), 35–42.

Smith, E., Bjorge, E., and Lang, A. (2020), 'Treaties, Parliament and the Constitution', *Public Law*, July 2020, 508–28.

Smith, J. (2012), 'The European Dividing Line in Party Politics', *International Affairs*, 88(6), 1277–95.

Smith, J. (2020), *Brexit Witness Archive interview*, 20 July (London: UK in a Changing Europe).

Soubry, A., Wollaston, S., and Allen, H. (2019), Letter to Theresa May, 20 February, https://twitter.com/Anna_Soubry/status/1098181942246367234 (Twitter).

Sparrow, A. (2016), 'What the Gove Camp Say About Why Gove Abandoned Boris Johnson', *Guardian*, 30 June.

Spelman, C. (2019), 'After Seeing What I've been Through, My Children Wouldn't Follow Me Into Politics', *Times*, 31 October.

Spence, A. (2018), 'Revealed: These 70 Tory MPs Support the Hard Brexit Group Led by Jacob Rees-Mogg', *Buzzfeed*, 8 February.

Spicer, M., and Hamilton, A. (2019), 'If Tory MPs Wish to Change the 1922 Committee No Confidence Vote Rules There is Nothing Standing in Their Way', *Daily Telegraph*, 13 April.

Spiering, M. (2004), 'British Euroscepticism', *European Studies*, 20, 127–49.

Starmer, K. (2018), '"Nobody Is Ruling Out Remain As an Option": Keir Starmer at Labour's Brexit Debate—Video', *Guardian*, 25 September, https://www.theguardian.com/politics/video/2018/sep/25/nobody-is-ruling-out-remain-as-an-option-keir-starmer-at-labours-brexit-debate-video.

Steerpike (2018), 'Boris Johnson's Speech to DUP Conference: "We Are on the Verge of Making a Historic Mistake"', *Spectator*, 24 November.

Stevens, J. (2018a), 'House of Unelected Wreckers', *Daily Mail*, 1 May.

Stevens, J. (2018b), 'It's Time to Pull Plug on the Lords', *Daily Mail*, 10 May.

Stewart, H. (2019a), 'Lord Young Quits Government Over Boris Johnson Proroguing Parliament', *Guardian*, 29 August.

Stewart, H. (2019b), Tweet of 22 May (@GuardianHeather), https://twitter.com/GuardianHeather/status/1131313196046925824.

Stewart, H., and Boffey, D. (2018), 'Tory Brexiters Planning to Reject Deal Even with Backstop Exit Clause', *Guardian*, 8 November.

Stewart, H., and Boffey, D. (2019), 'MPs Reject Boris Johnson's Attempt to Fast-Track Brexit Deal', *Guardian*, 22 October.

Stewart, H., and Elgot, J. (2019), 'MPs Vote to Seize Control of Brexit from May', *Guardian*, 26 March.

Stewart, H., and O'Carroll, L. (2018), 'Labour Delegates Back Keir Starmer Push for Public Vote on Brexit', *Guardian*, 25 September.

Stoker, G. (2006), *Why Politics Matters: Making Democracy Work* (Basingstoke: Palgrave Macmillan).

Streeting, W. (2019), Tweet of 20 March (@wesstreeting), https://twitter.com/wesstreeting/status/1108480028533293057.

Strøm, K. (1990), *Minority Government and Majority Rule* (Cambridge: Cambridge University Press).

Strong, J. (2022), 'Did Theresa May Kill the War Powers Convention? Comparing Parliamentary Debates on UK Intervention in Syria in 2013 and 2018', *Parliamentary Affairs*, 75(2), 400–19.

Stuart, G. (2018), 'Labour Must Not Betray Leave Voters Over Brexit', *Guardian*, 25 September.

Sullivan, W. (2019), 'Binary Indicative Votes Were Never Going to Achieve a Consensus', *Electoral Reform Society blog*, 29 March.

Sumption, J. (2016), 'The Limits of Law', in N. W. Barber, R. Ekins, and P. Yowell, eds, *Lord Sumption and the Limits of the Law* (Oxford: Hart).

Sumption, J. (2020a), 'Brexit and the British Constitution: Reflections on the Last Three Years and the Next Fifty', *Political Quarterly*, 91(1), 107–15.

Sumption, J. (2020b), 'Government by Decree—Covid-19 and the Constitution', *YouTube*, 27 October, https://www.youtube.com/watch?v=amDv2gk8aa0.

Sumption, J. (2020c), *Trials of the State: Law and the Decline of Politics* (London: Profile Books).

Sun (2016a), 'The Sun Says: Any Doubt About Theresa May's Commitment to Brexit Has Been Quashed—May Is the Capable PM We Can Be Proud of', *Sun*, 3 October.

Sun (2016b), 'The Sun Says: Theresa May Would Be Mad Not to Crush Pro-EU Saboteurs and Annihilate Corbyn's Labour', *Sun*, 5 November.

Sun (2017a), 'The Sun Says: This General Election Should Deliver a Thumping Tory Victory and Give Theresa May the Authority She Needs', *Sun*, 19 April.

Sun (2017b), 'The Sun Says: Tory Rebels Should be Ashamed of Themselves for Compromising Brexit After the Critical Commons Vote', *Sun*, 14 December.

Sun (2019a), 'Batten Down the Hatches…Set Course for a No Deal', *Sun*, 16 January.

Sun (2019b), 'Boris Johnson Announces His Brexit Deal With Jean-Claude Juncker', *YouTube*, 17 October, https://www.youtube.com/watch?v=xKmtPEsMyOk.

Sun (2019c), 'Brexsick of the Lot of You', *Sun*, 30 March.

Sun (2019d), 'The Sun Says: Odious John Bercow's Prejudices are Wrecking Brexit and Have Cost Him MPs' Trust', *Sun*, 10 January.

Sun (2019e), 'The Sun Says: Political Judges Must Face Scrutiny After Doing the Bidding of Braying Remainers', *Sun*, 25 September.

Sunak, R. (2022), 'Rishi Sunak First Speech as Prime Minister', *Gov.UK*, 25 October.

Supreme Court (2019), 'Watch Hearing: R (on the application of Miller) (Appellant) v The Prime Minister (Respondent): 19 September 2019, Afternoon Session', *Supreme Court website*, 19 September, https://www.supremecourt.uk/watch/uksc-2019–0192/190919-pm.html.

Swinford, S. (2016), 'Up to 40 Tory MPs Could Rebel and Back Move to Force Government to Reveal Plan for Brexit', *Daily Telegraph*, 5 December.

Swinford, S. (2017), 'The Brexit Mutineers: At Least 15 Tory MPs Rebel Against Leave Date with Threat to Join Forces with Labour', *Daily Telegraph*, 14 November.

Swinford, S. (2019a), 'How "Livid" John Bercow's Unprecedented Brexit Intervention Paves Way for Constitutional Crisis', *Daily Telegraph*, 9 January.

Swinford, S. (2019b), 'How Theresa May Rebuffed Calls to Set Resignation Date During "Frank" Chequers Summit over Brexit', *Sunday Telegraph*, 24 March.

Swinford, S., Hope, C., and Maidment, J. (2019), 'Exclusive: Theresa May Told by Chairman of 1922 Committee That Tory MPs Want Her to Quit Over Brexit', *Daily Telegraph*, 21 March.

Swinford, S., Wright, O., and Zeffman, H. (2019), 'General Election 2019: Nicky Morgan in Exodus of Moderate Tory MPs', *Times*, 31 October.

Syal, R. (2013), 'David Cameron May Vote for Amendment to His Own Queen's Speech', *Guardian*, 10 May.

Syal, R., Perraudin, F., and Slawson, N. (2016), 'Shadow Cabinet Resignations: Who Has Gone and Who Is Staying', *Guardian*, 27 June.

Syal, R., and Stewart, H. (2019), ' "I Fear for Brexit": ERG Dismayed by May Plan to Talk to Corbyn', *Guardian*, 3 April.

Sylvester, R. (2016), 'I'm Sure Theresa Will Be Really Sad That She Doesn't Have Children', *Times*, 9 July.

Syms, R. (2016), Tweet of 23 June (@RobertSyms), https://twitter.com/RobertSyms/status/746088128864260096.

Tapsfield, J., Groves, J., and Moore, C. (2018), ' "Oh Come All Ye Faithful!" Theresa May Sings a Carol on the Steps of No 10 As She Vows to Press on with "Doomed" Brexit Vote After Cabinet Crisis Talks, Despite Calls for Her to Delay It', *Daily Mail*, 5 December.

Tapsfield, J., Sculthorpe, T., and Dathan, M. (2017), ' "There is No Turning Back!" David Davis Warns Remoaner MPs They Will Face the Full Wrath of the Public if They Use Supreme Court Ruling to Block Brexit', *Daily Mail*, 24 January.

Thomassen, J., and Esaiasson, P. (2006), 'Role Orientations of Members of Parliament', *Acta Politica*, 41, 217–31.

Thompson, L. (2020), 'From Minority Government to Parliamentary Stalemate: Why Election 2019 was Needed to Break the Brexit Logjam', *Parliamentary Affairs*, 73(Supplement 1), 48–64.

Thompson, L., and Yong, B. (2019), 'What Do We Mean by Parliamentary Scrutiny of Brexit? A View from the House of Commons', in T. Christiansen and D. Fromage, eds, *Brexit and Democracy: The Role of Parliaments in the UK and the European Union* (Cham: Palgrave Macmillan).

Tickell, A., John, P., and Musson, S. (2005), 'The North East Region Referendum Campaign of 2004: Issues and Turning Points', *Political Quarterly*, 76(4), 488–96.

Tierney, S. (2019), 'Prorogation May Have Been Ill-Advised, But That Does Not Make It Unlawful', *UK in a Changing Europe blog*, 19 September.

Times (2016), 'Thin Gruel', *Times*, 20 February.

Tombs, R. (2019), 'Remainers Aim to Overturn Democratic Vote', *Sunday Express*, 27 January.

Tominey, C. (2019a), 'Brexit Plan C – the Malthouse Compromise: The Secret Tory Pact That Could Unite the ERG and Remainers', *Daily Telegraph*, 12 March.

Tominey, C. (2019b), 'No-Deal Brexit Now Expected from Boris Johnson as Dominic Cummings Sets "48 Hour" Whitehall Exit Plans Deadline in Shock to EU', *Daily Telegraph*, 5 August.

Tonge, J. (2017), 'Supplying Confidence or Trouble? The Deal Between the Democratic Unionist Party and the Conservative Party', *Political Quarterly*, 88(3), 412–16.

Tonge, J., and Evans, J. (2018), 'Northern Ireland: Double Triumph for the Democratic Unionist Party', *Parliamentary Affairs*, 71(Supplement 1), 139–54.

Tournier-Sol, K. (2014), 'Reworking the Eurosceptic and Conservative Traditions into a Populist Narrative: UKIP's Winning Formula?', *JCMS: Journal of Common Market Studies*, 53(1), 140–56.

Tusk, D. (2018), 'Remarks by President Donald Tusk After the Salzburg Informal Summit', *European Council website*, 20 September.

Uberoi, E., Baker, C., Allen, G., Roberts, N., Barton, C., Sturge, G., Danechi, S., Harker, R., Bolton, P., McInnes, R., Watson, C., Dempsey, N., and Audickas, L. (2020), *General Election 2019: Results and Analysis*, CBP-8749 (London: House of Commons Library).

Uhr, J. (2009), 'Parliamentary Opposition Leadership', in H. Patapan, P. 't Hart, and J. Kane, eds, *Dispersed Democratic Leadership* (Oxford: Oxford University Press).

UK Government and European Union (2018), *Political Declaration Setting Out the Framework for the Future Relationship Between the European Union and the United Kingdom* (London: HM Government).

UK Government and Parliament (2016), 'EU Referendum Rules Triggering a 2nd EU Referendum', *UK Government and Parliament Petitions website*, 25 November.

UK in a Changing Europe (2016), 'Response to Government Leaflet from The UK in a Changing Europe', *UK in a Changing Europe blog*, 8 June.

UK in a Changing Europe (2018a), *Cost of No Deal Revisited* (London: UK in a Changing Europe).

UK in a Changing Europe (2018b), 'Public Pessimistic About Prospect of Brexit Deal and Impact of Leaving EU, Major New Survey Finds', *UK in a Changing Europe blog*, 17 October.

UK in a Changing Europe (2019), *Brexit: The Manifestos Uncovered* (London: UK in a Changing Europe).

UK in a Changing Europe (2022), 'Can—and Should—Parliament Take Back Control from the Executive', *YouTube*, 4 April, https://www.youtube.com/watch?v=iEZNZ0guVys.

UKIP (2016), *Who Governs Britain?* (London: UKIP).

UK Parliament (2019), 'Parliament Sits on a Saturday to Debate the Prime Minister's Proposed Brexit Deal', *UK Parliament website*, 19 October.

Urbinati, N. (2019a), *Me the People: How Populism Transforms Democracy* (Cambridge, MA: Harvard University Press).

Urbinati, N. (2019b), 'Political Theory of Populism', *Annual Review of Political Science*, 22(1), 111–27.

Usherwood, S. (2018), 'The Third Era of British Euroscepticism: Brexit as a Paradigm Shift', *Political Quarterly*, 89(4), 553–9.

van Heerde-Hudson, J., ed. (2014), *The Political Costs of the 2009 British MPs' Expenses Scandal* (Basingstoke: Palgrave Macmillan).

Vasilopoulou, S. (2018), 'The Radical Right and Euroskepticism', in J. Rydgren, ed., *The Oxford Handbook of the Radical Right* (Oxford: Oxford University Press).

Walker, P. (2019), 'Boris Johnson Calls David Cameron "Girly Swot" in Leaked Note', *Guardian*, 6 September.

Walker, P., Stewart, H., and Elgot, J. (2016), 'Senior Lib Dems Confirm Backing for Second EU Referendum', *Guardian*, 20 September.

Walker, P., Stewart, H., and Elgot, J. (2018), 'McDonnell: New Brexit Referendum Should Not Include Remain Option', *Guardian*, 24 September.

Wall, S. (2008), *A Stranger in Europe: Britain and the EU From Thatcher to Blair* (Oxford: Oxford University Press).

Walsh, D. (2019), 'Would MPs Really Back a No Confidence Motion to Stop No-Deal?', *New Statesman*, 15 July.

Watt, N. (2009), 'Exit Stage Right: Pledge to Quit Big Party Alliance that Haunts David Cameron', *Guardian*, 29 May.

Watts, J. (2017), 'Labour Rules Out Working with Theresa May on Brexit Until She Dumps "No Deal" Rhetoric', *Independent*, 13 June.

Watts, J. (2018), 'Moderate Tories Warn Anti-EU "Purists" They Could Turn Against Brexit if Theresa May's Deal Is Torn Down', *Independent*, 17 November.

Watts, J., and Bale, T. (2019), 'Populism as an Intra-Party Phenomenon: The British Labour Party Under Jeremy Corbyn', *British Journal of Politics and International Relations*, 21(1), 99–115.

Waugh, P. (2019), 'Why Boris Johnson And Brexit Are Now In Limboland', *Huffpost*, 22 October.

Weale, A. (2018), *The Will of the People: A Modern Myth* (London: Polity Press).

Welby, J. (2019), 'Archbishop Justin Welby's Response to Invitation to Chair Citizens' Forum on Brexit', *Archbishop of Canterbury's website*, 27 August.

Wellings, B., and Vines, E. (2016), 'Populism and Sovereignty: The EU Act and the In-Out Referendum, 2010–2015', *Parliamentary Affairs*, 69(2), 309–26.

Whale, S. (2018), 'The Brexit Vote Explained', *The House magazine*, 22 November.

Whale, S. (2019), 'Brexit, Lies and Doctored Videotape', *The House magazine*, 17 December.

Whale, S. (2021), 'Whatever Happened to the 2011 Eurosceptic Rebels?', *The House magazine*, 24 October.

Wheeler, C. (2017), 'Five Days to Save Brexit: Vote Conservative or There Will Be Second Referendum, Says Davis', *Sunday Express*, 4 June.

Wheeler, M. (2016), 'Celebrity Politicians and Populist Media Narratives: The Case of Boris Johnson', in N. Jackson, E. Thorsen, and D. Wring, eds, *EU Referendum Analysis 2016: Media, Voters and the Campaign* (Poole: Bournemouth University).

White, H. (2015), *Parliamentary Scrutiny of Government* (London: Institute for Government).

White, H. (2022), *Held in Contempt: What's Wrong with the House of Commons?* (Manchester: Manchester University Press).

Wickham, A. (2019), 'There's a Secret Plan by Rebel MPs to Stop a No-Deal Brexit', *Buzzfeed*, 19 January.

Wilkins, C. (2020), *Brexit Witness Archive interview*, 22 June (London: UK in a Changing Europe).

Willumsen, D. M. (2017), *The Acceptance of Party Unity in Parliamentary Democracies* (Oxford: Oxford University Press).

Wintour, P. (2015), 'Jeremy Corbyn: Labour Will Campaign for UK to Stay in the EU', *Guardian*, 17 September.

Wintour, P. (2019), 'Rory Stewart Outlines "Alternative Parliament" to Stop No-Deal Brexit', *Guardian*, 7 July.

Working Group on Unification Referendums on the Island of Ireland (2021), *Final Report* (London: Constitution Unit).

Wright, O., and Coates, S. (2018), 'Tory Rebels Up in Arms After Theresa May Goes Back on Her Word', *Times*, 15 June.

Wright, O., and Waterfield, B. (2019), 'Brexit Vote Must Be Put on Hold, MPs Warn Theresa May', *Times*, 11 March.

YouGov (2016a), 'Corbyn Loses Support Among Labour Party Membership', *YouGov website*, 30 June.

YouGov (2016b), 'YouGov on the Day Poll: Remain 52%, Leave 48%', *YouGov website*, 23 June.

YouGov (2017a), 'Now That Theresa May Has Lost Her Majority in the House of Commons, Some Commentators Are Calling for Brexit to Be Negotiated by a Cross-Party Team, Including Representatives from Labour and Other Parties. Would You Prefer Brexit to be Negotiated by the Conservatives Alone or by a Cross-Party Team?', *YouGov website*, 12 June.

YouGov (2017b), 'The Supreme Court Has Ruled That Parliament Must Have a Vote on Whether the Government Can Invoke Article 50 and Start the Process of Leaving the European Union. Thinking About How Individual MPs Vote on this Issue, Do You Think They Should...', *YouGov website*, 25 January.

YouGov (2017c), 'Voting Intention: Conservatives 43%, Labour 25% (26–27 Mar)', *YouGov website*, 29 March.

YouGov (2022a), 'EU Tracker Questions: In Hindsight, Do You Think Britain Was Right or Wrong to Vote to Leave the European Union?', *YouGov website*.

YouGov (2022b), 'The Most Important Issues Facing the Country', *YouGov website*.

Young, A. (2019), 'Prorogation: Issues for the Supreme Court', *UK in a Changing Europe blog*, 16 September.

Young, A. (2021), 'The Prorogation Case: Re-Inventing the Constitution or Re-Imagining Constitutional Scholarship?', in D. Clarry, ed., *The UK Supreme Court Yearbook, Volume 10: 2018–2019 Legal Year* (Barlaston: Appellate Press).

Young, H. (1999), *This Blessed Plot: Britain and Europe From Churchill to Blair* (Basingstoke: Macmillan).

Zeffman, H. (2018), 'No Brexit Is More Likely Than No-Deal, Says Amber Rudd', *Times*, 21 November.

Zeffman, H. (2019), 'Boris Johnson Will Not Recall Parliament, Says No 10', *Times*, 19 August.

Index